The American
Catholic
Family

The American Catholic Family

JOHN L. THOMAS, S.J.

Member of the Institute of Social Order and the Department of Sociology, St. Louis University

Englewood Cliffs, N. J.

PRENTICE-HALL, INC.   *1956*

PRENTICE-HALL SOCIOLOGY SERIES
Herbert Blumer, Editor

PRINTED IN THE UNITED STATES OF AMERICA

02397

To

Mother

WHO SINGLEHANDED

RAISED THE SEVEN OF US

Preface

This book deals with the family system of the Catholic minority in American society. Specifically, it attempts to describe and to analyze the special problems Catholics encounter in maintaining their marriage and family ideals. This approach involves some understanding of the minority's present situation and the family values it embraces. Although it employs the Catholic frame of reference throughout, this book is not meant to be an apologia for the Catholic family system. Rather, it regards this system as a social fact; that is, it proceeds on the premise that there exists a sizable religious minority which cherishes these family values and attempts to maintain them. In other words, it simply states the values, describes the present position of the minority, and then attempts to outline the program which must be followed if the system is to be maintained intact.

Since every family system may be regarded as a practical program resulting from the more or less logical application of ultimate premises of value to a concrete social situation, this approach has been followed in dealing with the contemporary Catholic family system. Hence, the problem is briefly set in focus in Part I, and the value system of Catholics and their concept of marriage is outlined in Part II. Part III presents a description of the Catholic minority in terms of its diverse family backgrounds, its present social configurations, and the observed marriage patterns of its members. In Part IV, the major tension areas in the Catholic family as they appear in the records of broken marriages are analyzed. These first four sections, therefore, describe the ideal and the reality of the present Catholic family system. On the basis of this information, the requirements of a workable family program are discussed in Part V. The final chapter describes and analyzes the various movements which have been initiated by the minority in response to their family needs.

There is much that we do not know about the contemporary Catholic family. All available sources have been tapped, but numerous gaps in our information still remain. If one were to wait until all the evidence were in, however, the book probably would never be written. The major contribution of this book consists in its explanation of the Catholic position on the family and in its suggestions for future research on the intriguing problem of how a distinct cultural subsystem survives in a complex, transitional society.

It is impossible to acknowledge adequately my debt to all those who have contributed, directly or indirectly, to the writing of this book. Footnote references suggest some of the sources which have shaped my thinking. While a student at the University of Chicago, I acquired enduring obligations to W. Lloyd Warner, Everett C. Hughes, Ernest W. Burgess, William F. Ogburn, Herbert Blumer, Philip M. Hauser, and William F. Whyte. My research has been extensively aided by the considerate cooperation of numerous chancery officials, pastors, and leaders of Catholic Action who generously shared their time and experience with me.

I wish to thank the John Simon Guggenheim Memorial Foundation for a fellowship grant enabling me to study the process of acculturation among ethnic groups, and the Institute of Social Order, St. Louis University, which financed my family research and freed me for the writing of this book. A special note of appreciation goes to Rev. Francis J. Corley, S.J., for his careful reading of the text and his stimulating criticism.

JOHN L. THOMAS, S.J.

Table of Contents

ix

The American
Catholic
Family

PART I

A Preview

Minority Survival in a Complex Society

The wag who reminisced, "I was born young of a mixed marriage—male and female," was as wise as he was witty. We are all born "young" of a "mixed" marriage, and this explains why the family is such a universal human institution. Wherever men are found grouped together in community life, there we find the family. Universally, human nature is manifested bisexually—in male and female, mutually complementary partners in the reproductive act; and offspring are born "young," requiring nurture, protection, training, and instruction during long, formative years.

Wherever it exists, therefore, the family combines two basic functions. It controls sexual behavior for purposes of reproduction, and it provides for the organic social development of offspring. As a social institution, it is characterized by common residence, economic cooperation, and reproduction. These distinctive functions—sexual, reproductive, educational, and economic—invest the family with a many-sided utility rendering its universality inevitable. Hence, the family appears in every human society as the only workable adjustment to a series of essential human needs.

3

This does not mean that the family is similar and unchanging the world over. Man is a rational animal, not a creature of instinct. He is capable of working out many ways of satisfying his wants. As a social being, he tends to satisfy his needs through establishing relatively stable sets of patterned relationships called institutions. The "pattern" at any given time will depend on the available resources, on the way he defines the need to be satisfied, and ultimately, on his concept of the origin, nature, and purpose of himself and of society.

Consequently, the family as an existing institution will reflect the state of available resources, current definitions of sex and parenthood, and finally, prevailing concepts of the origin, nature, and purpose of man. Hence, family systems will differ *structurally,* that is, in the sets of relationships established to fulfill the various functions which the family performs in a given society; and *ideologically,* that is, in the way men think about these relationships and functions, and the values that they assign to them.

History and the contemporary world reveal a variety of family systems.[1] The simple familial unit of husband, wife, and immature offspring (the nuclear family) may exist as the only recognized type or it may be combined with other units into close-knit, larger aggregates (the extended family). Family functions may be extensive and inclusive so that the family becomes the primary unit for the exercise of such activities as worship, recreation, education, protection, production, and social intercourse, or they may be narrowed and reduced to the basic four enumerated above. Statuses and roles of family members may be variously defined, ranging from the subordination of wife and children in the patriarchal system to the more or less equalitarian ideal existing in the modern American family.

Each of these variations represents a way which men have found more or less satisfactory in fulfilling their sexual and parental needs. The range of possibilities is considerable, but it is not without definite limitations rooted in the character of the sexes themselves. To be sure, a specific family type is a cultural product, but the bisexual character of human nature is not the product of culture. The existence of male and female possessing mutually complementary reproductive attributes is the unchanging, elemental potential which is culturally channeled into distinctive familial statuses and roles in each instance. It is the fact that man is born "young" of a "mixed" marriage which provides the basis for every family system.

In a large, complex, rapidly changing society such as our own, divergent concepts of the family exist simultaneously. Although American families tend to resemble each other structurally, ideologically they may be poles apart. In structure, they tend to be small, relatively "closed" units composed of husband, wife, and immature offspring. In ideology, they vary widely according to the divergent value systems current in society. Is the contract which forms the basis of the family permanent or dissoluble at the will of the parties? Is it a natural contract or sacramental? Should the exercise of the reproductive drive be confined only to marriage? May its primary purpose be thwarted for the sake of obtaining secondary benefits? Does the mutual development and self-realization sought in marriage place a primacy on spiritual growth or is it narrowed to include only physical and psychic fulfillment?

There is no general agreement on these basic points. In the values which concern marriage and the family, we have what may be called a loosely integrated culture. That is, the cultural "blueprint for behavior" lacks unity and consistency. Concerning marriage and the family, society offers no relatively standardized prescriptions as to what must be done, ought to be done, should be done, may be done, and must not be done. Individuals are presented with socially acceptable alternatives in each of these categories, and they must make their choice in terms of their personal value system.[2]

Under these conditions, the existence of divergent family value systems in a culture becomes highly significant. Social customs and practices, at least in their origin, are the external expression of those ideals which people esteem and hold worthy of preservation. If these values are modified or rejected, the social conventions which lend them external expression will also tend to change. This shift may be slow. Social groups are generally conservative of established practices and may tolerate relatively wide divergence between accepted values and established behavioral patterns for a time. Eventually, however, social behavior tends to conform, or better, tends to give expression to the values which people have come to cherish. People tend to live as they think.

THE PROBLEM IN FOCUS

But what behavioral patterns develop in a society which includes sizable minorities embracing distinct and divergent family value systems? Or stated from the viewpoint of the subgroup, how does a religious minority which maintains distinctive concepts concerning the nature of man and his institutions secure the social realization of these concepts in a society which no longer accepts their validity as operative principles of organization and action? This is the question we propose to answer for the Catholic family. Specifically, then, we desire to study how American Catholics can maintain their marriage and family ideals in a society which does not fully accept these ideals and which, consequently, establishes institutions and practices that either oppose or fail to support them.

Hence, the present study resolves itself into an investigation of the family problems which a cultural subsystem encounters in a dominant society characterized by complexity and rapid change. Against the background of changing family patterns and competing value systems, Catholic families with their distinctive ideals stand out as a fairly well-defined subgroup. What conflicts and tensions are present? In what areas do the values, norms, and behavioral patterns prevalent in the dominant culture either oppose or, at least fail to support, the Catholic family ideal? To what extent has the Catholic family system integrated the structural changes associated with its modern urban environment? To what degree does it reflect the prevalent values, norms, and behavioral patterns? In brief, it is proposed to study how a cultural subsystem which does not choose to isolate itself preserves its values in a complex, changing society.

Since the statement that Catholic families constitute a distinct subsystem is a generalization which lends itself to some misinterpretation, it will be helpful to examine its meaning in greater detail. In the remainder of this chapter, therefore, the following points will be developed. First, the reasons for maintaining that Catholic families constitute a distinct subsystem will be briefly summarized. Second, we shall point out some of the limitations of this subsystem concept which result from the considerable diversity existing among Catholic families. Third, the transitional and culturally complex character of American society will be considered as further restricting the meaningfulness of the subsystem concept. Fourth, we shall describe briefly the general character of the problems which a subsystem will encounter in modern society. This involves some consideration of social change and the problem of integrating new behavioral patterns in terms of an accepted value system.

CATHOLIC FAMILIES AS A CULTURAL SUBSYSTEM

To say that Catholic families constitute a distinct cultural subsystem means simply that members of the Catholic Church can be identified as a distinct religious minority in our society. They embrace a common set of family values and associated practices which differ in some important respects from those generally accepted by the culture in which they live. And finally, these family ideals are based on a set of ultimate value premises which Catholics clearly recognize and cherish since they are authoritatively promulgated by a teaching church which Catholics believe is of divine origin. These characteristics enable us to distinguish the Catholic minority in American society. To be sure, although other groups may support essentially the same family ideals as the Catholic minority, in no other are these ideals and the ultimate value premises upon which they rest so clearly defined. Although individual Catholic families may manifest considerable divergence between ideal and practice, the Catholic minority, considered as a group, can easily be recognized by the following characteristics.

Religious Solidarity

Individual Catholics may differ in race, nationality, occupation, education, social class, and political affiliation, but they hold many things in common. They are members of one religious body, the Catholic Church. They embrace a similar religious creed, which not only teaches a definite system of values and life-goals, but implements and sanctions these by explicit and relatively detailed laws and directives. They share a common Christian heritage. Although this has been diversely channeled in different cultures, nevertheless, it retains an essential and profound continuity uniting the early Christian martyr, the medieval mystic, the Renaissance scholar, and the twentieth-century believer in a time-and-space-ignoring solidarity.

Several extrinsic factors have further intensified the minority status of American Catholics in the past. The rapid growth of the Church in America was largely the result of immigration. These Catholic immigrants faced the problem of establishing themselves in a society which had been pre-empted by Anglo-Saxon Protestantism. This placed Catholics on the defensive and intensified their minority status as immigrants. Further, throughout much of American history there has been a rather consistent current of "nativism," fomenting hatred against Catholics, Jews, Negroes, and immigrants. The over-all result has been that the Catholic minority, despite ethnic, political, and regional diversities, senses a general "consciousness of kind," leading to considerable group solidarity. At the same time, the non-Catholic public is kept acutely aware of the Catholic minority's existence in its midst.

Similar Family Ideals

Catholics embrace a unified, concise, and clearly defined set of values concerning marriage and the family. For example, they hold that the marriage contract is sacramental, that the marriage bond is intrinsically indissoluble, and that the marital union is the only legitimate channel for the exercise of the reproductive faculties. Further, they believe that the primary purpose of the generative faculties is procreation so that the physiological process of procreation must be respected in their use. Consequently, direct interference in this process, once it is voluntarily initiated by physical union in marriage, is considered morally evil. And finally, they maintain that the family is the fundamental social vehicle for the mutual development, perfection, and sanctification of its participant members.

In the dominant culture, most of these ideals are considered questionable. Dating and courtship practices which ignore the Catholic ideal of premarital chastity are rather generally promoted or tolerated. Civil divorce courts freely presume the right to dissolve the marriage bond. The use of contraceptives for purposes of family limitation has gained widespread social acceptance. An attitude toward the function of sex prevails which divorces it from its moral attributes, and elevates only its primarily physical aspects to the status of an important cultural value. Perhaps, from the Catholic viewpoint, the most serious divergence in the dominant culture is its tendency to secularize marriage and family values. This is to say, they are considered apart from their religious context and placed outside the direct domain of the moral law. It is not so much that religion and moral law are denied or rejected; they are simply judged not pertinent as guiding norms of practical action.[3]

As a result, there is considerable contemporary confusion concerning marriage and family values. Many strongly support traditional norms and behavioral patterns although they are disturbed by the practical necessity of meeting new situations. Others openly reject past solutions, but can agree on no general principles upon which to fashion a new approach. Consequently, whereas the Catholic minority possesses a clearly defined "design" for marriage, others take up a position intermediary between complete rejection of this design and a fairly close approximation to it.

In this connection, it should be noted that the social implementation of the Catholic family system entails the establishment of a whole series of practices which may be at variance with the practices promoted or tolerated by members of the dominant culture. In other words, marriage and family values have definite functional requisites. If they are to be operative, they must be translated into specific social relationships and these relationships, in turn, must be supported, or at least not hindered, by the customs, practices, and institutions within which they operate.

For example, if marriage is accepted as the only legitimate channel for the exercise of the reproductive faculties, it follows that all the relationships between the sexes from youth to old age must be regulated accordingly. This implies the establishment of distinctive customs and practices related to dating, courtship, and marriage. In addition to these, wider social support is required by way of education, literature, and recreation so that a total social "climate" is created within which it is possible for individuals to develop in conformity with the demands of their ideals.

It seems scarcely necessary to point out that since the Catholic concept of marriage and the family differs considerably from others, the attempt on the part of Catholics to implement their value system by establishing specific customs and practices, as well as by seeking wider cultural support, may lead to no little misunderstanding, confusion, and even conflict. When such cases arise, it is helpful to reflect that social programs represent the practical application of a value system to specific social situations. For example, when Catholics rise to the support of an organization such as the Legion of Decency, they do this because it represents to them an attempt in the practical order to create a social atmosphere within which it is possible for individual members of society to live up to the exigencies of the Christian ideal governing the relationships between the sexes. Obviously, in any given instance, a disagreement may arise in one of two ways. One may question whether a disputed practice or custom does implement or support a specific value; this is a mere disagreement over means. What is more fundamental, one may reject the practice because one implicitly rejects the value on which it is premised. This involves disagreement over ultimate purposes and goals.

Similar Ideology

At this point a third reason for considering Catholic families as a separate category becomes clear. Not only do their concepts of marriage and the family include distinctive features, but as might be expected, these concepts are based on ultimate premises or on an "ideology" presenting characteristics in many respects peculiar to Catholics. The term *ideology* as used here stands for those basic doctrines concerning the nature and goals of man and of society held by the group. It is highly important for the purposes of this study that the social implications of the Catholic ideology be thoroughly understood. When we analyze any social or cultural structure, several elements of primary importance are revealed. First, there is a basic, underlying ideology composed of the ultimate cultural goals. Second, there are derivative sets of values and purposes, that is, specific institutional objectives representing the culturally defined applications of the ideology to concrete social institutions such as the family. Finally, there are the institutionalized means or culturally patterned and acceptable procedures, that is, definite sets of social relationships established for the implementation of these institutional objectives.

Hence, in analyzing the Catholic family system, three primary divisions are to be kept in mind. First, there are the patterned relationships on the behavioral level, including those between husband and wife, parents and children, conjugal unit and extended family, and family and society. Second, there are the specific marriage and family values which these relationships embody and attempt to implement in the social system. Finally, there is the ideology representing the basic doctrines on the nature and purposes of man and society in the light of which the Catholic concepts of marriage and the family have been developed.

Briefly, you cannot understand the American Catholic family and its problems unless you understand the Catholic concepts of marriage and the family, and these cannot be understood apart from the Catholic ideology. It is on the basis of this hypothesis that we feel justified in devoting separate treatment to the study of Catholic families in America. Since Catholics share a common ideology, together with the family value system which derives from it, one may expect their patterned social relationships in this area, representing as they do, attempts to implement and institutionalize these same values, to be roughly similar. At the same time, it is evident that many aspects of contemporary culture are irreconcilable with Catholic family values, and to this extent, Catholic families may be held to constitute a distinct cultural subsystem.

LIMITATIONS OF THE SUBSYSTEM CONCEPT

It should be apparent that we have somewhat oversimplified the position of Catholic families in American society. In practice, they do not represent a clearly defined cultural subsystem, nor does the dominant culture present a unified set of doctrines, institutional objectives, and social practices totally at variance with the Catholic system. What we have is a complex culture in transition, and it is only through the analysis of prevalent trends that the increasing divergence of Catholic family values from the dominant system becomes apparent. In this sense, it may be stated that Catholic families are potentially a cultural subsystem, whereas the dominant culture tends to be moving toward a new definition of marriage and family values.[4]

Existence of Ethnic Minorities

There are several reasons why Catholic families do not constitute a clearly defined subsystem in American society. As this study will show, there are relatively large ethnic minorities among the Catholic group. Although the Melting Pot is boiling steadily, the process of assimilation is far from completed. To be sure, these ethnic minorities embrace a common Catholic ideology, but the derivative institutional objectives, as well as the social means used to implement these, reveal divergent cultural patterning indicative of their Old World origin. These differences are most apparent in the status and role of husband and wife, parent and child, and in the relationships between the conjugal unit and the extended family. Further, these minorities have erected a series of "cultural fences" such as devotion to the mother-tongue, prohibition on outgroup marriage, and parochial and ethnic organizations through which group solidarity is encouraged and traditional practices are fostered. Consequently, each of these groups faces the problem of preserving Catholic family values in its own way although there is increasing evidence that all these groups are coming to recognize their common interests as a cultural subsystem.

Social Implications of Catholic Values Not Clearly Seen

An additional reason for stressing the emergent character of the Catholic subsystem is that the social implications of their marriage and family values are not always clearly recognized even by Catholics themselves. Structural and technical changes have been occurring so rapidly in our society that the Catholic minority, immersed in the general cultural stream, has tended to "follow the crowd" in making necessary adaptations, excepting where such action clearly conflicted with obvious traditional Catholic values. The result frequently has been a confused, segmented, even superficial attempt to maintain specific marriage and family values while ignoring the fact that these values constitute an integral system requiring definite, institutionalized means and wide cultural support to become operative in the practical order. In other words, Catholics have been duly sensitive to the moral implications of their family ideals; they have been less perceptive in regard to their functional requisites. For example, they have strenuously opposed the use of contraceptives as immoral; at times, they have been less clear-sighted in facing the problems of wages, housing, and medical care which may render the task of parenthood unduly onerous in an industrialized urban society.

It should be noted that the failure to recognize the functional requisites of an accepted value system takes on special significance in a complex, loosely integrated society. This is seen clearly by contrasting such a society with a well-integrated one. In a well-integrated society, there is a fairly close relationship between institutionalized means, institutional objectives, and the underlying cultural ideology. The purposes and goals of basic institutions are clearly outlined and the approved means of reaching these are widely known. In this sense, a culture represents a "blueprint for behavior," or what Linton has termed "designs for living." In a complex, loosely integrated society, the cultural blueprint lacks unity and consistency, and individuals are presented with alternatives in each of these categories.

In practice, this means that the minority must formulate its own blueprint or design for living. Obviously, this can be done only if it clearly recognizes the functional requisites of its value system. There are several reasons why this becomes difficult in a complex, rapidly changing society. In the first place, although a minority may differ from the dominant culture either in ideology, institutional objectives, or behavioral patterns, it is primarily in behavioral patterns that minority group members tend to recognize their distinctiveness. Consequently, these behavioral patterns come to be regarded as values in themselves. They continue to be cherished by the minority long after they cease to implement group values. In other words, there is not only failure to adjust, but the critical, underlying divergence of ultimate values escape popular attention.

For example, the family can no longer exercise control over its adolescent members in the traditional manner. Movies, television, radio, and current literature are avenues of knowledge over which the contemporary parent has limited control. The introduction of facile and rapid means of travel has further limited this influence, since it has been a factor in taking recreation out of the home and away from parental supervision. Faced with these conditions, many parents ignore the changes and cling tenaciously to the traditional definition of parental roles as values in themselves. This means they content themselves with the reiteration of traditional values in the hope that their adolescent offspring will work out the social means necessary to achieve them.

But this is to neglect the fact that social means and practices are not the product of isolated individuals; they develop through group interactions oriented in terms of the dominant group's value system, and minority adolescents tend to follow. The result can only be confusion and strain between ideals and practice. The logic of the situation would demand that parents redefine their roles and prepare their children to meet the new situation by increased instruction and counsel coupled with new forms of supervision. Unfortunately, their experience has not prepared them to meet this challenge, and their feeling of inadequacy, together with a reticence about dealing with the subject of sex, hinders them from taking any constructive steps to implement the values they teach. The over-all result is that, whereas the divergence of the minority's value system is obvious, practice reveals a tendency to conform to prevalent standards.

At the opposite extreme, in a rapidly changing society new behavioral patterns which render the realization of the minority's values highly improbable may be thoughtlessly promoted or tolerated. Here again there is failure to recognize the functional requisites of a value system.

For example, society still lends theoretical support to the traditional ideal that sexual relations are to be exercised only in marriage. At the same time, dating and courtship practices are tolerated, if not promoted, which common experience and even superficial knowledge of the sexual drive of adolescents indicate are hardly consonant with the achievement of this ideal among the majority of the unmarried. In fact, some of these practices are based on the latent premise that the use of one's reproductive potencies is an amoral, personal affair to be regulated and adapted according to the individual's needs in a specific social milieu. Consequently, the insistence on traditional objectives, coupled with the toleration of contradictory practices, leads to considerable confusion and strain. The lack of logic in the whole procedure is best revealed when premarital pregnancy occurs. At once traditional sanctions are asserted on the assumption that this is a singular violation of morals, whereas the facts in the case reveal merely ignorance, carelessness, or chance failure in frustrating the consequences of actions which tolerated social practices and the immaturity of the agents render likely to occur.

AMERICAN SOCIETY AND THE SUBSYSTEM CONCEPT

A further reason for maintaining that Catholic families do not constitute a clearly defined cultural subsystem is that the dominant society in which they exist is far from exhibiting consensus in ideology, institutional objectives, and social means. This confusion tends to conceal basic divergence except in those areas where Catholic moral practices are clearly involved. American society is in transition, and perhaps in no institution is this more apparent than in the family.

Historians have documented the dissident Protestant provenance of the traditional American family system and its gradual secularization.[5] Social scientists have analyzed the changes in structure occasioned by the transfer from a rural to an industrialized urban environment.[6] They point out that the American family has modified many of its traditional functions. The extended family system is shifting in the direction of the nuclear type. The "patriarchal" form is evolving into the "democratic." Companionship rather than institutional values is being emphasized in popular evaluations of the family. The restriction of the exercise of the reproductive faculties within the confines of monogamous marriage, originally effected by Christianity, is showing signs of breaking down. Marriage is coming to be regarded primarily as a vehicle for the personality development of its participants. Compared with other countries in the western cultural tradition, more Americans eventually marry, they marry younger, and they marry oftener.

Change in Structure versus Change in Meaning

Clearly, the traditional family system is undergoing change in form and function. Moreover, these structural modifications are related to changes in ideology and institutional objectives, although this development is less often recognized. Indeed, analysis reveals that any change in family structure results in some modification of the meaning which the affected relationships will have for family members. For example, in the transfer from a rural to an urban environment, the domestic unit ceased to be the center of a common economic enterprise. Husband and wife were separated during working hours, their interests tended to become more diversified, and they did fewer things in common. As these relationships changed, their meaning to the spouses necessarily underwent some modification. Greater emphasis came to be placed on companionship and the mutual satisfaction of intimate emotional needs.

Reciprocally, a change in meaning leads to a redefinition and repatterning of relationships. If women are considered somewhat inferior to men, they are scarcely capable of real companionship in marriage. Their status and roles will be defined accordingly, and the husband-wife relationship will be oriented primarily around the needs of the male. If the marriage bond is considered nonsacramental, the marriage contract comes under the jurisdiction of the civil courts, and divorce with remarriage becomes a socially accepted pattern.[7] If the function of sex is separated from its moral significance, the relationships between the sexes both before and after marriage will undergo extensive change.

Since American society is far from static, this interplay of structure and meaning is a continuous process. Furthermore, changes in one institution call for adjustment in others. Hence, contemporary society offers the spectacle of constant and extensive change as people strive to adjust themselves and their institutions to new situations. However, this process of adjustment and change must be understood in reference to a wider frame of values. Initially, every culture is founded on an ideology, a set of specific doctrines concerning the nature and purposes of man and of society. These doctrines influence the form and functioning of the social order. When there is general consensus on the ideology, there tends to be a constant "strain" to orient institutional changes toward the achievement of these culturally approved goals. Obviously, even with universal agreement, the perfect implementation of an ideology would be possible only in a static society; in all others, man must settle for an approximation, an approach *toward* the ideal order.

Rapid Changes Obscure Shift in Meanings

In a complex sociey which embraces a plurality of cultural subsystems, rapid change tends to obscure the relationship between basic ideology and derivative institutional structures. Attention focuses primarily on the interplay of structure and meaning within a specific institution such as the family or the economic system. Meanwhile, the intricate web of relationships which constitutes the total social organization continues to undergo steady modification, since the sets of patterned relationships which we call institutions are all more or less interdependent in a given society. For example, the family system is affected by the economic system and vice versa. This interdependence becomes particularly significant under conditions of rapid change because the various elements of the culture may not change at the same rate. As a result, cultural "lags," or delays in the mutual adjustment of dependent institutions may occur. Under these circumstances, disorganization and frustration follow, for men are unable to reconcile the objectives of the various institutions in which they participate.

However, since attention is focused primarily on specific maladjustments within individual institutions, the significance of fundamental changes in the social system is ignored. By this we mean that attention is diverted from considering the relationship between ultimate values and the social means required to implement them in a given society. Interest centers on discovering the techniques of adjustment and adaptation as if these means were ends in themselves.

A good example of this process is offered in the development of the modern science of industrial relations. Attention is focused on the immediate job situation. Interest centers on discovering the techniques of adjustment and adaptation which can be used to make the worker feel satisfied and to give him "a sense of participation." This is a superficial approach to the problem. The first obvious question to ask is whether a policy which seeks to restore to the worker a sense of personal importance and dignity is even compatible with the organizational requirements of the modern productive process. Back of this question lies one which is even more fundamental. How are the ultimate value premises concerning the origin, nature, and destiny of man reconcilable with the technological and institutional compulsions of contemporary, large-scale economic organizations? Simply stated, this is merely suggesting that it is superficial to look upon the economic system as an end in itself, and consequently, before answering the question of *how* to adjust, one must ask the question: *Why* adjust?

Although few would deny that this approach characterizes most of modern man's encounters with change, there is little agreement concerning the nature of the maladjustment which results. To be sure, changes in man's control over the material forces of nature have developed so rapidly, adjustments have been required so extensively, and "lags" have been so apparent that it is understandable why many should see the basic need of our times as one of adjustment and adaptation. As we have indicated, this has led to a concentration on the processes of structural change and man's adaptation to them while neglecting to investigate the ideological premises, the value frame of reference in terms of which the adaptation was to be made.

Adaptation Without a Goal

In other words, so much effort has been spent on learning the techniques and methods of adaptation that the fundamental questions Why adapt? and Adapt to what? have not been raised. These questions can be answered only on the basis of an explicit ideology, that is, on the basis of doctrines concerning the nature and purpose of man and of society. Further, they imply that we make explicit the hierarchy of purposes and values in our culture. Short of this, the demand for adaptation appears aimless, a mere *ad hoc* "bread and the circus" approach to ease the frustrations of those who feel the maladjustment most severely. In practice, of course, adjustments and adaptations are always made on the basis of some premises although in a transitional society these may remain latent and unexpressed.

It is pertinent to investigate more fully the nature and significance of this failure to make explicit the ideology or ideologies on the basis of which adjustments have been made in contemporary society. We have already indicated the stress on techniques and methods of adaptation flowing from a preoccupation with the need for interinstitutional adjustments and also suggested that this preoccupation and stress obscured the relationship between ideology and derivative institutional objectives. The result was that specific institutional objectives were modified without clear recognition that the new objectives no longer represented logical derivatives of the traditional value system. In other words, they were based on different though unformulated doctrines on the nature and purposes of man and of society.

The institution of the family can serve as an illustration of what has happened. As we have seen, social scientists are unanimous in underlining the transitional position of the American family system. Although they are not clear about where it is going, they are sure that it is on the move. Frequently, what has not been made clear is that traditional marriage and family values were based on definite premises which cannot easily be reconciled with modern family trends. This is clear from a consideration of the original American family system. Even though the essential break with Catholic tradition occurred in the sixteenth century with the denial of the sacramental character of the marriage contract, the leaders of the Reformation continued to regard marriage as a sacred institution and as the only legitimate channel for the expression of man's reproductive drive. American traditional family values were based on this premise, and the relationships between the sexes were regulated according to it, at least in theory. To be sure, some of the early colonists placed marriage entirely under the jurisdiction of the civil authority, but they harbored few doubts concerning its serious character.

It was the rapid transformation of America from a rural to an industrialized urban society which set the stage for manifold changes in the traditional family structure. The status and roles of husband and wife, of parents and children, of conjugal unit and extended family were modified by the adjustments required to meet the changed situation. Theoretically, these changes could have taken place within the broad framework of the traditional value system. That is, institutional objectives could have been preserved although the social means implementing them would have been modified within limits. Actually, this did not occur because subtle changes had been taking place in the minds of men concerning their traditional ideology. They no longer agreed on a set of doctrines concerning the nature and purpose of man and of society. Consequently, traditional family objectives were deprived of their foundation; they were, so to speak, left suspended, lacking a common point of departure in an agreed value system. It is not surprising, therefore, to find them looked upon today as "relative" values subject to change with the rest of the social system.

Cultural Lag or Shift in Ideology?

In the light of this analysis, it should be clear that the confusion and contradiction concerning many marriage and family values revealed in the dominant culture today constitute something more than mere cultural lags. They indicate more than the failure of men's thinking and acting to adapt or adjust to rapid change. Lags and delays in adjustment do exist, but it is superficial to look upon them as only structural maladjustments, as temporary imbalances among various sets of social relationships, on the assumption that these latter are infinitely variable and imply no value referents.

Ultimately, confusion and conflict in practice can be reduced to divergence in value premises. It is because modern men no longer agree on marriage and family values that they disagree on cultural practices associated with them. It is relatively easy to document the confusion and conflicts existing in contemporary society, to point out that these have been occasioned by rapid social change, to conclude that the institution of the family is in a state of transition, but this explains very little. What must be explained is how the members of society have come to embrace different aspirational goals concerning marriage and the family, and why they frequently promote or tolerate practices which render the achievement of these aspirations improbable, if not impossible.

We have already set down the main elements of the explanation. Our position can be summarized as follows: When a complex society undergoes rapid change, the gap between traditional institutional values and observed practice tends to widen. Since the various elements of the cultural system are interdependent, a change in one institution calls for adjustment and adaptation in others. If there is delay or lag in adapting to change, considerable maladjustment can result. Ordinarily what happens is that structural adaptations are made without recognizing that the "meaning" of the affected relationships changes. As more and more structural changes are introduced, the gap between traditional institutional values and observed practices increases. Sooner or later, this discrepancy becomes obvious and traditional institutional objectives are called into question. If, as is the case in our culture, these objectives have been deprived of their foundation in an accepted ideology, there appears little reason for maintaining them. Traditional aspirational goals become "relative" values, little more than cultural rationalizations for what people do.

Cultural Discontinuities

Nevertheless, all members of society do not accept the change in aspirational goals. Indeed, the majority attempt to maintain the tradition-sanctioned institutional objectives, or at least some of them. Such persons find themselves in a serious dilemma. On the one hand, a specific cultural value is maintained and its violations strongly condemned; on the other, changes in structure and practice have occurred which make the frequent violations of the value-sanctioned behavioral pattern almost inevitable. When both cultural value and contradictory practice are strongly supported by public sentiment, the result is really a latent "cultural discontinuity." This means that the situation indicates the hidden conflict of contradictory aspects of two divergent value systems. In other words, a value is cherished without implementing the social means necessary for its achievement, and a set of customs and practices is adopted without openly recognizing the premises on which they are based. In a transitional society, these latent "cultural discontinuities" are frequently treated as merely conflicting aspects of the culture.

Actually, they are much more significant than that, and it is only through lack of what might be termed "social logic" that this is not widely recognized. Social logic implies that the functional requisites—that is, the relevant social means necessary to implement accepted values—are clearly perceived, and at the same time, that the premises upon which a given practice is established are recognized. Where such logic exists, people can distinguish between what may be called a cultural lag, requiring only the lapse of time for its solution, and a conflict of value systems demanding ultimate choice in life goals.

The family system in the dominant culture presents many examples of latent "cultural discontinuities." Traditional values are still advocated, and most people assume that they are operative. However, as social scientists clearly demonstrate, confusion and conflict are prevalent. The relationships between the sexes are scarcely determined in relation to traditional values, nor do these values receive support from the wider culture as expressed in literature, radio, television, movies, advertising, and so forth. In reality, there exists a whole series of alternate and competing family goals and associated practices. None of these is fully institutionalized, with the result that individuals may find themselves embracing contradictory goals and practices at the same time.

To summarize, this treatment of the contemporary family system is necessarily incomplete to the extent that we have prescinded from many factors which influence its structure and meaning. However, the aim has been to indicate that there is no basic agreement on marriage and family values in the dominant culture and as a consequence, the cultural subsystem status of the Catholic minority is less readily apparent. At present, Catholic families may be considered as constituting an emerging subsystem. Not only do they lack solidarity because they include distinctive, cohesive ethnic minorities, but

Catholics in general are frequently not fully aware of the functional requisites of the doctrines which they embrace. At the same time, their divergence from the dominant culture is made less apparent by the fact that there is no general consensus on marriage and family values. Nevertheless, an analysis of trends indicates increasing awareness of solidarity among Catholic families and a growing consciousness that new marriage and family values are developing in American society.

PROBLEMS OF A CULTURAL SUBSYSTEM IN A COMPLEX SOCIETY

The translation of religious dogmas and ultimate principles into practical social norms always takes place within a definite social context. Hence, the family system which Catholics develop depends not only on the inner logic of their family doctrine but also on the cultural setting within which it evolves. This suggests that Catholic families may encounter special problems in American society. Not only do they constitute a minority, but their family system is characterized by distinctive features not uniformly accepted by members of the dominant culture. It may be helpful at the outset, therefore, to outline briefly the principal problems which challenge a cultural subgroup in a complex, transitional society. Catholic families, like all American families, face the typical marriage problems inherent in our social system. However, as members of a religious minority which maintains a distinctive value system they must work out their adjustments and adaptations in a different frame of reference.

Theoretically, a minority can seek to maintain its family standards intact either by isolating itself from the dominant culture, thus controlling change, or it can attempt limited integration with the dominant group. Since American Catholics, with the exception of a few ethnic groups, are not isolated, only the latter alternative need concern us here. Three fundamental problems face the Catholic minority when it seeks

limited integration in the dominant culture. First, it must secure conformity to its family standards. Second, it must integrate necessary changes. Third, it must achieve social equilibrium without the assistance of related cultural institutions.
Although these problems will receive full treatment in later
sections, some indication of their implications at the outset
will clarify the basic issues with which this book attempts to
deal.

The Minority Must Secure Conformity to
Its Family Standards

Conformity tends to produce conformity in a society where
there is rather general agreement on ultimate values, family
standards, and related behavioral patterns. People agree on
how they ought to act in various social situations, and when
deviations occur from approved standards of conduct, the
offender is punished by loss of esteem or by the imposition of
more positive sanctions. At the same time, conformity is re-
warded so that, under such circumstances, to conform almost
constitutes the path of least resistance for the individual. Conformity is never merely automatic even in a simple society,
but granted the effect of past training, the mutual aspirations
and expectations of associates, and the average individual's
need for esteem and prestige, it is relatively easy to achieve
when general consensus prevails.

A minority which represents a distinct cultural subsystem in
a pluralistic society, however, cannot rely on the current social
mechanisms in securing conformity to its family standards.
Hence, it is faced with a threefold task. It must develop means
for assuring adequate knowledge of its family standards by
group members. Since knowledge does not necessarily lead
to conformity, effective motivation must be maintained. And
finally, there must be sufficient solidarity among group members to supply the mutual support which is lacking in the
dominant society. These requisites for survival imply considerable vitality and initiative in the minority. Catholic families
may never simply "follow the crowd," but their independence
and integrity can be maintained only if they are profoundly

attached to their system of beliefs and understand its practical implications in their daily lives. For this reason, several of the following chapters will be devoted to developing the Catholic system of values in some detail. Only in this frame of reference can one grasp the real nature of the problems which Catholic families face in American society.

The Minority Must Integrate Necessary Change

The problem of minority group survival in a static society would be relatively easy. The lines of divergence could be clearly drawn, and both ingroup and outgroup members could understand the practical implications of their basic differences. Once the general pattern had been set, the principal problem of the minority would be to "hold the party line." Innovations and changes could be uniformly rejected as incompatible with group standards. This facile solution is not possible in a society characterized by rapid and extensive change. New situations which call for a redefinition and reinterpretation of values are constantly presenting themselves. Established patterns of control are rendered obsolete or ineffective by the changed circumstances.

Under these conditions, the problem of the minority consists in discriminating between changes which are incompatible with the realization of its family standards and those which call for adjustment and adaptation. This approach to change involves a clear understanding of the difference between ultimate value premises and the social means used to implement them in a given situation. Failure to distinguish these leads to a hopeless conservatism in a changing society. In other words, what is required is the reapplication of basic premises to new social facts. Unless minority members are capable of doing this, they will either accept all change indiscriminately, even though it prove incompatible with their family standards, or they will attempt simply to ignore the implications of change by adhering to traditional practices. Either approach will prove disastrous. For this reason, in later sections a careful distinction is drawn between ultimate value premises and their varied social implementations.

The Minority Must Achieve Its Own Social Equilibrium

Since Catholic families operate within the social system of the dominant culture, their rejection on moral grounds of specific cultural practices such as divorce and contraceptives throws them out of balance with the total system. By this we mean that the rejected practice has evidently been introduced to answer a need within the system. Furthermore, once it has been introduced and established within the system, the social relationships which make up the system are "geared" or adjusted to it. Hence, when Catholic families reject it, they automatically let themselves in for a whole series of adjustments in other relationships associated with the rejected practice.

In other words, in rejecting the practice, Catholic families are rejecting the social equilibrium established in terms of it, and consequently, they must reestablish their own. Since the family system has such wide ramifications in the social structure, to reject a practice such as the use of contraceptives, which profoundly affects its present character, creates serious problems for Catholic families. Age at marriage, wages, housing, number of children, spending habits, and so forth are all affected by the practice, with the result that Catholics must make adjustments in all these areas or face the consequences. The requisites of an adequate Catholic family program will be treated in later sections, but it is well to keep in mind from the outset that although the problems of a religious minority in a complex, changing society are essentially moral, they have profound and extensive social implications which cannot be ignored.

SUMMARY

To recapitulate, this chapter has presented a brief overview of the position of Catholic families in American society. It has developed the reasons for considering them as a distinct cultural subsystem and has discussed some of the limitations of this subsystem concept which stem from the lack of solidarity among contemporary Catholic families. It further suggested that the meaningfulness of this concept is somewhat lessened because there is a lack of consensus concerning marriage and family values in the dominant culture. Finally, it has indicated some of the problems a minority faces in a complex, rapidly changing society.

From this chapter it should be clear that a subsystem can be understood only in terms of its ideology and its derivative institutional objectives. Hence, in the following section we shall develop briefly the Catholic doctrine on the origin, nature, and destiny of man, the Catholic concept of marriage, the juridical framework by which the Church implements this concept in canon law, and some of the functional requisites of this integral Catholic teaching on marriage and the family. Our purpose is not only to show the logical consistency of the doctrine, but to lay the foundation for an understanding of the position and problems of contemporary Catholic families.

Once this theoretical groundwork is made clear, we will be prepared to judge how well the Catholic family is achieving its ideals, what forces in modern society hinder the fulfillment of its objectives, what present-day programs are effectively supporting the Catholic ideal, and what basic problems must be met if the minority subsystem is to survive intact.

The Catholic family, like other families, must work out a *modus vivendi* in an industrialized urban environment. This calls for adjustment and adaptation, but the Catholic family is faced with the problem of developing these within a framework of values which keeps intact Catholic ideology and its derivative family objectives. Furthermore, since Catholic families constitute a minority group, they are unable to control the institutionalized means necessary to implement their marriage and family values. In fact, to Catholics, many contemporary practices such as civil divorce and the use of contraceptives appear as culturally patterned defects. Their widespread acceptance in the dominant culture merely raises the problem of the pathology of normalcy, since what is thus considered normal contradicts the purpose of man as Catholics conceive it.

Nevertheless, though the doctrinal divergence of these socially patterned defects are clear to every Catholic, the impulse to conform and the security which comes from doing as others do is bound to place a strain upon the individual Catholic. It seems likely that minority survival under these conditions will depend to a great extent on the strengthening of solidarity among Catholics. Then the force of conformity will operate to support group ideals, and the security of the individual will be rooted in the group.

PART II

The Catholic Concept of
Marriage

CHAPTER TWO

The Framework of Beliefs

The Catholic concept of marriage is based on a clearly defined ideology, a set of doctrines concerning the origin, nature, and purpose of man. It follows that an adequate understanding of Catholic marriage doctrine and practice implies some knowledge of this ideology. Catholic doctrine is not a series of disjointed statements. Rather, it is an organic body of religious truth in which one dogma cannot be adequately understood save in its relation to the others; a part cannot be denied without rejecting the whole. Consequently, this chapter will present a brief outline of the essentials of Catholic belief so that the intrinsic interdependence of all elements of the Catholic's philosophy of life may be understood. The purpose is to throw some light on the religious and philosophical climate within which the average Catholic views marriage and the family.

In this connection, it is well to observe that from the viewpoint of the individual, marriage and the family are instrumental; they are designed to serve him in the full development and realization of his being. Hence, they can be understood only in terms of his being and its destiny. Here, as in all human problems, the notion of the person is central. If we wish to proceed beyond the mere description of observed social phenomena, we must take up some position in regard to the person. Whether latent or expressed, our concept of the person will direct our research, orient our analysis, stand as the focal point of our synthesis, and operate as an ultimate value premise in our formulation of practical programs for social action.

It goes without saying that no adequate explanation or "defense" of the Catholic ideology is intended in the short space allotted to its treatment here. Nothing more is purposed than the statement of a clearly defined point of view so that the reader may perceive how the concept of marriage fits into the doctrinal whole. It is understandably difficult to grasp the rationale of many specific Catholic values and practices if these are considered segmentally, apart from the total system. Indeed, the characteristics of the Catholic family ideal derive so directly from the Catholic ideology that the present approach appears essential.

GENERAL STATEMENT OF IDEOLOGY

Catholic doctrine is based on reason, Scripture, and tradition. The role of each will become apparent from our analysis of the ideology. Briefly stated, the basic doctrines are as follows. First, there is God, a supreme, transcendent, intelligent being, pure act, the first cause, who created all things. Consequently, the visible world has not always existed, nor does it possess in itself the sufficient reason for its existence; it depends on God, the first cause. Although *how* God created the world is not known, the *fact* is held to be certain. Since creation is the act of an intelligent being, it has a purpose. This purpose can be known either by God revealing it, or by human reason which seeks in nature the essential tendencies of things and the reasons which explain them. Hence, the Catholic conception of the world is fundamentally teleological: the world and all created beings have a purpose.

In the visible world, being exists at many levels. We can distinguish inanimate matter, plant life, sentient life, and man, the rational animal. At each of these levels, things have their own constituent being, operate according to their own "laws," and possess their own intrinsic purpose. It is held that all created things have been placed at the service of man by his Creator. It is man's task to control and order them so that they contribute to his development and perfection. They are means, not ends in themselves; they are to serve all mankind, not a privileged few. Consequently, man, the human person, is the supreme value in creation. It is the achievement of his purpose and destiny which supersedes all secular purposes in the world.

It follows that a key-concept in the Catholic ideology is the definition of the origin, nature, and destiny of the human person. The average Catholic absorbs the basic elements of this concept early in life. Although his understanding of its implications and significance may never advance much beyond this stage, this early training gives an orientation to his thought which can be remarked throughout life. Man, a composite of body and soul, is created by God to know, love, and serve Him in this world and thus be happy forever with Him in the next. This definition is deceptively simple; its full explanation requires the aid of reason, Scripture, and tradition.

THE APPROACH FROM PHILOSOPHY

Let us start with what traditional Catholic thought tells us about human nature. Unfortunately, the term *nature* is one of the many words which, in modern usage, have taken on a variety of meanings. The term is used here in its philosophical sense to signify the "principle of action" in a being. Hence, we use the term *human nature* to signify the principle of action in man. It is that element in man which enables him to perform "human" acts. This meaning must be distinguished from much contemporary usage of the term through which it is employed in a primarily descriptive sense to signify little more than personality.[1] In this latter usage it is possible to speak of the "mutability" and "beginning" of human nature and to assume that man is not born "human," but becomes so in the process of developing his personality.

Our use of the term *human nature* to signify the principle of action in man, or that element in his being which enables him to perform human actions, reveals the ultimate constitution of man. It signifies the underlying source, the basic structure of his being which makes him capable of human activity. Used in this sense, human nature is not "mutable" nor does it have its beginning sometime after birth when the personality is developed. We are born human, that is, we possess a nature, a principle of action which enables us to perform human acts whether we ever live long enough to perform any or not. It is precisely because individuals possess this basic, constitutive structure that they can be classified as human.

There is more than a problem of semantics involved here since the use of the term *human nature* to signify little more than personality confines the study of man to little more than description. The principle of action, the human agent with his inherent potentialities and limitations, is ignored. When this happens, much of the activity of some social scientists consists in accumulating data on human activity, with little further analysis, obviously, on the tacit assumption that observed action does not imply a principle of action.

Human Nature

In Catholic thought, man is viewed as a composite of body and soul. Hence, the observed factual unity of man as an integral organism capable of both corporal and mental activities is taken into account. Although the primary source of the physical is matter (the body), and the primary source of the psychic is the soul, body and soul are but part-principles (elements) which in human nature are combined into the unity of a single nature by means of a substantial integration. The real subject of action in human nature, therefore, is not the body or the soul, but the person. This is the composite, unitary principle resulting from the substantial union of body and soul. It follows that the person is a subsistent being consisting of two really distinct substantial co-principles—soul and matter.

This concept of person should not be confused with the

psychological definition of personality in current use. Personality in this latter sense generally means the sum total of human functions and capacities, traits and aptitudes found in man. It possesses a functional unity which, in cases of severe personality disorders, can be destroyed. It may help to clarify the traditional concept of person to point out that the person can be considered under three aspects: empirically, the self as a unitary organism, observed at any present moment; historically, the self perceived by memory as the persisting unit running through life's experiences; metaphysically, the self considered in its nature and in its philosophically constituent elements.

To conceive of man as a composite of body and soul is to consider him as a true microcosm uniting within his person the essential realties of chemical elements, living plants, sentient animals, and spiritual intelligences. Although for purposes of study it is permissible by abstraction to consider his activity at any one of these levels, it should be emphasized that the principle of activity is the person. Human behavior and conduct are not to be equated with human nature; they presuppose a principle of activity which is the person.

Man is in contact with the external material world about him through the sense organs of the body. However, his knowledge does not consist of a mere collection of disparate sense perceptions. He possesses a spiritual faculty, the intellect, capable of arriving at the knowledge of the nature of things through the data supplied by the senses. Hence, although the intellect relies on the senses for its contact with the external physical world, its activities are not confined to their data. By means of his intellect, man forms concepts, formulates judgments, and perceives the connection between means and ends. He is conscious of the ability to choose between different means to achieve an end. He is conscious of the ability to act or not to act. He is capable of translating concepts and ideas into symbols and through the medium of language to communicate with others. All these activities and many others find their adequate explanation in the human person conceived as a psychophysical composite of body and soul. There is realism in this view since it does not neglect scientifically observable phenomena. Further, it proceeds beyond the mere description of behavior, on the hypothesis that observed activity implies a principle of action.

Since the spiritual principle, the soul, is immaterial, it bears no principle of dissolution within itself. Consequently, it can be destroyed or blotted out of existence only by annihilation, a power which belongs to the Creator alone. Related to this reasoning on the immortality of the soul is the observation that there is in human nature a craving for perfect happiness. This is so universal that it can only have been put into human nature by the Author of nature as a basic orientation of the creature to Himself. Since experience shows that perfect happiness is unattainable in this mortal life, it is argued that the soul must be immortal for, if this were not true, there would be a universal human craving for perfect happiness which would never be fulfilled, and human existence would be radically irrational.

Human Acts

Finally, it is maintained that independent of all human law, certain human acts are of their very nature good and deserving of praise; and conversely, some acts are of their very nature bad and deserving of blame. What measure or rule is offered to determine the good act from the bad act? It is held that the norm of morality is man's rational nature taken in its entirety. Hence, those actions are good which are in conformity with man's rational nature; those that are not in conformity with man's rational nature are bad. A consideration of man's rational nature taken in its entirety reveals three points. First, human nature is a composite of body and soul. Second, this nature is social, that is, it can attain its full development and self-realization only by living in society with others. Third, this nature is contingent, that is, the cause of its being and existence is not found in itself; it is dependent on its Creator. From this consideration of man's rational nature it follows that the individual has duties to himself, to his fellow men, and to his Maker.

In regard to himself, man must observe a hierarchy of values and so conduct his life that the spiritual is not made subordinate to the organic. For example, to imbibe to the point of drunkenness is an evil act in itself. It is not in conformity with man's rational nature since in getting drunk he fails to observe the hierarchy of values within himself by subordinating the spiritual and its powers to his bodily appetites. Likewise, in his dealings with his fellowmen, his actions must be in conformity with his social nature as this is revealed in the various social relationships which are established for his development and fulfillment. Consequently, it is a good act for a man to support his family, to aid his neighbor, to love his country, to respect the person and property of another. Conversely, it is an evil act to desert one's family, to lie, to steal, to murder, and to betray one's country. And lastly, as a contingent being, his actions must be in conformity to his nature as it is dependent on God. Therefore, acts of worship and reverence are good; acts of irreverence, such as blasphemy, are evil in themselves.

Although it is readily admitted that it is not always easy to work out and define the practical application of this norm of morality in specific cases, nevertheless, it does supply a fixed and immutable measure of universal validity. For example, in a complex, rapidly changing society, it may be difficult to determine what constitutes dishonesty in a commercial transaction; however, the principle that dishonesty is evil remains clear. Precisely because man is a social being, the specific application of this norm of morality in complex circumstances will be worked out by the social group. This leaves room for a certain relativity and development in application, but the important fact remains that the point of departure is a definite, recognizable universal norm.

Summary

To summarize, therefore, Catholics maintain that we can discover the following about human nature. Man is a composite of body and soul. As an integral organism, the person is capable of both bodily and mental activities. The soul, as a spiritual principle, is immortal. Since man is a contingent being, his existence implies a first Cause. For his full development and self-realization he stands in need of others; therefore, he is made to live in society. His mental activities imply a principle of action, the intellect. This is a spiritual faculty placed in contact with external reality through the data of the senses. Thus the person, as a psychophysical unity, is capable of coming to some knowledge of the world about him, of forming judgments, and of drawing conclusions. Although conditioned by biology and past experience, the person is capable of making free choices; consequently, he bears responsibility for his conscious actions. Actions are judged good or bad in relation to a norm of morality which is man's rational nature taken in its entirety.

This philosophical basis of the Catholic ideology must be kept in mind when considering the Catholic approach to marriage and family problems. Following in the tradition of Aristotle and Aquinas, Catholics tend to argue that quite independently of any dogmas of faith or of truths known only through revelation, a definition of human nature can be formulated in which all thinking men can concur. Furthermore, on the basis of this definition, general concepts concerning the nature and purpose of essential human institutions can be developed, with the result that irrespective of divergent religious beliefs, consensus concerning the general form and functioning of the social order can be achieved. Consequently, even in a complex culture, unity of action should result on the basis of those commonly accepted philosophical premises concerning which all can agree.

THE APPROACH FROM THEOLOGY

Turning now to the theological concepts upon which the Catholic ideology is based, we encounter concepts that depend upon revelation, and consequently, are particular to those who accept the fact of revelation. Revelation may be defined as the act whereby God speaks to men either directly through Himself or through His messengers. Hence, it should not be confused with the interior emotional experience of an individual. Rather, it is held that a personal God who is outside of and distinct from the recipient, at a definite time and in a definite place, makes a statement of truth to man. This statement is accepted as true because God has made it. Assent to this truth, therefore, is an act of faith. The faithful believe because of the authority of God "who neither deceives nor can He be deceived."

The Life of Grace

What does revelation contribute to the Catholic doctrine on the origin, nature, and destiny of man? According to revelation as understood by Catholics, when God created man, consisting of body and immortal soul, He added to this human nature a higher kind of life, a supernature. This supernature is a distinct principle of activity through which man can lead a supernatural life of grace. This supernature is a sharing in God's own life, and through it man is destined to supernatural union with God throughout eternity. This supernature is conceived, therefore, as something truly distinct from human nature. It is not merely human nature which has been improved, it is something superadded. It follows that human nature, man's body and soul with all their faculties, remains intact although a supernature has been added. Moreover, since the supernature is a superadded gift, a "gratia," human nature would not be destroyed if the supernatural life itself should be lost. Grace elevates and "informs" human nature, yet always remains separable from it.

The Fall

According to Catholic teaching, this was the nature of original man, of Adam, as he was created by God. However, this gift of supernatural life was given to Adam only on the condition of obedience to a special command. Since this command was disobeyed, God withdrew His gift of supernatural life so that Adam and his posterity were reduced to the merely natural "human" level of existence. Briefly, this is the doctrine of the "fall of man." Stated simply, it means the rejection and consequent loss of the gift of supernatural life. Because Adam, the first man, was the head of the human race, his rejection and loss of grace is transmitted to his posterity. Consequently, his descendants are born without the gift of grace. This is what Catholics mean when they speak of "original sin." It means essentially that human nature because of Adam's sin is deprived of the supernatural life of grace which God intended it to have.

The Redemption

As a consequence of the fall, human nature was incapable of attaining its supernatural destiny. What was needed was a redemption from sin, a restoration to the supernatural life of grace. This was accomplished in a marvelous manner by the "second Adam," Jesus Christ. Christ is God's own Son, the Second Person of the Blessed Trinity, who became incarnate, that is, took upon Himself our human nature and through His Incarnation, Life, Passion, Death, and Resurrection, atoned for Adam's sin and restored human nature to the life of grace. For each individual, this restoration is accomplished through union or incorporation in Christ. He is the source of supernatural life and grace, and only through union with Him can each individual share in the divine life. Specifically, the restoration of the supernature requires that each person be "born again" in Christ and live in union with Him who is the source of supernatural life. This new birth and continued union with Christ is accomplished through the system of rites called "the sacraments."

The Sacraments

Catholics believe that, although Christ lived on this earth for a relatively brief period, his redemptive work is carried on in space and in time through the Church which He established to teach his message of salvation and to dispense the graces which He had merited. This dispensation of grace to men is carried on primarily through the sacraments. A sacrament is defined as an outward, sensible sign instituted as a permanent rite by Jesus Christ to signify and effect by divine grace the sanctification of men. Stated briefly, a sacrament is an outward sign of inward grace instituted by Christ. In other words, there exist in the Church certain transactions of such a nature that they stand as signs of something spiritual. Further, they cause, confer, and contain what they signify. For example, in the rite of baptism, the outward pouring of water on the head of the recipient signifies the inner cleansing from sin and, in conjunction with the words, effects the restoration of supernatural life.

It might be well to note that this symbolism of visible sign and invisible reality runs all through Catholic thought. The visible creation signifies the existence of an invisible God—the Creator is known through His creation. In Christ, human nature veiled the Godhead. Human nature itself is composed of invisible soul and visible body. Consequently, Catholics do not find it strange that Christ should have used visible signs to signify and confer invisible grace. The premise upon which all of this thinking is based, of course, is that visible, material things are good. No part of God's creation is bad, because it stands as a visible sign of his creative act and because He can use it for the most spiritual of purposes. It follows that if there is evil, this is found not in material things but in their misuse.

This group of permanent rites instituted by Christ is called the sacramental "system." The term *system* is used because these rites can be thought of as constituting an orderly series. The first sacrament, baptism, is the New Birth by which the recipient receives supernatural life and begins to live the life of grace. As the young Christian develops in body and mind, he moves toward maturity, toward the "completion" of human nature. The sacrament of confirmation aids this "completion" in the supernatural life. It does not confer that life, but completes and establishes it so that the Christian becomes a "soldier of Christ," that is, has the virtue to imitate Christ in his life. In the sacrament of the Eucharist, the Christian receives strength or "food" for his soul through the reception of the Body and Blood of Christ under the species of bread and wine. He receives further help from the sacrament of penance through which he is strengthened against temptation and obtains forgiveness of sins committed, provided he has a firm purpose of amendment and is truly penitent.

Since the majority of Christians will assume the special responsibilities of the marriage state, the marriage contract has been raised or elevated by Christ to the dignity of a sacrament, thus conferring the spiritual assistance needed for Christian family living. At the same time, those who consecrate themselves in a special manner to the service of God in the priesthood receive the help needed for their office through the sacrament of holy orders. Finally, in the crisis of serious sickness and death, the Christian receives special assistance through the sacrament of extreme unction, the "last sacrament," as the final anointing rite is commonly called. Hence, the sacramental system can be conceived of as seven channels of grace flowing from Christ to the Christian throughout his life "pilgrimage." [2]

The Visible Church

Perhaps the most distinctive dogma in the Catholic ideology is the belief that Christ established a visible society or "church" whose function it is to carry on the work of teaching and sanctification which He began, and to whose rulers He gave the power to teach without error in matters touching on faith and morals. In other words, it is held that Christ founded a living teaching authority which, under the assistance of the Holy Spirit, transmits through all future generations His redemptive message and rites. Consequently, for the Catholic, divine revelation—God's message to men—is received through the written word, the Scriptures, *and* through tradition, that is, through the living teaching authority of the Catholic Church.

The significance of this belief in the existence of a church with infallible teaching authority concerning matters of faith and morals is of fundamental importance in the Catholic ideology. First, it guarantees a universal, unchanging, and timeless consensus in basic doctrines among all the faithful of every age and condition. Second, since it operates under the assistance of the Holy Spirit, it offers the faithful a set of absolute doctrines concerning which they can have no doubt or uncertainty. Third, as a living teaching authority it stands in the midst of each generation a vital witness to the truth, constantly repeating its basic doctrines on the nature of man. The result is that no matter how greatly the faithful of different epochs and divergent cultural backgrounds may disagree on immediate social objectives and the institutionalized means established to implement them, they always have the same point of departure; they operate within the same general frame of reference concerning ultimate values.

CATHOLIC IDEOLOGY AND SEX

This brief resumé of the basic content of the Catholic ideology has been necessary because it is precisely in these doctrines concerning the nature and destiny of man that divergent concepts concerning the nature and function of sex, and consequently, concerning the nature and purposes of marriage, are ultimately rooted. Marriage has "meaning" only in terms of sex, and sex has meaning only in terms of the person. In this connection, it should be noted that the term *sex*, considered comprehensively, signifies that human nature, like most higher forms of life, is expressed disjunctively in male and female. It is this property of maleness and femaleness which constitutes sex. Basically, this property indicates the possession of mutually complementary reproductive organs in male and female so that, in a sense, it can be stated that human nature is adequately expressed only in the reproductive couple. Moreover, the possession of different though mutually complementary reproductive organs has profound implications for male and female. Not only is their entire psychophysical unit diversely affected by its specifically sexual component, but their status and roles in society are related to this characteristic of sexual complementarity and to its specific function in the reproduction of the species.

Consequently, an adequate concept of sex implies this comprehensive approach. Sex signifies something more than the reproductive organs and the external manifestations of their activity. Rather, it signifies that human nature is manifested disjunctively in male and female through the possession of properties which bestow on each a different though mutually complementary function in the reproduction of the species. Hence, sex is a property of the person. Although the character and activity of specific reproductive organs may be studied in themselves, their use can be understood only in terms of the person.

In the following pages, we shall develop the Catholic concept of sex and the moral norms which govern its functions. This treatment is pertinent to the present study, but the necessary emphasis given to the subject here should not lead one to conclude that other areas of human conduct lack equal significance either for the development of the individual or for the integrity of the Catholic moral system. The basic moral principles which will be applied are relevant to all human acts. A discussion of their specific application to one area of human conduct offers but one illustration of how the integral moral system is developed.

Systems of Control

The personal factor is of paramount importance in considering the social consequences of the fact of sex. The reproductive drive is so powerful that every society has established restraints and controls lest this impulse lead individuals to actions considered disruptive of the social order. The formulation of these controls has not proved an easy task. Essentially, the problem consists in reconciling the need for control with the need for expression. Social order demands control; group survival requires expression. Considering the complexity of the problem and the various ways that one can conceive of the function of sex, it is not surprising that cultures differ greatly in the way they have defined their prohibitions and permissions.[3]

In general, two well-defined approaches have been followed in formulating a system of controls for the reproductive drive. The first is society-centered and does not seek to regulate the drive directly. It does not regard sexual phenomena from the person's point of view but rather from that of the social system. Because control of this powerful impulse is needed to maintain society's marriage, reproductive, kinship, status, and ceremonial systems, regulations are established in terms of these systems.

This approach to the regulation of sexual behavior is common to most cultures outside the Christian sphere of influence. Its point of departure, as we have indicated, is social rather than personal. Since sexual behavior is regulated in terms of other social phenomena with respect to which it is important, its morality is judged, not in relation to the person, but in relation to these other phenomena. For example, sexual relations are forbidden between certain classes of persons within the kinship group or clan; sexual advances are prohibited during certain ceremonials or at specified seasons or under designated circumstances. Generally these regulations are formulated and enforced to insure peace and order in the family, the clan, or the group. Outside these regulated areas, free expression of the sexual drive is permitted to the individual. In other words, sexual behavior in itself is regarded as nonmoral; one "sins" only when his action violates certain socially established patterns of conduct.

The second approach to the problem of control is person-centered and focuses on the drive itself. It seeks to establish a system of control which covers all the manifestations of the impulse under all circumstances. This is the Christian personalist approach, since it considers the drive from the point of view of the individual and weighs the consequences of its use or misuse in terms of the perfection of the person. This does not mean that the social consequences of the exercise of this drive are ignored, but the system of controls is formulated in terms of personal perfection, rather than social necessity, on the hypothesis that a well-ordered society is founded on well-ordered individuals. In practice, therefore, social control will appear to focus on the reproductive drive itself rather than on those specific manifestations of it which the group judges to be particularly disruptive of good order.

It should be emphasized that the point of departure and of return in this system is the human person. But it is the person

conceived of in terms of Christian values, that is, the person
having a transcendental goal, a destiny of eternal union with
God, made possible through the possession of supernatural
life. In terms of this transcendental goal, all other things are
considered as means (which does not at all signify, as is sometimes suggested, that they are *despised*). Hence, the development of personality and self-realization are conceived of as the
development and self-realization of the whole person. Specifically, the exercise of the reproductive faculty is developmental
only to the extent that it conforms to the nature and destiny
of the integral person.

The significant difference between these two approaches is
that the first conceives of morality of sexual behavior in terms
of some social phenomenon, such as marriage, kinship, and
so forth, in respect to which this behavior is important; the
second evaluates sexual behavior in terms of the human person. In the first, only those exercises of the reproductive faculty which possess recognized social significance have moral
pertinence; in the second, every free, conscious exercise of
the drive must be evaluated morally. In other words, every
thought, word, and action concerned with sex is regulated by
a personally supervised code which is devised with respect
to a creator, an integral personal destiny, and a social purpose.
Both approaches produce a set of culturally standardized practices which range through definitely prescribed or preferred
or permitted patterns of behavior to those definitely proscribed.
Hence, both solve the problem of reconciling the need for
control with the need for expression; in each approach, however, the solution is based on different premises.

These two approaches to the formulation of controls over
sexual behavior have been treated in some detail because the
problem of reconciling the need for sexual expression with the
need for its control is not easily solved in a complex culture.
American society, in particular, finds itself in a confused and
paradoxical situation. On the one hand, as a participant in the
broad stream of western Christian culture, American society
has followed the second approach and has traditionally based
its solution on the personalist concept of the function of sex.
On the other hand, numerous powerful and vocal groups in

modern society have rejected the original Christian view of the origin, nature, and destiny of the human person, with the result that for many, the personalist approach to sex has been deprived of its ideological foundation. Much of the confusion concerning the function of sex today has its origin in the fact that the traditional (and still theoretically approved) norms and practices have been erected on a concept of the person which is no longer accepted by some—and is no longer consciously recognized as the only logical basis for the Christian code by many more.

For the personalist approach to the control of the reproductive drive is logical and can become operative only if the human person is viewed in its integrity, that is, only if the person is considered capable of arriving at an objective norm of morality and is judged morally responsible for his acts to his Creator. In other words, this approach implies that there are moral norms governing the exercise of the reproductive drive and that the violation of these norms constitutes a moral evil or sin. This is the rationale of the personalist approach; to reject it is to render the norms and practices based on it meaningless and ultimately inoperative.

The Function of Sex

It seems scarcely necessary to point out that the Catholic approach to sex is personalist. However, since the Church's teaching on sex is not infrequently considered apart from its ideological context, it has been the subject of some misunderstanding, misinterpretation, and no little confusion. For this reason, it will be useful to develop this teaching in some detail. In considering the Catholic position, two preliminary observations must be kept in mind. First, Christianity teaches profound respect for the elevated dignity of the human body which, though corruptible, is destined for immortality (I Cor. 15:42-43). The body is not to be considered as merely "animal" or degraded, nor is any part or portion of the body to be judged unclean or evil. Likewise, the basic drives, forces, and potentialities of the body are not to be regarded as shameful or evil in themselves. The body was created as the instrument

and companion of the soul, together with which, as a component element, it forms the human person.[4]

Second, inner unity and order in man is not simply a static,
given reality—it is a dynamic state to be achieved and maintained by the right ordering of human impulses and acts. The
human person exists in a state of tension through a necessity
inherent in its very structure. To be sure, body and soul, the
two component principles of human nature, have an internal
proportion to each other resulting in substantial union, but
the body, since it is composed of matter, is subject to the laws
of matter, and consequently it offers the possibility of conflict
and opposition. As St. Thomas states: ". . . this conflict coming of opposed desires does not arise exclusively from sin, but
also from the necessity of matter. For since man possesses a
sensibility, he cannot but feel pleasure and desire for pleasur-
able things, and many of these are contrary to reason." [5]

This opposition is so real that according to Catholic teaching, a gift of supernatural grace is needed to compose the conflict. Our first parents possessed this grace in the state of innocence, but this preternatural gift was lost as a consequence of
the Fall so that today men find themselves in the tragic state
of tension so graphically described by St. Paul: "I see another
law in my members, warring against the law of my mind and
making me prisoner to the law of sin that is in my members"
(Romans, 7:23). As St. Thomas points out when speaking of
the virtue of temperance, which regulates, according to right
reason, the sensitive appetite in the pleasures of taste and
touch, these powers "can most easily bring unrest to the spirit,
because they belong to the essence of man." [6] It follows that
man is daily confronted with the arduous task of imposing
right order in the use of the pleasures of taste and touch. Because they are necessary for the development and survival of
the individual and the species, he cannot forego their use;
yet, because they represent the most powerful drives in his
nature, their use must be subjected to right reason lest they
destroy his inner order and disrupt the peace of the community.

With these considerations in mind let us take up the Catholic teaching on sex. The divine plan concerning the purpose

and function of sex is revealed in the opening pages of Scripture. Here the Creator shows that He desires to associate men with His creative activity by making the propagation and education of the human race depend on their free cooperation. Further, this cooperation was to be a work of love and hence, God created human nature in two sexes—"Male and female He created them." It follows that each individual possesses human nature in an incomplete manner. In order to reproduce and thus, perpetuate himself, the individual must be united with another of the opposite sex. Since man is a composite of body and soul, sexual differences extend beyond the physical; they affect the sensitive, intellectual, and moral aspects of the person.

A powerful drive within the sexes draws them together and impels them toward union. Hence, God appears as the Creator of the basic differences which characterize the sexes, of the powerful drive which leads them to unite, of the necessity of this sexual union for the propagation of the race, and finally, of the pleasures associated with this union. It follows that nothing in the sexual life of man is evil in itself, for it represents a divine work. If evil exists, it must consist in exercising one's sexual powers contrary to the divine plan. Man, as a responsible creature, must realize the order of reason in the realm of sexuality as in all other areas of his conscious activity.

Morality of Sex

To understand the Catholic position on moral rectitude in sexual behavior it will be helpful to keep clearly in mind a fundamental principle laid down by St. Thomas: "The more necessary something is, the more the order of reason must be preserved in it." [7] It is precisely because the sexual power is so noble and necessary, enabling man to cooperate with God in His creative activity, that it requires the preserving and protecting order of reason.[8] The order of reason demands that the imminent purpose of sexual power be not perverted but fulfilled (in marriage), that the inner structure of the moral person be kept intact (the primacy of the spiritual over the physical), and that justice between men be observed (the social significance of sex).[9] In other words, it requires the realization of the divine plan for sex, that is, the propagation of the human race under conditions worthy of the human person. Since sex is the property of intelligent, free, responsible beings, their union should not be restricted to the satisfaction of a mere biological impulse, but should be elevated to the dignity of a voluntary gift expressive of their mutual love.

Chastity and Modesty

According to Catholic teaching, it is the virtue of chastity which regulates, on the basis of principles drawn from reason and faith, the voluntary exercise of the sexual faculty in man. The Scriptural foundation for this teaching is found in the sixth and ninth commandments. The sixth states: "Thou shalt not commit adultery" (Exod. 20:14). The ninth states: "Thou shalt not desire thy neighbor's wife" (Exod. 20:17). Adultery alone is explicitly forbidden by the sixth commandment, but all actions which are intended to lead or which naturally lead to it, and all actions contrary to the orderly propagation of the race are implicitly forbidden. The ninth commandment forbids all lustful thoughts and desires.[10] These two commandments inculcate the virtue of chastity, and the six that of modesty also.[11]

Chastity may be defined as:

> . . . the moral virtue that controls in the married and altogether excludes in the unmarried all voluntary expression of the sensitive appetite for venereal pleasure. This pleasure is normally associated as well with the full exercise of the generative function as with the movements of the generative organs as they are preparing to function.[12]

Modesty, as it relates to the virtue of chastity, may be broadly defined as that habitual disposition which impels one to avoid everything which is likely to excite venereal pleasure contrary to right order either in ourselves or in others.[13] This virtue is not to be confused with chastity. It is the function of modesty to protect and stand guard over those avenues which experience has taught may lead to acts of unchastity. Chastity has absolute norms based on human nature considered in itself and consequently, valid for all times. The acts which chastity prohibits are clearly defined and unchangeable. On the other hand, external modesty is relative.[14] The acts which modesty prohibits cannot be deduced from any universal, a priori norm. This follows from the very function of modesty as defined above. Since modesty is to guard the avenues which lead to unchastity and experience shows that the dangers which threaten chastity differ according to persons, times, and places, external modesty will depend to a considerable extent upon these changing factors.[15]

It is well to emphasize that immodest acts must be avoided chiefly because of the dangers of unchastity. As we have indicated, the human person has difficulty in maintaining right order in the exercise of his basic drives. Experience teaches that one of the most imperious of these is the drive for venereal pleasure. Now venereal pleasure considered in itself is not evil, but once it is aroused, there is danger that an individual may consent to it, contrary to right reason, thus sinning against chastity. Consequently, modesty avoids those actions which common sense and experience show will either arouse or entail the danger of arousing venereal pleasure. True modesty is neither puritanical nor prudish, but realistic, stating simply: If you wish to avoid unchastity, you had better avoid actions which arouse venereal pleasure since experience teaches that this passion, once aroused, frequently entices consent.

To recapitulate, the use of the sexual faculties, like all voluntary activity of man, is subjected to moral norms. These norms take into consideration the nature of the sexual faculties and their essential purpose. Since God created human nature in two sexes, whose physical union is necessary for the propagation of the race, the exercise of the sexual faculties according to the divine plan is a morally good act. What is the divine plan for the use of the sexual faculties? It is maintained that this is discovered by considering the nature of these faculties. An analysis of the sexual organs reveals that they are ordained not primarily for the good of the individual, but for the good of the species. Consequently, in using his sexual faculties, man must respect their primary, essential purpose.

To use them while positively excluding their essential relationship to the species is to act contrary to the order required by right reason. To perform such an act is unreasonable and hence, morally wrong.

It should be noted that the moral evil of the act is in the will by which man chooses to exercise his sexual faculties contrary to right order. The sexual organs which are used are not evil any more than is the human body with its natural tendencies, phantasms, thoughts, looks, touches, and so forth. These become blameworthy only when they become the manifestation of a morally culpable act of the will. It is the conscious, deliberate choice to use the sexual faculties contrary to the moral law which constitutes sins of unchastity.[16] It is necessary to emphasize this point since "despite all contrary statements of principle, a smoldering subterranean Manichaeism casts suspicion on everything pertaining to physical reproduction as being somehow impure, defiling, and beneath the true dignity of man." [17] When dealing with the subject of sex, many find it difficult to take seriously the fundamental principle of revelation—"Everything created by God is good"—and think it through to its conclusion.

Chastity of the Unmarried

The practical application of this Catholic doctrine on the function of sex has resulted in the formulation of norms regulating sexual behavior in various life situations. All persons are bound to practice the virtue of chastity. As we have indicated, this altogether excludes the voluntary exercise of the sexual faculty in the unmarried and requires that it be used in accord with right reason in the married. Hence, masturbation is morally wrong because it represents the use of a faculty contrary to right order. Physical union outside of marriage is morally wrong for the same reason. In addition, such a union is a violation of justice. If one or both the parties are married, it is an act of injustice to the marriage partner, and if they are both unmarried, it is an injustice to the child that may result from their union.

A special problem arises in our culture, where adolescents

reach biological maturity several years before they become socially mature, that is, before they are considered old enough to marry. Under such conditions, the virtue of modesty plays a paramount role since it is only by guarding the avenues of thought, words, and actions which lead to sexual excitation that the adolescent can subject his developing sexual power to the control of reason. The Church's counsels in this area are frequently misunderstood by those who do not accept the Catholic doctrine on the function of sex. In reality, however, the Catholic insistence on modesty is logical since voluntary occasions leading to sexual excitation must obviously be avoided by those who are not free to perform the sexual act.

The problem of sexual control may become particularly acute during the engagement period.[18] The norms which apply to the situation are as follows. The couple are permitted those manifestations of mutual affection commonly regarded as proper to their situation in the culture. They are not permitted to seek sexual gratification before marriage and must refuse consent to any sexual excitation which may incidentally arise through the performance of permissible acts of affection during this period. Since individuals differ greatly, no more detailed norms governing this situation can be formulated. A profound appreciation of the virtue of chastity, some knowledge of the psychological differences between the sexes, and a sincere appraisal of past experience are the guides which Catholic teaching stresses in this difficult relationship.

Conjugal Chastity

The norms regulating the function of sex in marriage (conjugal chastity) may be broadly summarized as follows. Physical union in marriage is an objectively good act. It may be desired by either spouse for the purpose of showing love, procuring children, or physical release. Ideally, it should always be an act of mutual affection, a normal culmination of domestic love-making of the spouses, "two in one flesh." This follows from the very nature of the act considered in itself, for the essence of physical union is the communion of male and female in the joy of procreating love. Further, since the mutual gift in physical union is by its very nature a life-giving, procreating gift by which male and female mutually complete each other, mutually supply that which the other lacks in terms of generation, the very meaning of the act implies that each gives freely and unreservedly what they are able. This, in turn, implies that they place no obstacle to the natural process of procreation. To place a direct obstacle to the natural process of procreation is to deprive the mutual gift in physical union of its life-giving, procreating character. Under such conditions, the act of union loses its essential meaning since it no longer represents an act by which male and female lovingly complete each other—become one in a procreating act of love.

It is precisely this profound respect for the meaning of sex in human nature which furnishes the basis for Catholic thinking in this area. The Church's stand on contraceptives, which we shall take up shortly, as well as her teaching on premarital chastity, find their ultimate justification here. To continue our treatment of conjugal chastity, it should be noted that although the marital act is objectively good, right order requires that other factors be considered in its use. For example, during periods of sickness, fatigue, pregnancy, and so forth, justice and charity demand mutual forbearance and consideration. In general, since the act of physical union is good, all the acts leading up to and accompanying it are morally good. Here again, charity requires sincere respect for the attitudes and sentiments of the partner. When the partners do not wish to perform the marriage act, mutual manifestations of affection should be such as not to voluntarily lead to serious sexual excitation. Experience and a sincere respect for the physical and spiritual health of the partner serve as the best guides in this matter.

Birth Control

Perhaps no point of Catholic teaching on the function of sex is more sharply questioned than the Church's position on birth control. For this reason, it will be well to treat this subject in some detail. The Catholic position has been criticized as outmoded, contradictory, and even inhuman. The implication running through all this criticism is that the Church's position is merely a disciplinary measure and consequently, amenable to change. This is to misunderstand completely the reasoning on which the Church's position is based. Her stand on birth control follows logically from the Catholic teaching on the function of sex. It is for this reason that we have chosen to treat this subject here rather than in the chapter on marriage.

Any intelligent discussion of birth control must begin with a definition of terms and a clear statement of premises if hopeless confusion is to be avoided. In regard to terms, birth control may have many meanings, ranging from the planned limitation of offspring through virtuous continence to the control of fertility through the use of contraceptive devices. We shall use the term to include all deliberate acts which are aimed directly at the antecedent frustration of the fecundity of the conjugal act. Further, birth control may be considered from many different points of view: as a social phenomenon in its effects on the size and growth of population, as a physical and psychic phenomenon in its effects on the satisfaction and happiness of marriage partners, as a moral phenomenon in its effects on the moral character of the agent. We are interested here in birth control only in the last sense, that is, in its quality of moral goodness or evil.

A clear statement of premises is needed since a judgment concerning the morality of birth control is nothing more than the application of general moral principles to a specific act. Consequently, if we start with different general moral principles, our judgments concerning the morality of birth control will differ. This point needs to be emphasized. It is obvious that a materialist who maintains that man is merely a highly developed animal without the spiritual faculties of intellect and will and without an essential relationship of origin and dependence on his Creator is not going to arrive at the same judgment concerning the morality of birth control as will a Christian. In fact, if he reasons logically from his premises, the materialist will conclude that there is no morality involved and will evaluate the act in terms of his own satisfaction. It follows that any worth-while discussion of birth control with a materialist will immediately uncover differences in basic moral principles, and since these are based on our concept of the nature, origin, and destiny of man, the discussion must ultimately center on this point.

The premises upon which the Catholic position is based may be briefly summarized as follows. First, man has been created by God and stands in a relationship of essential dependence on Him. Second, as a reasonable being, man is to use things according to the plan the Creator intended in creating them. Man learns this plan by studying things in their normal and essential operations. Third, in regard to those things placed under his dominion, man acts reasonably when he uses them for his self-development and perfection in God's service. Fourth, God, the Author of Life, has not placed life or the principles of life under man's dominion. Man holds these in trust. Hence, man must respect his own life and that of others, and he is not permitted to destroy life merely for his own satisfaction. Likewise, man must respect the natural process of the generative act, in which he furnishes the co-principle of life, and he is not permitted to exercise his generative faculty while placing a direct, antecedent obstacle to its generative function. The function of sex has been entrusted to man primarily for the good of the species. The highly unique character of the sexual act derives first, from the fact that it is the act which the Creator has ordained for the propagation of the species and second, its fruitful exercise requires the special cooperation of the Creator, the Author of each new life.

Let us apply these principles to the act of birth control. It is obvious from a consideration of the specific constitution of male and female that they are prepared to cooperate with the Creator in the production of new life. They possess internal organs for the preparation of the principles of life and external organs for the union of these principles. Further, they are endowed with a powerful reproductive drive which strongly impels them to the exercise of this function. Both the internal and external organs, as well as the act by which they function, are called generative. Not that generation necessarily follows every act of sexual union, but the nature of the organs is such that their essential purpose is reproduction, and this can and does follow their exercise.

To be sure, the immediate result of sexual union is physical release, a temporary cessation of the reproductive drive, and a profound union of the partners, but these are consequent and accompanying effects of the generative act and clearly not the primary purpose of the generative faculties. Now, by definition, birth control is the performing of an act which is generative by nature, at the same time, frustrating its generative purpose by deliberately placing an obstacle to the natural generative process. In other words, the agent wills and does not will the generative act at the same time. Hence, he is not acting as a reasonable being. In fact, his action represents a contradiction in the practical order since he wills to perform the generative act, and at the same time, he does not will it inasmuch as he seeks to frustrate its primary, specific generative quality.

Further, this is a gravely sinful act. In the first place, it represents a serious deviation from an essential and necessary order in creation and therefore, from the Creator's plan in creating man, male and female, and endowing him with procreative faculties. Second, the unique and sacred character of the act by which man is enabled to cooperate with the Creator in the production of new life bestows special significance on the use of the generative faculty. Hence, man must have a sovereign respect for the natural process of procreation and for the inviolability of this process once it is set in motion. This respect forbids him to interfere with or disturb the natural relationship between physical union and procreation which exists in the total physiological process.

It follows that if man desires to perform the conjugal act, he may not interfere with the natural procreative process of this act. Whether generation follows or not, is not his to decide. Further, as long as he performs the act in conformity with its nature, he may act even when he knows that generation will not or may not follow. In so doing he is not acting unreasonably nor contrary to right order since the conjugal act possesses subordinate effects such as the fostering of mu-

tual love and the release of desire which may amply justify its
use. For example, to perform the conjugal act when one of
the partners is sterile either temporarily or permanently is not
in itself an unreasonable act nor does it represent a deviation
from the Creator's plan. The partners respect the natural procreative process of the act; the fact that generation does not
follow is beyond their control.

Periodic Continence

The specific type of interference in the procreative process
which the Church condemns in its prohibition on the use of
contraceptives will be seen more clearly from a consideration
of why the Church tolerates periodic continence or rhythm.
Granted the existence of serious reasons for limiting the number of offspring, periodic continence is permitted and at times
is to be counseled precisely because it leaves the natural procreative process intact.[19] As a matter of fact, in using rhythm
the couple are merely making use of a sterile period which
nature offers them. Since physical union serves additional purposes besides procreation, they are justified in performing
this act in order to satisfy these subordinate purposes. Through
increased knowledge of the procreative process, man has
learned that there are periods in which the act of physical
union and fecundity are dissociated. Consequently, in using
rhythm, the couple place no obstacle which restricts or violates the physiological process of procreation. The process remains intact although they are obviously limiting procreation.
On the other hand, let us suppose they use their knowledge of
the procreative process to increase their chances of having offspring. Hence, they perform the marital act only during that
period when fecundity is most likely to occur. Here again,
there is no question of positive interference in the physiological process. It is merely by choosing to have marital relations
during certain periods that they increase their chances of procreating. Whether the couple uses periodic continence to increase fecundity or to limit it, they do not interfere with the
relationship between sexual union and procreation. In either

case this relationship is respected since it is left up to nature itself.

It will be seen, therefore, that what the Church opposes in its prohibition of contraceptive practices is the positive and direct intervention in the process of procreation which the married couple have freely initiated by their physical union.[20] Hence, to clear up a misunderstanding which has frequently arisen concerning the Catholic position on birth control, we emphasize that the essential and primary evil of the act is not that it may hinder a possible fecundation. This may or may not follow the conjugal act and is quite independent of the will of man. The evil of the act consists essentially in its deordination, its deviation from right order. It is primarily an act by which man usurps dominion he does not possess by frustrating the essential purpose of this unique and noble faculty.

This traditional Catholic position has been forcefully and authoritatively stated by Pius XI in his encyclical on Christian Marriage:

> Any use whatsoever of matrimony exercised in such a way that the act is deliberately frustrated in its natural power to generate life is an offense against the law of God and of nature, and those who indulge in such are branded with the guilt of grave sin.[21]

He proves that the act is gravely sinful and against nature as follows:

> Since, therefore, the conjugal act is destined primarily by nature for the begetting of children, those who in exercising it deliberately frustrate its natural power and purpose, sin against nature and commit a deed which is shameful and intrinsically vicious.[22]

Hence, the Catholic position on birth control is founded on the order of reason and on authority. It does not represent merely disciplinary regulations promulgated for the direction of the faithful but rather, it is an obvious application of general moral principles to a specific act. As such, it is not within the power of the Pope or of Christians to change. Consequently, the rejection of the Catholic position implies either a lack of logic in reasoning or a denial of the basic moral principles upon which it is based.

The Virtue of Virginity

Finally, our discussion of Catholic teaching concerning the function of sex would not be complete unless we clarified a point of doctrine which has occasioned no end of confused controversy since the Renaissance and the Reformation. This is the Catholic position on the value of the virtue of virginity. The Council of Trent in its 24th Session defined this position by stating that "the married state is not to be preferred to the state of virginity or celibacy," and further, "it is better and happier to remain in virginity or celibacy than to be joined in matrimony." This comparison between the state of marriage and virginity runs all through Christian ascetical thought and has been the occasion of frequent exaggeration and misunderstanding for Catholics and non-Catholics alike. Even as early as Tertullian's time (160?–230?) the objection had to be met that in praising virginity the Christians condemned marriage. His answer to Marcion has been repeated down through the centuries: "We acknowledge and practice that holiness (virginity) without condemning marriage, not as if we preferred a good thing rather than an evil, but as preferring a better thing to a good." [23]

The comparison between marriage and continency is based on the familiar distinction between the precepts and the counsels. There are two degrees of morality set forth in the Gospels. First, there are the precepts, the moral laws, binding on all. These laws provide a wide margin of action for human freedom. To be specific, with the exception of certain circumstances, each individual is free to marry or not. Of course, once marriage has been contracted, the moral laws regulating this institution must be obeyed since the virtue of chastity must be practiced by married and unmarried alike according to their different circumstances. Second, in the counsels God invites some to a more perfect dedication of themselves in His service. Those who heed this invitation aspire to a way of life which is higher than that of the precepts. Through a life devoted to prayer, sacrifice, and the apostolate a state of life is assumed in which the individual strives to forget himself in order to dedicate himself to the service of God and his neighbor more completely. This renouncement of self is not imposed by God—it is offered as a free choice to the individual in the religious vocation and/or the priesthood.

The existence of this way of the counsels is not a condemnation of the way of the precepts. The fact that some generously renounce the goods of marriage in order to serve God more perfectly is no more a condemnation of marriage than the renouncing of ownership through evangelical poverty is a condemnation of private property. Christ Himself made the distinction between the way of the counsels and the precepts when pointing out to the rich young man the ways which lead to salvation. "But if thou wilt enter into life, keep the commandments!" . . . The young man said: "All these have I kept . . . what is yet wanting to me?" Jesus said to him: "If thou wilt be perfect, go sell what thou hast . . . and come follow me." [24]

Hence, anyone who accepts the Catholic doctrines on the nature and destiny of man is forced to conclude that the *state* of virginity which is consecrated to the service of God is higher and more perfect than the *state* of marriage lived according to the precepts. If man is created to serve God and this service admits of various degrees of completeness, then the state of life which involves the most complete dedication of service is clearly the higher and more perfect. Indeed, this conclusion is so obvious in the Christian frame of reference that it should cause little difficulty. Unfortunately, the premises upon which it is founded have been frequently misunderstood. In the first place, the virginity the Church holds up for admiration is not a fact, but an act. It is based not on a condition, but on a decision. Virginity considered as a virtue is established by the decision or vow to refrain forever from sexual union and its attendant pleasure. Consequently, it is not mere inviolateness as a psychic (and clearly not as a physical) factor which makes virginity a virtue.[25]

Further, the decision to remain virginal must be based on the right motives. As St. Augustine stated: "Virginity is honored not because it is virginity, but because it is consecrated." [26] Hence, the decision to remain virginal is "made praiseworthy only by its end and purpose, to the extent that it aims to make him who practices it free for things divine." [27] It follows that virginity which does not realize the purpose of being free for God and for divine things loses its meaning or, at any rate, does not possess the dignity for which virginity is honored by the Church. Virginity is esteemed not because the sexual appetite is considered impure and evil, but rather because the voluntary abstinence from what is in itself good and lawful frees the person for a more unrestricted service of God.[28] Finally, the Christian's decision to remain virginal is a direct affirmation of marriage as both a natural and supernatural good. This is clearly expressed in the Church's official prayer for the blessing and consecration of virgins. In this prayer we are told that those who forego the "honorable state of matrimony" and the nuptial blessing, nevertheless seek that which the sacrament of matrimony signifies, namely, union with Christ, the divine Spouse of every Christian soul.[29]

Once these premises are clearly understood, the logic of the comparison between the state of virginity and that of marriage becomes apparent. In practice, however, the problem is not so simple. It cannot be denied that in praising the merits of virginity many preachers and ascetical writers have either fallen into exaggeration or have neglected to develop proper esteem for the marriage state. The failure to maintain a position more in conformity with integral Christian doctrine can be explained in some cases as a reaction to the immoral practices of the times. This was particularly true in the early centuries of the Church's existence when the Christian minority was surrounded with a disorganized pagan culture and every convert to the new religion lived in imminent danger of death or exile. Furthermore, since the sexual drive is so universal and powerful, the practice of chastity, which is the virtue regulating the exercise of the sex function in accordance with right reason, has always been difficult. For this reason, it is given more frequent treatment in sermons and ascetical writing, with the result that proper balance is easily lost.

Finally, side by side with the true Christian view of sex the notion has always existed in some form that matter, or the body, or the visible world at large is somehow evil in itself. In early Christian times this doctrine was seen in the Manichaeans, a curious sect of Persian origin, whose influence was extensive. The Middle Ages witnessed many strange versions of the same notion best exemplified by the Albigenses and Cathari. According to these groups, food, marriage, and in fact, anything to do with the physical life of man, was evil owing to his fallen nature or even to the essential badness of matter. Right down to our own times a false Puritanism has persisted which either attempts to ignore the presence of the sexual drive in human nature or treats it as something wholly "carnal," "animal," or "dirty." [30]

Whatever form this opinion may take, whether it be the Manichaean condemnation of the body as essentially evil or the exaggerated asceticism which fears sex as the basic threat to sanctification, obviously places marriage in a very poor light. Granting that every culture must face the difficult problem of balancing the need for sexual control with the need for expression, the fundamental soundness of the integral Christian approach becomes apparent. All things that God created are good; evil comes from using them irrationally. It is the function of chastity, a part of the general moral virtue of temperance, to regulate the sexual appetite in accordance with right reason. Consequently, the virtue of chastity must be practiced in the unmarried and married state alike since the voluntary expression of the sensitive appetite for venereal pleasure must be rationally controlled according to one's state of life.

These brief and necessarily selective considerations of pertinent aspects of the Catholic ideology have prepared the ground for an understanding of the Catholic concept of marriage. As we have indicated, this concept is scarcely intelligible unless the Catholic doctrine concerning the origin, nature, and destiny of man is recognized. Once this point of departure is known, the Catholic position on marriage and the family will be seen to follow with evident logic.

In the following chapter we shall discuss the Catholic ideal and the juridical framework which the Church has established to implement and protect this ideal. This approach will enable us to understand the general frame of reference within which the individual Catholic views marriage and the family. This knowledge is necessary. Indeed, it is only by knowing the Catholic "definition of the situation" that we can understand the problems which the Catholic minority faces in our complex, changing society.

CHAPTER THREE

The Church and Marriage

When the Catholic Church was established, its first members—gentiles and Jews—were drawn from existing family systems in which they continued to live and through which they had been educated and conditioned. Christianity as a spiritual movement did not destroy these systems, but its teaching on chastity, sexual equality before God, and the sanctity and indissolubility of marriage worked as a powerful leven gradually transforming existing systems into some approximation of the Christian ideal. This was a long and arduous process characterized by numerous reverses, misconceptions, changing emphases, and only limited success.

The full implications as well as the profound social significance of the Christian concept of marriage emerged gradually out of the developing Christian synthesis. This represented elements of the Jewish, Greco-Roman, Egyptian (Coptic), Byzantine, Germanic, and Celtic cultures. It is not necessary here to retrace all the steps in the development of the Catholic teaching on marriage, but since it is sometimes implied that this doctrine was developed relatively late, attention should be called to the following points.

EARLY CHURCH DOCTRINE

By the time of Augustine (354–430) the marriage doctrine universally taught in the Church contained these essential elements. (1) Christian marriage was instituted by Christ. Since the primitive institution had become corrupted by pagan customs or by Jewish concessions, Jesus restored marriage to its primitive purity. (2) Marriage assures to the spouses the graces which will permit them to fulfill the duties of their state of life. (3) Christ Himself sanctified marriage, and the first manifestation of this was His presence and first miracle (the changing of water into wine) at the marriage feast of Cana. At each marriage this sanctification is renewed. The visible sign of this renewal is the benediction and other ceremonies of the Church. In this symbolism, the Church Fathers found the basis for all that was great in Christian marriage. Christian marriage must be holy, one, and indissoluble precisely because it is the symbol of the union of Christ with His Church. (5) The holiness and permanency of the contract entered into by Christian spouses has the same characteristics as the engagement of the Christian to the service of God, or of the priest to the service of the altar. Marriage, baptism, and ordination are frequently compared in sermons and writing.[1]

It was St. Augustine who formulated the classic definition of the three goods of marriage in his famous trilogy: *fides, proles, sacramentum* (loyalty, children, indissoluble unity). As he explains these terms, loyalty signifies that marriage is an exclusive relation between one man and one woman so that any form of infidelity by either party is sinful; children signifies that the purpose of marriage is the procreation and education of offspring, and this is one of its greatest blessings; indissolubility signifies that marriage is holy and permanent since the unity of man and wife in matrimony symbolizes the unity of Christ with His Bride, the Church.[2] Augustine's teaching on marriage exercised profound influence on the Catholic view of marriage throughout the Middle Ages. It was clarified and developed in the writings of St. Thomas Aquinas (1225?–1274) and received its final formulation in the Council of Trent (1545–1563).

MARRIAGE AS AN ACT AND AS A STATUS

The Catholic concept of marriage must be treated in some detail because it differs on certain specific points from most views accepted in our culture. To be sure, it has always been held throughout Christian history "that marriage should be monogamous, and ideally for life, with the obligation of fidelity equally binding upon both partners." [3] However, diversities of emphasis and attitude have been prevalent. Particularly since the Reformation, the divergence between the traditional Catholic view and that of the other Christian churches has widened.

Catholics define marriage as the lawful contract between man and woman by which is given and accepted the exclusive and perpetual right to those mutual bodily functions which are naturally apt to generate offspring.[4] Marriage is truly a contract since it involves a bilateral agreement between a man and a woman. By its nature the contract can be made only by male and female since the purpose of the contract is the supplying of mutually complementary sexual rights. The marriage contract can be considered under two aspects, as an act or as a state. Considered as an act, it is the formation of a bilateral contract, defined as a legitimate agreement between a man and a woman conferring the mutual, exclusive, and perpetual right both to acts which are of their very nature proper for begetting offspring, and to the sharing of life together. Marriage as a state is the conjugal union or state which arises from this act. This state may be defined as the legitimate union or society of a man and a woman for the purposes of generating and educating offspring and for mutual aid and companionship. Hence, the essence of the act of marriage is the mutual consent of the parties; the essence of the marriage state consists in the mutual sharing of life together.

ESSENTIAL PROPERTIES OF MARRIAGE

The contents and the nature of the marriage contract have been established and ordained by the Creator. Individuals are free to enter the contract or not, but they cannot alter its contents. The nature and essential purposes of the contract are independent of the wills of the contracting parties. If anything contrary to the essential nature and purposes of the conjugal union is expressed in the marital consent, it is maintained that there is no true marriage.[5] The specific qualities or properties of marriage are deduced from the primary object of the contract. In marriage, male and female are united as one principle for the purpose of procreation. This is the primary object of the contract. The conjugal union, to be sure, should be based on mutual love and affection; it supplies a suitable foundation for the control and expression of the sexual drive; it results in mutual actions providing pleasure of the highest kind; but all these things presuppose and take for granted the primary object of marriage; that is, those actions which are of their nature fitted for the generation of children.

In other words, a distinction must be made between objective functions and subjective purposes. The objective purpose or function of the marriage contract is that to which it is directed by its very nature or form. This is what the philosophers call the *finis operis,* the end or purpose of the thing considered in itself. Subjective purpose, however, implies conscious motivation. This is the personal motive or intention of the spouses in making and carrying out the contract. Philosophers call this the *finis operantis,* that is, the purpose or end intended by the one performing the work. It is clear that individuals enter marriage and establish a family for a great number of reasons. They seek love, companionship, social status and economic security, the avoidance of loneliness, escape from unpleasant surroundings or monotony, personal fulfillment and self-realization, and so forth. These subjective motives or purposes are not to be confused with the objective meaning and purpose of the marriage contract considered in itself. In fact, these subjective purposes have meaning and converge ultimately toward the primary and principal purpose of marriage, which is the generation and rearing of offspring.

Perhaps some of the confusion concerning this point has arisen because of the traditional terminology, which distinguishes between the primary and secondary purposes of marriage. The primary purpose is the procreation and rearing of offspring; the secondary purposes are companionship, the allaying of concupiscence, and so forth. This distinction of purposes has not been made with any implication as to their meaning and value to the individual. Rather it insists on the obvious biological fact that the marriage contract forms a union of persons of the opposite sex, and sex, taken in its integral meaning and significance, is the impulse to procreation. The secondary purposes, however important they may be, are orientated around this basic fact of sexual complementarity and receive their motivation and meaning from it.

This insistence on the generation and rearing of children as the primary purpose of marriage has not caused the secondary purposes to be neglected in Catholic teaching. Indeed, the Catechism of the Council of Trent when explaining "the reasons because of which man and woman ought to be joined in marriage" states clearly:

> The first is precisely the companionship sought by the natural instinct of different sex, and brought about in the hope of mutual aid, so that each may help the other to bear more easily the troubles of life, and to support the weakness of old age. The second is the desire of having children.[6]

Pius XI in his Encyclical on *Christian Marriage* states:

> This mutual inward moulding of husband and wife, this determined effort to perfect each other, can in a very real sense, as the Roman Catechism teaches, be said to be the chief reason and purpose of matrimony, provided matrimony be looked at not in the restricted sense as instituted for the proper conception and education of the child, but more widely as the blending of life as a whole and the mutual interchange and sharing thereof.[7]

Returning now to the consideration of the specific qualities
or properties of marriage deducible from the primary purpose
of the contract, it is apparent that closely related to the procreation of children is their physical and moral education. It
is from this child-rearing aspect of marriage that its two essential properties of unity and indissolubility are easily deduced.
It is maintained that the proper rearing of children requires
that there be one father and one mother in the home, and that
they remain permanently united.

Hence, polygamy in any form is considered contrary to the
nature of marriage since it renders impossible perfect marital
unity. The dissolution of the union between husband and
wife is wrong not only because it necessarily inflicts great harm
on the children, but because the mere possibility of obtaining
a divorce places an obstacle in the way of perfect union and
the desire to make the necessary adaptations inevitable in the
family cycle. Furthermore, since the primary object of the
marriage contract is the procreation and rearing of offspring,
the quality of unity and permanency in the home must be such
that it offers a fitting physical, emotional, intellectual, and
spiritual environment for the children. The marriage partners
are obligated to provide for more than the physical necessities
of their offspring. Through fostering mutual love and cooperation, they must create a family atmosphere conducive to the
full development of their children as future citizens of the
nation and of heaven.

In this connection it should be noted that neither the marriage contract nor Church teaching make any specifications
covering the number of children to be produced. Procreation
is a human act implying full responsibility on the part of those
who perform the act. Marriage partners should not engage in
physical union unless they are willing and reasonably capable
of assuming the responsibilities inherent in childbirth and
child-rearing. It is assumed that since children are one of the
great blessings of marriage and the privilege of cooperating
with the Creator in the procreative act is one of the noblest in
the marriage state, Catholic spouses will have the number of
children they feel they can reasonably support and rear. Ulti-

mately, the decision governing the number of children must rest on the mutual consent of the spouses. Their decision must be based on their condition and the exigencies of their state of life, for as Pius XII has pointed out, to enter the marriage state and to seek selfishly to enjoy its privileges while at the same time absolutely excluding (through periodic continence) the procreation of offspring is contrary to the very nature of marriage itself.[8]

Much misunderstanding concerning this specific point of Catholic teaching will be avoided if we recall the principles developed in our discussion of the function of sex. The use of the sexual faculty is a human act and is governed by the moral law. In marriage, this use represents the mutual, loving gift of one's procreative power in physical union. Consequently, if spouses choose to engage in physical union, they must respect the inviolability of the natural physiological process of procreation which they have initiated. Obviously, this does not mean that they are required to have all the children of which they are physically capable. It does require that they observe right order in the use of their reproductive faculties.

The Church's teaching on marriage does not ignore modern population problems.[9] It does demand that these problems be studied in their true perspective. The Catholic position concerning population problems is based on philosophical and religious premises integrally related to the whole Catholic concept of man and marriage. The rejection of the use of contraceptives as a solution to "overpopulation" represents a necessary conclusion derived from these basic premises. Hence, although it is admitted that serious individual and national problems may be occasioned by excessive population pressure, it is maintained that a solution in conformity with Christian moral norms must and can be found.

There has been a steady flow of "scare books" prophesying world-wide overpopulation and hunger since the end of World War II.[10] At the same time, the continuation of the baby boom in America has revived the discussion of optimum population theory. In this connection, it is maintained by some that the return of the traditional large-sized American family would be a calamity to the nation's prosperity.[11] Although an exhaustive treatment of population problems is not required here, a few observations appear in order.

First, in regard to world-wide overpopulation, experts call attention to various "danger spots." In these areas, population growth is outstripping the development of the means of production. Japan and Italy are classic examples of this situation. Although they can increase the productivity of their resources to a considerable degree, they will still have more people than they can supply with jobs that pay a living wage. In the present world situation, the "have-not" nations find it difficult to control the discontent and unrest arising from these conditions. As a result, they may well be regarded as "danger spots" worthy of serious attention.

As early as 1941, Pius XII pleaded that nations less richly endowed be given a chance to survive through emigration and access to raw materials. The Pope asked for "a better distribution of human beings over those parts of the earth which are capable of agricultural development—land which God created and prepared for the use of all" (May 15, 1941). Concerning access to raw materials, the Pope pointed out that "there is no place for that cold and calculating egoism which tends to hoard economic resources and materials destined for the use of all, to such an extent that the nations less favored by nature are not permitted access to them" (Christmas, 1941).[12] Unfortunately, since international trade is polarized around two power centers, the Soviets and the United States, it is unlikely that effective solutions will be developed until the conditions of "cold war" cease to exist.

Further, in technologically undeveloped countries, the rapid introduction of modern health programs can readily create a serious unbalance between population and productivity. One of the prime factors in population growth in these countries is not the increase of the birth rate but the lowering of the death rate, particularly in the younger age cohorts. Through the introduction of modern health care, population rises rapidly since more infants survive and increasing percentages reach the reproductive age. Under these conditions, serious population problems may arise unless effective steps are taken to increase productivity. Hence, health programs must be accompanied by adequate economic planning and development lest the application of American medical "know-how" to undeveloped countries should defeat its own purpose.

Those who advocate that the United States should make strict measures of population control a condition of continued assistance to these countries should reflect on the following points. First, the effective development and use of natural resources in most of these countries is restricted by lack of knowledge, skill, and financial support. The stabilization or decrease of population will not remedy this situation. Second, in urging many of these nations to restrict their population, we are in reality asking them to settle for a subordinate role in world history. The argument runs: if the Orientals continue to expand and increase, they will be a threat to the West; therefore, they must be convinced that it is to their advantage to limit their growth. It is highly improbable that the leaders of these countries are going to be convinced by this line of reasoning.

Finally, Americans who express concern over the continuation of the baby boom must realize that their belief in the beneficent effect of the small-family pattern on the national welfare represents a conclusion based on one version of an economic optimum theory of population. According to this theory, we have reached the right population size. Any change other than "a modest long-term population growth" would be a "calamity to the nation's prosperity." The soundness of this interesting conclusion obviously depends on the soundness of the premises from which it is derived. What are these premises? Briefly, it is assumed that the quantitative relationship between labor, capital, and resources yielding the highest per-capita product in any given economy can be known, that this relationship now exists in our system, and that any marked increase in population size would affect this relationship adversely.

How sound are these assumptions? Theoretically, it is conceivable that a certain quantitative relationship between these factors exists under an assumed set of conditions. The core of such theory is built on the two principles of the division of labor and the law of diminishing returns. When applied to an entire economic system, these principles presuppose some fixed relationship among the various productive functions of a nation's economic system. In short, with a given state of technology, a given base of resources, and given consumer tastes, the assumption is made of some specific proportion of labor to other productive factors that will yield the greatest per-capita output. As the theorists admit, the assumptions underlying this theory are that there exist indivisibilities of certain factors of production, that the quantity of other factors and the state of the arts are fixed at any one time, that people make the best use of given resources and knowledge, or, if there is a population change, no better use of existing resources and knowledge is made.

So much for the theoretical considerations involved. What do we actually know about the optimum relationship between these factors? It is clear that our economic system is the resultant of an extremely complex interplay of the components of these generalized factors. We can measure the influence of only a few of these with any precision. Even the measurement of these can be made only on the assumption of static conditions. In other words, we are not able to define optimum population size even for a static economic system.

But our economic system does not operate under static conditions. The system is characterized by rapid change in progress and efficiency. It is interesting to note that not even the most theoretically inclined population specialists have attempted to formulate a dynamic theory of optimum population. Hence, the statement that a return to the traditional large-sized family pattern would be a calamity to the nation's prosperity is clearly not scientific. It represents an opinion which the present state of our knowledge concerning the relationship between population size and the economic system does not enable us to verify.[13]

MARRIAGE IS A SACRAMENT

Catholics believe that when marriage is contracted by baptized Christians capable of making the contract, this marriage contract is sacramental since Christ has raised matrimony to the dignity of a sacrament. In a valid marriage between baptized persons, therefore, the contract is the sacrament.[14] This means that when two contracting parties, who are baptized Christians, contract to marry, this very exchange of consent by which the spouses give themselves to each other for the conjugal life is a sign and source of that peculiar grace by which "it perfects natural love, it confirms an indissoluble union, and sanctifies both man and wife." [15] This doctrine has far-reaching significance in the Catholic concept of marriage. First, the grace which is supplied is that which is needed for a union worthy of Christians. It is a supernatural aid available to the spouses for the exercise of all the rights, the accomplishment of all the duties, the enduring of all the burdens, the innocent enjoyment of all the benefits which such a union implies.[16]

Pius XI develops the authentic interpretation of this sacramental teaching as follows:

> By the very fact, therefore, that the Faithful with sincere mind give such consent, they open up for themselves a treasure of sacramental grace from which they draw supernatural power for the fulfilling of their tasks and duties faithfully, holily, perseveringly even unto death. Hence this Sacrament not only increases sanctifying grace, the permanent principle of the supernatural life in those who, as the expression is, place no obstacle (*obex*) in its way; but it adds particular gifts, dispositions, seeds of grace, by elevating and perfecting the natural powers in such a way that the parties are assisted not only in understanding but in knowing intimately, in adhering to firmly, in willing effectively, and in successfully putting into practice those things which pertain to the marriage state, its aims and duties. It gives them, in fine, a right to the actual assistance of grace, whensoever they need it for fulfilling the duties of their state.[17]

Although the demands of the Catholic marriage ideal are very high, God's help is made available to the wedded couple through the sacrament. The sacrament of matrimony is part of the seven-fold sacramental system through which the grace merited by Christ is dispensed to the faithful according to their needs. The vocation of marriage, therefore, draws its nobility from two sources. Not only are the spouses privileged to cooperate with their Creator in the propagation of the race, but they are united by a bond which is both the sign and the source of the graces needed for their state of life.

ECCLESIASTICAL MARRIAGE LEGISLATION

A further significant effect resulting from the sacramental nature of the marriage contract is that the Church claims jurisdiction over the marriages of all baptized persons. The Church is a special society established by Jesus Christ with a mission of salvation for all mankind. Individuals enter this society through the rite of baptism. By their membership they acquire new rights and obligations, and in matters pertaining to these they are subject to the jurisdiction of the Church. This jurisdictional power covers: (1) the imposition of conditions for the licitness and validity of the contract; (2) the establishment of impedient or diriment impediments; (3) the judicial jurisdiction over matrimonial cases even concerning the nullity of the bond; (4) the imposition of ecclesiastical penalties for failure to observe these laws. The civil authority has no direct or indirect power over the validity or licitness of the marriage of Christians although it is conceded the right to prescribe reasonable regulations for the protection of the public order, health, and safety, and also to pass laws governing the merely civil effects of the contract.

The laws regulating Catholic marriage are found in the canon law of the Church. This is an elaborate, well-reasoned, and thoroughly consistent system of law, the result of nearly two thousand years of development.[18] It has been clarified by the efforts of numerous competent commentators and by a series of official decisions of the Roman Rota, the Church's highest court of appeal.[19] Canon law specifies the conditions requisite to the validity and lawfulness of marriage (the impediments), the nature of the consent in the contract, and the form of celebration of marriage. Since these laws are sometimes misunderstood, a very brief explanation seems in place here.[20]

Canonical Impediments

The marriage contract, like any other contract, must consist of an agreement between parties who are legally capable of contracting with reference to the object of the contract. Where agreement (consent) or capability (eligibility) are absent, the marriage is void or invalid. That is, there is simply no marriage at all.[21] The specific circumstances which render a marriage contract either illicit (unlawful) or invalid (void) are called impediments in canon law. An impediment is a circumstance establishing a certain incapacity between two persons so as to affect the contract itself.

The Code distinguishes two types of impediments: prohibitory (impedient) and annulling (diriment). An annulling or diriment impediment both seriously forbids the attempted marriage and bars the valid contract. A prohibitory or impedient impediment seriously forbids, that is, renders unlawful or illicit a matrimonial contract, but it does not make it void or invalid. Thus if a couple marry and it is later discovered that a prohibitory impediment existed at the time the contract was made, the marriage is valid. However, if an annulling impediment existed, there would simply have been no marriage.

Canon law specifies three prohibitory impediments: certain vows of chastity, mixed religion (marriage between Catholic and *baptized* non-Catholic), and legal adoption in those states where civil law treats this as an impediment to marriage. The annulling or diriment impediments are: insufficient age, impotency, existing marriage bond, disparity of worship (marriage between a Catholic and an *unbaptized* non-Catholic), sacred orders, solemn religious profession, abduction, crime, blood relationship, affinity, spiritual relationship, and legal adoption if civilly it voids marriage.

These impediments represent the canonical specification of the factors which affect the capacity of individuals to make a marriage contract. As such they are general laws binding on all who come under the jurisdiction of canon law. However, in particular cases a relaxation of the law in the form of a dispensation may be granted provided due cause is demonstrated. A dispensation from a matrimonial impediment may be defined as the relaxation of a law which annuls or prohibits a marriage granted in a particular case by the legislator or by one who has received the power of doing so from the legislator.

The right of establishing matrimonial impediments is now restricted to the Roman Pontiff. He alone has the supreme and universal power to dispense from all ecclesiastical impediments. Others can dispense only if granted the power to do so by common law or special papal indult. Dispensations cannot be granted from what are considered the absolute provisions of the divine law; for example, in cases of impotency, consanguinity in the first degree of the direct line, or where the bond of consummated marriage between the baptized exists. On the other hand, impediments of ecclesiastical origin have often varied, and they can be dispensed by the authority which instituted them, although certain laws, owing to their extreme gravity, are never dispensed.[22]

Conditions for Valid Consent

Since marriage is a contract, it can be effected only by the agreement or consent of the parties. To enter a valid contract, the parties must be capable according to the law. The Code defines the factors which vitiate true consent. They are: want of the use of reason, defective knowledge of the object of the contract, mistaken identity, pretense or fictitious consent, duress and fear, and intention contrary to the essence of the marriage contract. Where these factors as defined in the Code are present, there is no true consent and consequently no marriage.

Conditions Required for Valid Celebration of Marriage

Finally, the Code defines the form of celebration of the marriage contract by stating that "only those marriages are valid which are contracted before the pastor or the Ordinary of the place, or a priest delegated by either of these, and at least two witnesses." [23] The purpose of this legislation is to safeguard the liberty of the contracting parties and to have assurance that the marriage has taken place validly. The presence of an authorized priest is not required for the administration of the sacrament since in matrimony the two contracting parties are the ministers of the sacrament. Indeed, up until the Council of Trent there had been no legislation on the form of marriage affecting its validity. The faithful had always been urged to secure the blessing of the Church on their conjugal union, but marriages celebrated without the presence of a priest were recognized as valid sacraments since the contract itself was the sacramental sign.

These "clandestine" marriages were open to abuse. The marriage could be repudiated, and it was difficult to establish with certainty the validity of the contract for there was no competent person present to make inquiries concerning the freedom of the parties to marry and the absence of annulling impediments. To put a stop to this abuse of a sacred contract, the first invalidating law was passed in 1563 and after some modification was adopted in the present Code. The law applies to all who are baptized in the Catholic Church. Catholics of the Oriental rites and all non-Catholics, when contracting marriage among themselves, are exempt from its provisions.

Premarital Instructions and Publication of the "Banns"

This canon law legislation covering capacity, consent, and form has been developed to safeguard the sanctity and validity of the marriage contract. For the same purpose, certain practices dealing with marriage preparation have been enforced by the Code. The pastor is required to make certain that there are no obstacles to the contemplated marriage by questioning each party separately concerning the impediments, freedom of consent, and understanding of Christian doctrine. In many dioceses of the United States, the couple are asked to fill out a set form or questionnaire covering the impediments and the usual obstacles to free consent.

On three successive Sundays or feast days of obligation before the marriage is to be celebrated, the names of those who are about to contract marriage must be announced at the principal mass, and the faithful are informed that they are gravely obligated to make known to the proper authorities any impediments or reasons why this couple should not marry. This is called publication of the "banns" and represents one further attempt to guarantee the validity of the contract. These banns must be published in the parish church of each place in which the parties dwell and, should the parties not be well known, in the parish church of each place where the parties have dwelt for longer than six months after reaching the age of puberty. Only the bishop can dispense from the publication of the banns.

Finally, the pastor must instruct the couple concerning the sanctity of marriage, the mutual obligations of husband and wife, and the duties of parents toward their children. The Code states that this instruction should be given "with due regard to the condition of the persons concerned." In those dioceses where pre-Cana or marriage preparation courses are commonly attended by engaged couples, the pastor may have to do little more than personally assure himself that the couple have understood what they have been taught. Where such marriage preparation courses are not offered, it is customary for the couple to meet with the pastor for three or four "instructions" shortly before the marriage is to take place.

ECCLESIASTICAL MARRIAGE COURTS

The Church laws respecting marriage are administered by a system of courts established by the Code of Canon Law for the universal Church. Since these courts are instruments of the spiritual governing authority of the Church, their jurisdiction is limited to matters within the proper and spiritual sphere of the Church, and their decisions have no civil effect but are binding on the faithful in the "forum of conscience." The purpose of the courts is to safeguard the dignity of marriage and provide for the spiritual welfare of the faithful. Provision is made for two types of court. There is an "annulment" court, which is concerned with cases in which the validity of the marriage contract is in issue or a dissolution of the marriage bond is sought. In some dioceses a second court, called the "separation" court, is established to deal with cases seeking permission to separate and live apart or to have recourse to the civil courts for separate maintenance or divorce. In many dioceses the functions of this latter court are handled directly by the bishop or his delegates without formal court procedure.

The Annulment Court

The annulment court deals with cases in which a dissolution of the bond of marriage is sought or the validity of a marriage is in issue. There are four divisions of the annulment court: the Roman court, the defect of form court, the documentary court, and the tribunal court. The Code clearly specifies the type of case these courts may handle. To avoid confusion in this complex subject, it will be best to consider the courts dealing with the dissolution of the bond cases and then those dealing with cases in which the validity of the bond is in issue. It should be noted that canon law does not use the term *divorce*. It uses the term *dissolution* in those cases where the bond of an existing valid marriage is set aside and the term *declaration of nullity* where it is discovered that what purports to be a valid marriage was invalid from the beginning.

Dissolution of the Bond. It has been the constant teaching of the Catholic Church that marriage is by nature indissoluble.[24] This means that the marriage bond cannot be dissolved by any human authority such as the contracting parties or the state. Furthermore, the valid marriage of two baptized persons (whether Catholics or not) when followed by consummation, is not only a contract resulting in a status as the civil law admits, but it is also a sacrament resulting in a relation-

ship terminable only with death.[25] Consequently, there is
never any question of the dissolution of the bond when dealing with valid, consummated marriage between baptized persons.

However, Church legislation does provide for dissolution of
the marriage bond in the following four instances: (1) unconsummated marriage, (2) the privilege of the faith, (3) unconsummated marriage in which one of the parties afterwards
takes solemn vows in a religious order, and (4) the Pauline
privilege. Since this portion of Church legislation is not very
well understood, we shall explain briefly how the ecclesiastical
courts handle such cases.

TYPE 1.   Cases of unconsummated marriage are handled by
the Roman court.[26] The court is so called because the cases
are not decided by the local chancery office but go directly to
Rome for disposition by the Pope. The procedure is as follows.
One of the spouses alleging sufficient reason, such as the im-
possibility of reconciliation, must petition the Pope for permission to start proceedings. If the permission is granted, evidence in the case is taken locally before the Roman court, and
the record is transmitted to Rome for consideration by a Committee of Cardinals acting as advisers to the Pope. He may ter-
minate the unconsummated marriage by a decree to that effect
if the evidence in the case so warrants it.

TYPE 2.   The privilege of the faith cases also come directly
under the Roman court. Such cases arise when there has been
a valid marriage in which one of the spouses was unbaptized
and a subsequent breakup of the marriage followed. If one of
the spouses is converted to the Catholic faith, a dissolution
may be granted to allow the convert to marry in the Church
provided two conditions are present. (1) It is morally impossible to reconcile the spouses. And (2), there is absence of
scandal in granting the dissolution. This privilege is granted
only by the Pope who acts on the evidence which has been
taken locally and transmitted to Rome.

TYPE 3.   Cases of unconsummated marriage in which one
of the parties wishes to join a religious order are rare at the
present time. The religious order petitions the Holy See for
permission to accept the individual as a novice and if the

permission is granted, dissolution of the marriage takes place on the profession of the solemn vows. Religious vows are "solemn" if they are so recognized by the Church. These are usual in religious orders as distinguished from religious congregations.

TYPE 4. The Pauline privilege cases occur when there has been a valid marriage between two unbaptized persons, the subsequent conversion to the Catholic faith of one of the spouses, and the refusal of the nonconvert to live in harmony with the converted spouse. When these conditions exist, dissolution is granted to allow the convert to remarry in the Church. These cases are handled by the local chancery office and the procedure is as follows. In a letter stating the fact of conversion, the convert asks the nonconverted spouse two questions: (1) whether he wishes to become a Catholic, and (2), if not, whether he is willing to live peaceably in marriage without interfering with the religious obligations of the convert. If no response is received within ten days or a negative answer is given to the second question, the convert may use the privilege. The former marriage is dissolved only at the moment of entry into the new marriage. This is called the Pauline privilege since it dates back to St. Paul in his dealings with the converts at Corinth.[27]

These four types of cases are true cases of dissolution of the marriage bond. A recognized valid marriage bond was dissolved and the parties to the contract were given the right to enter a new marriage. Cases falling under the first three types are not very numerous but the Pauline privilege is frequently used, particularly in missionary lands. Because of the confusion which exists concerning this subject of dissolution, it should be emphasized that, although these cases involved valid marriages, the marriage was either unconsummated (type one and three), or nonsacramental (type two and four, since they were contracted between baptized and unbaptized or between two unbaptized partners). A valid marriage contracted by baptized partners and consummated can be dissolved by no human power and by no cause other than death.

Declaration of Nullity. The second function of the annulment court is to deal with cases in which the validity of a

marriage is in issue. The court is asked to investigate whether
a valid marriage ever existed at all. Marriage contracts may be
null and void from the beginning because of some existing
annulling impediment, or from lack of proper consent, or from
substantial defect in the canonical form. When a supposed
marriage is found to be invalid, every effort must be made to
convalidate the contract by removing the invalidating causes.
In cases where this cannot be accomplished either because an
impediment exists from which there is no dispensation (for
example, the existence of a previous bond), or because the
parties refuse to live together, there are grounds for the spouse
who was not the cause of the impediment to seek a declaration
of nullity.

The Code has prescribed definite rules for dealing with
cases where the validity of marriage is in question, "lest man
should dare put asunder what God hath joined together, or
lest on the other hand he should declare valid a bond which
is null." [28] There are three divisions of the annulment court
which handle cases involving declaration of nullity. They are:
(1) the defect of form court; (2) the documentary court; and
(3) the tribunal court.

1. *The defect of form court.*   This court deals with cases in
which a Catholic attempts marriage by a ceremony other than
that prescribed by the Catholic Church. According to the
Code, if a Catholic goes through the marriage ceremony before someone other than a duly authorized priest and two witnesses, the ceremony is a nullity and there is no marriage. The
procedure in such cases is as follows. Proofs of the defect of
form are submitted to the court judge who acts as the delegate
of the bishop. If the evidence is conclusive, the judge, in the
name of the bishop, merely issues an official declaration that
there has been no marriage because of defect of form. Doubtful cases must be remanded to the tribunal court for a formal
hearing.

2. *The documentary court.*   This court handles cases in
which settlement depends on the mere presentation of documentary evidence. These cases involve certain antecedent annulling impediments clearly specified in the Code. If it is
shown that these were not dispensed and the marriage took

place, a declaration of nullity is granted by the judge of the court. The court has jurisdiction over the following impediments: consanguinity, affinity, spiritual relationship, adoption, bigamy, disparity of worship, holy orders, and solemn vows of chastity. Only one judge is necessary for hearing the evidence and disposing of the case. However, in all of these cases, the "defender of the bond," an officer of the court with the duty of opposing the granting of a declaration of nullity, must intervene in the proceedings. If there remains any doubt concerning the existence of any of these impediments, the case must be handled by the tribunal court.

3. *The tribunal court.* This court deals with cases which require a formal trial for disposition. It is concerned with all cases involving impediments which the Code has forbidden to be handled in a summary process by the documentary court and all cases involving matrimonial consent. The impediments falling under the jurisdiction of the tribunal court are: nonage, impotence, abduction, public propriety, and crime. Lack of consent cases include the following types. (1) What the parties agreed to was not a marriage since one or both parties intended to exclude an essential property of marriage. (2) One of the parties consented to the marriage only upon a specific condition and the condition was not fulfilled. (3) There was no valid consent for the reason that: one of the parties was incapable of consenting because of insanity or lack of knowledge of the nature of marriage; or one of the parties was mistaken as to the identity of the other party; or one of the parties was mistaken as to what was taking place; or one of the parties did not consent but was forced through fear to go through the form of marriage.

(a) *The judicial process.* The procedure of the tribunal court in handling all the above cases is as follows. A preliminary hearing is held to establish jurisdiction of the court over the persons in the case, to formulate the issues by pleadings, and to determine the existence of probable nullity. The cases in which these questions are resolved affirmatively must receive a formal hearing before a tribunal composed of from three to five judges. Attached to every court are two priests versed in canon law, known respectively as "the promoter of justice" and "the defender of the bond." The former is charged with safeguarding the public interest and procedural law; the latter must oppose every application for a decree of nullity. Litigants may, if they so desire, be represented by counsel of their own selection. There is, therefore, no such thing as an undefended action.

Once the evidence has been gathered, the record is given to the defender of the bond who, after studying it, formulates in writing his objections to granting a degree of nullity. After this, the advocates of the parties go over the record and add their written arguments and comments. The promoter of justice may intervene at any stage of the proceedings and add his written comments to the record. Finally, the court reviews and discusses the entire record and hands down its written decision.

(b) *The nature of the tribunal's decision.* Two concurring affirmative decisions are required before a petitioner is considered free to remarry. Consequently, if the decision of the court of first instance is in favor of nullity, the defender of the bond must appeal the case within ten days. An appeal lies from the court of a suffragan bishop to that of his archbishop and in cases originating in the latter, to the bishop's court which has been selected as the archbishop's appellate tribunal. If the appellate court affirms the decision, the petitioner is free to remarry. If the appellate court reverses the decision of the court of first instance, the case must be appealed to the Rota, the court of highest instance which sits at Rome. After going over the record, the Rota hands down its decision, and the case is closed except for the right to re-open it in the future upon the showing of new evidence.

If the decision of the court of first instance is against nullity, the petitioner may appeal. The parties may again be heard and further evidence may be advanced. A second decision against nullity normally closes the case, although the losing party may always appeal the case to the Rota. If the appellate court reverses the decision of the court of first instance and decides in favor of nullity, the case must be appealed to the Rota. When the courts hand down a decision, they do not say simply that the marriage was either valid or invalid. They use the formula: the nullity of the marriage in this case is established (*constat de nullitate matrimonii in casu*), or, the nullity of the marriage in this case is not established (*non constat*, etc.). This manner of stating the decision is used since the judges must decide the case only on the evidence presented in the court and they recognize how fallible they are under such conditions. A decree of nullity, therefore, does not put an end to a valid marriage. The decree merely constitutes an opinion on which the parties may act without sin. For a Catholic to deliberately deceive or mislead the court is futile since a decree so obtained would not justify remarriage.

(c) *Court costs.* The petitioners are required to pay something to cover judicial expenses unless they are granted the privilege of gratuitous representation.[29] Every tribunal has a schedule of fees specifying the amount to be paid by the parties for each judicial service and incidental cost connected with the process.[30] An example of annulment court costs in a large urban diocese runs as follows: If the case is heard before a one-judge court, the court costs are ten dollars; if before the three- to five-man tribunal court, the costs are twenty-five dollars. Of this sum, fifteen dollars are kept by the court of first instance, and ten dollars are sent to the court of appeal. For cases which are appealed to the Rota a charge covering advocate fees and printing costs is assessed.[31]

If the parties are poor, they may be granted the privilege of free representation or a reduction of the ordinary expenses.[32] For example, the tribunal court in the same diocese was dealing with 479 cases during the years 1950–52 inclusive. Of these cases, 301 or 63 per cent were paying their own expenses, and 178 or 37 per cent were too poor to pay anything. During the year 1952, the Rota handled 188 cases, of which 68 were granted and 120 refused. Of the total number, 71 cases, or 37 per cent, were handled free of charge. Out of the 68 granted, 22 cases, or 32 per cent, were too poor to pay anything; out of the 120 refused, 49 cases, or 41 per cent, were too poor to pay.[33]

Number of Cases Handled by the Annulment Courts. Some

understanding of the annulment courts function can be gathered by considering the number of cases it handles each year. A study of six major annulment courts having jurisdiction over approximately 4.36 million Catholics reveals that during the three-year period 1950–52 inclusive their combined average annual case load ran as follows: Their documentary courts handled approximately 200 cases; their defect of form courts dealt with a little over 2000 cases; their tribunal courts handed down 107 decisions; and these courts also assisted in obtaining the Pauline privilege for 60 cases. This was the combined average annual case load for these six major annulment courts.

The most interesting information uncovered by this study was the relatively large number of cases handled by the defect of form courts. It appears that the number of Catholics who attempt marriage "outside" the Church is rather large. It will be recalled that the cases handled by this court have attempted an invalid marriage, have obtained a civil divorce, and are now seeking an official declaration of the invalidity of this attempted marriage in order to enter a valid Catholic marriage. Since the Church law concerning the form of marriage applies to all baptized Catholics, it is possible that many of these cases involve Catholics who have received little or no instruction in their faith up to this time. At any rate, this study suggests that invalid marriages constitute a serious problem for the Catholic minority.

The Separation Court

This court is concerned with cases in which one spouse seeks permission to live apart from the other. The validity of the marriage is not questioned and no dissolution of the bond is sought, but permission is asked for the temporary or perpetual right to cease cohabitation (separation *a mensa et thoro*—from bed and board—as opposed to separation *a vinculo matrimonii* —from the bond of marriage). The marriage contract obliges the partners to cohabitation or the leading of their conjugal life in common unless some just reason excuses them from doing so. Cohabitation normally implies the habitual sharing of bed, board, and home and the mutual companionship and assistance required for the full attainment of the primary and secondary ends of marriage.

Although the Church does not recognize the dissolution of a valid, consummated marriage among the baptized, provision is made for the cessation of cohabitation in those cases where the good of one or both the spouses requires it. Considerable confusion has arisen because historically this permission to separate was loosely called divorce, and even today there is the possibility of some misunderstanding since permission is sometimes granted to resort to the civil courts for the legal implementation of the ecclesiastical separation decree. In such cases, even when permission is granted to obtain a civil divorce, there is never any question of the dissolution of the marriage bond. Consequently, the parties are not free to contract a new marriage in the Church.

Grounds for Separation. Separation may be either temporary or permanent. Outside the rare case when perpetual separation on the mutual consent of the two parties is sometimes granted by the Holy See because both spouses wish to embrace some form of religious life, the only recognized cause for permanent separation is adultery. The Code states that adultery on the part of one of the spouses, without breaking the bond, gives to the other spouse cause for separation, even forever, unless he himself consented to the crime, or has been responsible for it, or has condoned it expressly or tacitly, or has committed the same crime. There is tacit condonation when the innocent spouse, knowing the adultery, has freely continued to treat the guilty one with marital affection; condonation is presumed when the adulterous party has not, within six months, been sent away, or departed from, or duly denounced.[34]

Although adultery offers the only recognized grounds for permanent separation, there may be good reasons why the couple should live apart for a time. In the words of the Code: "if one of the married parties becomes affiliated with a non-Catholic sect; if he gives the children an education which is not Catholic; if he leads a criminal and disgraceful life; if he is a grave danger to the other's soul or body; if his cruelty renders common life too hard; such and similar causes will give the other spouse the right to withdraw by appealing to the ordinary of the place (the bishop); or even of his own authority if they are proved with certainty and there is danger in delay.[35]

Hence, the Church does not force people to cohabit where intimacy is harmful to one of the spouses or to the children. If the cause of the separation ceases to exist, common life is to be resumed since the marriage contract obliges the spouses to cohabitation. Unfortunately, these temporary grounds are never removed in many cases and the temporary separation results in a permanent one. In such cases, there is a natural tendency to have recourse to the civil courts for a decree of separate maintenance or a civil divorce.

Recourse to Civil Divorce Courts. Since the problem of divorce is particularly acute in the United States, the Church in this country has formulated specific norms regulating the action of the faithful in this regard. Married persons are forbidden to have recourse to the civil tribunals in order to obtain separation from bed and board unless they have previously consulted the appropriate ecclesiastical authority.[36] Further, Catholics are directly and positively forbidden to approach courts to seek the dissolution of their marriage bond. Moreover, the censure of excommunication, to be incurred automatically upon the violation of the law, is inflicted upon those Catholics who attempt another marriage after obtaining a civil divorce from a valid marriage bond.[37]

Permission to seek a civil divorce is granted by the Church for only two types of cases. As we have seen, where the Church through the annulment court has judged a marriage invalid or dissolved, a civil divorce may be obtained and the parties are free to remarry. Second, in separation cases where the innocent party would suffer serious civil law disadvantage, such as grave threat to substantial property rights which only a civil court may remove, resort may be had to a civil divorce. Of course, this civil divorce does not dissolve the marriage bond. The divorced spouses are admonished to avoid occasions such as company keeping which might lead them into an invalid marriage and consequent excommunication. In many states, a decree of separate maintenance offers sufficient protection to the aggrieved party, and permissions for civil divorce are relatively few.

Judicial Procedure in Separation Cases.   In handling separation cases the bishop may exercise his authority in an administrative manner or by judicial procedure. In most dioceses the former practice is followed, but a few have established a separation court and require a judicial procedure. The outstanding separation court in the United States is maintained in the Chicago Archdiocese. The court sits the year round and employs twenty judges who represent the Cardinal-Archbishop and act in his name. The court has two divisions. The first, employing eighteen judges, sits daily and deals with petitions to separate and requests for permission to resort to the civil court for separate maintenance. The second, employing two judges, has the additional power to decide requests for permission to seek a divorce in the civil courts. The judges are priests who have been trained in canon law and have passed an apprenticeship period in the court system. The court handles approximately two thousand cases each year.

The procedure of the court is as follows. Any married person over whose marriage the court has jurisdiction may petition the court for relief. After the preliminary information is secured, a date is assigned and the initial hearing is held usually within ten days after the docketing of the case. The parties are summoned by letter, and their refusal to appear, if interpreted as contempt of court, may deprive them of the right to receive the sacraments of the Church. Cases are usually heard and decided by one judge. The hearing is informal, and every attempt is made to work out a solution in cooperation with the parties. Additional witnesses may be called in at the discretion of the judge, and he may refer the parties to a doctor or psychiatrist if he judges they can be aided in this way. Each case is given as much time as is needed. There are no court charges.

The principal purpose of the hearing is to reconcile the parties where this is possible. Particularly where there are no adequate grounds for separation, an attempt is made to reconcile differences so that the couple may assume harmonious cohabitation. Where reconciliation is impossible and there are grounds for separation, permission may be granted to live apart for a specified time or permanently. In case of the latter, recourse to the civil courts may be permitted for obtaining a separate maintenance decree.

If permission to seek a civil divorce is sought, the case is transferred to the division of the separation court empowered to grant relief. In case of dissatisfaction with this court's decision, either party may request a rehearing. This request is never refused. The court judges prefer to function as marriage counselors rather than judges. Their aim is to save the marriage, and when this is impossible, to work out a solution in conformity with justice and Church law. One of the indirect effects of the separation court has been a greatly increased interest in marriage and family problems and widespread support of movements such as pre-Cana, Cana, and the Christian Family Movement within the Archdiocese.

SUMMARY

This brief outline of the Church's teaching on marriage and the juridical system which has been established to implement and sanction this doctrine in the practical order shows us the value frame of reference within which the Catholic family operates. Our concern has been to clarify the basic premises and positive norms which enter into Catholic thinking on the function of sex, the purposes of marriage, and the meaning of family life. This gives us the specifically Catholic elements in the minority's "definition of the situation." We now know how Catholics "feel" about sex, marriage, and the family.

Lest it be objected that we have been dealing merely with ideals and well-formulated theories, attention should be called to the remarks on the unique character of Catholic belief in an authoritative teaching Church. Catholics believe that the Church was established by Christ to dispense the sacraments and to teach. Furthermore, the Church is organized to teach. Through its schools, retreats, missions, Sunday sermons, pastoral letters, and numerous publications, as well as through its administration of the sacraments, the Church keeps the basic elements of Catholic doctrine constantly before the minds of the faithful.

The extent to which individual Catholics succeed or fail in putting this teaching into practice is not at issue here. The point is that the average Catholic has a fairly adequate understanding of what the Church teaches concerning marriage and the family. If he fails in practice, he is conscious of his failure. If he tries to rationalize his failure (and who doesn't?), this very need to rationalize indicates his knowledge of the ideal. Consequently, it must be admitted that the Church's teaching is a vital, operative force among the faithful. Ultimately, their problems must be defined in terms of this teaching.

PART III

Characteristics of the
American Catholic Family

CHAPTER FOUR

Family Backgrounds

The broad framework of family ideals and structure outlined in the preceding chapters has been accepted by practicing Catholics down through the centuries. However, the incarnation of the Catholic ideal in a definite culture, its translation into specific human relationships, has produced a variety
of family types. These represent what we might call national
or cultural approximations of the ideal. They are workable
systems of family relationships developed in distinct social
"climates," and evolving out of man's constant effort to channel
the satisfaction of his basic needs according to acceptable patterns of action. Hence, the traditional German Catholic family
differs from the French, the Italian, or the Irish, and even
within the same cultural group, the family relationships of
the various social classes may reveal marked differences.

In other words, even when the ultimate cultural goals and
the specific institutional objectives of diversely circumstanced
groups remain the same, the institutionalized means or culturally patterned and acceptable procedures which they establish for the implementation of these objectives may differ considerably. The status and roles of husband and wife, parent
and child, may be variously defined even within the frame-

work of monogamous marriage. The farmer's wife—and the farmer's daughter—may take a different view of the family than their urban, cliff-dwelling sisters. An Irish husband and father is not expected to exercise his headship of the family in the same manner as his German or Polish contemporaries.

The typical modern couple do not model their marriage expectations on the same lines as their colonial ancestors or even as their grandparents. Basic needs, ideals, and life-goals may remain essentially the same; their personal and social implications and their implementation in concrete relationships undergo modification in terms of different cultural emphases and changing circumstances. The family unit, although fundamental, is only one of the institutions through which man satisfies his elemental needs. It affects and is affected by all his other goals and relationships.

The fact that the Catholic ideal of marriage and the family has been actualized differently in various cultures has considerable significance for our understanding of the modern American Catholic family. The Catholic Church in America, somewhat like the nation itself, has grown primarily through immigration. There were Catholics in America, some 35,000 of them, at the time of the Revolution. The Louisiana Purchase and the annexations following the Mexican War added several hundred thousand primarily French- and Spanish-speaking Catholics. However, the major growth of the Catholic population resulted from the heavy flood of immigrants coming at first from Ireland and Germany; later, from southern and central Europe and the Americas.[1]

These immigrants brought with them their own cultural approximations of the Catholic ideal of marriage and the family. As alien groups in a dominantly Anglo-Saxon Protestant culture, they tended to cluster together in close-knit national aggregates, thus retaining many of their traditional traits and prolonging the process of acculturation. Today, with the exception of the Spanish-speaking groups and perhaps the French Canadians of the New England States, this process is well under way. However, for a better understanding of the contemporary Catholic family, it will prove helpful to review briefly some aspects of the immigrant "problem" in the past.

IMMIGRATION AND ASSIMILATION

As the poet Walt Whitman pointed out long ago, "America is a nation of nations." Nearly all races and nationalities of the world have contributed to her population, although the great majority of immigrants have been furnished by Europe. During the years 1820–1923, net immigration totaled approximately 30 million. Three major waves of immigration may be singled out. The first, arriving during the years 1830–1860, drew primarily upon the British Isles and northwestern Europe. This was the period of heavy Irish and German immigration although large numbers from these countries continued to arrive throughout the century. The second wave entered the country during the era of industrial expansion which characterized the post-Civil War period. Southern and eastern Europeans started arriving at this time, but the major source was still the British Isles and northwestern Europe. Finally, beginning in the late 1880's and culminating in the enormous influx of 1900–1910, a third wave poured in from southern and eastern Europe.[2]

After World War I, Congress passed restrictive laws drastically curtailing immigration. When these went into effect in the mid-twenties, the great epoch of American immigration was closed. Since that time, a large proportion of immigrants have entered from Canada, Mexico, and the Americas. During the late thirties, a considerable number of political refugees arrived from Europe.[3] Following World War II, America started receiving a limited number of displaced persons, but their settlement has been accompanied by systematic social planning so that modern immigration resembles the old in few respects.

The Nativist Reaction

The entrance of immigrants into American society has long been a subject of deep concern to "native" Americans, although as Handlin discovered when preparing to write a history of immigrants in America, "the immigrants are American history."[4] Periodically, nativist groups capitalized on religious and racial prejudices to arouse violent opposition to immigrants. The Native American party (Know-Nothings) stirred up bitter feelings against immigrants in general and Catholics in particular from 1840 to 1860.[5] In the late eighties and early nineties, Know-Nothingism reappeared in the form of the American Protective Association (A.P.A.).[6] It appeared again after World War I as the Ku Klux Klan, an organization which set out to promote, by violence if necessary, native, white, Protestant supremacy. It waged a vicious campaign of hatred against Catholics, Jews, Negroes, and immigrants for nearly two decades.[7] In action, it was more anti-Catholic and anti-immigrant than anti-Negro.[8] That anti-Catholic nativism is a hardy perennial can be seen from the fact that the American Protective Association in the late 1890's counted at least a million members and in the 1920's approximately one-fourth of the men of the United States eligible to join the Klan were included in its membership.[9]

The Assimilation Process

In his provocative study of the American character Denis Brogan remarks, "America denationalizes quickly. Does it nationalize?"[10] The answer depends to a large extent upon what one means by the term *nationalize*. A review of the various theories developed to explain the integration of the immigrant into American culture reveals an increasing awareness of the complexity of the problems involved in assimilation. The early belief in facile and relatively rapid Americanization displayed little understanding of the nature, origin, development, and survival potential of established cultural patterns. The majority of immigrants reaching our shores were not infants nor were they incapable of organizing to preserve some measure of solidarity among themselves.

The Melting-Pot Theory. It was precisely because they miscalculated this tendency of immigrants to establish an in-group solidarity with considerable survival potential that the early theorists of assimilation could advance their hypothesis of rapid "Americanization" or inevitable fusion in "God's Crucible," the "Melting Pot" where the great Alchemist melts and fuses all with his purging flame.[11] Although the theory enjoyed great popularity, it proved too optimistic in its prediction of steady fusion. Not only did the great Alchemist seem to be ignoring some of the minority groups altogether, but many ingredients in the Pot appeared highly resistant to the "purging flame!"

Forced "Americanization." Hence, during World War I, a veritable crusade was launched to Americanize the immigrant. Minority peoples were to be transformed into "old line" Americans at once. The Americanizers were confused in their thinking and vague in their choice of terminology.[12] Actually, they desired to force the immigrants to divest themselves immediately of their heritage and to take over a standardized American pattern for their lives. As Panunzio pointed out, such assimilation tended to be merely standardization.[13] It was largely a negative process of denationalization aptly described by John Collier's remark that it "rather indicates the taking over of the richly variegated cultural life of the many peoples coming to our shores and reducing them all to a dull, deadly Puritan drab." [14] This itch to enforce conformity has frequently plagued Americans. Some historians even look upon it as a carry-over from Puritanism.[15] At any rate, the crusade was soon recognized as spurious Americanization.[16] One writer has summarized the program as follows: "One part ability to read, write and speak English; one part the Declaration of Independence; one part the Constitution; one part love for apple pie; one part desire and willingness to wear American shoes; and another part pride in American plumbing will make an American of anyone." [17]

Cultural Pluralism? At present, the diversity and complexity of the processes involved in "becoming an American" are more clearly recognized. Assimilation is viewed as a slow process in which both the host culture and the minority undergo modification while working toward an eventual unity which implies synthesis, not integral absorption. It is not assumed that complete fusion of cultures is a necessary optimum. The nation will be richer in its cultural composition if the best that each group has brought can be conserved. Since the nature, character, and personality of the minority groups have evolved out of a culture different from our own, effective cultural transmission requires that the fundamentals of their heritage be preserved for some generations. Hence, the time element necessary in processes of assimilation is recognized, and the *de facto* diversity of our population growing out of traditional white-colored demarcation and the variety of cultures associated with the national origins of our immigrant stock is acknowledged. Although this approach represents a considerable advance over the traditional American provincialism which saw in all cultural differences the necessary marks of inferiority, and its rejection of the ethnocentrism characterizing previous theories is commendable, it tells us very little about the actual process of assimilation.

Assimilation and the Three Constituent Elements of Culture. What changes has the culture of the minority groups undergone? The best approach to this problem is to examine the nature of culture itself. An analysis of social and cultural structures reveals several elements of primary importance. First, there is a basic, underlying ideology composed of the ultimate cultural goals—the elemental doctrines on the nature and destiny of man and of society. Second, there are derivative sets of values and purposes, specific institutional objectives, representing the culturally devised applications of the ideology to concrete social institutions such as the economic system, the family, the state, and the church. Third, there are institutionalized means, culturally patterned and acceptable procedures, definite sets of social relationships established for the implementation of these institutional objectives.

A comparison of immigrant and American cultures according to these three constituent elements reveals what transformations are required of the immigrant cultures if true Americanization is to be achieved. First, an analysis of basic, underlying ideologies reveals fundamental similarity. This should surprise no one since these immigrants are all products of the broad stream of Western culture. Their concepts of the nature and destiny of man agreed with the traditional American outlook, and many of these groups had fought long and bloody battles for freedom and independence. Consequently, their incorporation into the American cultural pattern encountered no obstacles in this area.

Second, there were no substantial differences in regard to the specific derivative institutional objectives defined in their cultures. These immigrants were strongly family-centered and conservative. Their peasant background had inured them to hard work and frugality. They were anxious to achieve economic independence and ownership—enduring peasant drives which constant past frustration had only served to enforce. What they sought was an opportunity to work, to raise their families, and to worship without becoming a burden to anyone. If their necessary concentration on securing a living tended to blind them somewhat to their wider political responsibilities as citizens, it should be recalled, as Tom Paine once remarked, that "hunger is not a postponable want." Besides, there was the barrier of language, lack of experience in American ways, and the general attitude, all too often strengthened by everyday experience, that they were outsiders who had not yet qualified for full participation in American affairs. The important point is that their derivative institutional objectives were consonant with traditional American cultural patterns so that the process of integrating them into American society encountered no serious obstacles in this respect.

Third, the institutionalized means, or culturally patterned and acceptable procedures, established for the implementation of these institutional objectives differed considerably among the various immigrant cultures and, in turn, distinguished the immigrant groups from the remainder of American society. It was these relatively superficial, though highly visible aspects of culture combined with a language barrier that slowed down where it did not totally eliminate communication, which made the immigrants' culture appear so alien to the unsophisticated, provincial American mind. The enthusiasts of the melting-pot theory with their faith in the mystic fusion of the "best" in all cultures, the crusaders of the Americanizing decade with their itch to enforce conformity, and some of the cultural pluralists with their laudable respect for cultural differences have all tended to concentrate on this third element of culture, with the result that they have little understood the problems which the immigrant faced and have missed the significance of his reaction to them.

The Immigrants' Basic Problem. Granted that the immigrant arrived with a basic ideology and a set of institutional objectives not foreign to traditional American culture, he did possess a complex of social relationships established for the implementation of these objectives quite alien to American society. His problem, therefore, was to maintain his basic institutional objectives while repatterning the means needed to implement them. In itself this problem is a difficult one, as the shift from a rural to an urban way of life has revealed in our own country, but for the immigrant it was complicated by additional factors.

First, there was his language which limited his facility to learn new ways, inhibited his mobility, and marked him for discrimination, if not contempt. Second, he was crudely and mercilessly exploited—in construction gangs, stockyards, mines, steelmills, and factories as well as in housing and general living conditions. Third, the natives whom the immigrant encountered were frequently no models of civic or domestic virtue. It was all very well for the Americanizers to speak of the "good old American virtues." What the majority of the immigrants saw, crowded together as they were in the large industrial centers at the turn of the century, was widespread and open corruption in city politics, ruthless exploitation of the worker and his family in industry, and shocking disregard for morality in social life. Hence in the immigrant's mind, Americanization came to be synonymous with demoralization.[18]

Refuge in Group Solidarity. This experience not only increased the immigrant's tendency to withdraw into the security of his own group, it further motivated him to strengthen the existing barriers to wider participation in society. It was this tendency to establish small ethnic enclaves which most accentuated the cultural variations of the immigrants in American eyes. Actually, these differences existed at a relatively superficial level, and their perpetuation through group action could only be a temporary expedient since second and third generation ethnics were only partially subjected to minority group influence and found themselves in position to choose new practices for the implementation of traditional objectives.

A perceptive overview of the immigrants' history, therefore, reveals that minority groups, forced as they were to solve the problem of acculturation under adverse circumstances and with little intelligent aid from the dominant group, faced their situation with considerable acumen.[19] The formation of some measure of group solidarity cushioned the shock of culture conflicts, helped bridge the gap between generations, and permitted the gradual, though steady introduction of new customs and practices while retaining the traditional institutional objectives. Under the circumstances, it is difficult to see what alternatives were available to these groups.[20]

CATHOLIC IMMIGRANTS

It is against this background of immigration, nativist bigotry, and evolving attitudes toward assimilation that American Catholic families must be studied. Only in this frame of reference can we analyze some of the unique characteristics of these families and arrive at an understanding of the specific problems which they face in contemporary society. There are those who argue that since immigration ceased in the twenties, and second and third generation ethnics are becoming rapidly acculturated, their immigrant origins are no longer significant.[21] This is to ignore the facts of history. The Catholic Church in the United States is largely an immigrant church and her members bear the stamp of their origin to this day.

What percentage of the immigrants were Catholic? Since official government statistics do not report the religious affiliation of the immigrants, we must rely on estimates. Table 1 presents the findings of one of the most exhaustive attempts to estimate the percentage of Catholics among the immigrants.[22] Although both the total Catholic population and the number of Catholic immigrants are clearly underestimated, it appears that the over-all picture presented by this study remains substantially correct.[23] As Table 1 reveals, membership in the Church grew from a mere handful of 35,000, scattered throughout the colonies in 1790, to the largest single religious

TABLE 1

CATHOLIC IMMIGRATION AND THE GROWTH OF THE CHURCH BY DECADES

Decade	Catholic Population	Catholic Immigration During Preceding Decade
1790.............	35,000	
1820.............	195,000	77,000
1830.............	318,000	54,000
1840.............	663,000	240,000
1850.............	1,606,000	700,000
1860.............	3,103,000	985,000
1870.............	4,504,000	741,000
1880.............	6,259,000	604,000
1890.............	8,909,000	1,250,000
1900.............	12,041,000	1,225,000
1910.............	16,363,000	2,316,000
1920.............	19,828,000	1,202,000

group in the country in 1920. This growth was primarily the result of the heavy influx of Catholic immigrants throughout the century.

What has happened to these different immigrant groups and their descendants? To what extent have they maintained their national traits and group solidarity? In answering this question we must separate the immigrants into three broad categories: the "Old" Immigration, the "New," and those from the Americas.[24]

The "Old" Immigrants

The large Irish and German Catholic aggregates of the Old Immigration have become thoroughly acculturated so that they display few national traits and little specifically ethnic solidarity. There are still centers which are predominantly Irish or German, but these are primarily the result of original national settlements and the tendency of people in the same socioeconomic class to reside near each other. In the past, German Catholics struggled valiantly to preserve their language and traditions, but the fierce anti-German propaganda campaign during World War I seriously weakened these aspirations. Well before this time, however, the inevitable Americanization process had set in among the German immigrants with the result that today, even in the relatively isolated German rural centers of the Midwest, we find not German-Americans, but Americans of German descent.[25]

At the present time, it is difficult to estimate the number of Catholics of Irish and German descent. Members of both these strains have married rather freely outside their national group. Suffice it to point out that the total Irish immigration to this country numbered approximately 4 million. At least two-thirds of these immigrants were Catholic and their peak year for arrival was over one hundred years ago (1851), so we may conclude they have numerous descendants. Approximately 6 million Germans immigrated to America. It is estimated that 1½ million of these were Catholic and their peak year for arrival was over seventy years ago (1882), so that they too must have numerous descendants.[26]

The "New" Immigrants

The major Catholic national minorities today are composed of members of the New Immigration and their descendants and the Spanish- and French-speaking groups from the Americas. We shall present a brief description of the more prominent minorities and then go on to discuss their patterns of acculturation. Among the Catholic minorities of the New Immigration, those of Polish and Italian background are the most numerous.

The Poles. Polish immigrants and their descendants number about 6 million today. Their heaviest concentration is in the middle eastern states and those bordering on the Great Lakes, although some are to be found in almost all sections of the country.[27] The great majority of Poles have remained faithful to the Church although a strongly nationalistic dissident sect, the Polish National Church, has attracted considerable numbers.[28] Polish Catholics maintain approximately 900 parishes and 600 parochial schools in addition to an active Polish-language press, some 10,000 Polish dramatic, literary, singing, social, religious, and athletic societies and various national Polish organizations with a membership totaling about 800,000.[29] Because the Polish immigrants moved rapidly from a close-knit peasant community to an industrialized urban environment, early studies advanced dire predictions of widespread family disorganization.[30] However, these predictions have not been realized primarily because of the efficiency of the Polish parish organization and the deep religious faith of the immigrant.[31] Some of these parishes grew to tremendous size during the years of heavy immigration. For example, by 1899, St. Stanislaus Kostka parish in Chicago had 50,000 members and some fifty different church societies. In the neighboring parish of St. John Cantius there were an average of 500 marriages per year from 1905 to 1915.

The Italians. It is estimated that Italian immigrants and their descendants number approximately 6 million. For the most part, Italian immigrants to the United States came from the south of Italy.[32] Most of them entered the country through the port of New York and many of them never went very much further.[33] Those who did tended to settle in highly congested areas near their compatriots from the home village in Italy, thus forming "Little Italys" in almost every major American city. Although the vast majority of Italian immigrants were professing Catholics, their indifference to the practice of religion has long been a subject of concern to American churchmen.[34] Many factors were involved in this problem. The Italian immigrants were generally poor and settled in urban slums or mining towns. They were seldom accompanied by their clergy as were many of the other minorities. The majority were poorly instructed in their faith and did not have any tradition of building and supporting church institutions on their own initiative. Finally, their clannishness, further intensified by considerable animosity on the part of other groups, kept them from affiliating with established parishes. As a result, there is rather general agreement that considerable numbers have abandoned the practice of their traditional religion.[35] For example, in 1939, one student of the problem estimated that of the 6 million Italian Americans, 2 million were fervent Catholics, 1 million had abandoned the practice of their religion, and 3 million were doubtful. He predicted that this latter group would sever all connections with the Church in the next generation unless adequate steps were taken to insure their instruction and integration into parish life.[36]

The Czechs and Slovaks. Immigrants and their descendants from Czechoslovakia number about 1,750,000. They are located chiefly in the states of Pennsylvania, Illinois, Ohio, New York, Wisconsin, Nebraska, and Texas. About 50 per cent of the Czechs settled on the land and have become prosperous farmers. The Slovaks tended to cluster in urban areas. It is estimated that between one-half and two-thirds of the Czechs are fervent Catholics. They maintain 120 parishes, most of which have a flourishing parochial school. The majority of Slovaks are Catholic. They maintain over 200 parishes and are noted for the strength and vitality of their various religious, social, athletic, and cultural organizations.

The Croatians and Slovenes. Yugoslav immigrants and their descendants number approximately one million. Of these, it is estimated that the Croatians number 500,000, the Slovenes, about 300,000, and the Serbs, about 200,000. They are distributed throughout the country, but their chief centers of settlement are the states of Illinois, Minnesota, California, Nebraska, Iowa, and Colorado. Most of the Croatians and Slovenes are Roman Catholics; the Serbs are Eastern Orthodox. At the present time, the Slovenes maintain some forty-five, and the Croatians some thirty-three parishes, while considerable numbers of both groups are affiliated with other parishes.

The Magyars. There is little agreement on the exact number of Magyars (Hungarians) and their descendants. Immigration statistics are particularly unreliable here, and present estimates range from a conservative 300,000 or 400,000 to 1.5 or even 2 million.[37] Over half the Magyars are Catholic and they maintain fifty-eight active parishes located chiefly in Pennsylvania, Ohio, New Jersey, New York, Connecticut, and Indiana. Second and third generation Magyars are a socially mobile group and they tend to be acculturated rather rapidly. As distinguished from the Poles, Slovaks, and Czechs, they maintain few specifically ethnic organizations so that it might be said that their cultural fences are down.

The Lithuanians. Estimates of the number of Lithuanian Americans differ greatly but it seems safe to state that there are at least 500,000 in the United States today. Research indicates that all but 30 per cent are practicing Catholics.[38] There

are 120 Lithuanian parishes located primarily in the East and
Great Lakes region. The largest center is Chicago with a
Lithuanian American population of approximately 100,000. In
spite of the strong nationalistic spirit of the immigrants, second and third generation Lithuanians tend to adopt American
customs very quickly. The arrival of considerable numbers of
displaced persons from the homeland has reawakened interest
in the language and history of the mother country, but it is
doubtful whether this will have any appreciable effect on the
younger generation.

The Greek Uniates. Finally, the New Immigration included
a large number of uniate Catholic families rather broadly classified as Ukranians.[39] There are some 632,000 of these, about
equally divided between the jurisdiction of the Ukranian
Greek Catholic (Byzantine Rite) diocese of Philadelphia and
the Greek Rite diocese of Pittsburgh. Their major settlements
are in Pennsylvania, although they are found in most of the
principal industrial centers of the East and Great Lakes region
as well as in Los Angeles and San Francisco. They maintain
approximately 350 parishes and numerous schools. Second and
third generation Ukranians reveal the same general tendency
toward Americanization as do other groups of the New Immigration. This may create a special problem for them, however, since Americanization frequently involves a preference
for the Latin rite.

ASSIMILATION AND THE "NEW" IMMIGRANTS

We have seen that the large groups of Irish and German
Catholics and their descendants have, with few exceptions, become thoroughly Americanized. To what extent has this been
true of the minorities included in the New Immigration? Perhaps this question can be answered best by setting up a continuum at one extreme pole of which can be located the ethnics
who remain in well-integrated national parishes and at the
other, those who have moved out of the national parish communities and affiliated with other parishes. Between these two
extremes can be placed the ethnics who are members of what

might be called "marginal parishes," namely, those parish communities which are becoming "mixed" through the entrance of outside elements.

Function of the National Parish

All our studies show that the national parish has been and continues to be the core institution in the maintenance of group characteristics for the members of the New Immigration.[40] As long as the national parish retains its vitality, group consciousness will remain relatively intact, although some of the characteristic marks of nationality will undergo transformation. In other words, if one wishes to discover how well various groups have retained their distinguishing ethnic traits and what their chances for survival as identifiable social entities are, one must look to the influence and vitality of the national parish community. If these centers remain vigorous and active, the members of the group will display distinct ethnic characteristics, and there is good reason to believe that they will continue to do so in the future. Conversely, if members of the group move out of the sphere of influence of the national parish, they readily lose their distinguishing ethnic traits and cease to be identifiable as ethnics.

The function of the parish in maintaining solidarity among Catholic minority groups follows from the fact that the national parish is much more than a religious institution. If in the Old World the churches had served as the rallying point for nationalism among most of these groups, this role became intensified in the New. The national parish, through its numerous associations, schools, and prohibitions on outgroup marriage, erected a series of structural fences to keep the ethnic individual closely articulated to the community. Further, the village-community rather than the nation had been the traditional integrating unit for the immigrant in his homeland. He tended to think of himself not as a Pole, or a German, or an Italian, but as a man from a certain village and a certain parish. "Companilism" the Italians call it—a deep loyalty to that which falls within range of the village bell tower. In the New World the parish most closely resembled the Old World com-

munity. Hence, solidarity with the national parish remained
the measure of the individual's solidarity with his ethnic group.
Although there is little doubt that the national parishes operated effectively in slowing down the assimilation of considerable numbers, it should never be forgotten that they were instrumental in preventing widespread initial disorganization.[41]

Indexes of Group Solidarity

In searching for evidence of group cohesiveness and national
survival, we have employed the following indexes: (1) the
prevalence of the use of the mother-tongue in the home,
church, and school; (2) the persistence of distinctive religious
and social customs; (3) the adherence to ethnic associations;
and (4) the rate of outgroup and/or mixed marriages. These
indexes were used because they not only represent visible
marks of ethnic diversity but they imply the existence of those
solidary bonds which traditionally have held these groups together. In practice, the existence of the traits implied in the
first three indexes appear basic to the maintenance of ethnic
solidarity because it is doubtful whether the traditional prohibition of outgroup marriage can long be effective without
them. This is particularly true since we are dealing for the
most part with members of an urban industrial society in which
personal associations leading to marriage tend to develop along
occupational and social class lines.

Returning now to our example of a continuum of acculturation, let us look at the general characteristics of the groups
which we have situated at various points along this line. At
one extreme are those members of a group who have moved
away from the ethnic center, the parish. Judged by our four
indexes, it is found that these retain few visible marks of their
national origin. English is adopted almost exclusively, particularly in parent-child relationships. The reading of foreign
language literature, participation in ethnic associations, the re-
tention of distinctive religious and social customs, and the
prohibition on outgroup marriage are usually dropped.[42] There
is apparent a strain for external conformity with the dominant
group and a marked tendency to disclaim former ethnic attach-

ments. The exceptions to the latter were certain politicians and professional people who played up their ethnic backgrounds when this was likely to prove beneficial. It was interesting to note in this connection that such individuals separated their children from ethnic influences so that as one astute observer remarked, "They wear their nationalism on their sleeve, not in their heart."

The "Marginals"

Ethnics who are members of marginal parish communities present an interesting example of how rapidly solidarity based on national minority sentiments breaks down once the community is invaded by outsiders. Frequently, the invasion is preceded by the movement of young or socially mobile ethnic families away from the area of original settlement. In some instances this may be occasioned by new industrial developments within the area, attracting workers from the outside. At times, the invasion of adjacent areas by groups considered lower in the socioeconomic scale precipitates a mass exodus out of the ethnic community. Since the majority of these national groups are located near the industrial sections of our large urban centers, they are particularly vulnerable to such invasions. Furthermore, slum clearance programs and the tendency of the urban white population to move to the suburbs, abandoning the urban centers to less fortunate newcomers, also threaten the solidarity of the ethnic community. When such conditions occur, national traits tend to disappear rapidly. The rate of outgroup marriage increases almost at once. The use of the mother-tongue is confined to the home and even there it is employed only by the elders. Whatever distinctively ethnic associations endure are patronized primarily by the older members of the group. It is only a matter of time when all traces of the old ethnic community will disappear completely.

The "Solidarists"

At the opposite extreme of our acculturation continuum are found those families who have remained within the sphere of influence of the national parish. Contrary to popular belief, these communities are still numerous and have continued to play a vital role in the preservation of national minorities.[43] Since this is the case, it will be necessary to study the general characteristics of these groups in some detail. Although various ethnic groups present distinct patterns of acculturation, and indeed, within most of the groups there exist marked subdivisions depending upon local and regional differences, nevertheless, clearly defined general trends are apparent in all these groups.

Language. Perhaps the most obvious is the tendency of second and third generation ethnics to become illiterate in their mother-tongue and passive in its use. That is, they are unable to read, write, or speak it fluently, although many retain an "ear" for the language and can understand it when it is spoken. This means, of course, that they are unable to transmit it to their children. Publishers of foreign language newspapers find the bulk of their readers among the older generation and the DPs. Teachers testify that first-grade children are frequently unable to understand the simplest directions given in the mother-tongue. Many pastors find that young people tend to avoid church services in which the mother-tongue is used and flock to those in which English is spoken. Efforts to retain the use of their language have been more successful among some groups than others and there exist some compact, relatively isolated communities where all the members of the group are acquainted with their mother-tongue, but the general consensus among competent observers is that third and fourth generation ethnics are ceasing to be bilingual.

Ethnic Customs. Many religious and social customs have disappeared or are well on the way to disappearing. It appears that modern urban living with its fast tempo, its diversions, and crowded living conditions no longer allow place for them. Many of these customs grew out of the small rural community existence of the Old World and were primarily meaningful only in this frame of reference. People caught up in the demands of a modern industrial society find little time for the celebration of numerous local or national saints and heroes nor can they approach the great feasts of Christmas and Easter with the same leisurely spirit as in a rural community. This represents a loss of much that was wholesome and truly human in a way of life, and it is regrettable that in a society where all institutions are geared to the exigencies of the economic system, no meaningful substitutes are forthcoming. During our research we discovered that many ethnics of relatively high income chose to retain residences far beneath their financial status chiefly because they liked the spirit of the old community.

Associations. In regard to ethnic associations, it should be observed that some groups traditionally displayed small preference for such associations. One explanation advanced by some ethnic leaders is that these associations thrive mainly among those groups which were national minorities in Europe; that is, among groups such as the Poles, Czechs, Slovaks, Slovenes, Croatians, and so forth. It is maintained that these groups had long struggled for cultural survival and had established associations for that end. Further, even though living in America, many of these groups were strongly influenced by the desire to "liberate the fatherland," and much of their activity was directed toward keeping attachment to the Old World vital among the immigrants.[44] This explanation appears plausible considering the nature of many of these associations and the fact that relatively few have been established among such groups as the Italians and Magyars whose history reveals no struggle for cultural survival. At any rate, where they have been established, ethnic fraternal and cultural organizations are still vigorous although they display less emphasis on separatist national loyalties and greater willingness to cooperate in larger community and diocesan activities. In general, their attitude is less defensive than formerly, reflecting, no doubt, the slackening of opposition from the outgroup.

Problem of Outgroup Marriage

The prohibition on outgroup marriage is still maintained by most groups attached to the national parish.[45] Since outgroup marriage often implies marriage with one not of the faith, there can be little doubt that this prohibition is enforced by the Church's attitude toward mixed marriage. Nevertheless, the primary sanction appears to be the attitude of the group. Interviews revealed that many ethnics rationalized their attitude by stating they felt "clashes of temperament" would result from outgroup marriage although they agreed that some combinations were more likely to succeed than others. In general, young people are told that they will be happier if they marry "their own." One interviewee reflected the prevalent attitude when discussing a particular outgroup marriage, "I asked her why she picked out this fellow when there were so many fine boys among our own group."

Two types of data on ethnic marriage patterns have been gathered. First, there is the information gleaned from going over individual parish marriage records. This process is time-consuming in the extreme so its use has been confined to several representative parishes in each region. The second type of data is based on the number of mixed marriages in the national parishes. These data do not reveal the total amount of outgroup marriage but they do reveal the religious solidarity of the group, and there is a close parallel between the rates of outgroup and mixed marriage.

Outgroup Marriage Rates in the Active Ethnic Parish. Table 2 presents the mixed and outgroup marriage rates of

TABLE 2

MIXED AND OUTGROUP MARRIAGE RATES OF AN ETHNIC PARISH
FOR SELECTED YEARS

Years	Total Marriages	Mixed Marriages	Outgroup Nonmixed	Total Outgroup
1923	108	2	2	4
1926	109	4	6	10
1935	128	11	11	22
1940	155	10	8	18
1945	109	8	13	21
1950	109	9	11	20
Total	718	44	51	95

a single ethnic parish for selected years. According to our research, the rates for this parish are fairly representative of those ethnic parishes in which the members are bilingual, lower middle-class, and not totally isolated from nonethnics.

National parishes in which the use of the mother-tongue is still predominant or which are surrounded by other national parishes usually show a lower rate of outgroup marriage. Table 2 reveals small variation in the total outgroup marriage rate starting with the year 1935. The percentages for the years cited are: 17.2, 11.6, 19.3, and 18.3, respectively. The exception for the year 1940 may be explained by the advent of war since an unusual number of marriages (155) were performed during this year. Other parishes studied reveal the same phenomenon.

It will be noted that the outgroup marriage rate closely parallels the mixed marriage rate (53.7 and 46.3, respectively). Investigating these rates further, we see that females are much more inclined to outgroup marriage than males. In 70.4 per cent of the mixed marriage cases, the Catholic party was the wife, and in 82.4 per cent of the nonmixed outgroup marriages, she was the ethnic involved. These rates point up a tendency which appeared in all our studies; when there is outgroup marriage, it is the female rather than the male who tends to select her mate from outside the group. This does not necessarily signify that the female is less conscious of group loyalties than the male. The same phenomenon occurs in mixed marriage rates in general yet it would seem contrary to what we know about the religious characteristics of women were we to conclude that they value their religion less than men. A more plausible explanation would seem to be that the average female has less freedom in her choice of a mate, with the result that she cannot afford to be as selective as the male.

Our conclusion from this set of data is that the active ethnic parish reveals no marked trends toward increased outgroup marriage. There are some indications, however, that members who are about to contact a mixed marriage move out of the ethnic community, and consequently, their marriage does not appear in the parish register. On the other hand, not all outgroup marriages represent a loss to the group. The ethnic community is capable of assimilating outsiders and since the ethnic involved is so frequently the wife, it appears likely that the children will be reared according to ethnic group patterns and consequently in ethnic solidarity.

Mixed Marriages in Predominantly Ethnic Centers. Let us turn now to the data dealing only with mixed marriages. Table 3 presents the findings for ten adjacent, roughly coter-

TABLE 3

PERCENTAGE OF MIXED MARRIAGES IN TEN RELATED PARISHES

Parish	Per Cent Mixed Marriages
Diocesan (Territorial)	6.2
Ethnic (Old Immigration)	4.6
Group I (New Immigration)	.5
Group I (New Immigration)	.0
Group II (New Immigration)	2.2
Group III (New Immigration)	1.5
Group III (New Immigration)	1.4
Group IV (New Immigration)	2.3
Group V (New Immigration)	.0
Group VI (New Immigration)	2.5

minus parishes. One is a diocesan (territorial) parish, one is a national parish formerly composed of Old Immigration ethnics, and the remaining eight parishes represent six different groups of the New Immigration. The total number of families is 4,084. We have presented the data for this cluster of parishes because it brings out clearly the low percentage of mixed marriages found in those areas where large numbers of ethnics have settled together. The diocesan parish was established by a national group of the Old Immigration, but at present there are few of their descendants living in the district so that the parish is made up almost entirely of members of the New Immigration. It will be noted that its percentage of mixed marriages is considerably higher than that of the newer ethnic parishes. This seems to confirm our hypothesis that some ethnics who enter mixed marriage feel ill at ease in their own parishes so they take up membership in the diocesan parish when this occurs. Although it was impossible to check the total outgroup marriage rate in all these parishes, there were indications that it was correspondingly low. Again, almost all the marriages in the diocesan parish involved intergroup marriage, leading to the conclusion that outgroup marriage even between Catholics was a reason for some to join the nonethnic parish.

Mixed Marriages in a Typical Industrial Urban Center. Finally, Table 4 presents the mixed marriage percentage for all

TABLE 4

MIXED MARRIAGE PERCENTAGES FOR ALL THE PARISHES IN LARGE
MIDWESTERN URBAN CENTER

Type of Parish	No. of Parishes	No. of Families	Percentage Mixed Marriage
Diocesan	22	23,774	15.2
Old Ethnic (National)	9	9,029	15.8
New Ethnic (Group I)	17	16,060	2.9
New Ethnic (Group II)	5	1,710	3.6
New Ethnic (Group III) ...	3	1,977	9.5
New Ethnic (Group IV) ...	1	291	10.7
New Ethnic (Group V)	2	1,545	13.9

the parishes in a large Midwestern urban center. It will be noted that the percentages for the diocesan and "Old Ethnic" national parishes are approximately the same. In other words, although the "Old Ethnic" parishes are still juridical national parishes, there is no evidence of nationalism in their mixed marriage rates, and we can safely conclude that their specifically ethnic solidarity has disintegrated. The five parishes in Group II are small parishes constituted by five distinct ethnic groups, but we have summarized the data for them under one heading since their percentages were similar. It will be noted that Groups IV and V have relatively high mixed marriage percentages for ethnic parishes. These two groups represent minorities in which a considerable number are non-Catholics so that the percentage of mixed marriage is not necessarily an indication of ethnic outgroup marriage.

To summarize, therefore, ethnics of the New Immigration can be identified primarily by their cohesiveness as expressed in nationalist organizations and ingroup marriage. Further, this solidarity is apparent only among those who reside in communities clustered around the national parishes. Bilingualism and distinctive national customs are gradually disappearing even in these centers. Finally, prejudice against the immigrants and their descendants has subsided so that one of the fundamental external supports of group solidarity has been removed.

In the light of these facts, it seems safe to predict that although many of the old ethnic centers will remain vigorous for some time to come, increasing numbers of third and fourth generation ethnics will move away from the group. If present trends in urban population movements continue, more and more ethnic parishes will become marginal and gradually cease to be identifiable ethnic centers.

Immigrants from the Americas

As we have pointed out, American Catholic immigrant minorities can be placed in three categories: members of the Old and New Immigration and those from the Americas. Outstanding among this latter group for their cultural cohesiveness are the French Canadians.

French Canadians. It is estimated that these immigrants and their descendants number between 2.5 million and 3 million.[46] Their major settlements are found in New England, the Eastern Seaboard, and the states of Illinois, Wisconsin, and Michigan. The majority have entered the United States since 1870, for prior to that time the typical French Canadian immigrant spent a few months or a few years working in the States and then returned to Quebec with his savings. Although they have few cultural or spiritual ties with France, the French Canadians have succeeded in preserving their French institutions and customs to a remarkable degree. Even in the United States the life of the typical French Canadian centers chiefly around his parish and his home. Working on the premise that "qui perd sa langue perd sa foi," they have always stressed the national parish, French-speaking parochial schools, the French-language press, and numerous social and cultural associations.

At present the French Canadians constitute a distinct cultural subgroup, but there is some question how long they can maintain their language and customs intact. Like other immigrant groups, their efforts to achieve higher economic and social status will present them with a painful dilemma. On the one hand, there can be little social and economic mobility unless they acquire mastery of English; on the other, they will be reluctant to drop their mother-tongue since they consider such a step a repudiation of their ancestral culture. This is particularly true for the French Canadians since they consider their language, culture, and religion as constituting an inseparable whole so that one element cannot be dropped without imperiling the survival of the others. In America the drive for a better standard of living and a higher social status is part of the national ethos. There is evidence to suggest that the French Canadians will succeed no better than other national minorities in their efforts at cultural survival. At present, however, their eastern settlements represent a cohesive, close-knit cultural subgroup.[47]

Spanish Americans. Americans of Mexican ancestry number approximately 3,500,000 persons in the United States.[48] About 90 per cent of the group live in the Southwest and the remainder have settled in or near urban centers in Illinois, Michigan, Minnesota, and Ohio. There are at least four major types to be considered: old native group, new native group, "wetbacks" (Mexican workers who have crossed the frontier illegally), and Mexican Nationals or contract laborers. Although there is some intermarriage with other groups, the Spanish Americans tend to keep their language and their customs intact. With the exception of the old native group, they are uniformly poor, suffer marked discrimination in education, law, and social life, and are the victims of widespread and flagrant exploitation in the economic sphere.[49]

Most of this group are Catholic but their poverty, the necessity of moving from place to place to find employment, and the difficulty they experience in adapting to a wholly alien culture tend to produce considerable indifference to religious practice among many. The family is the basic social unit in their lives, but American customs and practices leave them confused and insecure. Their traditional family patterns appear outmoded, yet they have learned no substitutes. As a result, parents are bewildered and uncertain, and the young lack guidance and motivation; whereas all efforts to help them encounter the barriers set up by prejudice, discrimination and segregation.

Puerto Ricans. Somewhat similar in culture to the Mexican group are the Spanish-speaking immigrants from Puerto Rico.

They started arriving in large numbers only after 1940.[50] At present they number over 500,000, about 80 per cent of whom are located in New York City. The net total immigration since 1950 has been over 50,000 a year, and it appears that this high rate will continue for some years to come. As our latest immigrant arrivals, the Puerto Ricans find themselves at the bottom of the socioeconomic ladder. The most serious problem the Puerto Rican family faces is the virtual nonexistence of family living accommodations at rentals that they can afford. During the last few years, New York City has been in a period of "slum making" and must be prepared to face the social and moral consequences which arise when such conditions are tolerated.[51] In general, the Puerto Rican immigrants are in the first stages of acculturation and are facing the same discriminations and misconceptions which have been applied to other new groups upon their arrival. It is too early to hazard any predictions concerning their eventual adjustment to their new environment.

Significance of the Catholic Minority's Immigrant Origin

This brief review of immigrant history and of the major minorities in the American Catholic population throws some light on the variety and diversity we discover among American Catholic families. In a later chapter we shall discuss some of the practical consequences of this cultural diversity for Catholic family life. It will suffice here to point out a few general characteristics resulting from their immigrant past. First, the Catholic immigrant groups faced the problem of establishing themselves in a society which had been pre-empted by Anglo-Saxon protestantism. This put the Catholic families on the defensive and intensified their minority status.

Second, Catholic families, with the exception of the Irish, encountered a language barrier which slowed down their economic, social, and political integration, intensified their dissimilarity with the dominant group, and motivated them to settle in relatively closed communities clustered around their national parish. As a result, the Irish have been the first to be assimilated, their clergy have composed the majority of the hierarchy, and in a sense, the Irish have acted as an intermediate group between the dominant Protestant majority and the minority Catholic groups. To be sure, this leadership of the Irish has not gone unchallenged. It was strongly contested by the Germans in the latter part of the nineteenth century when Irish-German rivalry aroused considerable animosity between the two groups. Fortunately, the minority status of both in American society forced them to work out an amicable solution.

Third, since the majority of Irish and German families arrived during the last century, they were well established before the new immigrants arrived. Consequently, they tended to look upon themselves as "natives," and to acquire many of the prejudices of the dominant group concerning the later arrivals from central and southern Europe whom they considered "foreigners." This attitude has led to considerable feeling between certain national groups and has further intensified the tendency of some to isolate themselves in an effort to preserve their language and other cultural traits. A manifestation of this was the multiplication of national parishes and parochial schools which placed heavy burdens on immigrant families.

Fourth, the process of acculturation requires time, it involves a clash of cultures, and it produces a generation or two of marginal individuals. The factor of time is self-evident. The mature immigrant could not immediately discard his alien culture even if he had so desired. Further, a clash of cultures was inevitable as soon as the immigrant attempted to adjust himself to American society. This conflict became most apparent in parent-child relationships so that the process of acculturation frequently produced marginal men. Second and third generation ethnics found themselves partially integrated in two cultures. They were neither Americans nor aliens, but something of both. Under these circumstances some chose complete rejection of their alien cultural past and became more American than the natives. Others retreated into cultural ghettoes, seeking security in the preservation of the past. Others experienced personal and social disorganization. For all, the process involved a period of strain and tension, focusing their attention upon their own problems rather than upon those of the community or the nation.

Finally, the fact that the Catholic minority is composed of families at different stages of the acculturation process and retains various degrees of group solidarity has resulted in its having only limited influence on American culture in general. However, even if it had presented a united front, the late arrival of many of its members in addition to their initially low social and economic position would have restricted its influence in this regard. For the most part, the American culture was developed under Puritan Protestant auspices and with the gradual breakdown of this influence, it has become highly secular in character. This does not imply that it is necessarily antispiritual or promaterialist. Rather, it is a complex culture tolerating great individual freedom and, under the influence of its economic system, it is frankly utilitarian in its general outlook.

As a result, although the Catholic family enjoys a maximum of religious freedom, many institutions such as civil divorce, and some accepted practices such as the use of contraceptive birth control, lend no support to the Catholic family ideal. Hence, Catholic families must formulate and put into practice particularly in the realm of chastity and family life certain moral ideals considerably at variance with the dominant culture. As we have indicated, it was precisely because many ethnic leaders were distressed by the moral ideals and practices which they encountered in the lower ranks of society that they reacted by building strong group solidarity around the national parish and its organizations. With the gradual disintegration of these old solidarities, there is appearing increasing awareness among all ethnic families of a common bond of unity with other Catholic families. This appears in youth movements, marriage and family organizations, and various religious and social activities.

CHAPTER FIVE

The Catholic Family Today

Our review of the origins and nationality background of American Catholic families suggests several further questions concerning the Catholic population. How many are there? Where are they? What are their characteristics? We shall try to answer these questions on the basis of whatever data are available, but it should be noted at the outset that the information is far from complete. Although the religious composition of the population is conceded to be among the most significant determinants of human behavior, the item on church affiliation or religious preference has never found a place on the census population schedule in this country. This is unfortunate since we must rely on estimates or relatively small samples for our information concerning numbers, percentages, and distribution of the various religious groups.

The same sources must be used if we would study the relationship between religious affiliation and marriage, divorce, the birth rate, education, occupation, and social status. To be sure, a "Census of Religious Bodies" was conducted in 1906, 1916, 1926, 1936, and 1946 (unpublished), but the word census is somewhat misleading in this context. Data were secured by questionnaires addressed to the various church organizations, not by an enumeration of the population. As a result, there is general agreement that some denominations were under-reported, the figures for some were exaggerated, and only those organized under an ecclesiastical hierarchy were fairly adequately canvassed.

INADEQUACY OF CATHOLIC POPULATION DATA

Our statistical information on the American Catholic family has neither the completeness nor the reliability that we might desire. We are not sure how many Catholic families there are nor do we know their average size, annual income, or socio-economic status. What information we have, however, reveals some general characteristics of the Catholic family which merit our further attention. Many specifically Catholic family problems appear to be closely associated with the relative number of Catholics in a given region or community and with their economic and social status. As members of a minority group, Catholic families must contend with a variety of opposing forces and circumstances in their effort to realize their family ideals. In this chapter we shall present a general outline of the situation, a broad frame of reference for locating the Catholic family in American society.

Problem of Definition: Who is a Catholic?

How many Catholics are there in the United States? The answer to this question implies an acceptable definition of a Catholic. Theoretically, a definition of Catholic might include all those who express a "preference" for the Catholic faith. Most opinion polls use this definition of Catholic probably because it is difficult to obtain more detailed information. According to Catholic doctrine, all those are Catholic who have been baptized in the Church since baptism is the sacrament which initiates the supernatural life of grace in the soul. This is a workable, sufficiently clear definition, and Canon

Law uses it in determining the jurisdiction of specific Church legislation.

Unfortunately, this definition has limited usefulness for a study dealing with the association of religious affiliation and family practice. Some individuals may be baptized in the Church but later receive no instruction in Catholic doctrine and may have no further association with the Church. Others may receive some slight instruction in Catholic doctrine and may remain affiliated to the Church up through the first reception of Communion, and then have no further connection with Catholic worship or reappear only on the occasion of their wedding or some major feast. Still others may be baptized and instructed but later "lose" the faith, that is, they may simply drop all connection with the Church or affiliate with a Protestant sect. Others may be cut off from active participation in the life of the Church because they have contracted an invalid marriage which excludes them from the reception of the sacraments. Others may be characterized as "dormant," that is, they maintain their "preference" for the Catholic Church, but any one of a variety of reasons may dissuade them from active participation in the religious community.

Diversity of Participation Among the Faithful

Finally, even among those who are actively affiliated with the Church there is considerable diversity in the degree of participation in religious observances and activities. This ranges all the way from those who do no more than maintain a more or less faithful observance of the prescriptions to attend Sunday Mass and receive the Paschal Communion to those who are frequent in the reception of the sacraments, faithful attendants at various religious services, and active in parish organizations. Further, there is evidence to show that the degree of participation differs according to sex. Reporting on his study of religious practice in a Southern Parish, Fichter states:

> Sex differences among these 8,363 people studied show the expected predominance of female observance in every age category. . . . Our statistics show that the proportion of males

to females is as follows: out of every 100 persons: who go to
confession, only 36 are males; who attend evening services,
30 are males; who attend special Lenten services, 24 are males.[1]

The same study revealed a difference in the degree of formal
religious observance between the various age groups and in
particular, between the married and single.[2] Members of the
10-19 year age cohort were the most observant, while those in
the 30-39, were the least. Fichter's data on the married are
in substantial agreement with Kelly's findings on Florida Catholics. "For all married people, there is a certain falling off in
religious observance between the ages of thirty and thirty-
nine. Except for this decline, increasing age generally brings
with it a more faithful observance of religious duties." [3] Although these studies include rather select groups (one parish
in New Orleans, the native white married couples in Florida),
it is probable that the same differentials exist in varying degrees among the Catholic population as a whole.[4]

It follows that in evaluating various estimates of Catholic
population size, the definition of Catholic used in making the
study is of prime importance. As we have stated, most pollsters
use "religious preference" in their research. This may yield a
higher estimate than the official definition of "baptized in the
Church," since it is conceivable that an individual might express a preference for a specific religious body without seeking
formal affiliation. On the other hand, pollsters would not include in their estimates those baptized Catholics who had
abandoned their faith and affiliated with a Protestant denomi-
nation.

The Official Catholic Directory's *Estimates*

The Catholic population estimate which we shall use is
based on the statistics presented in *The Official Catholic Directory*. These statistics are obtained from the various diocesan chancery offices throughout the country which, in turn,
obtain their data from the pastor's report of each parish in
the diocese. It is not clear what definition of Catholic is used
in making out the parish record. In some dioceses very thor-

ough parish censuses are taken and the number of baptized Catholics in each parish is fairly accurately reported. In others, the number is estimated and usually includes only those who actively participate in parish life. Under the circumstances, it is difficult to evaluate *The Catholic Directory*'s data, but it seems safe to maintain that the over-all Catholic population figure presented in *The Directory* for the past few years represents a fairly accurate estimate of the more or less active Catholic population in the country. An analysis of the birth, death, and marriage rates listed in *The Directory* leads to the conclusion that its population estimates are reliable within a margin of 10 per cent.[5]

According to *The Directory*, the Catholic population of the country as of January 1, 1953, was 30,329,427.[6] In other words, approximately one-fifth of the nation's population was affiliated with the Catholic Church. This represents a vast increase since the first Federal Census of 1790 when Catholics numbered only about 35,000, or less than one per cent of the total population. We have seen that much of this growth was associated with immigration, and we described this characteristic of Catholic families in the last chapter. However, we cannot grasp the present significance of Catholic population growth unless we consider the distribution of Catholics throughout the country. The pattern of their concentration and scattering, though easily explained in terms of their history, adds further complexity to our over-all picture of the American Catholic family.

THE CATHOLIC CHURCH IS URBAN

For reasons which we need not go into here, the majority of Catholic families tended to settle in the large industrial centers. The point has often been made that the Catholic Church in America is primarily an urban church. Evidence for this assumption can be gathered from a comparison of church statistics and the census reports. Using the 1940 reports, since it was on the basis of these that the estimates for Catholics were made, we find that approximately 43 per cent of the nation's population were classified as rural. This includes both the rural-farm (23.2 per cent) and the rural-nonfarm (20.5 per cent) population.[7] Of the Catholic population, only 19.4 per cent are classified as rural (farm and nonfarm), and according to estimates of the Catholic Rural Life Conference, only about 8 per cent of the Catholic population now live on the land as full-time farmers.[8]

Although the secularizing tendencies of urbanization are a commonplace in modern sociological literature, it should be noted that the evil effects of this concentration of Catholic families in large industrial centers have been somewhat mitigated by other important factors. Concentration has made possible the construction of a church and school system without parallel in the world. There is some question that this could have been managed if Catholic families had been dispersed equally throughout the country. Even today in the 9,641 Catholic rural parishes and missions, only 17.9 per cent have Catholic elementary schools, and 3.2 per cent have Catholic high schools.[9]

THE CATHOLIC POPULATION IS REGIONALLY CONCENTRATED

Another characteristic of Catholic families is their high concentration in certain areas of the country. Approximately 75 per cent are located in 20 per cent of the territory. Roughly speaking, this is the area north of the Ohio River and east of the Mississippi Valley region. The other 25 per cent are scattered throughout the remaining territory with rather heavy concentrations in Louisiana and those sections of the Southwest where the Spanish-speaking population is relatively high. Table 5 shows the trends in this distribution for the past four decades. The population figures are based on the statistics presented in *The Catholic Directory* for the years cited. The regional classification is based on the sixfold division developed by Odum in his well-known study of regionalism.[10]

The table shows that the Northeast region, which includes the twelve states of Maine, New Hampshire, Vermont, Massa-

TABLE 5

DISTRIBUTION OF CATHOLIC POPULATION ACCORDING
TO REGIONS, 1921–51

Year	North-east	Middle States	North-west	Far West	South-east	South-west
1921	50.8	30.6	4.2	4.5	5.7	4.2
1931	50.3	30.0	4.3	5.0	5.4	5.0
1941	49.2	30.2	4.0	6.2	5.4	5.0
1951	46.7	28.9	3.5	9.0	5.4	6.5

chusetts, Rhode Island, Connecticut, New York, New Jersey, Delaware, Pennsylvania, Maryland, and West Virginia, contains approximately 50 per cent of the Catholic population. However, its proportion has been decreasing steadily in the past few decades. The Middle States region, which includes Ohio, Indiana, Illinois, Michigan, Wisconsin, Minnesota, Iowa, and Missouri, contains the next largest proportion of Catholics although here too, the proportion is slowly decreasing. The Northwest region, which includes the Dakotas, Nebraska, Kansas, Montana, Idaho, Wyoming, Colorado, and Utah, has never had a high percentage of Catholics and with the general loss of population which some portions of this region have been experiencing in the past two decades, even this small proportion is decreasing. The Far West region includes four states: Nevada, Washington, Oregon, and California. Its percentage has doubled since 1921, reflecting the over-all growth of population during these decades. The Southeast region, which includes the eleven states of Arkansas, Louisiana, Mississippi, Alabama, Tennessee, Kentucky, Georgia, Florida, the Carolinas, and Virginia, has always been regarded, with the exception of Southern Louisiana, as solidly Protestant. In fact, even the 5.4 percentage is misleading since approximately 77 per cent of this is found in the two dioceses of New Orleans and Lafayette located in the southern half of Louisiana. The Southwest region, which includes the four states of Texas, Oklahoma, New Mexico, and Arizona, has shown some increase in the proportion of Catholics it contains. Since the majority of Catholics in this region belong to the Spanish-speaking group, this growth probably reflects the increase of immigration from Mexico during the past few decades.

SOME SOCIOECONOMIC CHARACTERISTICS OF
THE CATHOLIC POPULATION

Thus far we have seen that the Catholic population is primarily urban and concentrated in the Northeast and Middle States regions. What information do we possess on the education, occupation, and economic status of this population? Unfortunately, the only data available are based on opinion-poll studies and, as we shall see, these leave much to be desired in scientific objectivity so that their formulations must be regarded as tentative. However, we shall present a résumé of their findings as the best now available on the subject.

The first study was reported by Cantril in 1943.[11] It is based on two surveys conducted by the American Institute of Public Opinion and two by the Office of Public Opinion Research between March, 1939, and December, 1940. These surveys represent a total of approximately fourteen thousand cases based on a "social" rather than a "political" or "voting" cross-section of the population.[12] The information reported covers only the relationship between religion, education, and economic status.

The second study was made under the auspices of the Department of Research and Education of the Federal Council of the Churches of Christ in America and was conducted by Wesley Allensmith of Princeton University at the Office of Public Opinion Research of Princeton's Department of Psychology. The findings are based on a "voting" cross-section representing approximately 12,400 cases contacted between November, 1945, and June, 1946.[13] This study offers information on education, occupation and economic class. It should be noted that since it is based on a "voting" sample, a large number of nonvoting Protestant Negroes are not represented.

A third study is based on a "social" cross-section survey conducted in 1952 and comprises approximately three thousand cases. This is a survey of religious beliefs, practices, and attitudes made for *The Catholic Digest* by Ben Gaffin & Associates, a nationally recognized marketing and opinion research organization.[14] In the following tables the pertinent data on

education, occupation, and economic status presented in these
three studies are summarized for purposes of comparison.

TABLE 6

RELATIONSHIP BETWEEN RELIGION AND EDUCATION

Study	Religion	High School Incomplete (or less)	High School Graduates (or more)	College Graduates
Cantril	Catholic	58.1	41.9	8.6
	Protestant	51.3	48.7	14.8
Federal	Catholic	57.0	43.0	7.0
Council	Protestant	50.9	49.1	15.7[a]
Gaffin	Catholic	55.0	45.0	5.0
	Protestant	48.0	52.0	10.0

[a] Data incomplete. This figure is based only on Methodist, Baptist, Presbyterian, Lutheran, Episcopalian, and Congregational bodies.

Religion and Education

The typically American belief in equal opportunity for all
has led to the establishment of a remarkable public and private school system making at least a high school education
available to all. Americans have traditionally placed great faith
in the possibilities of human betterment through education.
American industry has constantly increased its demands for
educated employees. And in our open class system, education
still remains the most easily available "ladder" for social mobility. Hence, it is important to know how the Catholic minority compares with other groups in regard to formal education.

Although due allowance must be made for the tentative
nature of the data, the percentages given in Table 6 are consistent in showing that the Catholic population tends to have
less formal education than do members of the Protestant bodies. This finding is in conformity with what we would expect
on the basis of the relatively recent immigrant origin of a
considerable percentage of Catholics. However, the differences are not as great as is frequently assumed, since they
range between 5 and 7 per cent in all categories. According
to the three studies reported here, between 41.9 and 52 per

cent of the Protestant membership and between 41.9 and 45
per cent of the Catholics had received a high school education
or more. The percentage of college graduates ranged between
5 and 8.6 per cent for Catholics, and 10 and 15.7 per cent for
Protestants, although, as the table indicates, this latter figure
is based on an incomplete coverage of Protestant bodies. In
the light of these data, it seems safe to conclude that an increasing percentage of second and third generation ethnics
are making use of the educational opportunities offered in
this country.

Religion and Occupation

In Table 7, which presents the data on the relationship be-

TABLE 7

RELATIONSHIP BETWEEN RELIGION AND OCCUPATION

Study	*Religion*	*Business and Professional*	*White Collar*	*Urban Manual Workers*	*Farmers*
Federal	Catholic	14.0	23.0	55.0	8.0
Council	Protestant	19.4	18.6	41.7	20.3
Gaffin	Catholic	16.0	17.0	64.0	3.0
	Protestant	22.0	16.0	52.0	10.0

tween religion and occupation, we have only the findings of
the Federal Council and the Gaffin studies since Cantril does
not report on occupational status. The figures in this table per-
tain to the principal breadwinner in the case of each family
interviewed. In evaluating the data it should be recalled that
opinion polls usually reveal some subjectivity in the classification of occupations, and the relative status of various occupations varies from region to region. However, the over-all
picture is clear. Relatively few Catholics are occupied on
farms and from 55 to 64 per cent are found among the urban
manual workers. If the white collar, business, and professional
classes are taken together, however, it is interesting to note
that both studies present approximately the same percentage
for Catholic and Protestant groups.

Religion and Economic Status

The classification of individuals or families into the economic categories of "Upper," "Middle," and "Lower" is apparently a highly arbitrary procedure. Interviewers are usually

TABLE 8

RELATIONSHIP BETWEEN RELIGION AND ECONOMIC STATUS

Study	Religion	Upper	Middle	Lower
Cantril	Catholic	9.0	50.0	41.0
	Protestant	14.0	52.0	34.0
Federal	Catholic	8.7	24.7	66.6
Council	Protestant	13.8	32.6	53.6
Gaffin	Catholic	11.0	55.0	34.0
	Protestant	19.0	50.0	31.0

told to make an appraisal of economic class on the basis of
certain external symbols such as dress, type of house, residential area, possession of luxury items, and so forth. Subjectivity is further increased by the injunction to appraise
economic status on a relative basis, that is, in terms of the
interviewee's community rather than on an absolute basis in
terms of the whole nation. Consequently, the data presented
in Table 8 should be judged to represent little more than rather
broad estimates of obviously vaguely defined economic status.
Further, since the Cantril and Federal Council studies are
based on a "voting" cross-section, they will tend to reveal
somewhat fewer Protestants in the lower economic status than
would be the case if they were based on a "social" cross-
section.

Considering the findings of these studies with the aforesaid
limitations in mind, we find they lend some confirmation to
the prevalent assumption that the Catholic population is in a
lower economic status than Protestants, although the difference does not appear as great as commonly believed. The
Cantril and Gaffin studies differ from that of the Federal Council in placing approximately 50 per cent of both Catholics and
Protestants in the middle class. It would seem that until more
scientific indexes for the ascription of economic status are

formulated and accepted by pollsters, it will be safer to draw few conclusions about the relationship of religion and economic status on the basis of their findings.

SOCIAL STATUS OF THE CATHOLIC POPULATION

Closely related to education, occupation, and economic status is the social status of an individual. All large and complex societies possess some type of social status system by which people are placed in higher and lower positions in accordance with a stratification scale growing out of the value-patterns of each society. Even in a democratic society, social status is important since both experience and research reveal systematic differences in life style among upper, middle, and lower class families. Because of the profound influence which family life exerts on its youthful members, variations in family background result in children learning somewhat different motives and ways of behaving, ideas and beliefs, attitudes and values.[15]

Social Status and Ethnic Background

What do we know about the social status of American Catholic families? In addition to education, occupation, and economic status, two further determinants of social status have special pertinence for the Catholic family. These are religious affiliation and ethnicity. Belonging to a specific ethnic group may affect the social status of the family primarily in two ways. First, the family may suffer discrimination because of its ethnic origin. As we have seen, the members of the New Immigration were uniformly looked upon as foreigners by the dominant group and those who had arrived earlier. Further, Spanish-speaking groups, Orientals, American Indians, and Negroes have been set off as groups apart in most sections of the country so that their participation in the social life of the larger community is reduced to a minimum.

Second, ethnic families which have maintained strong group solidarity for the preservation of their cultural heritage tend to form a variant subsociety within the larger society. Such groups possess their own internal system of stratification and specify the ways in which group members may participate in the main class system. The French Canadian group in the East furnishes a typical example of this phenomenon. In general, therefore, the importance of the ethnic character of the family for their social status will depend on the social position of the group, the degree of ethnic solidarity, and the prevalent attitudes toward the group in the region where the family resides. Specifically, ethnicity is no longer important for the Irish and German families of the Old Immigration; it tends to modify downward the social status of most others.[16]

Social Status and Religious Affiliation

Religious affiliation has some effect on the social status of the family although regional differences must be considered. Among the Protestant groups, denominations tend to be socially evaluated. It is commonly recognized that there is a rough classification of denominations corresponding to the class structure. For example, Warner states that Episcopalians and Unitarians generally rank higher than Methodists and Baptists. However, in the South, the Methodist Episcopal Church often enjoys a position like that of the Episcopal Church in most other communities. Congregationalists, Presbyterians, and Christian Scientists tend to be drawn from the middle class.[17]

Where does the Catholic Church rank in this hierarchy? In the first place, it should be noted that the Church tends to draw its members from all ranks of society although because of the ethnic origin of so many of its constituents in this country, its membership will be predominantly middle and lower class. Second, because of the traditional Protestant background of American society and the peculiar regional distribution of the Catholic population, regional differences are paramount. Community studies point this out clearly. In the wide regions where "fundamentalist" Protestantism is strong and Catholics are few, the Catholic family has almost no social status. One study of a mid-west community states: "Of all the religions in the world, Catholicism is considered by most Plainvillers to be the most 'non-Christian.'" [18] The scattered Catholic families living in such communities cannot be considered to be articulated in the main class system at all.

In communities where somewhat similar attitudes persist but where Catholics are more numerous, Catholic families tend to be articulated into the social system on an unstable basis and only to the extent that their religion is kept private and unobtrusive. Catholic families tend to constitute a group apart because of their religion. As the Lynds remark when discussing religion in Middletown: "A major cleft among these twenty-eight groups marks off Catholics and Protestants, there being roughly fifteen Protestants for every Catholic in the city." [19] They note the unobtrusive character of Catholic participation in the social system. "The Catholic Church pursued in 1935 the same quiet, resolute, inconspicuous course as in 1925. It is not involved in local politics or any other public aspect of Middletown's life." [20]

In regions where Catholic families are more numerous and bigotry has given way to tolerance, religion plays a smaller role in determining social status. In the North Prairie community of "Jonesville" the seven churches, ranked in order of the class level of their congregations, were found to be: Federated (Congregational and Presbyterian), Methodist, Lutheran, Catholic, Baptist, Free Methodist, and Gospel Tabernacle.[21] In this community, although Catholic families were found in all the classes, the majority were, according to Warner's classification, "upper-lower-class" ethnics.

In the East and Great Lakes region where the bulk of Catholic families are located, religious affiliation and ethnic background have been closely associated as determinants of social class. We have seen that for the families of the New Immigration the church more than any other structure served to organize the group as a community system. Each new group that entered started life in America near the bottom of the social heap and for some time led a marginal existence, partly submerged in an ethnic subsystem and partly articulated in the wider social structure. With the passage of time, the ethnic family bettered its occupational status, acquired an increasing number of material symbols of success, including a better residence, extended its formal and informal contacts in society, and gradually underwent changes in behavior modes.[22] As a result, even in the tightly structured "Yankee City" society, Warner discovered Catholic families in all but the "upper-upper" class, although the majority were classified in the middle or lower classes. This finding can probably be generalized providing allowance is made for a decreased social class consciousness outside the East and the marked social mobility of ethnic minorities in the past two decades.

THE CATHOLIC BIRTH RATE

A further differentiating characteristic of the Catholic family concerning which we possess some information is that of the birth rate. It may be assumed that because Catholic moral teaching forbids the use of contraceptive devices in limiting conception, the Catholic birth rate will tend to be higher than that of others located in the same social circumstances. Further, one would expect this differential to be greatest among those socioeconomic classes where contraceptives are known to be used most effectively. What few studies have been made tend to support these hypotheses.

For example, one study included 40,766 urban couples in Wisconsin married between the years 1919–1930. Only those couples were reported in which the husband was under 30 years old and the wife under 25 at marriage. Approximately 35 per cent of the cases represented valid Catholic marriages in which both partners were Catholic. An analysis of the confinement rates of these 40,766 couples between 1919 and 1933 revealed that the fertility of the Catholic couples surpassed that of the non-Catholic couples in all comparable categories.[23] However, the study also revealed that the fertility of the Catholic couples during this period declined at a faster rate than that of non-Catholic couples. This would seem to indicate that Catholic couples were starting to react to modern urban conditions during the twenties in somewhat the same manner as non-Catholic couples had done a decade or two earlier.

Several field studies carried out in cooperation with the Milbank Memorial Foundation and covering native white families in five urban areas are summarized by Notestein as follows:

> It is clear that class for class, the Catholics are more fertile than the Protestants, although the differences are greater among the families of business men than among those of unskilled laborers. In the latter class the proportions of large families are the same. It is equally clear that both religious groups exhibit the characteristic inverse association between fertility and occupational status, although the association is stronger among Protestants than among Catholics.[24]

A further study dealing with differential fertility among 41,498 native white couples in Indianapolis offers the most detailed information we have on the association between fertility and religious affiliation.[25] This study was conducted in the summer of 1941 and included virtually every household in Indianapolis. The report dealing with factors affecting fertility includes only native white families in which neither the husband nor wife had been married before and in which the wife was over forty-five years of age. Of the 41,498 couples in the fertility sample, 80 per cent were classified as "Both Protestant," 10.8 per cent as "Both Catholic," 5.8 per cent as "Protestant-Catholic Mixed Marriages," and 1.0 per cent as "Both Jewish." On the average, Catholic couples were 18 per cent more fertile than Protestant unions, the mixed Protestant-Catholic marriages were 10 per cent less fertile than the Protestant, and the Jewish couples were 25 per cent less fertile than the Protestant marriages. It should be noted that the Jewish couples constituted a very small sample.

An analysis of fertility by rental value of the dwelling unit, rent paid by the couple, and educational attainment of the husband and wife revealed the usual inverse relation of fertility to socioeconomic status among both Protestant and Catholic couples. The authors summarize these differences as follows:

> Although the fertility rates of Catholic couples tend to exceed those of Protestant couples at most socio-economic lev-

els, this may not be true at the lowest rental-value levels. At all events, the proportionate excess of the fertility rates of Catholic couples definitely tends to decrease with lowering of socio-economic status. Thus, at rental-value levels of $80 and over, the rate for Catholics is 43 per cent higher than that for Protestants. At the $15-19 rental-value level, it is only 12 per cent higher. On the basis of the wife's education, the fertility rate for Catholic couples exceeds that for Protestant couples by 40 per cent at the college level, but by only 3 per cent at the grammar school level. On the basis of the husband's education, the comparable figures are 39 per cent and 7 per cent. Catholic couples of "Both College" status are 35 per cent more fertile than Protestant couples of comparable education. On the other hand, the fertility rate for Catholic couples of "Both Grammar School" status is only 3 per cent higher than that for Protestant couples of the same limited education.[26]

On the basis of these data we can conclude that as of 1941 Catholic couples in Indianapolis were more fertile than Protestant. We do not know whether this difference applied generally nor whether it maintains since World War II. There is some evidence for the belief that increases in nuptial fertility ratios since 1940 have tended to be proportionately heaviest among categories of highest fertility.[27] It is not known what changes have occurred in the fertility of Catholic couples. In general, it seems safe to state that among urban Catholic couples fertility is less controlled than among Protestants and it appears that the fertility of both religious groups reacts to similar environments in the same direction although this is less true for Catholic than Protestant units.

Finally, there is ample evidence in Louisiana of fertility differentials between ethno-religious areas.[28] Families in the French, Catholic portion of Louisiana have much higher rates of reproduction than those of the Anglo-Saxon, Protestant portion. The fertility ratio of the urban population in the French section is 344 as compared with 244 for the non-French sector, and for the farm population the fertility ratios are 574 and 530, respectively. This fertility differential is found in all residential categories. Thus, in cities of from 10,000 to 100,000 population, the ratios are 303 and 230, respectively; in cities of from 2,500 to 10,000, the ratios are 371 to 269, respectively; in towns and villages between 1,000 and 2,500 population the ratios are 389 and 306, respectively. It is interesting to note that these fertility differentials maintain for both white and Negro families residing in the two areas.

THE STRUCTURE OF CATHOLIC FAMILIES

Up to this point we have discussed the Catholic ideal of marriage and the family, the immigrant origin of the American Catholic family and the process of acculturation associated with that background, the distribution of Catholics according to region, occupation, education, economic status and social class, and finally, the fertility differential manifested by Catholic couples in selected areas. A word remains to be said on the structure of Catholic families. It might be assumed that because of their different family ideals and immigrant origin, the status and roles of husband and wife, parents and children would be expressed differently in Catholic families. With certain notable exceptions which we shall take up presently, this does not appear to be true.

Although it tends toward conservatism, the modern Catholic family reflects rather faithfully the pattern of relationships between husband and wife, parents and children typical of the stable families in the socioeconomic class to which it belongs. There is the same drive for increased companionship of husband and wife, greater equality in the status of women, and diminishing expression of parental authority. Nor should this come as a surprise since Catholic families are subjected to the same cultural molding and pressure as other families in the social system, and it is only where clearly defined moral values are at issue that differences will appear.

The major exceptions to this generalized pattern are those ethnic families which have maintained close solidarity with the national group. Even in regard to these we must be careful to distinguish among groups and between generations within each group. As we have indicated, the majority of new immigrants came from small towns or rural villages. The recognized family structure was patriarchal in the sense that the father was the acknowledged head of the family. This status was reinforced by the fact that in a peasant society the family constitutes a productive unit managed by the father. The subordinate position of the wife and children in such a structure is what we might call "situational," that is, it follows from their position as assistants to the father in a common economic enterprise. Since the ultimate success and social status of the family demands that the economic enterprise function smoothly, considerable stress is placed upon rules and work-functions rather than on emotions and personal sentiments. In such a family structure, parental authority is strong and effectively sanctioned by the attitude of the group.

Lest we regard this family pattern as wholly alien to American cultural traditions, it should be recalled that the early American family presented a similar structure.[29] However, with the shift from a rural to an industrialized urban society, this earlier patriarchal system gradually evolved into the more equalitarian system that we have today. In like manner, to the extent that immigrant families become articulated into the American social structure they tend to assume the features of the families with which they associate. As we have seen, the process of acculturation has advanced rapidly among the descendants of the New Immigration so that most second and third generation ethnic couples reveal the same marriage patterns as their American contemporaries. To be sure, some members of the older generation reflect former patterns but in a dynamic society where group solidarity can be maintained only by quasi-segregation, interpersonal contacts are multiplied rapidly and the "strain for consistency" which operates in every culture enforces conformity among all but the segregated.

The Spanish- and French-speaking minorities constitute cultural subgroups meriting separate treatment. Particularly in the East, the French Canadians have maintained remarkable solidarity up to the present. However, their family structure has undergone some modification in its changed environment. The typical immigrant came from a rural society made up of landholding families.[30] Their change to an urban environment has created some shift in roles and has somewhat lessened the dependence of the children on the father. There is also evidence to show that the extended kinship group plays a smaller role in family affairs. In general, however, there has been an attempt to keep the social structure closely tied in with the traditional family-parish unit.

The Spanish-language minority of Mexican origin has not chosen segregation but has been subjected to it in most sections of the country. However, the traditional Mexican family structure was so closely interwoven with Mexican community social life that the family has not endured transplanting in America without considerable disorganization. The typical Mexican immigrant remains somewhat confused by the changed situation. The status and role of the wife has undergone modification in the more progressive families although in most she is still subordinate to her husband in all respects. It is difficult to describe the position of Mexican women either in our society or in Mexico. On the surface, it is a man's society. Women have little legal status and are expected to confine their interests entirely to the home and the family circle. However, within this sphere she enjoys a good deal of power and prestige. One student of the culture described her position as follows: "As the *madrecita*, entitled to respect and homage, she may actually dominate, in all matters that affect her children. Hers may be the deciding voice in every important decision. As grandmother she may develop into a despot, benevolent or otherwise." [31]

Undoubtedly, our problem in trying to understand the position of women in such societies arises from the tendency to identify the defined rights and accepted roles of women in a given society with the prestige which they enjoy. We forget that some societies may value women very highly yet have rigid definitions of permissible male and female roles. In analyzing the position of women in a given society, we must proceed beyond definitions to the study of actual practice. While studying American ethnic groups, the writer discovered that although most of them insisted that the husband was undoubtedly the head of the family, the husbands themselves admitted that under present conditions, their wives really "ran" the family. As one social worker remarked, "If you want to know what one of these families is going to do, ask the mother!" In this connection, Marshal Foch once observed of the typical Frenchman, "Contrary to what the Napoleonic Code states, husbands generally follow the advice of their wives—and nine times out of ten, this shows good sense."

SUMMARY

The inadequacy of religious population data must be admitted. The census does not supply this information. Pollsters generally use "religious preference" as the basis for their calculations. Various church bodies tend to supply only more or less reliable estimates. Nevertheless, by combining the results of polls, estimates, and localized studies, a fairly reliable picture of the Catholic minority's general characteristics can be drawn. The Catholic population tends to be urban. It is regionally concentrated in the industrial centers of the East and Great Lakes region. An analysis of its education, occupation, and economic status characteristics shows it to be primarily middle and lower class. What may be termed "the social status of Catholics" is in conformity with these three characteristics except in those sections of the country in which ethnic background and religious affiliation affect social status downward. The Catholic birth rate tends to be affected by the same social factors as the general population, but the Catholic birth rate runs consistently higher in all comparative categories. With the exception of a few ethnic groups, the structure of Catholic families is the same as other families of similar social position.

Although this information is somewhat general, it will prove helpful in analyzing the problems which the Catholic family faces in America. The family experiences the impact of a culture according to its position in society. It is important, therefore, to know where Catholic families are located and what characterizes their position in society, if we are to understand their special problems.

CHAPTER SIX

Marriage Patterns

In every known society, outgroup marriage is regulated by group sentiments of approval or disapproval. The degree of encouragement or discouragement shown an outgroup marriage is determined by the current evaluations of the ranking of other groups, cultures, classes, races, and religions. Hostile attitudes range from ridicule and scorn to absolute prohibition. These attitudes, usually strengthened by group self-consciousness, ethnocentric propaganda, and isolation, are the means which the group uses to prevent the dissipation of its forces and the dissolution of its traditions by outgroup influences.

As members of a religious minority, Catholics may become involved in various types of outgroup marriage. In this chapter we shall discuss some of these and present the available information on their prevalence and general characteristics. The problem of religious outgroup marriage is important since there is danger that a minority will not long survive as an identifiable social entity if a sizable proportion of its members enter outgroup marriages.

TYPES OF OUTGROUP MARRIAGE

The term *marriage type* is used loosely here to cover several categories based on distinctions found in Canon Law. The possible types are: (1) the union of two Catholics in a valid marriage; (2) the union of a Catholic and a non-Catholic in a valid marriage. This is commonly called a mixed marriage and presents two possible combinations. The union may involve a Catholic and a baptized non-Catholic or a Catholic and an unbaptized non-Catholic. (3) Finally, there may be the union of two Catholics or of a Catholic and a non-Catholic, baptized or not, in an invalid marriage.

In regard to this last category, we have seen that according to Catholic teaching a marriage contract may be null and void from the beginning either because of some existing impediment, or from lack of proper consent, or from a substantial defect in the canonical form. Hence, an invalid marriage is not based on a sacramental contract and consequently, there is no marriage bond established so that in reality it is no marriage at all but only the simulation of one. Obviously, these unions are considered gravely sinful. Catholics involved in such unions have serious obligations to regularize their relationships, but until they do so, there is no valid contract and hence, no marriage.

The church imposes heavy sanctions on Catholics engaging in invalid marriage. They are stigmatized as living in public sin and are excluded from the sacraments. As a result, these unions are likely to be very unstable since the Catholic parties are urged by their friends, relatives, and the Church to either regularize them where this is possible, or break them up at once. It follows that any research on marriages involving Catholics must carefully distinguish between valid and invalid unions. Many otherwise excellent studies have lost much of their value by failing to make this distinction.

In the second category we have used the term mixed marriage as it is commonly employed in everyday speech. In canonical literature, however, the term is used strictly for marriages between a Catholic and a validly baptized non-Catholic.

The impediment which then exists is called "mixed religion" (Canon 1060). If the non-Catholic party is unbaptized, the impediment is called "disparity of cult" (Canon 1070). We have treated these two cases under the general heading of mixed marriage because our data do not distinguish between them.

EARLY CHURCH LEGISLATION AND MIXED MARRIAGE

Since Catholics have often existed as minority groups, we need not be surprised that the problem of interfaith marriage has been the subject of a great deal of Church legislation from earliest times. The points of primary concern in this legislation were the danger of loss of faith to the Catholic party and the requirement that all the children of the faithful be instructed in the Catholic religion. Inasmuch as there is some tendency today to consider the Church's solicitude concerning mixed marriages as of relatively recent origin, it may be well to consider briefly the history of the problem.

In the first place, there is no clear statement in the New Testament concerning mixed marriages. Since the early Christians were not numerous, it is reasonable to suppose that there was a considerable number of mixed marriages in the beginning. The first official notice we have found is in the Council of Elvira, Spain, in 306. Christian girls were forbidden to marry pagans, Jews, and heretics.[1] The Emperor Constantine in 339 forbade the marriage of a Christian and a Jew under pain of death. Later emperors mitigated this legislation but called such unions adulterous and they are so regarded in the Justinian Code. The council held at Laodicaea somewhere between 343 and 381 forbade all marriages between Christians and heretics. We know that Saint Augustine and Saint Ambrose clearly opposed such marriages. However, it is not clear whether these marriages were regarded as invalid in the first five centuries of Christianity. We know that in the tenth and eleventh centuries, marriages between a Jew and a Christian were regarded as invalid in many countries. In the twelfth century, the Decrees of Gratian enjoyed wide acceptance and they inferred that marriages between a Catholic and a non-Catholic were invalid. The Great Scholastics opposed this concept and maintained that only the marriage of a Catholic with an unbaptized non-Catholic was invalid. In accordance with this doctrine we find Clement VI in 1346 approving the Decrees of the Synod of Pressburg (1309) stating that the marriage of a Catholic with an heretic was illicit, not invalid. Before the Reformation, there is no record in Canon Law of dispensations for either disparity of cult or mixed religion.

The missionary activity in the Orient activated the question of disparity of cult, and Gregory XIII (1572–1583) granted permission for dispensations. Against the Protestant heretics the Church showed considerable severity. The general rule was to grant no dispensation for marriage to a heretic unless the heretic first renounced his heresy (Benedict XIV, "Magnae Nobis," 1748). A decree of 1624 forbade pastors to witness such mixed marriages without a dispensation from the Holy See. This was equivalent to a prohibition, since after the Council of Trent a marriage was invalid unless witnessed by a priest. However, in Germany, England, Poland, and the Netherlands, the custom grew of freely marrying mixed couples without a papal dispensation and without demanding the abjuration of heresy. Many leading theologians maintained that once the custom was established it should be permitted. Pius VI (1775–1799) allowed a priest to be a material witness at such marriages providing he had secured the necessary promises concerning the faith of the Catholic party and the religious instruction of the children. The Bishops of the United States obtained permission to grant dispensations for mixed marriage around the middle of the eighteenth century.

PRESENT LEGISLATION REGULATING MIXED MARRIAGE

At the present time, the Code of Canon Law clearly sums up the attitude of the Church concerning mixed marriages:

Everywhere and with the greatest strictness the Church forbids marriages between baptized persons, one of whom is a Catholic and the other a member of a schismatical or heretical sect, and if there is added to this the danger of the falling away of the Catholic party and the perversion of the children, such a marriage is forbidden also by the Divine law (Canon 1060).

Pius XI comments on this Canon in his encyclical letter covering Christian marriage.

If the Church occasionally on account of circumstances does not refuse to grant a dispensation from these strict laws (provided that the divine law remains intact and the dangers above mentioned are provided against by suitable safeguards), it is unlikely that the Catholic party will not suffer some detriment from such a marriage.[2]

In his encyclical to the American hierarchy, Pius XII repeats the same admonition.

With regard to those marriages in which one or the other party does not accept the Catholic teaching or has not been baptized, we are certain that you observe exactly the prescriptions of the Code of Canon Law. Such marriages, in fact, as is clear to you from wide experience, are rarely happy and usually occasion grave loss to the Catholic Church.[3]

REASONS FOR THE CHURCH'S OPPOSITION TO MIXED MARRIAGES

There is no need to enlarge further on the official attitude of the Church toward mixed marriage. The cumulative experience of centuries enforces the belief that mixed marriages involve special hazards. The reasons advanced for this may be summarized briefly as follows.

First, differences in religious beliefs furnish the basis for fundamental differences in the individual's value system. Love does not resolve these differences. On such practical issues as the use of contraceptives, the indissolubility of marriage, mari-

tal fidelity, and the sacramental nature of the marriage contract, the Catholic Church takes a position quite different from
that tolerated or promoted by the dominant culture.

Second, the religious training of children can cause conflict
in mixed marriages. The Church insists that the children be
trained as Catholics and where there are Catholic schools, the
children are to attend these schools.

Third, although the influence of the kinship group is diminishing, there is still considerable pressure exerted by the nearest of kin in regard to religious tolerance. This in-law interference becomes apparent not only in directing the religious
affiliation and training of children, but also in excluding the
divergent party from full acceptance in the kinship group.

Fourth, church loyalties and family loyalties frequently clash
where there are divergent beliefs. Every system of belief makes
demands of time, interest, and money on its members. Where
husband and wife have different church loyalties, the door is
open to disagreements which are hard to resolve since they
are based on emotion-loaded religious beliefs.

Finally, the spiritual unity of the marriage is seriously compromised. Marriage is meant to be a life partnership in which
each partner supports and works for the temporal and spiritual
welfare of the other. In mixed marriage, religion is more likely
to be a bone of contention or, at best, a skeleton in the closet
rather than a unifying bond.

VALID MIXED MARRIAGES

Considering the official attitude of the Church toward mixed
marriages and the known hazards which such unions necessarily involve, one might conclude that few Catholics would
venture to enter them. Statistics show that this is far from the
case in the United States. Although we do not know the total
number of mixed marriages involving Catholics, we do have
fairly accurate data on the *valid* mixed marriages which occur.[4]
These data are available in all chancery offices throughout the
country and a reasonably accurate listing of them year by year
can be found in *The Official Catholic Directory*. Since we shall

take up the problem of invalid marriages later in this chapter, we shall confine our present remarks to valid mixed marriages alone.

Mixed Marriage Rates

What is the mixed marriage rate of Catholics in the United States? During the decade 1940 to 1950, valid mixed marriages accounted for between 25 and 30 per cent of all Catholic marriages. Complete data for the thirties are not available, but a study of the valid marriages in fifty dioceses during this period revealed an over-all mixed marriage rate of approximately 30 per cent.[5] In other words, during the last two decades, mixed marriages have been accounting for between one-fourth and one-third of all valid Catholic marriages. This figure for valid mixed marriage alone suggests that the recently advanced "triple-melting-pot" theory has limited utility. According to this theory, assimilation in America will take place within three separate "melting-pots" based on the cleavage which exists between the three major religious groups, namely, Protestants, Catholics, and Jews.[6] Although religious differences may function as the chief basis of assortive mating in some communities, this does not appear to be true on a national scale.[7]

Characteristics of Mixed Marriages in the United States

Two characteristics of mixed marriages in the United States should be signalized. First, Catholic girls tend to enter such marriages more frequently than do Catholic boys. In the chapter dealing with minority groups we pointed out a similar pattern for outgroup marriage involving ethnics. The Bishops' study mentioned above found the ratio was 60-40 throughout the ten-year period, 1932–1941. The Indianapolis survey uncovered an even higher percentage of Catholic brides in the mixed marriages studied.[8] In his study of one city parish, Schnepp discovered the ratio was 60-40 for all valid and validated mixed marriages.[9] Fichter's "Southern Parish" had a ratio of 73-27 for the valid mixed marriages.[10]

Second, mixed marriage rates vary greatly from one section of the country to another. The range is from over 70 per cent in the diocese of Raleigh to less than 8 per cent in the diocese of Corpus Christi.[11] Even within the same diocese or the same city, the rates for different parishes may differ widely so that national or diocesan averages tell us very little about the rates in individual parishes.

Factors Influencing the Rate of Mixed Marriages

What are the principal factors which determine the rate of mixed marriage for Catholics? Research indicates that they may be reduced to three: (1) the percentage of Catholics in the total population; (2) the presence of cohesive ethnic subgroups; and (3) the socioeconomic status of the Catholic population in the community. We shall treat these factors separately, although it may be difficult to determine their specific influence on the rate of intermarriage in any given community.

Percentage of Catholics. First, the proportion of Catholics in the total population greatly influences the intermarriage rates of Catholics in different sections of the country. The relative scarcity of prospective marriage mates within one's own religious group leads to a high rate of intermarriage wherever ethnic and/or social status differences do not prevent occupational and social contacts. For example, in the dioceses of Raleigh, Charleston, Nashville, Savannah-Atlanta, and Natchez, where the Catholic population is 2 per cent or less of the total, the mixed marriage rates are 70.2, 65.4, 62.1, 64.1, and 60.8, respectively. On the other hand, in the dioceses of Corpus Christi, Lafayette (La.), Providence, Fall River, and Santa Fe, where the Catholic population is from 50 to 70 per cent of the total, the mixed marriage rates are 7.9, 15.3, 18.6, 16.3, and 11.2, respectively. There is no need to seek further evidence on this point but we hasten to add that the relative percentage of Catholics in the population is not the sole factor determining the rate of intermarriage as many seem to believe.

Cohesive Ethnic Groups. The second factor is the presence of close-knit ethnic subgroups in the community. In the chapter dealing with national minorities we have shown how well the prohibition on outgroup marriage operates in those parishes where ethnic solidarity is strong. However, there are many factors combining to produce this effect—fidelity to the group, social status of the ethnic minority, religion, language, and transplanted national prejudices. The important point to be noted is that it is not religion alone nor the relative number of prospective mates available in the religious group which determines the intermarriage rate.

For example, Catholics in the diocese of Amarillo, Texas, constitute approximately 7 per cent of the population. The intermarriage rate of Catholics is 20.8 per cent. Indianapolis, with a slightly higher percentage of Catholics, has a mixed marriage rate of 45 per cent. The reason for the difference in the mixed marriage rate is obvious. The diocese of Amarillo has a large subgroup of Spanish and Mexican Catholics; the diocese of Indianapolis contains no cohesive ethnic minorities. One might compare the dioceses of San Antonio and Marquette (Mich.). Both have approximately the same percentage of Catholics in the total population (30 and 28 per cent, respectively). Their mixed marriage rates are quite different (4.8 and 38.4, respectively). San Antonio includes a large ethnic minority which has little outgroup marriage.

The effect of ethnic minorities on intermarriage rates is even more pronounced if one considers individual parishes. We first arrived at our conviction of their importance while making a study of intermarriage rates in different sized cities. Drawing samples from the Great Lakes and Middle West regions, we studied 25 parishes in each of the following categories: 100,000 and over, 25,000-100,000, 5,000-25,000, and 5,000 and under. Table 9 presents the results of this study. It should be noted

TABLE 9

PERCENTAGE OF MIXED MARRIAGE ACCORDING TO SIZE OF CITY

Population of City	Number of Parishes	Number of Families	Percentage of Mixed Marriages
100,000 and over	25	36,353	14.9
25,000-100,000	25	15,000	24.2
5,000-25,000	25	16,624	21.4
5,000 and under	25	9,431	19.6

that the percentages given in this table are not mixed marriage rates but rather the percentage of mixed marriages found in the parishes at the time the study was made. Since there are a considerable number of mixed marriages which end in divorce or cease to be classified as mixed marriages either because the non-Catholic partner is converted or the Catholic party no longer chooses to be identified as a member of the Church, the percentage of mixed marriages in a parish has been found to be between 5 and 20 per cent below the mixed marriage rate.

As Table 9 reveals, the percentage of mixed marriages found in cities of 100,000 and over was surprisingly low. The assumtion has been that the rates would increase in direct ratio to the size of the city. What had caused the break at the "100,000 and over" level? A more intensive comparative study of the individual parishes indicated that the major ethnic subgroup concentrations were in the larger cities of the territory from which the samples were drawn. It was discovered that those large urban parishes in which minorities were located uniformly had low percentages of mixed marriages. Hence, the conclusion that the presence of these groups in the community is an important determining factor in the rate of intermarriage.

Socioeconomic Status. A third factor appears to be the socioeconomic class of the Catholic population in the community. Intermarriage rates seem to be closely related to socioeconomic status. This hypothesis is advanced tentatively since adequate statistical support is still lacking. However, we have made studies of several communities which furnish rather substantial evidence that the hypothesis is well founded. For example, using graded rental areas as a rough measure of socioeconomic status, we studied the intermarriage pattern of 51,671 families distributed in thirty parishes of a large urban center. Table 10 gives the results of this study. It should be pointed out that percentages in the table are relatively low since they record the percentage of mixed marriages found in the parishes at the time of the study, not the mixed marriage rates. This study gives every indication of a rather close association between socioeconomic status and intermarriage since

TABLE 10

RENTAL AREAS AND PERCENTAGE OF MIXED MARRIAGES

Rental Area	Percentage of Mixed Marriages
Lower	8.5
Mixed Lower and Middle	9.1
Middle	12.0
Mixed Middle and Upper	16.3
Upper	17.9
Suburban	19.3

the percentage increases from 8.5 in the lower rental areas to 19.3 in the suburban parish.

Trends in Mixed Marriage Rate

Is the Catholic mixed marriage rate increasing? Complete information for many sections of the country is lacking on this point. It is known that there was a considerable increase in mixed marriages during both World War I and World War II. Some dioceses registered an increase of from 5 to 10 per cent for valid mixed marriages during the wars. Judging from the several dioceses in which the records are complete, it appears that a steady but gradual increase has occurred since 1910.

However, since intermarriage rates vary so greatly in different sections of the country, it would be unsafe to venture a generalization on the basis of such inadequate data. On the other hand, there are cogent reasons for thinking there will be a gradual but steady increase of marriages between Catholics and non-Catholics in the future. Some of the factors which will influence this trend are the following.

First, as we have seen, the solidarity of ethnic subgroups has operated as a strong check on outgroup marriage. The decline in immigration, the horizontal and vertical mobility characteristic of our population, and the increased cultural contacts facilitated by modern means of communication will make it increasingly difficult for these groups to maintain their isolation and ingroup loyalties. The melting pot is a reality although the boiling process may take longer than was at first believed necessary.

Second, mixed marriages have a cumulative effect. The children of mixed marriages tend to marry those outside their religious group more often than do the offspring of ingroup marriages.[12]

Third, the attitude of Catholic and Protestant young people toward mixed marriages seems quite tolerant. Landis reports a study of students' attitudes on marriage in which more than 50 per cent of approximately 2,000 students said that "other things being equal" they would marry into a different faith.[13] We have given the same attitude test to 224 Catholic college students in a Catholic institution and found that 33 per cent of the boys and 40 per cent of the girls would marry one of another religious group, "other things being equal." Of course, these are attitude tests and do not tell us what these same young people will actually do when the occasion arrives and parental and pastoral pressure is brought to bear on them. However, the figures are indicative of an attitude which definitely does facilitate contacts leading to intermarriage.

Fourth, it is generally agreed that the family and the church have less control than formerly over youth. Increasing individualism and the widespread acceptance of the romantic view of love have tended to make the choice of marriage mates a strictly personal affair.

Stability of Mixed Marriages

Are mixed marriages less stable than other unions? Several studies carried out in widely separated areas of the country seem to prove conclusively that they are. For example, Landis studied 4,108 mixed and nonmixed marriages among the parents of college students in Michigan. Approximately one-third of these marriages were Catholic or mixed. The percentage of marriages broken by divorce or separation for the various categories was: both parents Catholic, 4.4; both parents Jewish, 5.2; both parents Protestants, 6.0; mixed Catholic-Protestant, 14.1; both parents no religion, 17.9. The mixed marriages presented an interesting pattern. Where the husband was Catholic and the wife Protestant, the rate was 20.6; where the wife was Catholic and the husband Protestant, it was only 6.7.[14]

In another study, the 6,548 families of public and parochial school children in Spokane, Washington, were used for an analysis of marital status. This study revealed a divorce rate of 3.8 among Catholics, 10.0 among Protestants, 17.4 in mixed marriages, and 23.9 among families where there was no religion.[15] A third study analyzed the marital status of 13,528 families of mixed and nonmixed background in Maryland and discovered a divorce rate of 6.4 among Catholics, 4.6 among Jews, 6.8 among Protestants, 15.2 among mixed marriages, and 16.7 where there was no religion.[16]

Unfortunately, the value of these studies is somewhat lessened by two important considerations. First they were dealing only with those mixed marriages in which there were children. Since childless marriages appear to be more unstable than others, they would have obtained higher divorce rates if these had been included in their studies. In our studies of broken valid mixed marriages, we have found that over 40 per cent of the couples were childless. Second, these studies did not distinguish between valid and invalid mixed marriages.

It must be obvious to anyone who understands the significance of the religious sanctions imposed on invalid marriages that a good number of such unions have every chance of being eventually repudiated by the Catholic party. For example, we found that in 6,744 divorces involving Catholics from the Middle West region, 60.4 per cent of the unions were based on invalid marriages in the first place. More specifically, a study of all the mixed marriages in thirty parishes well distributed throughout the State of Michigan, where it is presumed most of the subjects of the Landis study had residence, showed that 39.2 per cent were invalid. It follows that the differential divorce rate found among the mixed marriages in the aforesaid studies may be partly accounted for by the high number of invalid marriages which they included. On the basis of these studies, therefore, we cannot conclude that valid mixed marriages are necessarily more unstable than other valid Catholic marriages.[17]

Factors in the Breakdown of Mixed Marriages

What are the main factors in the breakdown of mixed marriages? Landis states that the chief source of friction in the mixed marriages which he studied centered around the religious training of the children.[18] On this point his findings agree with the results of an earlier somewhat limited study of mixed marriages conducted by Baber who found that half the conflicts in such marriages arose from religious differences.[19] Both of these studies were dealing with mixed marriages in which there were children. This general belief that the chief source of friction centers around the religious differences of the partners as manifested in direct quarrels over religion or over the religious training of the children, finds only limited confirmation in our studies. However, contrary to Baber and Landis, we have analyzed only valid mixed marriages and also marriages in which over 40 per cent had no children.

Our studies show that the factors leading to marital breakdown in these mixed unions are not so obviously related to religion. Out of approximately 1,200 broken mixed marriages analyzed, only a little over 10 per cent traced their problem to quarrels over religious differences. On the other hand, adultery was the final factor in the breakdown of over 50 per cent of these cases.

Our conclusion is that religious differences are factors in marital instability not primarily because they lead to direct quarrels over religion. As a rule, people do not argue about religious differences even, or especially, in mixed marriages. Religious beliefs by their very nature involve the emotions to such an extent that it is impossible for most people to argue about them with any degree of calm or objectivity. As a result, after a few attempts, most couples give up trying to talk over their religious differences. Finding this approach rather hopeless, they silently agree to disagree. Hence, the unstabilizing effects of religious differences develop in more subtle ways. The real problem is basic disagreement over the nature and purposes of marriage. Ultimately, this appears in quarrels over family limitation, marital infidelity, and so forth.

Mixed Marriage and the Practice of Religion

What effect do mixed marriages have on the faith of the Catholic party? There is rather general agreement that Catholics in mixed marriages are less fervent in carrying out the religious practices demanded by their faith than are the general run of Catholics. Studying the effects of mixed marriage in a large urban group, Leiffer discovered that over 50 per cent of the men and approximately one-third of the women in these marriages had either dropped all church affiliations or had not attended any church within the past year. Many others admitted that they went to church very irregularly.[20] Leiffer did not distinguish between valid and invalid mixed marriages but the picture which he presents is appalling.

In his Southern Parish study, Fichter found that less than 60 per cent of the Catholics in mixed marriages attended Mass on Sunday and approximately two-fifths did not make their Easter duty.[21] Schnepp discovered that in 22 per cent of the cases where the wife was Catholic and in 47 per cent where the husband was Catholic, the families were not practicing their religion.[22] Coakley's detailed study of his parish in Pittsburgh clearly corroborates these findings.[23] The Bishops' Committee on Mixed Marriage estimated that between 20 and 30 per cent of the Catholics involved in mixed marriages gave up the practice of their faith.[24] On the other hand, Kelly's study of Catholic families in the diocese of St. Augustine shows relatively little difference between the Catholic marriages and the valid mixed marriages in the general practice of the faith.[25]

Our studies clearly indicate the deleterious effects of mixed marriage on the religious practice of the Catholic party. Large samples have been analyzed from various sections of the country with the following results. Of all the valid mixed marriages studied, approximately 25 per cent had lapsed in their practice of the faith, another 20 per cent attended church services only from time to time and the remaining 55 per cent could be classified as fervent Catholics.

Unfortunately, this does not present the whole picture of the effect of mixed marriage on the faith of the Catholic party.

The studies and figures we have presented are based on valid mixed marriages which have survived for some time and in which the Catholic party has retained allegiance to the Church at least to the extent of admitting membership. Extensive studies of Catholic religious practice, carried out in many different dioceses and covering several hundred thousand marriages, show a marked discrepancy between the number of mixed marriages to be found in a diocese and the mixed marriage rate for the diocese. This discrepancy varies from 5 per cent up to 20 per cent.

How is this difference between the mixed marriage rate and the percentage of mixed marriages discovered at any given time to be explained? First, we know that the mixed marriage rate has not varied a great deal in the past several decades so that the proportion of valid mixed marriages in the diocese should correspond fairly well with the mixed marriage rate. Secondly, we know that there are a small number of valid mixed marriages in which the non-Catholic party has been converted.[26] However, the two factors of slight variation in mixed marriage rates in the past and of converts after marriage can account for a relatively small percentage of the discrepancy discovered in many dioceses. It seems logical to conclude, therefore, that from 5 to 15 per cent of these mixed marriages have either been dissolved by divorce or have so completely severed connection with the Church that former affiliation is no longer acknowledged.

Mixed Marriage and the Religious Training of Offspring

What religious training do the children of mixed marriages receive? The studies of Coakley and Schnepp indicate that a considerable number of children born in valid mixed marriages are not baptized or are baptized in a Protestant sect. Further, many do not attend Catholic schools although these are available. Leiffer discovered that the same situation existed among the mixed marriages which he studied. He states, "The main sufferers from the tensions resulting from interfaith marriages are perhaps not the parents, who have more or less consciously entered into this situation, but the children who have had no choice in the matter." [27] Both Leiffer and Landis point out the dominant role of the mother in the religious training of the children. [28]

Our research has uncovered such marked differences from parish to parish that it is difficult to advance any generalizations in this field. From 5 to 20 per cent of the children were found to be either unbaptized or baptized as Protestants. Whereas about 70 per cent of the non-Catholic partners were found to have kept their promises in regard to the religious practice of their Catholic spouse, between 40 and 50 per cent oppose the attendance of their children at religious schools. A conservative summary of the effect of mixed marriage on the religious instruction and training of the children would be to state that approximately 40 per cent of all children born of mixed marriages are either unbaptized, or are baptized in a Protestant sect, or are baptized only, that is, they receive no formal instruction in the faith.

It is impossible to ascertain how much of this failure is due to lack of firmness on the part of the Catholic party. Leiffer hints that the failure may be mutual. "The recorded interviews made clear what is apparent in the statistics quoted above, that the most common pattern in marriages between people of different religious background is the development of indifference toward the Church. Not only is religion omitted from conversation, it does not even enter significantly into the thinking of parents. Usually this is reflected in lack of religious training for the children." [29]

INVALID MARRIAGES

Up to this point we have been dealing primarily with valid mixed marriages. What information do we possess concerning invalid marriages? First, it should be noted that it is difficult to obtain adequate data covering the number and characteristics of invalid marriages. Since these marriages are contracted "outside" the Church, they are not recorded in parish or chancery records. At the same time, civil authorities gather no information concerning the religious characteristics of those applying for marriage licenses. Further, the status of these unions is frequently modified either through divorce or convalidation. Consequently, there is a wide gap between the rate of invalid marriages and the percentage which is found to exist in any given parish.

Finally, in many cases what data we have are quite inadequate. Frequently, our information does not permit us to distinguish between invalid marriages involving two Catholics and those involving a Catholic and a non-Catholic party, nor do we know what percentage could be validated or what impediments exist in those cases where validation is not possible.

However, we have sufficient evidence to suggest that invalidity looms as a major problem for the Church in America. It has special pertinence for our study of Catholic families since, together with mixed marriages with which it is closely associated, it indicates one of the major avenues through which solidarity in a religious minority is broken down. Table 11 presents a typical picture of what we find when we analyze the marriage pattern of urban Catholics. It should be noted how widely parishes differ in both mixed marriage and invalidity.

The percentage of valid mixed marriages varies from a mere 1.4 per cent to 35.2, and the percentage of invalid marriages from 9.9 to 34.7 per cent. The parishes in the "poor apartment" category have a higher percentage of invalid marriages (27.8 per cent) than either the "marginal" (16.0 per cent) or "better residential" (15.8 per cent) parishes. This difference was to be expected since studies in personal disorganization as evidenced by suicide, crime, and broken homes have discovered a similar differential. Although the data are not complete for all the parishes, the close association between invalidity and mixed marriage is apparent. We have had occasion to mention this association when discussing the instability of mixed marriages. The data leave no room for doubt on this subject. For example, of the total number of mixed marriages found in 132 parishes, 39.6 per cent were invalid.

TABLE 11

MIXED AND INVALID MARRIAGES IN 18 SELECTED SUBURBAN PARISHES

Type of Parish	Valid Marriages		Invalid Marriages		
	Total Valid	Per Cent Mixed	Total Invalid	Per Cent of Total	Per Cent Mixed
POOR APARTMENT					
I (1857 families)	1339	13.2	518	27.9	77.6
II (1079 families)	805	8.4	274	25.4	52.8
III (844 families)......	650	4.8	194	22.9	58.7
IV (1434 families)	1080	17.6	354	24.6	71.2
V (1500 families)	1024	20.9	476	31.7	70.6
VI (810 families)......	530	1.4	280	34.7	...*
MARGINAL (lower-middle)					
I (1389 families)	933	17.5	456	32.8	69.2
II (2744 families)	2110	8.6	634	23.1	56.1
III (1942 families)	1942	5.6	194	9.9	53.5
IV (1758 families)	1502	27.3	256	14.5	...*
V (3717 families)	3323	7.0	394	10.6	...*
VI (1665 families)	1485	35.2	179	10.7	...*
BETTER RESIDENTIAL					
I (1672 families)	1240	16.2	432	25.8	69.4
II (1885 families)	1650	15.2	235	12.5	75.7
III (1845 families)	1630	10.7	215	11.6	69.0
IV (2120 families)	1801	13.7	319	15.0	64.9
V (945 families)	755	21.8	190	20.1	...*
VI (937 families)	839	19.7	98	10.4	...*

* Data not available.

Number of Invalid Marriages

How many invalid marriages take place each year? As we have indicated, we must depend on indirect evidence and estimates in arriving at the annual figure. The Bishops' Committee estimated that each year between 15 and 25 per cent of all marriages involving Catholics were invalid. This estimate appears to be well substantiated. Besides the evidence based on parish studies which we have already considered, additional information can be gained from other sources. For example, an analysis of the dispensations granted for mixed marriage reveals that between 20 and 30 per cent of these marriages had originally been contracted invalidly and the dispensation was being obtained at the time they were being convalidated. Since mixed marriages constitute between 25 and 30 per cent of all Catholic marriages, this means that a relatively large number of marriages were initially invalid.

Further, all the major diocesan chancery courts handle several hundred "defect of form" cases each year. These are cases in which a Catholic has been involved in an invalid marriage, has been civilly divorced, and now wishes to contract a valid marriage in the Church. The defect of form court studies the cases and when the evidence warrants it, issues a statement that the previous union was invalid and the party is free to enter a valid marriage. To grasp the full significance of the evidence for a high rate of invalid marriages based on convalidation and defect of form cases, it must be recalled that parish surveys show that only a relatively small percentage of invalid marriages are eventually validated and what studies we have on instability reveal that not over 15 or 20 per cent are dissolved by divorce. One must conclude, therefore, that the total number of invalid marriages is surprisingly high.

Factors Affecting the Rate of Invalid Marriages

What are some of the factors which determine this relatively high incidence of invalidity among Catholics? We have already indicated the principal one. Many Protestants preparing to contract marriage with a Catholic either refuse to make the promises required by the Church in such cases or are opposed to a Catholic marriage ceremony. If the Catholic party agrees, the marriage is performed in the presence of a Protestant minister or a justice of the peace and is consequently invalid.

A second major factor is the prevalence of divorce in our society. According to Catholic doctrine, a valid consummated marriage cannot be dissolved by divorce. However, with the prevalent high rate of divorce in America, it is to be expected that some Catholics will attempt marriage with a divorced person. Such an attempt can involve either another Catholic or a non-Catholic. In either case, if the previous marriage was valid, it could not be dissolved by a civil divorce and the attempted second marriage is invalid. There is good evidence to show that many marriages are invalid because of the existence of a previous marriage bond. An analysis of 7,233 invalid marriages drawn from different sections of the country showed that approximately 28 per cent were invalid because of the existence of a previous bond.

Finally, a third factor is general religious indifference. Particularly among some second and third generation ethnics there is a tendency to dispense with a religious ceremony at marriage. In such cases, one or both the parties have not been actively affiliated with any parish, and because they are poorly instructed in their religion, they are unwilling to undergo the inconvenience and expense of a religious ceremony. The result is an invalid marriage.

Effects of Invalid Marriage on Religious Practice

What are the effects of invalid marriage on the religious practice of the Catholic parties and their children? We do not know how many invalidly married Catholics still attend Mass or remain affiliated to some parish. Because of their invalid marriage, they are forbidden to receive the sacraments, and consequently, they are constantly reminded that they are living apart from the communion of the faithful. However, since a considerable number of these marriages could be validated and are not, we must conclude that there is little likelihood of active religious participation in such cases.

There is some information on the religious instruction and training of the children from such unions. Coakley states that in his parish only 40 per cent of the children in such unions are baptized Catholics, and a mere 3 per cent attend Catholic schools.[30] In our research on this subject, we have found that approximately 30 per cent of the children are unbaptized, 13 per cent are baptized as Protestants, and the remaining 57 per cent are baptized as Catholics. The fact that over 50 per cent were baptized as Catholics does not mean that they will receive further religious training. It has been found that many Catholics who are otherwise quite indifferent concerning the practice of their faith insist on the baptism of their children. Once the child is baptized, their solicitude for its religious life seems to subside.

An exception must be made for those well-instructed Catholics who are involved in an invalid union which cannot be validated, usually because of the existence of a previous valid bond. Such cases frequently represent tragic examples of divided loyalties. On the one hand, they would like to participate actively in the sacramental life of the Church, on the other, they do not see their way clear to dissolving their present invalid union. Under such circumstances, they often compensate for their personal loss by insisting on the religious practice and training of their children.

SUMMARY

Outgroup marriage represents a perennial threat to the survival and solidarity of a religious minority in any society. The problem is particularly acute for American Catholics since, with the exception of a few ethnic minorities, Catholics are not isolated from the rest of society, and the popular attitude toward marriage in general, compounded as it is of romanticism and individualism, presents no effective check to the contracting of mixed unions. As a result, the valid mixed marriage rate varies between 25 and 30 per cent. There is good reason to believe that this rate will gradually increase. There is ample evidence to show that mixed marriages are highly deleterious to the religious life of both the marriage partners and the offspring. Even more ominous is the high incidence of invalidity. Such unions automatically exclude the Catholic partner from sacramental union with the faithful, and their harmful effects on the religious instruction and training of children is beyond question.

It follows that any serious study of the American Catholic family must be deeply concerned with this problem of outgroup marriage. A religious minority must work to prevent the dissipation of its forces and the dissolution of its traditions by alien influences. Just as the final step in the process of acculturation is amalgamation or intermarriage, so the disintegration of solidarity in a religious minority is heralded by the rate of outgroup, that is, mixed or invalid marriages.

PART IV

Family Breakdown

CHAPTER SEVEN

The Disorganized Family

The extensive and rapid social changes characterizing society during the past century have affected both the goals and the structure of the traditional American family. The status and roles of husband and wife, parents and children have been slowly modified in the process of adapting the family to its urbanized environment. In the past few decades there is increasing awareness that the family's adjustment is not proceeding smoothly. Divorce and juvenile delinquency rates offer scant grounds for illusion on this point. At the same time, there are numerous indications of confusion and lack of consensus concerning traditional family values.

Although there is rather general agreement that the family institution is in a state of transition, opinion is sharply divided as to whether the emerging "democratic" family represents the final stage in a long evolutionary development or the first step in the breakdown of a culture. The latter hypothesis finds strong precedent in the history of the Greek and Roman family systems; the former is based on the belief that with the passage of time the family, as a primary institution answering fundamental human needs, will work out a satisfactory equilibrium in its changing environment. It seems scarcely necessary

173

to point out that a truly scientific approach demands that we modify our hypotheses to fit the facts no matter how annoyingly these facts may prove counter to our cherished preconceptions.

Catholic families in a complex, changing culture are subjected to the same pressures as other families in society. Although Catholics may have a clear concept of family values, as a minority group they are not in position to establish the social practices which will adequately implement these goals. For this reason, Church leaders in recent times have expressed great alarm over the changing family situation. In 1930, Pope Pius XI issued an encyclical letter on Christian marriage in which he clearly reiterated the traditional Catholic concept of marriage and the family, decried the errors and vices threatening the realization of this concept in modern society, and broadly outlined a program designed to meet present-day family needs.

This encyclical letter had great repercussions throughout the Church. Seminary courses were revised to acquaint young clerics with the marriage problems of the day. Marriage courses were introduced in the Church's schools. Study clubs were organized for the discussion of courtship and marriage. Eventually, the Cana Conference for the married and the pre-Cana Conference for the engaged were organized in all the major cities throughout the country. Finally, more stringent regulations in regard to premarital instructions for the prospective couple were issued in most dioceses. It is apparent that the hierarchy believe the Catholic family ideal is being threatened. Indeed, in their statement on the Christian family in November, 1949, the American bishops affirmed that "the lethal danger to the family is neither chimerical nor remote. It is a present danger, more fearsome than the atom bomb." [1]

STUDIES OF MARITAL ADJUSTMENT

What do we know about success and failure in Catholic families? We have already indicated the threat to the Catholic ideal represented by mixed and invalid marriages. Do we know how well the Catholic family is adjusting to its modern environment? Judging from the case loads of social workers, the records of marriage counseling centers, the findings of parish surveys, and the testimony of chancery officials and experienced pastors, modern Catholics are having their share of critical family problems. Unfortunately, in spite of the very considerable effort that has been made to study marital success in America, little information is available on the Catholic family.

Limited Coverage

The majority of studies have dealt with variously selected samples of urban, well-educated, middle class Protestant families.[2] This is not necessarily a reflection on research workers since social scientists are not always free to work where they choose. Bernard remarked on this point several decades ago.

> Studies of normal families, depending, as they must, upon voluntary co-operation, will probably always select an exceptionally intelligent, well-educated group. Average people can seldom mobilize their intelligence and emotions sufficiently to co-operate in a study of family relations, dealing, as such studies so frequently do, with emotional sore spots.[3]

Of course, some justification for equating the typical American family with the middle class family of scientific marriage literature can be offered. It is frequently maintained that although the middle class does not represent all American families, nevertheless it represents the largest group in society. Further, those families which are considered below the middle class in the social structure of contemporary American society are modeling their family attitudes and modes according to the general middle class pattern.[4] This argument is not without some foundation in fact. However, it seems more in conformity with the real situation to state with Hill that the reasons for drawing generalizations from data on the middle class family "is simply that information concerning this group was easiest to obtain." [5]

Inadequate Definitions

There are several objections to drawing generalizations from data based on these middle class family studies. In the first place, it is difficult to define what is meant by middle class in this context. It appears to include a rather vaguely delimited socioeconomic "middle" group. Second, such a loosely defined category will obviously embrace a considerable variety of family types and patterns in our complex culture. Hence, a representative sample of middle class families would have to be drawn with great care, but most of these studies have depended on the voluntary cooperation of selective groups. Third, there is little agreement on the criteria used to judge marital success.[6] In spite of the effort that has gone into family research, science has uncovered surprisingly little about the factors which contribute to happiness in marriage.[7] Much of this failure can be traced to the inability of scientists to agree on what constitutes success and happiness in marriage.

This same disagreement concerning acceptable criteria plagues the marriage prediction studies.[8] It is obvious that one can neither measure nor predict marital success unless one has an idea of what constitutes this success, but what is not always so clearly understood is that criteria of marital success are based on premises implying definite family values and goals. To be sure, the crux of the problem of marital prediction is where Burgess has indicated.

> But so far, it has been rather difficult to say whether these problems which the interviewer is able to predict will be disruptive or whether the couples will be able to solve them. This seems to depend in large part upon the adaptability of one or both members of the couple. The factor which we have not adequately identified, either in statistical or clinical prediction, is the characteristic of adaptability, or a capacity for problem solving. We need a better definition and measurement of adaptability.[9]

But it is precisely in trying to measure adaptability that fundamental differences in definitions and value systems make

their appearance. Adapt whom to what? Not any kind of adaptability is acceptable. We must know the nature and the legitimate goals of the adaptee as well as the requisites of an institution, such as the family, which necessarily involves others.
We can readily agree that adaptability and the capacity for
problem solving should be viewed in terms of personality development, but this statement is meaningless unless we can
agree on a definition of personality since development obviously implies the perfecting of a nature in relation to its
goals.[10] Hence, the attempt to measure what might be called
the couple's "potential of adaptability" brings us right back to
the problem of establishing valid criteria of marital success.
Because criteria imply value premises and there is little agreement on these, studies of marital success tend to be segmental
and noncumulative; that is, the findings of one study seldom
serve as the basis upon which future research can be constructed.

Applicability of Findings to Catholic Families

These limitations of marriage-success studies should not lead
us to ignore the excellent scientific techniques they have developed and the valuable contributions they have made toward
understanding the modern family. However, since they have
been based primarily on middle-class Protestant families, the
applicability of many of their findings to the Catholic family
remains questionable. As we have indicated, the Catholic family has its own system of ultimate values, and marital success
must be measured in terms of these goals. Personality development for the Catholic implies both natural and supernatural
growth within a clearly defined frame of values. Consequently,
not only are the dimensions of marital success somewhat differently defined for the Catholic couple, but their motivation
in seeking this success receives special reinforcement from
their religious life. It follows that their potential of adaptability is increased for, as Burgess has pointed out, the determination to succeed is an important factor in marital adjustment.[11]
This would appear to be an obvious conclusion if we grant
that individuals are normatively orientated; that is, they not

merely respond to sense stimuli but make an effort to conform their activities to internalized ideals.

In other words, as previous chapters have demonstrated, Catholics maintain that the family is founded on a sacramental contract characterized by perpetuity, indissolubility, and mutual fidelity. Marriage furnishes the institutional framework within which the sexes work out their mutual complementarity. The primary end or purpose of marriage is the procreation and education of offspring. Its secondary or concomitant purposes are companionship, and the mutual support and sanctification of the spouses. This is the "philosophy" of marriage promulgated by the Church and practiced by the faithful from the beginning of the Christian era. Down through the centuries, with inspiration and insight, a body of laws governing marriage has been formulated which constitutes the unique juridical framework within which Catholic marriages operate today. Hence, it seems logical to conclude that Catholic marriages constitute a separate field for investigation. More specifically, granted the belief in the indissolubility and the sacramental nature of the bond, one would expect to find a different pattern of marital adjustment and family breakdown among Catholics.

DISORGANIZED CATHOLIC FAMILIES

To know how well the Catholic family is adjusting to its modern urban environment, therefore, we must study the Catholic family itself. Research based on non-Catholic families will supply helpful insights, techniques, and comparative data. Only a study of Catholic families themselves in terms of their defined marriage and family ideals will uncover the critical problems which they face in contemporary society. In this chapter we shall discuss some of the characteristics of disorganized Catholic marriages and compare our findings with those of other studies in this field. The following chapter will analyze the factors involved in the breakdown of these marriages. We shall present the data in considerable detail because our research has uncovered some significant facts concerning

maladjustment. Knowledge of these will help us understand
the impact of the dominant culture on the Catholic subsystem.

Since separation or divorce constitute a valid criterion of
maladjustment in marriage, we have analyzed a large number
of broken Catholic marriages in an effort to discover the factors which contributed to the breakdown.[12] The couples involved in these marriages were well aware that their marriage
bond was indissoluble and consequently, that they were not
free to enter another marriage. It may be presumed, therefore,
that the maladjustment was serious and relatively insurmount-
able. Although some of these couples were later reunited, at
the time they were studied, they had reached the parting of
the ways. Life together had proved too difficult for them and
they were seeking permission to live apart.

Source of the Data

The couples involved in the study were all members of the
Chicago Archdiocese. At the time, this comprised the counties
of Cook, Lake, Du Page, Kankakee, Will, and Grundy in the
state of Illinois. This area is almost coterminous with the city
of Chicago and its immediate environs. The immediate source
of the data was the records of the Archdiocesan separation
court. We pointed out in a previous chapter that the Church
may deal with petitions for marital separation in one of two
ways. Either the decision is made by the bishop and granted
through an administrative decree or else the case is handled
by a regular judicial procedure in which both parties are cited
and their case is heard by a judge or by several judges who
hand down the decision.

The Chicago separation court includes a staff of twenty delegate judges who are empowered to hear cases and hand down
decisions which are binding on the parties. The decision of
one judge suffices except when he recommends divorce permission or is in doubt concerning the advisability of such
permission. In these cases, referral must be made to a special
division of the court composed of two judges who have special
delegation to grant permission for obtaining a civil divorce.
The judges in the separation court are parish priests who have

special training in canon law and family counseling. Each judge devotes several days a week to the work of the court.

The necessity of appealing to the chancery court whenever a separation is contemplated is incumbent upon all Catholics living in the Archdiocese. They are informed of their obligation by public decrees, announcements from the pulpit, and in the confessional. Hence, all the faithful who wish to remain Catholics in good standing will have recourse to the court if the need for separation arises. Refusal to have recourse to the court or to accept its decision bears heavy sanctions. The recalcitrant party is forbidden the use of the sacraments and in case of death is refused Christian burial. This is a severe penalty for the faithful. It can be assumed that all who are other than nominal Catholics will attempt to conform.

Over one thousand couples brought their marriage problems to the chancery court each year during the forties. We have used the cases dealt with between the beginning of 1942 and the beginning of 1948 as the basis for our study. A sample of two thousand cases was selected from this total and furnishes the material for the present analysis. Since the data on these marriages are filed in folders arranged in alphabetical order according to the name of the husband, the following method was used to secure a representative sample. The total number of cases was divided into groups of twenty each and every third group was selected for analysis.[13]

The case records supply information on the name, address, religion, parish, occupation of breadwinner, date, place and officiant at marriage, length of acquaintanceship and engagement, age at marriage, duration of marriage, number of children, source of petition for separation, and finally, the factors which are judged to have contributed to the breakdown of the marriage.

Reliability of the Data

How reliable is this information? In the first place, it should be pointed out that the separation court is not to be compared to an ordinary civil divorce court. The parties appearing in the court know that the court has no competency to deal with the marriage bond itself and hence, there is no question of the right to remarriage during the life of the two parties. Further, the court stresses the moral obligation of earnestly seeking a reconciliation whenever this is possible. If permission to separate is granted, the parties must agree to avoid "keeping company." They are warned that any perjury in giving their testimony renders them unworthy to receive the sacraments. Therefore, in appearing before the court the parties are seeking a spiritual good which depends on their honesty in giving testimony.

It might be remarked that Catholics who take their cases to the court are those to whom the practice of the faith represents a real value for which they are willing to make sacrifices. Members of the Church who do not have this firm appreciation of spiritual values will simply take their marital difficulties to the civil courts and obtain a divorce without the Church's permission. This is particularly true where one or both parties contemplate remarriage. They realize that remarriage automatically excludes them from the sacraments so there is no point in having recourse to the chancery court.

In general, the reliability of data based on the testimony of individuals may be evaluated in two ways. One may question the veracity of the witnesses or one may question their ability to give adequate and pertinent testimony. In regard to the first question, there seems no valid reason to doubt the veracity of the witnesses in most cases used here. The partners present the case as they see it. Since they are seeking a spiritual good dependent on their telling the truth, there seems little point in doubting their good intentions.

However, the response to the second question is not so clear. Many people are not capable of analyzing a situation in which they are intimately involved. The incidents leading to the breakdown of the family have been very painful to at least one of the parties and hence, all their thinking about related factors may be deeply emotional. Under such conditions, there is a tendency for mere suspicion to take on the trappings of reality; incidents that happened over a long period of time are massed together, and their cumulative effect can be quite at odds with reality. Then too, there is always the temptation of self-justification and self-righteousness. Guilt is all too frequently rationalized and misdeeds made to appear less culpable by stressing the shortcomings of the other party. Wounded pride is no aid to clear self-analysis.

On the other hand, the evidence is taken in the presence of both parties. A comparison of the conflicting testimony and a demand for proof of allegations lightly made has a healthy, sterilizing effect on the emotions and the free play of imagination. The esteem in which the judge is held because he is also a minister of God plays a considerable role also. Further, the judge has been trained in taking and weighing evidence through years of study and experience so that a few well-placed questions from him usually reminds the parties that he is seeking the truth and is not interested in emotional display.

In spite of this earnest attempt to get at the real "facts," it must be admitted that in a certain number of cases the evidence in the records presents merely the immediate or proximate factors leading to the breakdown. Perhaps a protracted investigation of such cases might uncover all the factors which have contributed to the failure of the marriage. However, whether it be successful or not, there are certain elements which it is difficult to quantify and measure. Among these "imponderables" perhaps the most important, as we have suggested, is the will of each party to make a success of the marriage no matter what obstacles may occur.

The best that the records can reveal is an account of the factors which were instrumental in causing the breakdown, and these will necessarily be presented as they appear to the subjective view of the parties involved. In analyzing any social process it is difficult to isolate and measure with precision all the variables involved. Nevertheless, these court records, representing as they do the testimony of the partners, plus the insights and interpretations of the counseling judge, offer information which will substantially advance our understanding of Catholic marriage problems.

Representativeness of the Data

How representative of American Catholics is the population from which these cases were drawn? This is a difficult question to answer, considering our limited knowledge of many characteristics of American Catholics in general. However, a consideration of the following points will throw some light on the group studied. The cases are drawn from a population which is largely urban. Catholics are a minority, but a large minority, representing approximately 40 per cent of the population. The vital statistics of the archdiocese reveal that we are dealing with a vital sector of American Catholicism.

At the time of the study, over two thousand priests were actively engaged in ministering to the needs of the faithful. Parishes numbered over four hundred and some 8,500 sisters were engaged in teaching and nursing. Eight colleges and universities were located in the area with an enrollment of approximately 22,000 students. The thirty-nine high schools in the area had an enrollment of around 16,000 students. Parochial elementary schools numbered 375 with an enrollment of over 158,000 students. There were some twenty Catholic general hospitals in the area and sixteen schools of nursing with a student body of over 1,500. The mixed marriage rate of 20 per cent was below the national average, which at the time was running between 26 and 30 per cent.

It is more difficult to prove that the population is representative of American Catholics in regard to ethnic composition. There are no adequate statistics available covering the number of Catholics in the various ethnic groups. However, census reports may throw some light on the problem. The census classifies foreign-born whites by country of birth. In 1940 there were over 670,000 foreign-born whites in the area. These were divided into 35 categories according to countries of origin. The ten main groups were: Poland (17.7); Germany (12.4); Italy (9.9); Russia (9.2); Sweden (6.9); Irish Free State (5.2); Czechoslovakia (5.0); England and Scotland (4.3); Lithuania (3.9); Austria (3.9); all the others had less than 3 per cent of the total foreign-born white population each.[14]

A comparison with the statistics for the total number of foreign-born in the United States reveals striking similarities. The top 10 per cent were: Germany (15.1); Italy (13.3); Poland (8.4); England and Scotland (7.8); Russia (7.5); Irish Free State (7.0); Canada non-French (5.8); Sweden (3.8); Austria (3.6); Mexico (3.0).[15] A study of these percentages reveals that the area from which the cases were drawn has a fairly representative share of the foreign-born. It has considerably more than the national average of Poles but less than the national average of Italians. The other nationality groups correspond rather closely. On the basis of these statistics one may conclude that the area studied is fairly representative of the large industrial centers of the country, and, as we have seen, the majority of American Catholics are located in these areas.

Hence the value of our data on broken Catholic marriages may be summarized as follows. They are drawn from an urban population in which the Catholic minority is relatively large and vigorous. This population is characteristic of American industrial regions in its ethnic composition. The information in the records has been gathered by trained investigators and contributed by couples motivated by religious ideals. However, the cases may not be representative of Catholic families in general for two reasons. First, they are couples in which at least one of the partners values the practice of religion so highly that considerable sacrifice will be made in order to conform to Church laws. Second, they are couples facing marital difficulties of a serious nature since the parties are either living separately or are contemplating doing so.

COUPLES IN TROUBLE

What do we know about the couples coming to the chancery court with their problems? Are they typical Catholic couples that just haven't managed to adjust? Who are they? From what level of society have they come? Under what circumstances did they marry? What kind of family have they established? These are some of the questions we shall answer in this chapter. Previous marriage studies have uncovered a number of traits which proved significant for adjustment in marriage. We want to discover to what extent the couples in our study possessed these traits.

Our primary aim, therefore, is to describe and compare our findings with those of other studies. This is the method of presenting this descriptive information: After a brief discussion of the reasons why a particular characteristic may be considered pertinent to marital adjustment, the findings of other studies will be analyzed and compared with our own data. In this way, significant differences may become apparent and, at the same time, the cases we are studying will be seen in their proper perspective.

Ethnic Characteristics of the Group

There are two reasons for gathering information on the ethnic composition of the group. We want to know whether there are ethnic or nationality differences in marital stability and whether intergroup marriage results in instability. It is widely recognized that the statuses and roles of family members are defined somewhat differently in the various ethnic groups. This suggests the possibility of culture conflicts when intergroup marriage occurs. On the other hand, it might be argued that ethnics who had separated from the group to the extent of choosing a mate from outside the group have already lost most of their attachment to their national culture.

More pertinent to maladjustment in marriage, perhaps, is the fact that the process of acculturation does not proceed uniformly among all members of a specific ethnic minority. In some measure, acculturation is associated with the number of generations minority families have lived in America. However, this is by no means the only factor involved in cultural adaptations concerning marriage and family patterns. Of equal importance are the degree of isolation, the amount of education, the persistence of bilingualism, and the effectiveness of nationality organizations and propaganda.

Consequently, even when marriage takes place within the group, the spouses may have dissimilar marriage expectations owing to the different degrees of Americanization they have experienced in the melting pot. This would appear in conflicting concepts of marital statuses and roles. For example, the subordination of women in marriage, prevalent in the culture of many European ethnic groups, is bound to conflict with the American concept of the "democratic" family implying relative equality between the sexes. In such cases, the male, as the member of the family who stands to profit most from the traditional view, is more prone to cherish the culture which protects his prerogatives of dominance than is the female who sees in the new culture an opportunity for freedom.

This would explain, in part, the increasing number of women seeking separation on grounds of drunkenness and abuse. There may be a culture conflict here which is not always recognized. According to American standards, the actions of the husband may be judged selfish and unreasonable, whereas he is merely following the role of arbitrary dominance as head of the family which his culture has taught him is one of the prerogatives of the male. He is angered and indignant when his actions are called into question and since his wife is not carrying out the role that he has been taught was customary for the woman, he accuses her of being a "poor" wife, of being "no mother to his children," and of being carried away by new-fangled, "modern" ideas.

Limitations of the Data. Unfortunately, the court records do not supply all the information that might be desired on the ethnic composition of the group. Nationality had to be estimated from the family name and the parish of origin of each partner. This method is subject to error, but in the opinion of the court judges it was quite reliable for members of the major national groups. A large number of the parishes in the diocese were national parishes embracing members of one ethnic group. Particularly in the past, many parishes tended to include only one national group, and since the separation court's record contained the parish of origin, it was possible to arrive at the national background of the marriage partners in most cases with only a small margin of error.

This method of ascertaining nationality, however, gives no information on length of residence in America so that the generation represented in the case is not known. Knowledge of this is admittedly helpful in judging the degree of acculturation among ethnics. Nevertheless, as we have indicated, this is not the only index nor necessarily the most significant one. Indeed, as far as marriage expectations are concerned, it seems in many cases to be minor. Knowledge of all the factors previously enumerated are necessary if one is to judge the possibility of a cultural clash in marriage.

Hence, incomplete as the data on ethnic composition admittedly are, we present them not only because of their general descriptive interest, but also because they may aid in understanding some of the problems which these broken marriages reveal. It should be obvious, of course, that the mere existence of outgroup marriage is not a problem in itself. Tension may arise when one or both of the partners possess not merely different but conflicting concepts of the status and roles of family members. Frustration and strain arising from ethnic disparity are not the product of ethnic differences as such but develop out of the clash which may arise when these differences are not resolved and become elements of conflict rather than of completion in the marriage relationship.

Ethnic Background. Table 12 presents general information on the individual spouses. The percentages for the four major nationality groups are given for both male and female.[16] The remaining national groups were not treated separately since they each contained too few cases to justify detailed analysis. The table shows relatively high percentages for those of

TABLE 12

DISTRIBUTION OF SPOUSES ACCORDING TO ETHNIC ORIGIN

Ethnic Origin	Male	Female
Irish	27.5	28.7
German	25.3	21.6
Polish	13.8	16.9
Italian	10.9	10.8
Others	22.5	22.0

Irish or German extraction. Together, these two groups constitute half the cases appearing before the chancery court. Although there are no available data on the exact percentage these groups represent in the total Catholic population of the Archdiocese, reliable estimates suggest that they are overrepresented here. However, one may not conclude on the basis of these statistics alone that Irish and German Catholics experience more marital difficulties than do other Catholics. A plausible alternative explanation may be that they are more obedient to the laws of the Church and more willing to submit to the Church's legislation concerning separation procedure.

Outgroup Marriages.   Owing to the possibilities of culture conflict developing in outgroup marriages, it is of interest to note that approximately 43 per cent of the cases represented such unions. In this respect, some unexpected rates appeared among the major ethnic groups and among the sexes within these groups. Table 13 presents the proportion of outgroup marriage for both sexes of the major national groups.

TABLE 13

DISTRIBUTION OF OUTGROUP MARRIAGE ACCORDING TO NATIONALITY AND SEX

Nationality	Husband	Wife
Polish	15.9	31.2
Italian	39.2	39.2
Irish	39.8	42.2
German	57.3	49.8
Others	50.7	49.7

The Polish male displayed the least tendency to marry outside his national group. The Polish female showed the same tendency but to a much less marked degree, outnumbering the male two to one in such unions. Although our research indicates that ethnic females enter outgroup marriages more often than males, the ratio revealed in the court records appears unduly high.[17] The highest rate of outgroup marriage was found among those of German descent. Here too, the rate differed between the sexes, although it was the German male who showed the greatest tendency to enter outgroup unions.

The Irish and Italian groups were intermediate between the two extremes represented by the Poles and Germans, and there was little difference in the rate for the two sexes. To the extent that these couples are representative of their national groups, some conclusions in regard to ethnic solidarity may be drawn.

It would follow that the Poles maintain the greatest degree of solidarity and the Germans the least, with the Italians and the Irish displaying about equal degrees. However, previous studies suggest that our cases contain an unexpected number of Italians involved in outgroup marriages, and there is every reason to believe that the general ingroup marriage rate of Italians is higher than would be indicated by the present figures.

Types of Marriage

We have already discussed the possibility of marital conflict developing out of mixed marriage. Table 14 presents the type of marriage represented by the marriage cases appearing before the separation court. Since conversions which take place

TABLE 14

DISTRIBUTION OF CASES ACCORDING TO TYPE OF MARRIAGE

Type	Percentage
Husband and wife Catholic	75.9
Husband non-Catholic	12.7
Wife non-Catholic	4.5
Husband convert	3.4
Wife convert	3.4

at the time of marriage are frequently viewed with suspicion, it was judged useful to record them separately.

In approximately three-fourths of the total cases both partners were Catholic. In another 6.8 per cent both partners were Catholic, but one was a convert at the time of marriage. Although the mixed marriage rate for the area was roughly 20 per cent during the previous decade, only 17.2 per cent of the cases represented mixed marriages. This should not lead one to conclude that valid mixed marriages are more stable than other marriages. It will be noticed that in only 4.5 per cent of the mixed marriage cases the wife was the non-Catholic party.

In other words, it appears that this type of mixed marriage was underrepresented and the reason is obvious. There is a bias in our data here owing to the fact that we are dealing with the records of a Catholic court to which it is unlikely that non-Catholic parties would have recourse since they will not feel bound by Church legislation. Furthermore, since the majority of petitioners to the court are the wives, it is evident that mixed marriages in which the wife was the non-Catholic partner would be inadequately reported. On the basis of our data, therefore, one can draw no conclusions concerning the relative stability of mixed marriages although mixed marriages involving a Catholic wife and a non-Catholic husband are apparently well represented.[18]

The percentage of converts at marriage is of interest because it is believed that many of these conversions at marriage may have been occasioned more out of a desire to please the Catholic party than through conviction. This does not necessarily imply insincerity. However, since many Catholics still insist they will never marry "outside" the Catholic Church, meaning they will never enter a mixed marriage, it is possible that the non-Catholic party who has no serious religious convictions may undertake conversion without fully calculating the cost of perseverance. Once the honeymoon is over and routine replaces novelty in daily habits, the "conversion" may appear in its true form, a meaningless, external ritual. The final outcome may be a mixed marriage in reality though not in form.

Length of Acquaintance Before Marriage

Studies in marital adjustment have found some association between length of acquaintance before marriage and success in marriage. For example, Burgess and Cottrell enumerate length of acquaintance before marriage as an item which has certain predictive value for adjustment in marriage. They maintain that the highest correlation is secured when the couple were acquainted two years or more.[19] They find a "direct positive relation of length of acquaintance with marital compatibility."[20] Popenoe, in a study comparing certain background items for several hundred unhappy married couples and a control group of several hundred happy married ones, discovered that the unhappy couples had an average length of acquaintance of 20.15 months; the control group, of 28.30 months.[21]

On the other hand, Terman designates length of premarital

acquaintance as of small importance since it shows only a slightly significant relationship to the happiness of one or both of the spouses.[22] Indeed, he states that "the most striking thing disclosed by our data is the almost negligible relationship between marital happiness and length of premarital acquaintance." [23] A careful analysis of his findings, however, indicates that a premarital acquaintance of three years or more gives the highest positive correlation with husband's happiness and one year or more for wife's happiness.

Locke's study of happily married and divorced persons shows that the proportion of happily married and divorced men for given lengths of acquaintance were about the same, whereas married and divorced women differed considerably.[24] He concluded that length of acquaintance is not a very important item in the marital adjustment of husbands, but a year or less is very unfavorable for wives.[25]

Catholic Couples. Table 15 presents information on the length of acquaintance for the couples appearing before the separation court. It is apparent that a considerable portion of the couples married after a relatively brief acquaintance. Ap-

TABLE 15

DISTRIBUTION OF CASES ACCORDING TO LENGTH OF ACQUAINTANCE

Length of Acquaintance	*Percentage*
Less than 3 months	6.6
3 to 6 months	11.0
6 to 11 months	27.0
12 to 35 months	19.2
35 months or more	36.2

proximately 17 per cent were acquainted for less than six months, and about 45 per cent for less than one year. On the other hand, over 36 per cent were acquainted for three years or more. It would seem that nearly half the couples do not meet the minimum prerequisite for length of acquaintance before marriage.

Duration and Length of Acquaintance. However, if the data on the length of acquaintance make any contribution to our knowledge of family adjustment, it should be revealed in the length of duration of the marriage. The length of premar-

ital acquaintance has been judged significant on the premise
that it is necessary for the future marriage partners to know
each other well before marriage. A consequence of this increased knowledge derived from continued acquaintance
would be to obviate incompatible unions to a considerable
degree. If this reasoning is correct, we should expect to find
that a relatively high percentage of marriages contracted after
a brief acquaintance would break down more quickly than
those entered into after a longer acquaintance period. This
follows since theoretically the former will encounter difficulty
as soon as the incompatibilities which should have been discovered before marriage become apparent.

The association between duration of marriage and length
of acquaintance revealed in Table 16 would seem to substantiate this hypothesis. Among the couples who had been acquainted for less than six months before marriage, well over

TABLE 16

DISTRIBUTION OF CASES ACCORDING TO DURATION
OF MARRIAGE AND LENGTH OF ACQUAINTANCE

	Length of Acquaintance Before Marriage				
Duration of Marriage	Under 3 Months	3-5 Months	6-11 Months	1-2 Years	3 Years and Over
Under 1 year	23.3	22.2	12.4	9.7	12.3
13 months to 5 yrs. ...	28.5	26.4	30.4	29.1	29.0
6-10 yrs.	18.8	25.0	22.3	20.4	23.6
11-15 yrs.	13.5	11.8	16.9	16.8	14.5
16-20 yrs.	6.0	6.4	8.7	12.1	10.9
21 yrs. & over	9.8	8.2	9.3	11.8	9.5

one out of five broke up within the first year of marriage. This
is almost double the percentage of those who were acquainted
for longer periods. The fact that over one out of five of these
short-acquaintance marriages broke up within twelve months
of their wedding date seems to indicate that they had entered
marriage with undue precipitation. On the other hand, those
who had been acquainted for more than six months all presented the same pattern for duration. Perhaps Terman is correct when he observes that "right" judgments are about as
likely to be made within the first year of acquaintance as
thereafter.[26]

Our study, therefore, lends some support to the belief that a short acquaintance before marriage is related to marital instability. However, this would seem to be true only in those cases revealing an acquaintance period of less than six months. Particularly when dealing with relatively young couples, marriage counselors are on safe ground when they advise an acquaintance period of more than six months.

Length of Engagement

The term *engagement* or *betrothal* can be defined in various ways. There may be an external, formal rite including a formal promise to marry pronounced before witnesses such as the relatives or a representative of the Church. Ordinarily, the external rite consists in the giving of the engagement ring, by which rite the couple declare to the public that they have exchanged promises to marry. However, the external rite is not necessary. The essential point is the time at which the couple come to a definite understanding that they are to be married.

Previous Studies. It is in this sense that the term is used in many studies seeking significant background items in marital happiness. For example, Terman found a moderately high positive correlation with marital happiness for an engagement of six months or longer for the husband and three months or longer for the wife. Those engaged for five years or more had the highest average happiness score. However, since he had only 22 cases in this latter category, his findings should be used with caution.[27] Burgess and Cottrell found the highest positive correlations when the engagement extended for three years or more. They state that as duration of engagement increased, the proportion of marriages with "poor" adjustment declined from 50 per cent for under 3 months to 11 per cent for 2 years and over, while the percentage with "good" adjustment increased from 25.7 per cent for under 3 months to 62.6 per cent for 2 years and over.[28]

Popenoe found that the duration of engagement for unhappy married couples was 7.51 months; for the happy, it was 12.46. He observes that the number of unhappy married couples who had married on the spur of the moment "without any engagement," was eight times as great as among the control group.[29] Locke concludes from his study that an engagement period of 6 months or over is highly associated with marital adjustment for men; a period of 12 months and over is very favorable for women. In terms of average length, he found that happy married men reported an engagement of 10.2 months compared with 7.3 months for divorced men. This was a 40 per cent longer engagement. Married women reported an average engagement of 12.0 months as against 7.1 months for divorced women. This was a 69 per cent longer engagement.[30]

In the present study, the term *engagement* is taken to signify more than just a definite understanding between the two parties that they will eventually marry. In other words, it is a formal engagement with some external signs in the form of a ring or an announcement to friends and relatives. It follows that there will be a considerable number of couples who will report no formal engagement.

Catholic Couples. According to the data presented in Table 17, approximately 50 per cent of the couples either had not

TABLE 17

DISTRIBUTION OF CASES ACCORDING TO LENGTH OF ENGAGEMENT

Length of Engagement	Percentage
No engagement	35.6
Less than 3 months	14.3
3 months to 6 months	20.2
6 months to 11 months	22.1
11 months and over	7.7

been formally engaged or had been engaged for less than three months. Only about 8 per cent had been engaged for more than one year. If the findings of Burgess and Cottrell, Terman, Popenoe, and Locke can be accepted, it would seem that the present cases displayed very unfavorable engagement characteristics. However, since there is no clear definition of the term *engagement* in these studies, the data may not be comparable.

As might be expected, the length of premarital acquaintance was closely related to length of engagement. For most of the other characteristics studied, the cases which had not been engaged reveal few significant differences from the engaged group. Later in this study we shall see that "forced" marriages, that is, marriages occasioned by pregnancy, present a marked exception since approximately 70 per cent of these cases had not been engaged.

It seems proper to point out that research findings on the correlation between length of engagement and adjustment in marriage must be used with great caution since the term *engagement* does not signify the same thing in all studies. Further, on the basis of the present study, one must conclude that formal engagement has little connection with the type of maladjustment which may occur in the marriage. Since information on the engagement characteristics of the total Catholic population from which our cases were drawn is not available, it is impossible to affirm that a formal engagement is correlated with good marital adjustment although the high percentage of cases in which there was no engagement or an engagement of three months or less leads one to suspect that there may be some relationship.

Age of the Spouses at Marriage

There is general agreement among students of the American family that marriage at early ages tends strongly to lead to subsequent unhappiness. Just what constitutes "early" or "premature" age at marriage is the subject of some dispute. In 1940 the median age of those marrying for the first time was 24.3 years for the groom and 21.6 for the bride.[31] The trend in the last decade has been toward earlier marriage so that by 1949 it was estimated that the median for men had dropped to about 22.7 and for women, to about 20.3.[32] It is to be noted that the median age at marriage for both grooms and brides is lower in rural areas than in urban, that it is lower in the South than in the Northeast, and that it varies according to class levels and probably according to ethnic groups.[33]

Previous Studies. Because of the many variables involved in this diversity of age at marriage, many studies dealing with early age at marriage as a factor in marital maladjustment will be applicable only to the group studied. For example, Hamilton discovered that the proportion of unhappy marriages for both men and women was approximately twice as high among those who married before the age of 25 as for those who married between the ages of 30 and 34.[34] It must be obvious that this generalization applies only to the very select group with which Hamilton was dealing. The same caution must be expressed in regard to the findings of Davis. She states that when both bride and groom were under 21 at marriage, the percentage of wives later regarding themselves as unhappy in marriage was seven times as great as at the ideal age combination. In cases where the bride was under 19 or the groom under 24, the risk of unhappiness was found to be more than three times as great as at the ideal age.[35]

Although there is considerable diversity for age at marriage in different sections of the country, among rural and urban dwellers, and among the various social classes, the general evidence of research studies seems to indicate that marriage at early ages tends strongly to lead to subsequent unhappiness. In these studies the term *early* would signify under 19 or 20 years for the bride and under 22 years for the groom.[36]

For example, Locke discovered that the differences between the mean age at marriage of married and divorced women was very significant, that is, 21.5 to 19.9 years, respectively. Married and divorced men also differed significantly in the mean age at marriage (24.1 and 23.2 years, respectively). He found that marriage before the age of 18 was very unfavorable for women; for men, marriage below 21 was unfavorable. The optimum age of marriage for women was between 21 and 29; for men, it was between 24 and 29. Terman's findings are less conclusive. He discovered a negligible correlation between happiness and age at marriage except for wives who marry under 20 and possibly for husbands under 22.

Burgess and Cottrell are much more explicit, stating that there seemed to be no doubt regarding the unfortunate effects of very early marriages in the great majority of their cases. Wives under 19 and husbands under 22 tend toward poor marital adjustment. In a study of 1,051 marriages, Landis found that the divorce rate decreased as the age at marriage increased. The divorce rate was six times higher for marriages in which both were under 21 than for those in which both were 31 or over at marriage. Where one spouse was under 20 and the other over 20 at marriage, the divorce rate was higher than if both were over 20 years old at marriage.

Relationship to Instability. The question may be asked whether marriage at an early age is the cause of marital unhappiness or merely a symptom of emotional instability. Terman tends to look upon it as the latter without, however, excluding a certain degree of causal relationship. Popenoe tends to consider early marriage as symptomatic since he maintains that only the emotionally unstable and the rebellious defy custom and marry young. On the other hand, Burgess and Cottrell hold that there is a causal relationship between early marriage and marital unhappiness. They argue from the nature of things: general unpreparedness of the young spouses for obligations, haste, opposition of relatives and friends, and so forth. It is not necessary to pursue this discussion further at this point. However, as we shall show, in many "forced" marriages one or both of the parties are relatively young, and this possibility of premarital pregnancy should be taken into consideration when judgment is passed on the adjustment potential of couples who marry at early ages.

Catholic Couples. The age of husband and wife at marriage for the separation court cases are presented in Table 18.

TABLE 18

DISTRIBUTION OF CASES ACCORDING TO AGE OF HUSBAND AND WIFE AT MARRIAGE

Age at Marriage	Husband	Wife
Less than 18 years	.6	7.0
Less than 19 years	2.8	17.7
Less than 20 years	6.7	28.7
Less than 21 years	13.0	39.6
Less than 23 years	32.7	59.5
Less than 25 years	51.9	73.2
Less than 27 years	68.0	83.0
Less than 30 years	80.6	90.5
Less than 35 years	91.7	95.8

Approximately one-third of the husbands were 22 years old at the time of marriage. This indicates a rather high percent-

age in an age-group considered by many to be immature for
marriage. Among the wives, 7 per cent were married before
they were 18 years old and nearly 40 per cent were married
at 20 years or under. Further, only 27 per cent married at 25
years and over. This would indicate that the wives in the
group married at comparatively early ages. Indeed, if we are
to trust the findings of the studies which have been cited, we
would predict a considerable degree of maladjustment for
over one-third of them. However, the age at marriage of the
cases in the present study was found to differ in no significant
degree from the age at marriage of the total population in
that area. Since the cases studied were representative of the
general population in regard to this characteristic, it can be
questioned whether a deviation from the general pattern of
age at marriage has any predictive value for subsequent marital adjustment.

Two Hypotheses Possible. It is well to recall that our evaluation of the factor of age at marriage can be based on two
different premises. On the one hand, we may hold that a
flexible person adjusts more readily in marriage, and since one
is considered more flexible in early than in later life, those
who marry at an earlier age have a better chance of meeting
the adjustments required in marriage. On the other hand, we
may hold that maturity is associated with adjustment in marriage, and since maturity has some relation to age, those who
are older at marriage have a better chance of adjusting in marriage. Let us analyze some of the characteristics of these cases
to see which of these hypotheses can be substantiated.

Significant Variables. In the first place, it should be noted
that the age at marriage for specific ethnic groups is quite
distinct. Those of Italian descent tend to marry at earlier ages
than others and those of Irish descent tend to marry later.
These differences are particularly marked for the brides although they are significant for the grooms also. This fact
should be kept in mind when evaluating the age at marriage
characteristic of a given population. Further, although some
studies have discovered considerable variation for the age at
marriage of different socioeconomic classes, the present study
found a tendency for only the upper white-collar classes to

marry later but there were no significant differences between the lower white-collar, the skilled, semiskilled, and unskilled classes.

Husband's Age at Marriage and Number of Children. It is generally assumed that children can be a stabilizing factor in marriage. Table 19 shows that there is a close relationship be-

TABLE 19

DISTRIBUTION OF CASES ACCORDING TO NUMBER OF CHILDREN AND AGE OF HUSBAND

	Age of Husband at Marriage				
Number of Children	*20 and Under*	*21-22*	*23-24*	*25-29*	*30 and over*
None	23.5	29.5	32.6	35.8	50.4
1 child	29.2	26.5	28.7	29.0	23.1
2 children	22.3	20.9	16.8	18.3	15.7
3 children	11.2	9.9	9.5	8.9	6.2
4 children	6.9	5.6	5.5	4.7	1.8
5 or more	6.9	7.6	6.8	3.1	2.6

tween age at marriage and the number of children per family whether we consider the age at marriage of the husband or the wife. In the case of the husbands, the percentage of childless families increases through the five age classes from 23.5 per cent for those marrying at twenty and under to 50.4 per cent for those marrying at 30 or later. On the other hand, the percentage of families having three or more children decreases from 25 per cent to 10.6 per cent.

Wife's Age at Marriage and Number of Children. Since the childbearing span of the female normally extends approximately from her fifteenth to her forty-fifth year, the age at marriage for the wife can be expected to have a close relationship with the number of children per family. However, it appears from the data presented in Table 20 that other factors besides that of age operate to limit the birthrate in late marriages. The percentage of childless families increases through the five age classes from 25.9 for wives who married at 18 or under to 64.0 per cent for those who married at 30 years or later. At the same time, the percentage of cases having three or more children decreased from 24.8 to 1.6 per cent. The significance of Tables 19 and 20 should be pondered by all those

TABLE 20

DISTRIBUTION OF CASES ACCORDING TO NUMBER OF CHILDREN AND
AGE OF WIFE

	Age of Wife				
Number of Children	18 and Under	19-20	21-24	25-29	30 and Over
None	25.9	26.9	34.6	40.6	64.0
1 child	26.5	32.5	26.2	27.1	21.7
2 children	22.8	19.2	18.0	17.6	12.7
3 children	8.8	10.7	10.2	8.6	1.6
4 children	8.1	4.8	5.5	2.6	.0
5 or more	7.9	5.7	5.5	3.4	.0

who advocate late marriage on the premise that the couple will
be more mature. According to Catholic teaching, children are
considered one of the "goods" of marriage and a childless marriage is to be viewed as a misfortune rather than a goal.

Husband's Age at Marriage and Duration. Data on the
duration of marriage should throw some light on the relative
marital stability of the various age groups. In other words, it
may be assumed that if age at marriage is associated with
marital happiness, this should be revealed in the length of
time the couple remained together. Tables 21 and 22 present
some pertinent data on this subject. According to Table 21, it
would seem that husbands who entered marriage between the
ages of 20 and 25 were most capable of achieving adjustment
in the early years of marriage since only a little over one-third
broke up within the first five years of marriage and approxi-

TABLE 21

DISTRIBUTION OF CASES ACCORDING TO AGE OF HUSBAND AND DURATION
OF MARRIAGE

	Age of Husband				
Duration	20 and Under	21-22	23-24	25-29	30 and Over
Less than 1 year	12.0	12.7	11.3	13.7	17.0
Less than 5 years	43.6	39.9	36.6	42.8	50.6
6-10 years	17.0	19.1	21.0	27.8	23.1
11-15 years	17.8	18.8	15.5	12.4	13.9
16-20 years	9.3	10.4	15.2	7.8	7.7
21 years and over	12.3	11.7	15.6	9.0	4.4

mately 40 per cent endured for more than ten years. Those who married at 30 years or later apparently encountered serious problems early in marriage since over 50 per cent broke up within the first five years.

Wife's Age at Marriage and Duration. An analysis of the data presented in Table 22 shows that unions in which the bride was between the ages of 20 and 25 were least likely to

TABLE 22

DISTRIBUTION OF CASES ACCORDING TO AGE OF WIFE AND
DURATION OF MARRIAGE

	Age of Wife				
Duration	18 and Under	19-20	21-24	25-29	30 and Over
Less than 1 year	14.6	12.1	12.4	11.8	23.3
Less than 5 years	42.4	41.4	38.5	45.2	57.1
6-10 years	17.7	21.5	23.0	25.6	25.9
11-15 years	18.3	14.4	16.8	13.0	10.0
16-20 years	10.7	11.7	10.5	7.8	4.2
21 years and over	10.7	11.0	11.2	8.4	2.6

break down within the first five years (38.5 per cent), whereas when she was 30 years old or over, about 57 per cent of the marriages did not survive the first five years. In general this information on marriage duration supports the hypothesis that people marrying at a later age are less adaptable than those marrying earlier so that when marital problems arise they find it difficult to work out satisfactory solutions and the marriage disintegrates quickly.

Age at Marriage and Factors in the Breakdown. Finally, age at marriage can be studied in relation to the factors involved in the breakdown of the union. In the cases studied, there appeared some association between the age at marriage and infidelity. The rate of infidelity on the part of the wives decreased from 8.5 per cent for those who had married at 18 years or younger to .7 per cent for those who had married at 30 years or over. In the case of the husbands, the percentages ran from 25.5 per cent for those who had married at 20 years or younger to 11.0 per cent for those who had married at 30 years or older. On the other hand, drinking tended to be a more important factor in marital breakdown for the older age categories. Further, when the husband was under 23 years or the wife under 21, there was an increasing percentage of cases showing marked irresponsibility.

How important is the factor of age at marriage? It seems that it can be easily overemphasized. Clearly there is little evidence in the present study which would lead one to encourage late marriages unless one conceives the ideal family as either childless or nearly so. On the other hand, there was some evidence of immaturity among those who married relatively early. Here as elsewhere, *virtus stat in medio*. The extremes of age (over 30 years) and of youth (under 20 for the bride, under 22 for the groom) should be avoided, due respect being had, however, for ethnic, regional, and social class differences.

Relative Ages of the Spouses

Of what importance is difference in age between spouses? There is a rather general belief that ideal marriage demands that the husband be a little older than the wife, although this age difference should not be too great. Terman does not consider this point important. He believes "a great deal of nonsense has been written about the risks entailed by marrying . . . out of one's age."[37] It would seem, on the basis of present knowledge, that it is rather difficult to defend any age relationship between spouses which does not appear as a predominant tendency of the group. The cultural heritage of a group more than anything else determines what its marital standards regarding age will be.[38]

The General Average. A study of the general population from which our cases were drawn reveals the following pattern: in 8 per cent of the cases the spouses were the same age; in 10 per cent of the cases the bride was older; and in 82 per cent, the groom was older. In a study of marriage licenses granted in Philadelphia in 1931, Bossard found that in 10 per cent of the cases the spouses were the same age; in 10 per cent, the bride was older; and in 80 per cent, the groom was older.[39] In the cases appearing before the separation court, 14.5 per cent of the spouses were the same age; 11.4 per cent of the brides were older; and 74.1 per cent of the grooms were older. Although these studies show that the over-all pattern is roughly similar, the present study contains a significantly higher percentage of cases in which the couples were the same age.

Minor Importance. How does age difference affect the marriage relationship? In general, our study bears out Terman's conclusion. An apparent exception appears in the category of infidelity but if allowance is made for the relationship of this problem with early age at marriage, age difference between the spouses seem relatively unimportant. For example, the highest percentage of infidelity (27.8 per cent) on the part of the husband occurred in those cases where the spouses were the same age; the lowest (12.0 per cent), when the husband was 6 years or more older. For the wives, the highest percentage (5.8 per cent) occurred in those cases where the husband was 6 years or more older; there were no cases of infidelity on the part of the wife in those cases where she was 6 years or more older. In the majority of these cases, the offending spouse was relatively young at marriage so that infidelity appeared to be related to age at marriage rather than the age differences of the spouses.

Husband's Occupation

Various studies show that there is some relationship between family stability and occupational status. Weeks studied divorce rates by occupation and found that by dividing occupations into professional, proprietary, clerical, skilled, semiskilled, unskilled, and unemployed, there was a steady increase of the divorce rate from the professional to the unskilled. The unskilled showed a decreasing rate but it seems that if he had included separations, "the poor man's divorce," he would have found an increasing rate in this class also.[40] Ogburn studied census data and summarized the literature for information on divorce and separation. He concluded that higher education and larger incomes are associated with what he calls "more united families." [41] What elements produce greater unity in these families is not clear from his studies. On the other hand, Terman found that "the correlation of income with happiness scores is zero." [42]

It is evident that we must await the findings of further research before the relationship between occupational level and family stability is adequately understood. However, there is rather general agreement that family customs and attitudes differ considerably among the various socioeconomic classes. It may be assumed that these differences would be reflected in marital adjustment. Although occupational class is only one of the variables used in assigning social class membership, it is usually considered basic. Since the chancery records supply information only on the occupation of the husband, we have used that as the basis for our classification.

A seven-way breakdown of occupations has been used for classifying jobs as follows: (1) Dependents—no acceptable, regular employment; (2) Day laborers—jobs requiring no special training; (3) Semiskilled laborers—jobs requiring some training; (4) Skilled laborers—jobs requiring skill and experience; (5) Lower white-collar group—jobs not primarily manual but requiring moderate education and skill; (6) Upper white-collar group—jobs requiring considerable education, experience, and mental capacity; (7) Professional group—jobs requiring professional training.

Unfortunately, the occupational level of the total Catholic population from which the cases were drawn is not known so that the data presented in Table 23 must be accepted as primarily descriptive. The heaviest concentration of cases is

TABLE 23

DISTRIBUTION OF CASES ACCORDING TO OCCUPATIONAL CLASS OF HUSBAND

Occupational Class	*Percentage*
Dependent	1.0
Day labor	26.8
Semiskilled labor	24.0
Skilled labor	22.9
Lower white-collar group	15.3
Upper white-collar group	8.6
Professional group	1.2

found in the "day labor" category and there is a steady decrease through the rest of the groups. Approximately 75 per cent of the cases fall in the "blue collar" classes and only about 10 per cent can be classified as upper class. Although the distribution of cases according to occupation may not be representative of all American Catholics, with the exception of the relatively high percentage found in the "day labor" category, it probably represents the Catholic population of the area fairly well. As we have seen, the cases were drawn from an industrialized urban area containing large ethnic aggregates so that strong representation in the working classes was to be expected.

Number of Children Involved

Studies of divorce have generally paid particular attention to the number of children in the broken family. This interest developed not only out of concern for the welfare of the children, but because children were thought to be a unifying factor in the family. There can be little doubt that, in many cases, marital difficulties do not reach the divorce courts because of the desire of one or both the parents to keep the family intact for the sake of the children. This was probably more true of former times than at present, but it still is a powerful motive in the lives of many unhappy married couples.

On the other hand, there seem to be marriages that would have continued if it were not for the presence of children. The husband who deserts as soon as his wife becomes pregnant is not rare among the lower working classes. In mixed marriages, children can become a divisive rather than a unifying factor, since their religious education and training may be the occasion of disagreement between the spouses while at the same time offering an excellent opportunity for in-law interference.[43]

Previous Studies. Terman, Burgess and Cottrell, Bernard, Landis, and Locke found little or no relationship between the presence of children in the family and marital happiness and success.[44] Since all these studies with the exception of Locke's were based on samples including only married couples, some feel that their findings would have been different if divorced couples had been included.[45] Perhaps the opinion of most writers on this subject can best be summarized by saying that children are a unifying factor in most marriages, but that there are notable exceptions which must be taken into consideration. In the majority of cases the young couple look forward to having children. Normally, the maturing expansion made possible by the coming of children strengthens the marriage relationship.

Childless Marriage and Divorce. The proportion of divorced couples who are childless has long been a subject of comment in marriage literature. One of the earliest statistical studies of American divorce problems found that in 1928 more than 60 per cent of divorced couples had no minor children.[46] A careful study of the available divorce statistics by Jacobson showed that in 1948 the proportion of childless couples seeking divorce was approximately the same as in 1928.[47] The relative frequency of divorce varied inversely with the number of children under age 18 in the family. For childless couples, the divorce rate was 15.3 per 1,000 married couples; where there was one child, it was 11.6; two children, 7.6; three children, 6.5; and four or more children, 4.6.[48] Unfortunately, the best available data are far from complete so that these figures represent estimates obtained by piecing together whatever information could be obtained from various state and county records.

TABLE 24

DISTRIBUTION OF CASES ACCORDING TO NUMBER OF CHILDREN IN THE FAMILY

Number of Children	Percentage
No children	35.3
1 child	27.3
2 children	18.5
3 children	9.0
4 children	4.8
5 or more	5.1

Catholic Couples. The data presented in Table 24 are not restricted to the number of children under age 18 so that our findings are not wholly comparable to studies based on civil divorce court records. Approximately 35 per cent of the couples appearing before the chancery court reported no children in the family. Although allowance must be made for the lack of comparability between the studies, it would seem that Catholic couples seeking separation are less likely to be childless than couples having recourse to the civil courts. The fact that approximately 65 per cent of the cases reported one or more children indicates that a large number of children are involved in the tragedy of broken marriages among Catholics. In fact, about one out of every ten couples reported four or more children.

Duration of Broken Marriages

A survey of divorce statistics for the country shows that about two-fifths of all divorces and annulments are granted to couples married less than five years, and one-fourth to those married for from five to nine years.[49] In other words, about two-thirds of the divorces take place within the first ten years of marriage. The percentages presented in Table 25 show that

TABLE 25

DISTRIBUTION OF CASES ACCORDING TO THE DURATION OF THE MARRIAGE

Duration	Percentage
Less than 6 months	6.6
6 months to 11 months	7.1
1 year to 5 years	29.2
6 years to 10 years	22.4
11 years to 15 years	15.2
16 years to 20 years	9.7
21 years and over	9.8

our cases conform rather closely to the national pattern. Over 6 per cent separated within the first six months and another 7.1 per cent, before the end of the first year. Approximately 43 per cent broke down within the first five years of marriage and 65 per cent within the first ten years. Only about one out of each ten broke up after twenty years of marriage. It would be

reasonable to assume that causes of tension and conflict which
disintegrate a union very quickly would be different from
those which cause separation or divorce in later life. We shall
discuss this subject after we have dealt with the factors involved in the breakdown of marriage.

Source of the Petition for Separation

Since the law assumes that the "innocent" party is the only
one who has the right to petition for divorce, there has always
been considerable interest shown in whether the petitioner
for divorce was the wife or the husband. This assumption of
law that the petitioner must come into the court with "clean
hands" is no longer valid. In the civil courts, the wife is the
plaintiff in three out of every four cases, but there is no reason
to assume that the proportion of "innocence" and "guilt" in
marital maladjustment follows the same distribution. Since
the majority of divorce actions are uncontested, the frequency
with which the wife assumes the role of plaintiff may be explained by the belief that divorce is more readily granted to
the wife, the desire of the wife to secure support, or the attempt to protect the reputation of the wife and avoid a family
scandal.

In over four-fifths of the cases appearing before the chancery court, the wife was the plaintiff. Without going into the
ultimate causes of the maladjustment at this point, it is interesting to note the association between the partner who acts as
plaintiff and the alleged cause of the breakdown. In cases
where drinking, adultery, and mental cruelty were involved,
the petitioner was usually the wife. In most of the other cases,
there is a better distribution of husbands and wives as plain-
tiffs. In general, our data indicate that regardless of which
party may have acted as the principal agent in the breakdown,
it appears that the wife feels the greatest need to have her
changed marital status approved by the Church authorities.

GENERAL SUMMARY OF CHARACTERISTICS

The general characteristics of the cases appearing before the separation court can be summarized as follows. The national groups are not equally represented. Those of Irish and German descent make up about 50 per cent of the cases, a figure which seems to be out of proportion to their representation in the total Catholic population of the area. Considerable differences were discovered in the rate of ingroup marriage for the various national minorities. The Polish group manifested relatively little outgroup marriage, while those of German extraction displayed about the same percentage of outgroup as ingroup marriage. The Irish and Italian groups were midway between these two extremes with a ratio of about two to three for outgroup marriages. This same pattern was evident in the rate of mixed and convert marriages. These cases represented 25 per cent of the total, with the German and Polish group again at the extremes.

The length of acquaintance before marriage seemed to be shorter than desirable for optimum adjustment in marriage since 45 per cent of the cases were acquainted for only one year or less. As would be expected from this fact, the number of those who had no formal engagement or a very brief one was high. Approximately 50 per cent of the cases reported no engagement or one of less than three months.

The age at marriage of the group would seem to be somewhat lower than that demanded for optimum adjustment although it compared favorably with the general population. About 33 per cent of the husbands were 22 years or younger, and approximately 40 per cent of the wives were 20 years or under at marriage. The age differences of the spouses seemed to follow the general population pattern. However, there was some evidence of a relatively high percentage of those who were the same age.

The cases were drawn predominantly from the laboring classes. Only about 25 per cent were classified as "white-collar" workers. This information is valuable because most studies on marital adjustment have dealt primarily with the "white-collar" classes. The number of children in these families was relatively high. Only about 35 per cent were childless, and nearly 20 per cent had three or more children. Many of these marriages had endured for a long period. Nearly 60 per cent lasted for five years or more; however, approximately 14 per cent did not last one year. These cases were similar to those appearing before the civil divorce courts in that 80 per cent of the petitions were initiated by the wife.

CHAPTER EIGHT

The Disintegrating Factors

The search for causal factors underlying marital tension is no mere fad of the modern social scientist. Plutarch in his *Lives* reports the story of a Roman divorce in which the husband was being chided by his friends, saying: "Is she not discreet? Is she not beautiful? Is she not fruitful?" The Roman held out his shoe, saying: "Is this not handsome? Is it not new? But no one of you can tell me where it pinches my foot." And the wise Plutarch observes, "as a matter of fact, it is great and notorious faults that separate many wives from their husbands; but the slight and frequent frictions arising from some unpleasantness or incongruity of characters, unnoticed as they may be by everybody else, also produce incurable alienations in those whose lives are linked together." [1]

Only a bold spirit indeed would attempt to trace the intricate chain of causality leading to the breakdown of marriage in our modern complex society. When investigating maladjustment in the dynamic, emotion-loaded relationships which constitute marriage, the cautious scientist's retreat to the use of some noncommittal term such as "factor" rather than "cause" seems amply justified on grounds other than mere philosophical skepticism. Just as it is difficult to isolate and evaluate

211

the causality of the various elements which contribute to the building of a successful marriage, so too, the factors involved in the breakdown of marriage lend themselves to no facile analysis.

Perhaps the psychiatrist, working through the night like a patient Penelope, may succeed in unraveling the close-knit threads in the web of some one individual's life, but who would lightly assume the task when two or more lives are closely interwoven, and the threads have become hopelessly tangled? Surely, the prudent scholar will proceed with misgivings, and the honest, with qualifications. This warning is not an invitation to despair. On the contrary, considerable knowledge and insight have been gained concerning the factors leading to marital breakdown. The fact that it is often impossible to distinguish clearly between cause and effect in a dynamic, reciprocal relationship like marriage does not invalidate all analysis of the situation.

STUDY OF MALADJUSTMENT IN MARRIAGE

Marriage involves the human person in a unique set of relationships, and consequently the analysis of marital maladjustment necessarily presupposes a definition of the human person and the nature of the marriage state. Since there is limited agreement concerning both, studies of maladjustment in marriage frequently proceed on different premises and reach different conclusions. The result can only be confusion, particularly when the duly qualified statements of the researcher, stripped of their context and limitations, are purveyed to the public as scientific "facts." For this reason, it will be worthwhile to review some of the possible approaches to the problem before discussing our own findings on marital breakdown among Catholics.

Fulfillment of Requisite Roles

One may proceed by studying the individuals constituting the termini or poles of the relationship, and from a more or less a priori analysis of the various roles they must fulfill, possible areas of tension can be pointed out. For example, in marriage there is the intimate union of two complementary sexes fulfilling the role of husband and wife, father and mother. On the assumption that successful marriage is based on the mutually compatible function of the male and female in these various roles, one could predict that disagreement over definition of roles or the refusal of one of the partners to fulfill a required role would create a tension situation. Whether this situation would develop into serious marital trouble would depend upon the reaction of the mate.

Perhaps if we had a deeper understanding of human nature and a clearer knowledge of how personality develops, it would be possible by this method alone to uncover the roots of marital tension with relative ease. The approach could be developed in this way. First, from an analysis of human nature as developed in a given culture we could arrive at a fairly adequate concept of the requisites of marital success. This would enable us to define in some detail the roles of the sexes in marriage. Further, we might be able to establish a rank order of roles in a given culture ranging from roles which were absolutely essential for the continuance of the union down through those which were more or less auxiliary.

When faced with an actual case of marital maladjustment, the procedure would be as follows. Investigate the interrelationships, ascertain the role that is not being fulfilled, estimate the seriousness of the tension by the rank of the unfulfilled role, and then turn attention to the nonfunctioning party. Presupposing an adequate knowledge of how personality develops, one could find out why this individual is not carrying out the necessary role, and by proper manipulation and education, changes could be introduced which would remedy the situation.

This approach has some value. It rightly emphasizes the general requisite functions which must be fulfilled somehow if the marriage is to endure. Unfortunately, there are many limitations in such a method of discovering and dealing with marital tension. If man were a creature of instinct, it would be relatively easy to determine his roles in marriage. Any deviation would promote tension or frustration, and the work of discovering the cause of maladjustment would be a relatively simple task. But man is not a creature of instinct, he is a rational animal. Consequently, he is culture-laden, and, we might add, value-ridden. Instead of following set patterns of action, man has shown tremendous adaptability in satisfying his needs.

Not that human nature is totally malleable, as some would seem to assume, but from culture to culture, and even within the various strata of the same culture, man displays great variety in the way he satisfies his needs. Nowhere is this more manifest than in the relationship of the sexes. Although the elemental needs of the male and female are clearly determined by their nature, the fulfillment of these drives in the existential order admit of wide variation. There are limits, but the area within these limits gives free play to the extraordinary capacity for adaptation found in the rational animal. This all adds up to saying that in any given culture, the objective factors leading to marital tension are highly relative.

Natural Incompatibility

To be sure, it is not only what happens, but to whom it happens that is significant in marriage. However, analysis sometimes proceeds on the premise that some persons are simply incompatible by "nature." The term would seem to imply that through some stroke of bad luck, two people otherwise quite normal possessed traits which in combination proved markedly irreconcilable. If only they had married somebody else, all would have been well. The underlying assumption here is that some people "fit" or are compatible by nature and others are not. If the wrong types get mated there is bound to be trouble. Such a line of reasoning is mistaken not only in its premise of the natural compatibility of certain persons, but also in its neglect of the potential of adaptability which the rational creature is known to possess.

As Chesterton somewhat facetiously remarked, if divorces are to be granted because of incompatibility, then nobody will stay married since man and woman are by nature incompatible.[2] The point is that, in analyzing marriage breakdown, it is important to investigate not only the mutually inharmonious traits, for some of these will be present in every union between male and female, but also the potential of adaptability possessed by each of the partners. A factor which causes tension in one marriage seems to cause none in another.[3]

Elements of an Adequate Analysis

It follows that any worthwhile study of marriage problems must reveal awareness of the following points. First, tension in marriage is always to be viewed as bi-polar. There are always two or more persons involved; that is, either husband and wife, or parents and children. Tension should never be considered from only one person's point of view. There is action and reaction. As we have indicated, people are highly adaptable. Some readily adjust to inharmonious situations. Consequently, it is of supreme importance to investigate how all the parties involved in the situation have reacted to it.

Second, marital adjustment must be considered as a situation with a history. This implies something more than uncovering the past chain of events which have created the present tension. Many problems leading to marriage breakdown must be analyzed under several aspects, each with a history of its own. Under one aspect the problem may be viewed as a fairly autonomous episode with a beginning and history of its own. For example, in cases of infidelity it is relatively easy to trace through the steps leading up to the new love-interest. This gives us the pertinent circumstances and the rationalizations which accompanied the deviant action.

Next, we must consider the problem in the context of the marriage itself. At this point, a careful distinction should be made between two further aspects of the problem lest we fall into the subtle trap of treating the episode as a mere symptom. First, we may proceed on the assumption that the infidelity was occasioned by some dissatisfaction with the marriage. Our assumption may or may not be verified by subsequent investigation. At any rate, we would here be considering the symptomatic aspect of the episode. Second, we must consider the cumulative reaction of the spouses to the problem. This gives us the present state of the marriage. It is frequently forgotten that many episodes so modify marital relationships, the personalities of the spouses, and the social character of the family that their symptomatic character ceases to be meaningful. They have now become major causes of maladjustment in the marriage, and to treat them as mere symptoms of some underlying causal factor is to imply that marriage is a static affair.

Finally, two categories of maladjustment in marriage should be distinguished: those brought about by actions which are considered wholly antagonistic to the primary purposes of marriage as these purposes are defined in a given culture, and those arising from actions not defined as fatal to marital unity. When a tension situation of the first type arises, the interested parties immediately think of it in terms of separation or divorce. For example, adultery on the part of the wife creates a situation almost always considered in terms of separation or divorce. On the other hand, talkativeness, poor housekeeping, and so forth, are generally considered troublesome, and often present occasions for quarreling, but they are seldom thought of in terms of divorce.

The importance of this distinction will be apparent if we consider the wide range of adaptability in man. Historically, marriage mates have adapted themselves to many types of marital tension. Adjustment was possible because their culture defined for them what situations were to be endured or rejected in marriage, and they adapted themselves accordingly. Consequently, it is important to know how people classify tension situations in a given culture if we wish to understand marital conflict. Actions which are thought of immediately in terms of divorce do not motivate married people to make adjustments. On the other hand, situations not immediately identified with marital breakdown may be met with all the resources of adaptability present in the rational creature.

Failure to make this obvious distinction renders some studies of marital dissatisfaction of questionable value. Given the nature of male and female, it is evident that there will necessarily be found in any marriage a considerable number of tension-causing factors. This seems to be a law of social life. It follows from the very character of marriage as an intimate union of interacting personalities. To tabulate in long statistical sequences all the little frictions and tensions found in the normal happy marriage without attempting to distinguish those which strike at the very essence of the marital union as defined by the interested parties, seems to be much ado about nothing.

Uncovering the Basic Factors in the Breakdown

The attribution of causal significance to any one given factor in marital breakdown is admittedly difficult. By the time marriage partners have reached the point at which they decide to separate, a whole series of incidents in word and action have accumulated. These are often recited to the counselor with no attention to time, causal sequence, or relative importance. What is the real root of the trouble? At times, the couple themselves do not know. At times, even the experienced counselor is unable to discover the real source of disharmony and has to sum up his opinion of the case under the empty, cover-all of "incompatibility."

However, in most cases it is possible to get at the real sequence of events and uncover the basic factors in the maladjustment. In this connection it may be observed that there is a good deal of confusion in much of the current writing dealing with marriage breakdown. Many flippantly dismiss such factors as drinking and adultery as "symptoms" and seek for "causal" factors either solely in the marriage itself or in the depths of the individual's personality. This approach appears quite scientific and sophisticated although in reality it is superficial and may lead to mere nominalism. In the first place, factors such as drink and adultery are not always symptoms of dissatisfaction with marriage. Circumstances and factors extrinsic to the marriage frequently play an important role in their incidence. Further, given the confusion in which social psychology finds itself today, it must be evident that the

"causal" factors advanced to explain the "symptoms" will only
be a reflection of the particular theory which the writer happens to hold concerning the development of personality. Since
there are many conflicting theories, there will be many "explanations" of marital failure.

As we have indicated, the symptomatic character of factors
such as drinking and adultery is only one of the aspects which
must be considered. When these factors make their appearance
in marriage, they tend to operate as relatively autonomous
causes in the breakdown. Individuals may have an "affair" or
start drinking for any one of a number of reasons, but once
they do, a chain reaction is usually started which creates an
entirely new situation. The whole intricate web of marital
and parental relationships undergoes modification. Unless this
process is arrested or reversed, the resulting situation will further motivate and promote the deviant action of the offender
and the disintegrating reaction of the spouse. It is this process
which must be understood if we would uncover the operative
factors in the breakdown.

Briefly, this is our position on the assignment of basic factors in marriage breakdown. We ask what factor started the
chain of events which led to the disintegration of a union presumably founded on love between two people who were more
or less compatible in the beginning. To be specific, we have
considered drink as a basic factor in marriage breakdown in all
those cases in which the partner's drinking pattern was modifying personal, family, and social relationships. In some cases
drinking was alleged together with several other factors, but
it was obvious that the partner's drinking had not modified
basic family relationships. Only in such cases can it be considered a mere symptom and not a basic factor in the breakdown. Why do people drink? Mankind has been looking for
the answer to that question for a long time, but one fact seems
quite well established; the habit of drinking is not due to
specifically marital frustrations in the majority of cases.[4] Perhaps it is most meaningful to say that the use of alcohol is a
readily available, socially acceptable, and convenient "crutch"
or "escape" for individuals in all walks of life.

FACTORS IN THE BREAKDOWN

In analyzing broken marriages, it is helpful to set apart for separate treatment certain categories which contain cases characterized by obviously atypical features. Hence, we have divided the couples appearing before the chancery separation court into two broad, generic groupings. The first includes all those marriages which were entered into under apparently normal conditions. This group represents approximately 80 per cent of the cases. The second group contains all those marriages which were contracted under circumstances seemingly more or less unpropitious to success. Here are placed "war marriages," marriages in which the bride was pregnant at marriage (forced marriages), marriages in which offspring were absolutely excluded from the beginning by one or both parties, and marriages of widows and/or widowers.

This preliminary grouping of cases into two categories is based on the hypothesis that the attribution of certain causal factors to marital disintegration is meaningful only to the extent that the peculiar circumstances identifying various "types" of marriage are taken into consideration. This is to say, such factors as adultery, desertion, drinking, and incompatibility have quite different significance as they occur in war marriages, marriages in which the bride was pregnant, and marriages in which children were excluded from the start. It is maintained that the peculiar nature of such marriages renders them singularly unstable; in fact, they carry in themselves from the very beginning, predisposing elements of instability. For this reason, it is held they should be studied apart from those marriages in which, to all appearances, the union is entered into fully, seriously, and under circumstances which make the endurance of family life both possible and likely.

In the remainder of this chapter we shall analyze the marriage cases which have been placed in the first group. These cases represent what we consider to be the typical maladjusted Catholic marriage. The marriages placed in the second group will be studied in a subsequent chapter.

Table 26 presents an over-all picture of the disintegrating

TABLE 26

DISTRIBUTION OF CASES ACCORDING TO FACTORS INVOLVED IN
THE BREAKDOWN OF MARRIAGE

Factor	Percentage
Drink	29.8
Adultery	24.8
Irresponsibility	12.4
Temperaments	12.1
In-laws	7.2
Sex	5.4
Mental	3.0
Religion	2.9
Money	.8
Unclassified	1.7

factors appearing in the typical cases having recourse to the chancery separation court. The importance of drink and adultery as disintegrating factors is readily apparent. Together they account for almost 55 per cent of the cases. Further, the first four categories listed include nearly 80 per cent of all the cases studied. We shall describe each category at some length and then present the general characteristics of the broken marriages which were found in each so that the real significance of each factor may be grasped. Our purpose here is to let the reader face marital tension as it actually appears in marriage. Whether one wholly agrees with the system of classification is not too relevant. What is important is to visualize some of the real problems the average marriage counselor must deal with in practice.

Drink

Drinking accounts for 29.8 per cent of the cases. The term *drink* is used here to cover those cases in which drinking appeared as the major factor in the maladjustment. Drinking as such never appears alone in marriage breakdown. The excessive use of alcohol bears in its train serious consequences for the family. To be specific, alcohol in any form costs money. It is not surprising, therefore, to find that drinking and nonsupport account for 37 per cent of the cases in this category. Further, drinking often leads to physical cruelty and abuse. At times, not only the wife but also the children are made to suffer physically. One of every three cases in this category alleged drink and abuse as the main factor in the disintegration of the family. Another result of drinking is the association with doubtful characters of the opposite sex leading to the presumption of adultery. Nearly one out of every five cases presented this pattern. In only a few cases was the wife guilty of excessive drinking.

It appears from the data that a large percentage of these cases could not be classified as "alcoholics." Rather, they were periodic drinkers or "weekenders" holding fairly steady jobs. Many of them spent much of their after-work leisure in taverns with the "boys"; others seemed to assume that they had an inalienable right to a Saturday night "drunk" after a week of work. In a few cases, home conditions were such that the husband remained away as long as possible and eventually fell into the habit of drinking with the gang.

The cases included in this category of drink presented some interesting characteristic differences. As we would expect from other studies, national patterns were in evidence with the Irish and Poles well represented. Classified according to occupation, the "blue-shirt" classes furnished proportionately more cases than did the "white-collar" classes. However, the problem of drink affected the various classes in different ways. The lower occupational classes showed relatively high percentages where drink was accompanied by nonsupport and abuse, while drink and infidelity was higher in the upper classes. The number of children found in these families is higher than in any other category. In fact, only 19 per cent of the cases were childless, while approximately 36 per cent of the two- and three-child families, 54 per cent of the four-child families, and 42 per cent of the five-or-more-child families in the entire study were found in this category.

Adultery

According to Table 26, adultery is the second most common factor precipitating family dissolution. It appears in nearly one out of every four cases. The husband is the transgressor in four of every five cases. From the point of view of the analyst, cases involving infidelity present a difficult problem. In the first place, it is not always possible to interview both parties. The offending partner frequently refuses to appear since he may have no desire for reconciliation. Even when both parties are present it is difficult to cut through the mutual recriminations in order to get at the essential facts in the case.

Although this is true, it should be pointed out that the present tendency to look upon adultery as a mere symptom of frustration in marriage appears somewhat superficial. To be sure, there are cases in which infidelity follows an unhappy marital experience. There are cases of the "innocent" partner refusing marital rights or contributing little in the way of companionship. On the other hand, in many cases this hypothesis simply does not square with the facts.

It is time that this unrealistic causal analysis of infidelity be abandoned. We must face the fact that some individuals are unstable and easily tempted; others, either because of past patterns of conduct or present circumstances, find monogamy both trying and monotonous. Given the manifold opportunities for infidelity offered in contemporary society, such individuals easily get involved in extramarital affairs. Of course, such persons tend to rationalize their position. In adopting a line of action not sanctioned by their religion or by society, they find it necessary to project the blame onto their spouses.

The cases included in this category present some distinctive characteristics. As in the marriages affected by drink, national differences are apparent here. The incidence of infidelity is relatively low among Polish males, Italians of both sexes, and Irish females. Divided according to occupations, the "white-collar" classes contributed relatively high percentages. In general, the birthrate was high and the unions endured for a considerable time indicating that these marriages appeared to have made a fair initial adjustment. Age at marriage appeared as a significant factor. When the husband was the offender, the highest relative percentages occurred in those cases in which he was under 25 years at marriage. When the wife was the offender, the rate of infidelity decreased in direct relation to her age at marriage. Of course, it is difficult to determine the real significance of the factor of age in this category since it is obvious that in our society the opportunities for infidelity decrease somewhat with age.

Irresponsibility

The third largest category, accounting for approximately one out of every eight broken marriages, includes couples classified as irresponsible or immature. All cases in which one or both partners displayed a complete unwillingness to accept the responsibilities of marriage as they are defined by the Church and the standards of our society were placed under this heading. Unfortunately, the data for some of these cases are not very revealing. This is particularly true for those cases in which the husband has escaped his responsibilities by deserting. Many of these individuals had a history of periodic desertion before the final break. Of course, there was question of nonsupport in all such cases, and it is probable that the desertion was primarily an attempt to escape further family obligations in this regard. These cases of desertion, however, represent only a small proportion of the marriages included under this heading.

Many of the cases appeared poorly adjusted to all of life's problems, often displaying a childish refusal to face reality. For many, the fact that they had entered marriage seemed to indicate little more than that they could cohabit without scandal or fear of the law. At times, neither partner accepted any new obligations or duties because of the marriage. There were cases here where the wife was "dating" others two weeks after the wedding ceremony. In some, the husband still spent most of his nonworking hours with the "boys" at the tavern or pool hall. Most of the marriages occurred at a relatively early age. There were many one-child families but few large ones. A high percentage of cases was found in the unskilled class, suggesting that further investigation would reveal irresponsibility reflected in other activities.

The traits we encounter in these cases are often character-

ized as immaturity, and they are clearly indicative of that, but
the use of this term can lead to considerable confusion and
misunderstanding. It would be well to ask: What constitutes
maturity? As the term immaturity is popularly used, it would
signify little more than youth and inexperience. This would be
something quite different from the spirit of irresponsibility
which characterized the cases placed in this category. A couple
might well be young and inexperienced and even a little naive
about some of the realities of life but still make an excellent
adjustment in marriage as long as they were willing to accept
responsibilities and attempted to adapt themselves to changing circumstances.

The individuals falling into the present category were not
merely young or inexperienced; rather they displayed a peculiar, selfish disregard for the rights of others. They did this,
seemingly, not so much out of malice as out of mere intellectual and moral shallowness. They were children in the sense
that they were never "socialized." They seem never to have
learned that as social beings their actions affected others. They
ignored the fact that as members of society they were responsible for the consequences of their actions. It would be of great
interest to learn something of their family backgrounds. Are
we dealing here with basic personality defects? Are these the
products of poor family training? Or are these the victim-
products of our complex civilization, the refuse of our "sensate
culture," what Marx once characterized as that useless mass,
the *lumpen Proletariat?*

Unfortunately, the data throw little light on the true nature
of these cases. All the marriage counselor uncovers, as a rule,
is the irresponsible personality. When the case appears it is a
simple matter to learn the apparent reason for the breakdown
of the marriage: the husband gambles, he doesn't come home
from work until late at night, he spends all his time with the
"boys," he goes away for days at a time; or, the wife runs to
the tavern, she is a hopeless housekeeper, she wants a "good
time" without responsibilities. These are the reasons and they
are apparently valid, but neither the case records nor the available literature on the subject tells us how people "get that
way."

Clash of Temperaments

The fourth largest category includes all those cases where a clash of temperaments had occurred in the marriage. This group represented a little over 12 per cent or almost one out of every eight cases. The term usually employed to characterize these couples is incompatibility, but this designation of maladjustment has been used so loosely by the civil courts that it has lost all meaning other than a convenient cloak for obvious collusion. Strangely enough, a clash of temperaments frequently occurs in marriages characterized by traits which would have led us to expect fairly satisfactory adjustment. The members of this group are not irresponsible and seem well adjusted in society. They do not commit actions which render them markedly odious to the married partner. The essential roles of support and sexual companionship seem to have been adequately fulfilled. Nevertheless, the partners find it impossible to get along together.

These are generally puzzling cases. There are a number of conflicts mentioned, it is true, but none of them taken separately seems sufficient to explain the breakdown. In many cases there appeared little basis for the frequent quarrels which occurred, and the couple admitted this. In other cases, it appeared that the couple had grown apart rather than together with the lapse of time. In some cases, this disunity had not been noticed when the children occupied most of the wife's time; but as they grew up and she was forced to seek greater companionship with her spouse, it was discovered that their former intimacy no longer existed. They had managed without each other for so long that now when they needed each other most, one of them found the intimacy intolerable.

The clash of temperaments revealed in these cases manifested itself in a great variety of ways so that a degree of arbitrariness is necessarily present in placing them all under one heading. Accusations of jealousy, "mental" cruelty, "queerness," neglect, selfishness, meanness, of being "hard to live with," are clearly relative and signify quite different things to different individuals. This became evident when positive mani-

festations were cited. It would seem that the basis of the conflict should be placed in the frustration of some latent expectation arising either from the union or from life itself.

A consideration of the general characteristics of this group
reveals that a marked disparity in age may have played some
role in the maladjustment. About 30 per cent of the husbands
were six or more years older than their wives. The skilled and
lower-class white-collar occupational groups supplied relatively
high percentages in this category. The birth rate was relatively high, and the unions continued for some time, indicating that the differences in temperament may not have been
apparent at first and may have arisen from some frustration
arising later. After all, mere differences in temperament or
character traits need not lead to conflict. Adjustment and adaptation are required in every marriage since the sexes have
undergone different cultural conditioning and possess diverse
constitutional components. Conflict arises only when the couple refuse, or are no longer capable of making, the routine
adjustments required by cohabitation.

Although none of the remaining categories accounts for as
much as 10 per cent of the cases, several of them figure prominently in the popular thinking and writing about marriage
breakdown. Most of these categories can be handled rather
briefly but because of the general interest in the subject, special treatment will be given to cases involving in-law problems.

Sexual Incompatibility

Under the heading of sexual problems have been placed
only those cases in which marital relations were rendered almost impossible by the refusal or incapacity of one of the
partners. Although there is little doubt that the failure to
achieve good sexual adjustment can and does lead to a great
deal of frustration in married life, this failure does not appear
as a direct common cause for the dissolution of the marriages
studied here. The prevalent assumption that sexual incompatibility lies at the root of most marital difficulties is a classic
example of putting the cart before the horse. From the inti-

mate nature of the sexual act, it is only to be expected that difficulties arising from other factors will ultimately be reflected in this relationship. The implicit assumption that the human race, or at least, Western man, had to wait until the middle of the twentieth century to be taught the "right" sexual techniques strikes the writer as somewhat preposterous.[5]

Just what part the failure to achieve satisfactory sexual adjustment may play in the series of causes leading to marital disintegration is open to debate. The distinction between cause and effect is particularly difficult to make in such cases. At any rate, the majority of couples appearing before the chancery court did not recognize sexual incompatibility as an important factor in their maladjustment. Hence, the factor of sex appeared as a disturbing element only in the nearly complete absence of all sexual relations.

The failure to have marital relations in some cases was owing to the physical incapacity of one of the parties. In the majority of cases, however, at least when the wife seemed to be at fault, failure to have relations resulted from her downright refusal. In some instances she alleged frigidity; in others, however, it appeared that she had entered marriage for security or some other motive and had no intention of engaging in actions which might entail future burdens. Perversion and sex crimes were the charges most often leveled against the husband. In many cases these charges were backed up by giving proof of arrest for violation of morals. As a rule, these marriages broke up very quickly. About 75 per cent were childless. It would seem that selfishness precluding any consideration for the partner was the basis for much of the difficulty on the part of the wife. The failure of the husband could be traced to serious defects of character in most instances.

Religious Differences

Religion as a factor in the breakdown of marriage was surprisingly rare although 17 per cent of the cases involved mixed marriages. As we have seen in the chapter on mixed marriages, the unstabilizing effect of such unions does not appear in direct quarrels over religion but in more subtle ways which disclose basic disagreement over the nature and purposes of marriage itself. For the cases reporting religion as a major factor in maladjustment, the conflict appeared in two major areas: the education of the children and the refusal of freedom to practice religion.

The first area will obviously be one of frequent conflict in mixed unions where children exist. The Catholic parent has the obligation to educate all the children in the Catholic faith and at marriage the non-Catholic party signs a promise agreeing to this. However, when children arrive it is possible for the non-Catholic party to deny the validity of the promises made at marriage and to refuse consent to the baptism and Catholic training of the children. Where the Catholic partner remains firm, breakup of the family may result.

The second area of conflict, namely, the refusal of freedom to practice religion, seems to occur only in cases where the non-Catholic party nurses quasi-fanaticism. In such cases the Catholic party is presented with the alternative of relinquishing the practice of religion or breaking up the marriage. An analysis of this "fanaticism" frequently revealed that the point at issue was not so much the external practice of religion as the system of values nurtured by this practice. For example, the refusal of one of the partners through religious convictions to consent to the use of contraceptives was found to have aroused a hatred of the religion which promoted this conviction.

The national group including the highest percentage of mixed and convert marriages also revealed the highest percentage in this category. This was the German group which accounted for 45 per cent of the cases. Eighty per cent of these unions involved mixed marriages and about 15 per cent, convert marriages. The data on length of acquaintance indicated some hasty marriages since 30 per cent were married after an acquaintance of six months or less. The age at marriage showed fewer than the average early marriages for both husband and wife. The age differences were normal. The occupational class most affected was the lower white-collar group. There were relatively few children involved in these marriages. One-third were childless, 50 per cent had one child, and there were no large families. In point of duration, these cases broke up a little sooner than the general average, approximately 18 per cent within the first year, 47 per cent in the first five years, and an additional one-third in the next five years.

Mental Illness

The category of mental illness includes all those cases in which one of the parties had been institutionalized or judged mentally ill by a competent psychiatrist. Our data are not sufficient to establish any classification of the types manifested. In general, the motive for seeking a separation was fear of physical violence and the desire for security. The general characteristics of this group indicated stability. There were relatively few marriages after a brief acquaintance, and more than the average were engaged before marriage. The data on age of husband at marriage showed that over 30 per cent were thirty years or more at marriage, and very few were under 22 years. The age of the wife revealed the same tendency to late marriage. Indeed, a very high percentage were 27 years or over at marriage. The age differences were less marked than for the general average. The lower white-collar occupational class produced almost double the expected percentage of these cases. As a rule, the trouble was manifested rather late in the marriage. Only one-third broke up in the first five years, and 50 per cent endured for ten years or more. Over 30 per cent of these families had three or more children.

Money

Disagreement over the use of money was found to assume demoralizing proportions in few Catholic marriages. In less than one case out of a hundred did such disagreement lead to major marital conflict. Because "money" is so frequently cited as a major factor in marriage breakdown, a clear definition of terms is called for. In the present study, the term "money" is used to cover only those cases in which conflict arose over the use of money, that is, concerning either its investment or the way it was to be spent by the partners.

It appears that those who cite money as a major cause of breakdown use the term to cover nonsupport. It is obvious that if a husband refuses to support his wife, there will be quarrels over money, but it seems rather meaningless to classify this as anything but nonsupport. Consequently, many cases which have been classified under drink, adultery, and irresponsibility in the present study might have been loosely assigned by others to the general category of money. Although the cases falling under the heading of money are too few to justify detailed analysis, the present study has made some contribution to the clarification of terms.

In-Laws

Finally, the problem of in-laws has been reserved for more detailed treatment because of the broad interest this topic generally arouses in popular discussions of marital adjustment. What would happen to some after-dinner speakers and cartoonists if a form of marriage were devised to do away with in-laws? The mother-in-law theme, in particular, provides an inexhaustible source of humor. Of course, there is a more sombre side to the picture. In-laws (and again the mother-in-law leads the field) are accused of driving untold numbers to drink, desertion, and despair. At times, this approach takes on the character of a vitriolic attack against the whole female "species," as in Wylie's *Generation of Vipers.* Again, as in Strecker's *Their Mothers' Sons,* "moms" who refuse to cut the "golden cord" are made accountable for the high incidence of neuroses in the armed services and marriage. Fact or fiction, the in-law theme, like the weather, is a recurrent topic of conversation.

Previous Studies. Students of the problem are in virtual agreement that in-law adjustment constitutes one of the most persistent problems encountered by young couples in achieving marital happiness. For example, in a study of 409 couples who had been married an average of twenty years, women mentioned in-law relationships second, and men, third among six areas calling for adjustment in marriage. In another study of 544 couples in the early years of marriage, in-law relationships were given first place in the list of difficult areas requiring adjustment.[6] The relatively high rate of incidence, however, offers no gauge of the problem's seriousness. Most cases in these two studies characterized themselves as happily married. In general, most studies indicate that in-law adjustment is a problem of early marriage; it is occasioned most frequently by the wife's family; it involves the mother-in-law more often than other members of the respective families; and successful adjustment in this area is closely related to happiness in marriage.[7]

The Problem in Focus. Before presenting our findings on this question, a few preliminary observations are in order. First, for the average happily married couple, in-laws are not "problems." On the contrary, they are normally looked upon with esteem and affection. Of course, in the early months of marriage, while both parents and newlyweds are getting used to their new roles, mutual adjustments will be required.

Second, when in-law problems do arise, one must not make the a priori assumption that the in-laws are the cause of the conflict situation. There seems to be a general tendency to blame them in all cases. This is an uncritical assumption not squaring with facts. Frequently, immaturity or the past experience of one of the spouses with their own family renders them inimical to all in-law contacts.

Third, the in-law problem is complex in its nature and its origin. It may arise out of the very situation. For example, living with the parents after marriage or having a parent in the home can give rise to problems frequently solved only by a change in the situation. Over-identification with one's parental family, frequent in early marriage, may cause resentment. Religious, cultural, ethnic, or social class differences, especially if they are accompanied by latent nonacceptance of the "outsider," may give rise to tensions and antagonism coloring all in-law relationships.

Fourth, the incidence of in-law conflicts in a given culture is no indication of the control of the extended family or of the

amount of their "interference." In many cultures the control
and consequent "interference" of the extended family is persistent and extensive, but there are few in-law "problems" because young couples have been reared to accept this patterning of family relationships. In an industrialized urban culture,
however, the nuclear family (composed of husband, wife, and
immature offspring) is supposed to form a relatively autonomous unit brooking no interference and maintaining a husband-
wife "companionship" ideal which appears extremely chary of
even emotional attachment to the extended family group.
Under such circumstances, opportunity for conflict, particularly from the side of the overpossessive parent or the immature newlywed, can be expected to be prevalent.

The Extent of the In-law Problem. The question is frequently asked: Do in-laws break up many marriages? The
usual answer is: Not if the couple are fairly secure in each
other's affections and are mature enough to discuss their families objectively. Of course, this is not really an answer, since
we would like to know how often situations arise in which
failure to work out satisfactory relations with in-laws leads to
breakdown of marriage. On the basis of the present study it
can be stated that at least among Catholics, such failure occurs
in less than 10 per cent of marriages which end in separation.
It appears, therefore, that when it occurs, the problem of
in-laws, like that of money, may lead to considerable tension
and may call for extensive adjustment by one or both spouses,
but it is usually resolved short of marital breakdown.

In order to uncover all possible manifestations of unsatisfac-
tory in-law relationships, the following analysis includes all
those cases appearing before the chancery court in which in-
law problems figure more or less prominently. In slightly less
than 50 per cent of these cases, failure to resolve the problem
appeared as the primary factor in the breakdown. In the remaining cases other unstabilizing factors were present together
with the in-law problem so that it was impossible to judge
what role the latter had played in causing the marriage to
disintegrate.[8]

It might be well to note here that when dealing with marriage cases in which in-law interference is alleged by one of

the parties, every effort must be made to ascertain at what stage of marital conflict the alleged in-law interference occurred. Very frequently, in-laws are obliged to step in and protect their blood relative from abuse and mistreatment. The offending party, through a later rationalization of his conduct, will insist that all would have been well had in-laws not "interfered." This process of "telescoping" cause and effect occurs in most personalized accounts of marriage problems. Once a couple start to weave the tangled threads of discord into the web of their lives, the entire pattern of their relationships takes on a different design. Where did the trouble start? One must have the patience of Job to unweave the snarl. At times relationships have reached such an impasse that the only solution is to declare a moratorium and have the couple make a fresh start.

General Description of the Couples. The in-law cases revealed some interesting traits which merit further consideration. The most striking feature to be noted is that the in-law problem was characterized by national differences. It involved those of Polish and Italian descent proportionately oftener than others and at about the same rate for ingroup and outgroup marriages. For example, although a husband of Polish descent was involved in only 13.8 per cent of the total group of broken marriages, he was involved in 20.3 per cent of the cases experiencing in-law trouble. Likewise, a wife of Polish descent was involved in only 16.9 per cent of the total group but in 23.9 per cent of the present cases. This characteristic was somewhat less marked in those of Italian descent, the percentages being 10.9 compared to 13.1 for the husbands, and 10.8 compared to 14.1 for the wives. These national differences can be explained in terms of different family systems. Traditionally, the Poles and Italians have cherished an extended family system so that the modern trend toward the nuclear type, completely autonomous and self-sufficient, creates special problems of adjustment.

Length of acquaintance and engagement, age at marriage and age difference characteristics of the in-law group presented few marked deviations, and all differences from the total group ran in the direction of greater marriage stability, if we are to credit the findings of marriage-prediction experts. For example, 40.1 per cent were acquainted for three years or more before marriage as compared to 36.1 per cent of the total group; only 29.7 per cent married without an engagement period compared to 35.6; only 7.2 per cent of the husbands were under twenty-one at marriage as compared to 13.0; and 55 were thirty years or over as compared to 45.1 per cent; 34.2 per cent of the wives were under twenty-one at marriage as compared to 39.6; and only 6.8 per cent of the wives were older than their husbands as compared with 11.4 per cent of the total group.

The white-collar classes were somewhat more affected by the in-law problem than were the working classes. Although they were only 25.1 per cent of the total group, they contained 29.3 per cent of the in-law group. This finding is unexpected inasmuch as the necessity of "living in" with the parental family would seem more common among the working classes. Actually, it was found that the problem of "living in" accounted for only 9.5 per cent of the cases with in-law difficulties. Where it did occur, however, it was among members of the working classes in two out of three cases.

The in-law group differed most widely from the total group in the two closely connected characteristics of number of children in the family and duration of marriage. Approximately 42 per cent of the in-law cases were childless, 37.4 had one child, and only 8.5 had three or more children. The comparable percentages for the total group were 35.3, 27.3, and 18.9 per cent, respectively. The data on duration of marriage give even more convincing evidence that the in-law problem occurs very early in marriage. Approximately 24 per cent of these marriages broke up within the first year, 64.4 per cent within the first five years, and only 15.8 per cent endured ten years or more. The comparable percentages for the total group were 13.7, 42.9, and 33.9, respectively. These figures speak for themselves. When there is an in-law problem, some acceptable adjustment is worked out early in marriage, or the partnership fails.

Who Interferes with Whom? Perhaps the most disputed question in this whole in-law situation is who causes the trouble. Popular belief assumes that the mother-in-law is generally the troublemaker. Landis, in the study previously mentioned, states that of 116 husbands and 160 wives reporting various in-law relationships causing friction in their marriages, 42 per cent of the husbands and 50 per cent of the wives claimed it was the mother-in-law. Our findings do not picture the mother-in-law quite so unfavorably. She appears as the sole in-law factor in 38.7 per cent of the cases; in the remainder, two or more in-laws are involved in the situation.

An additional disputed point is whether the families of husband or wife figure more prominantly in in-law problems. It is generally maintained that in-law friction is a feminine pattern because mother-in-law, sisters-in-law, and wives are involved more frequently than are males. Our findings lend some support to this hypothesis. The wife's in-laws figure in 47.7 per cent of the cases; the husband's, in 38.3 per cent; and in-laws from both sides, in 14.0 per cent.

This breakdown of cases enables us to take another look at the mother-in-law situation. Of all the cases involving the wife's relatives, her mother was featured as the sole factor 44.3 per cent of the times; in those involving the husband's relatives, his mother appeared as the sole factor in 45.9 per cent.[9] However, if we consider only the cases involving the mother-in-law, we find that the wife's mother appeared in 54.6 per cent of the cases. This figure follows from the fact, as we have indicated, that a higher percentage of the wife's relatives were involved in the total number of cases.

It has been suggested that a description of the persons involved in in-law problems does not establish the direction of the cause-and-effect relationship. In itself it does little more than outline the active agents, the two polar points of conflict. Such information will scarcely satisfy those whose censorious proclivities compel the assignment of guilt in all cases. It must be recalled that in-law problems arise as conflict or tension situations between two or more people. This situation becomes a marriage problem only to the extent that both marriage partners are involved. For example, in the typical mother-in-law problem situation, "mom" is a menace only to the extent that she controls her offspring or, stated in another way, only to the extent that her offspring immaturely values the parental bond more than the marriage bond. It is precisely the inability of one or both marriage partners to stand on their own feet that makes in-law interference effective.

Of course, this is only stating the obvious. Realism impels one to point out that competition between the long-standing parental bond and the newly formed marriage bond can create tension. Through the manipulation of unscrupulous, selfish, or well-intentioned but domineering parents, this tension can grow until it leads to breakdown of the marriage. Further, where a pattern of overdependence on the parent has been maintained up to marriage, there is every danger that it will continue. Unless there is understanding and cooperation between parents and the "outside" partner in these cases, serious trouble may arise. Sometimes the wedding sets the stage for a long overdue weaning process, but it is well to remember that the weaning process, whether in infancy or later in life, is successful only if the parent takes the initiative.

Some Typical In-Law Situations. It may prove helpful to review briefly a few of the typical situations in which in-law conflicts arise. As we have indicated, the much-discussed case of newlyweds living in with parents does not generally lead to the breakdown of the marriage. It does create considerable tension, if for no other reason than that modern urban dwellings do not have sufficient space for two families. Tension can also be increased by the very proximity of the two households. On the other hand, the situation is generally recognized to be temporary or, at least, modifiable, so that the couple frequently chooses to move as an alternative to continued conflict.

A more serious and difficult situation may arise when one of the parents lives in with newlyweds. Difference in age often leads to difference in outlook and customs. However, among normally mature people the situation, while not always mutually satisfactory, is generally manageable.

Real trouble occurs in those cases in which the parent (generally the mother) resents the loss of the economic and/or emotional support of her child through marriage. In this situation, experience shows that such women can be utterly ruthless, stopping at nothing to regain monopoly over their child. Subtle remarks, innuendo, persistent criticism, false accusations, feigned sickness, tears, and assuming a martyr's role are the chief techniques they employ to achieve their ends. Frequently the only solution lies in breaking up the unhappy threesome. In practice, this involves making a choice between parent and marriage partner—unfortunately, the parent does not always lose.

There is also the phenomenon of "momism" of which Wylie and Strecker have written. This can be a mother-daughter or a mother-son combination and is equally disruptive of marriage in either case. Actually, the daughter or son reared in such circumstances is incapable of mature marriage relationships. Dependence is so deeply interwoven into their personality from childhood that they are lost without "mom." Obviously, they should never have married, but in the ordinary course of events they do. Not only are they incapable of fulfilling their partnership role in marriage, but "mom" has no intention of losing her child through marriage. When the husband is involved, case histories reveal a pattern of nonsupport, infidelity, irresponsibility, and frequent desertion back to "mom." The mother-daughter combination generally ends with the females taking a stand against all males. When the marriage counselor gets the case he learns that the husband is "oversexed," a "beast," a "drunkard," and so forth.

At times, in-law problems arise because of immaturity in one or both marriage partners. When both are immature, in-laws from both families tend to become involved. The marriage remains unstable, since it never has become an adequately autonomous unit, with the result that major decisions are frequently made by the in-laws, and necessary adjustments are avoided by having recourse to overhelpful parents. Immature partners tend either to exaggerate or to minimize the significance of the marriage bond. That is, some childishly resent their spouse's customary and normal affection for parents and are unduly upset if in-laws attempt to counsel or assist. On the other hand, some seem to forget that marriage implies the establishment of a new social unit, and they merely strive to integrate their partner into their parental family group. If these attitudes are stubbornly retained, real marriage conflict can follow.

Finally, there is the situation of nonacceptance by the parental group. This nonacceptance can be based on religious, national, cultural, or social class differences. Even when clearly recognized and foreseen, these differences create tension in marriage—although they constitute no basic threat to stability if the partners are mature. Further, it is usual for nonacceptance to disappear when the parents see the couple enjoying real happiness.

This treatment of the in-law problem has by its very nature emphasized the "outlaw" aspects of in-law relationships.[10] It would be misleading and unrealistic to dismiss this topic without pointing out that most in-law relationships are maintained with a minimum of friction on both sides. For every marriage breaking up through in-law "interference," one could easily point out many saved by parental aid. The nuclear family is no social ideal. Kinship bonds are prime realities which can be ignored only at the expense of a stable family system. That they should be exploited by the selfish or prove harmful to the immature surely constitutes no grounds for their neglect. People implicitly recognize this truth. To be sure, they may joke about some in-law situations, but the general tendency of mature marriage partners is to respect the kinship bonds of their mates even when they find it difficult to understand them.

SUMMARY

It may be helpful at this point to summarize briefly our findings on the factors which have entered into the breakdown of the typical cases appearing before the chancery separation court. Approximately 55 per cent of these marriages broke up because of drink or adultery. These two factors manifest the spouse's failure to fulfil one or both of the two major roles of marriage partner, namely, that of bread winner and sexual companion. The data show that most of these marriages were not contracted lightly and thoughtlessly nor did they disintegrate readily. In other words, the union was taken seriously, and there seems to have been an earnest effort to make it succeed. Failure was admitted only when, through the refusal of one of the spouses to fulfil an essential marital role, the marriage lost all semblance of a real union and deteriorated to a mere external form or became an instrument of physical and moral harm to the partner and the children.

Although the evil effects of drink are readily obvious, nevertheless, this failure does not necessarily strike at the affectional bonds which constitute the very meaning of the union for the partners. Hence, considerable toleration and endurance were often displayed by the nonoffending party as is evident from the data on the number of children and the duration of marriage. From the information gathered in this study, we are forced to conclude that in the majority of cases the problem of drink is not one which arises specifically from the marital union. Rather, it would seem to be a product compounded of national and cultural differences and the present industrial civilization.

In regard to Catholic marriages, however, this much is clear; the present trend toward greater equality and independence for women, implying as it does a weakening of the foundations upon which the prerogatives of male dominance in the marriage institution were based, has caused many wives to be less tolerant and less long-suffering than formerly. It is possible that the relatively high percentage of marriages which break up because of drink is as indicative of this trend as it is of any change in the drinking habits of the average husband. It seems scarcely necessary to add that this phenomenon of drink in the modern world requires a great deal of research as a problem in its own right.

The problem of adultery is clearly one associated with the institution of marriage. Both from tradition and religious teaching, the average Catholic is trained to look upon this as the act *par excellence* which destroys all affectional bonds between the spouses. For this reason it strikes at the very heart of the union and is aptly judged the most flagrant violation of the marriage promises. The non-offending party is not inclined to show much patience or tolerance here. Quite contrary to drink, adultery is a direct offense against the marriage partner, and both society and the Church vindicate the right to discontinue cohabitation. Despite the public opprobrium connected with this act, our data show that it is the cause of the breakdown in a relatively high percentage of Catholic marriages. Here again, the records suggest that if we can judge from the statistics on the length of acquaintance and engagement, the number of children in the family, and the duration of the marriage, these unions gave every indication of being fairly stable from the beginning.

However, it was remarked that a rather high percentage of these cases were relatively young at marriage. This was true for both sexes. It is possible that the lack of experience and maturity evidenced by youth, although leading to seemingly excellent adaptations in the early years of married life, may be manifested later in marriage by the search for new experiences and outside or extramarital contacts. The records show that in many cases of youthful marriage, a period arrived after several years of married life when one of the spouses grew restless and eager for new experience. There was evident a vague feeling that they felt they had missed something in marrying young. They believed they were settling down too soon. They were still young and attractive and could get others to notice them, whereas their partner was expecting them to act like an "old married couple."

In some adultery cases there was evidence that the partners had grown apart rather than together as their marriage progressed. The wife had concentrated on the work of raising the children to the neglect of her husband, and he had sought affectional attachments in other quarters. Unfortunately, there is little specific information in the records concerning the sexual relations of the couple before the offense was committed. However, the couple did not recognize sexual incompatibility as a factor, and since the number of children per family was relatively high, it seems plausible to assume that neglect or temporary indifference rather than sexual maladjustment was the underlying cause of the deviation.

There was no information on the number of cases in this category in which the wife was working or had worked during the war period. It is possible that the unusual conditions existing during the war when it was not uncommon for both spouses to be working away from home, or when the husband was thrown into contact with a large number of the opposite sex while at work, may account for the relatively high percentage of cases falling under this heading.

The analysis of the other factors associated with breakdown supplied valuable information of both a positive and negative nature. The factor of religious difference was found to be of less importance in marital failure than might have been assumed. This was evident from the study of the cases specifically listed under religious conflict and from the study of all the cases of mixed and convert marriage. However, mixed and convert marriages presented a distinct pattern. They had a significantly low birth rate and an extremely high percentage of cases involving adultery. Although the number of these cases was not unrepresentative of their proportion in the Catholic population of the area, there may be a bias in our data on mixed marriage since it is not clear that the non-Catholic partner had recourse to the separation court when marital problems arose.

In-law trouble did not prove as prevalent as modern literature and propaganda imply. Temperamental differences, which apparently play such a large role in the civil divorce courts, have a relatively limited field here. Immaturity, as characterized by irresponsibility, accounted for a fair percentage of cases but further research would be required before an adequate picture of this group could be drawn. The category of mental illness was presented for the purely factual information it conveyed. The category of sexual adjustment dealt only with those cases in which marriage relations were refused or proved impossible and did not directly investigate the association between marital happiness and sexual adjustment. Finally, the data showed that disputes over money accounted for very few cases of marital failure.

CHAPTER NINE

Some Special
Characteristics

There are several items of special interest represented in the marriage cases appearing before the chancery separation court. For example, it was discovered that the various national groups displayed distinctive characteristics in some courtship and marriage practices so that, to the extent that these cases were representative of their national groups, they reveal interesting patterns of acculturation. Further, the mixed marriage cases provided some valuable information when they were analyzed according to which spouse was the Catholic party. Although there were only a limited number of cases in which one of the partners was a convert at marriage, they have been analyzed separately since the data indicate that such marriages constitute a distinct group. Finally, it was discovered that if cases of marriage failure were divided according to length of duration, considerable insight could be gained concerning the various factors which disrupted the union at different stages in the family cycle. Hence, the present chapter will be devoted to a description of these traits in the hope that it will increase our understanding of the American Catholic family and some of the problems it faces.

Since there is little information available on the characteristics of successful marriages in the general Catholic population of the area, it is impossible to compare our findings on broken marriage with those obtained from the study of a successful group. Such information would make it possible to study differences and perhaps uncover factors of vital importance to successful family life. Until research is further advanced, an alternative must be used. We can take the general average of the total group as a standard or norm with which to compare the detailed information obtained from analyzing the characteristics of the various categories. In this way it is possible to study the degree of deviation from the average.

In other words, we can assume that the average represents a uniform distribution of traits, and we can observe whether the particular category being studied is underrepresented or overrepresented in various traits. In general, the data reveal the existence of "patterns" in the different categories. That is, the variations of percentages do not occur as isolated phenomena but rather, when a variation is noted in one item, it becomes apparent that a somewhat similar variation occurs in several other categories.

GENERAL CHARACTERISTICS OF THE FOUR MAJOR GROUPS

Four major national groups have been singled out for special treatment. Although no information was available on the specific generation the members of these groups represented, two of the groups, the Poles and Italians, were members of the New Immigration, and two, the Irish and Germans, were members of the Old. Consequently, it would be safe to assume that we are dealing with second and third generation ethnics in the Italian and Polish groups and probably fourth and fifth in the others. At the same time, the data show that even when this factor of generation is not more precisely determined, some very obvious differences exist in the marital habits of the major national groups considered in this study.

The Irish

The pattern for the group runs as follows. When both parties were Irish, the number of marriages in which both spouses were Catholic was well above the average with a corresponding decrease in the percentages for mixed and convert marriages. In regard to length of acquaintance and engagement, there was a marked tendency for marriage after a relatively long acquaintance and engagement period. The age at marriage for both bride and groom was much more advanced than for the average, and there was some tendency to marry a spouse of the same age.

In occupational status, the Irish showed a tendency to higher percentages in the "white-collar" classes. The number of families having one or more children, as well as the number of unions which endured for more than five years, was considerably above the average. Concerning the factors precipitating the breakdown, the Irish showed a relatively high percentage for drink and mental breakdown and low percentages in adultery on the part of the wife, in-law trouble, and religion. There were many less cases than might be expected involving war marriages, exclusion of children, and widows.

The Poles

When both spouses were of Polish descent, there were almost no mixed or convert marriages. Few marriages were contracted after a brief acquaintance, and there was a corresponding tendency to have a formal engagement lasting relatively long. The age at marriage followed the average with the exception of a relatively high percentage of brides between 18 and 21 years and a correspondingly high percentage of husbands who were older than their wives.

The occupational status of the husbands revealed high percentages in the manual labor classes and low percentages in the clerical classes. The number of children and the duration of marriage for these cases ran fairly close to the average. Among the factors in the breakdown, drink had a high percentage, but there was a correspondingly low percentage for adultery. There were no cases in which religion was a major factor in the breakdown. This group revealed more than the normal amount of in-law trouble. There were fewer cases of war marriages and marriages excluding children than were to be expected, but there was double the amount of expected cases involving the widowed.

The Germans

Cases in which both partners were of German descent displayed a relatively high percentage of mixed and convert marriages. The percentages for length of acquaintance and engagement followed the average rather closely although there was some tendency to have low percentages in the extremes. In occupational status, the percentages were relatively high in the clerical and professional classes and correspondingly low in the working class categories.

The number of children and duration of marriage traits showed little deviation from the normal with the exception of a relatively high percentage in the class having two children. Concerning the factors which entered into the breakdown, drink ranked low but adultery was relatively high. As was to be expected from the amount of mixed marriage, religious differences played a more important role than they did among the other groups. Irresponsibility and in-law problems showed a comparatively low percentage. There were well over the expected number of war marriages and unions in which the bride was pregnant at marriage.

The Italians

When both partners were of Italian descent, there were almost no mixed or convert marriages. There was double the expected amount of marriages after a brief acquaintance but also more than the expected amount after a long acquaintance. The characteristics of the group in regard to engagement followed the general average. There was a marked deviation from the other groups in regard to age at marriage. This was true for both spouses. In general, this group had a tendency to enter marriage at a much younger age than the general average and presented a striking contrast to a group such as the Irish.

Information on occupational status revealed a relatively high percentage in the laboring classes, particularly at the unskilled level. However, there were a few more than expected in the professional class, although it should be noted that this class was quite small in the general total so that this high percentage may have little significance. In regard to the number of children, the percentages for the childless and one-, three-, and four-child family indicated that there were less than the average number of children involved in the majority of families. By contrast, however, there were well over the expected number of cases having five or more children.

This phenomenon was paralleled in the data on the duration of marriage. There were high percentages in the first- and five-year brackets and, at the same time, a relatively high percentage lasting over twenty years. An analysis of the major factors in the breakdown revealed that both adultery and drink were underrepresented, and irresponsibility, clash of temperaments, and in-law problems were overrepresented. There were no cases in which religion was a factor in the breakdown. The number of cases involving war marriages was relatively low, and there were few cases in which the bride was pregnant at marriage.

Findings of Other Studies on These National Groups

It is evident from this brief description of the major national groups studied that significant differences did exist in the cases representing these minorities in the chancery separation court. A review of the rather limited literature dealing with the specifically ethnic traits of these groups reveals that our findings here agree substantially with the observations of others who have worked in this field. For example, Park pointed out the strict regulations which the Italian community imposed upon marriage and the relations of the sexes leading

us to expect few "forced" marriages and little infidelity.[1] Ware
has indicated the patriarchal characteristics of the Italian family and the tendency of the young to break away from this
control.[2] Our data offered some evidence of this in the relatively high percentage of cases that had married after a comparatively brief acquaintance and also in the proportion revealing marked immaturity and irresponsibility in marriage.
Warner has indicated that among all the ethnic groups there
is a movement on the part of the wives toward greater equality in marriage.[3] As we have suggested, it is possible that the
relatively high percentage of cases breaking up because of
drink may be an indication of this demand for more consideration on the part of women.

Warner's description of the various ethnic groups indicates
a considerable amount of drinking among the working-class
Irish, and relatively high percentages of outgroup marriage
among the upper classes. There were some indications that
this pattern was exemplified in the cases studied. As Ware
has stated, hard drinking is recognized as an Irish practice by
all social workers.[4] Whether this is merely a stereotype handed
down from the past, we have no way of knowing for there is
little tested knowledge on the drinking habits of the various
national groups.

Furthermore, there may be no close connection between the
amount of drinking in a group and the number of marriages
which are disrupted by drink. Marital breakdown always involves at least two people, and the reaction of the nondrinking
partner may be as important as the habit itself in determining
whether a given marriage will end in failure. It may be that
some wives are more tolerant than others in regard to drink;
they may enter marriage with different marital expectations
so that the common "cumulative pattern" so often observed in
these cases may not get started.

By this we mean that the reaction of the wife may be one
of acceptance rather than a factor that motivates the husband
to further drinking. As a result, marital tension does not increase quantitatively and qualitatively as it must when nonsupport, lack of companionship, suspicion of infidelity, and

loss of prestige in the community conspire to turn the spouses against each other, thus increasing the tendency of the erring partner to seek refuge in drink.

Because of their numbers and their strong ethnic solidarity, Polish immigrants and their descendants have been more thoroughly studied than any other group. Park has pointed out the strong parish and community grouping of the Poles in this country, a situation which leads to limited outgroup marriage.[5] He further indicated the tendency of the Poles to maintain their language with the result that the Americanization process has been slowed down among them and their advance in occupational status has been restricted.[6] Our research on acculturation among the ethnic groups and the findings of the present study on broken marriages clearly substantiate this thesis.

THE ETHNIC FAMILY IN "THE POLISH PEASANT"

However, our research does not confirm the prediction concerning the breakdown of monogamous marriage among the Polish peasants in America, as found in Thomas and Znaniecki's monumental work.[7] Since this classic study analyzed the acculturation process of one major ethnic group and attempted to formulate "social laws" applicable to others, it will be worth while to describe and evaluate their approach in some detail. The contribution to the social sciences of this outstanding work has been manifold and is recognized by all. Unfortunately, some of the methodological concepts advanced by the authors have been adopted uncritically by others, with no great advantage to the social sciences.

Our primary interest lies in their treatment of the Polish American family, but implicit in this treatment is an hypothesis concerning the function of religion in society which is highly pertinent to the present study. Our description and analysis of the American Catholic family is fundamentally an investigation of the effects of a specific set of religious beliefs and practices on a minority composed largely of immigrants and their descendants who have been forced to adjust to new cultural patterns. The authors of *The Polish Peasant* have developed a more or less widely accepted theory on the motivating force of religious beliefs in the individual's life. Let us study their theory as they presented it, for if it proves to be a correct analysis of the situation, then there is little chance that the Catholic minority will long survive in American culture.

Serious Maladjustment Predicted for the Polish Family

Thomas and Znaniecki summarize their study of the conjugal relations existing among Polish-Americans as follows:

> Thus, in general the marriage situation among the American Poles looks quite hopeless when judged by the standards of the permanent and exclusive conjugal bond. Numerous causes contribute to the progressive dissolution of the monogamous marriage-group, and there are no important and general reconstructive factors.[8]

If in 1920, at the conclusion of this study, there was present, on the one hand, "progressive dissolution of the monogamous marriage-group" and, on the other, "no important and general reconstructive factors," one would expect to find relatively greater marital disintegration among the American Poles today. This is particularly true if we consider that Thomas and Znaniecki specifically discount any of the forces which might fortify the conjugal bond. They point out that, as a result of the breakup of the wider family institution found in Poland, "marriage almost ceases to be a social institution, and the old socially sanctioned attitudes upon which the strength and permanence of the conjugal bonds were based lose most of their practical influence." Hence, for American Poles, "marriage rests almost exclusively upon the temperamental attitudes of the individuals, not upon their obedience to social rules." And the authors produce documents allegedly showing that "none of these attitudes is sufficient to form a permanent basis for the family."[9]

Further, the immigrant will find great difficulty in substituting new social ideals and norms for the crumbling old insti-

tutional foundations of family life. The abstract principle of
duty has, according to Thomas and Znaniecki, little practical
influence on the Polish immigrant. Love as a cultural product
demanding exclusive attachment to one individual is also ex-
ceedingly rare among the peasants. Economic ideals, although
they demand a certain amount of stability, do not guarantee
the unity of the conjugal bond. Finally, social progress and
the desire for prominence, although they can operate as positive moral forces, affect only a minority and are appreciable
only when the parents have passed through the "stormy period" of youth. For these reasons

> . . . the moral status of the average Polish-American
> individual or marriage-group in matters of conjugal life can
> be thus briefly characterized as that of a very unstable balance
> of temperamental attitudes and personal habits, which deter-
> mine whether the traditional social schematization—now al-
> most reduced to a mere form—will be preserved or not.[10]

Stability of the Typical Polish Family

Considered in the light of the above predictions, the future
of the Polish-American family in 1920 looked gloomy indeed.
Fortunately, the last three decades have not borne out the
contentions of the writers. In the first place, it must be admitted that the Polish-American population today is not generally considered less monogamous than the average run of
Americans. In fact, from what evidence is available, it may be
inferred that the conjugal bond is much more stable among
them than among almost any other comparable group.

Although it would be difficult to obtain information on the
total number of Polish Americans in this country, the census
reports do supply information on the number of foreign-born
Poles. Since the authors gathered much of their data on family disorganization from Chicago, we shall use this city to
study the validity of their predictions. According to the 1940
census for Chicago, of the 672,705 foreign-born whites in the
city, 17.1 per cent were Poles.[11] This was the largest foreign-
born white group in the city. Nevertheless, the Poles do not
appear in relatively large numbers in the domestic relations

courts of the city, although, according to the predictions of Thomas and Znaniecki, that was to be expected.

Further, if we assume with the authors that the majority of Poles in this country maintain some connection with the Church, statistics gathered on Polish-American Catholics should be of some help in discovering the state of monogamous marriage among them. The findings of our study on marriage conditions in the dioceses of the Great Lakes region are very enlightening. Statistics were gathered on approximately three hundred parishes, a considerable number of which were Polish. The data on separation and divorce indicate that the conjugal bond is more stable among the Polish-Americans than among other American Catholics of comparable socioeconomic status. It is difficult to reconcile this evidence with Thomas and Znaniecki's predictions.

Finally, our study of broken marriages based on the records of the chancery separation court indicates no relatively great demoralization among the Polish-American Catholics of the Archdiocese. Separation cases involving those of Irish and German descent greatly outnumber the cases involving those of Polish descent. Further, as we have shown, among the factors entering into the breakdown of the marriage, the Poles had the lowest percentage in which adultery appeared as the main factor in the disruption of the union. These findings indicate no widespread demoralization among the American Catholic Poles in the very region from which the authors drew much of the data for their predictions.

Why the Prediction Failed

In the light of this evidence we are tempted to ask why the predictions of the authors failed to materialize. Others have questioned the defensibility of applying to society in general conclusions which are based on the study of Polish peasants. Blumer has questioned whether the theoretical conceptions in this work are really derived from the material at all, contending that they have no essential dependence on the documents employed.[12] In his penetrating analysis he goes further and questions "both the logical and methodological adequacy of the concepts of 'attitude' and 'value.'" Yet these concepts are basic to the methodological formula designed by the authors to yield "laws of social becoming." [13]

In his comment on Blumer's *Appraisal,* W. I. Thomas admitted that "the concrete materials of the volume are not adequately correlated with the methodological scheme." However, he went on to explain:

> I approve our separation of attitudes and values, or psychological sets and tendencies to act, on the one hand, and the external stimuli to action on the other, and of our general description of the interaction of these factors, but I think we went too far in our confident assumption that we shall be able to lay bare the complete and invariable nature of this interaction and thus determine the *laws* of "social becoming." [14]

Since human material is never stable, he concludes, "we should therefore not speak of social *laws* but seek to establish high degrees of *probability* in the interaction of attitudes and values." [15]

It would appear that the authors did not achieve "high degrees of probability" with regard to Polish-American marriage values and attitudes. Perhaps the most obvious reason for their failure was that they did not associate statistical methods and controls in their use of documents. Although admitting this defect, Thomas justified his position as follows: "This would have been difficult in view of the character of the materials, which for the most part were found ready made and were not systematically prepared." [16]

This is quite true with regard to the use of letters and, perhaps, of life-histories. However, in studying the breakdown of the conjugal relation in Polish-American families, they employed for the most part materials supplied by the Legal Aid Society in the city of Chicago. [17] Some attempt should have been made to ascertain just how representative of the Polish-American population as a whole were the cases which they studied. Since there is no indication that this was done, one questions the defensibility of using the term "average" Polish-American when making generalizations based on such highly selected cases.

Inadequacies of Their Conceptual Formula

Prescinding from this admitted defect in their approach to the problem of social change, let us consider the conceptual formula which was basic to their interpretation of change in the conjugal relations of the Polish peasant in America. The authors quite rightly contend that, in treating the problem of social change, both the objective factors, which they have chosen to call "values," and the subjective factors, which they have named "attitudes," must be taken into consideration. Feeling that the subjective factors had been too much neglected, Thomas and Znaniecki insisted that the attitudes of the recipient human agent must be ascertained, since recipients did not react uniformly to the same objective factor, as in the natural sciences, but differently at different times because of their different attitudes.

No one will quarrel over their insistence on the old scholastic adage: *Quidquid recipitur, ad modum recipientis recipitur* (Whatever is received, is received according to the disposition of the recipient). The problem, however, consists not only in ascertaining the attitudes of the recipient and how they change, but primarily in judging the relative motivating force of conflicting attitudes in the same agent. It would seem that the assumption that one attitude simply replaces another attitude in the agent when the social values change is far too simple an explanation of reality. The problem is basically one of the conflict of attitudes and the discernment of their motivating force.

Further, there is the problem of two or more social values calling forth the same attitude in the same agent. Thus, if one social value is removed, it is not necessary to postulate a change in attitude, since the second social value then becomes operative and the individual will act in the same way as before in a given situation. Failure to see that attitudes can be enforced by various sets of values operating at different levels of consciousness can lead to serious misinterpretation of social phenomena.

For example, the authors state that "sexual indulgence as

such has no meaning of 'wickedness' attached to it; only its
bearing on the family system made it condemnable or contemptible." [18] This statement reveals slight knowledge of Polish character, since their experience in dealing with the
"average" Polish-American must have acquainted them with
the fact that the average Polish-American felt seriously obliged
to admit his sexual indulgences in confession in order to obtain
peace of mind. Further inquiry would have shown them that
the feeling of guilt arose not only from committing an act
which the community judged "condemnable or contemptible"
but from an attitude, based on a value, that this act was sinful
or wicked.

In other words, two social values were operative: the sanction of the community and the sanction of religion. In peasant
life, within the close-knit family and community structure of
the primitive group, it is possible that the sanction of the
community was uppermost in forming the attitude of the individual. At the same time, however, the sanction of religion
was operating, for it would be otherwise impossible to explain
the delinquent's recourse to confession in the primitive peasant
society.

When the individual migrates and the sanction of the kinship and community group becomes weakened, the other
value, namely, the sanction of religion, comes to the fore and
enforces the attitude. It is obvious that the force of the religious sanction may be weakened in the process of migration,
since the immigrant may be forced to live under circumstances
which seriously threaten his moral life. [19] In addition, there
may be a period of transition during which the immigrant is
cut off from active contact with his church, a fact that can
lead to a still further weakening of the religious sanction. But,
as the authors point out, Polish immigrants were quick to
establish a parish wherever possible. [20]

It would seem that Thomas and Znaniecki were too much
impressed by the state of temporary disorganization consequent upon settlement in a new country. More specifically,
since their general theory led them to expect a weakening of
the conjugal bond, they found it easy to accept the cases of
marital disintegration appearing in the records of the Legal

Aid Society as typical. Their reasoning was as follows: The disorganization of the Polish peasant in America is due to the decay of the large-family system, to the weakness of the Polish-American community, and to the novelty of American legal standards. They maintained that the marriage group had formerly been held together not through the personal responsibility of the individuals involved but rather by the power of the large family (kinship group) and the larger community (church and state).

In America the sanctions of the large family and community were greatly weakened and, because the individual was not accustomed to taking the personal responsibility for maintaining the conjugal bond intact, great demoralization was to be expected. In other words, with the increase of individualism among the immigrants and the lessening of external family and community sanctions, marriage ceased to be a social institution, and its stability rested on the none-too-stable temperamental attitudes of the individuals.[21]

Effect of Religious Belief Is Misconceived

As we have pointed out, the authors have taken a far too simple view of the subjective factors in human action. Their theory seems unable to treat in an adequate way the absolute strength of a given attitude, the possibility of a conflict between attitudes, and the obvious fact that an attitude may be enforced by different values at the same time. For instance, they state that the relations between husband and wife were defined in a specific way by the large family and community in Poland. Impelled by their desire for recognition, individuals accepted this traditional definition. In the absence of the larger groups, this desire no longer operates effectively, and the individual follows the traditional definition only if it conforms to his natural tendencies and habits. This is true because "there is no social prestige behind this definition and no higher motive which would induce the individual to accept and maintain it when it disagrees with his temperament and habits." [22] This is to say that they do not consider the possibility that the traditional definition was also sanctioned by the religion of the individual, so that, when the one sanction became ineffective, the other became operative.

The inability to take into account the subjective aspect of religion and its strength in shaping the attitudes of the individual is one of the great weaknesses of their approach. They seem to have been satisfied with considering religion as an external institution which exerts pressure in much the same way as does any other. This does not seem to square with reality. For example, they state that abortion is considered "shameful—probably because resorted to mostly by unmarried girls," forgetting the very real subjective effect of the strong religious prohibition upon the individual.[23]

Further, they maintain that as a check on sexual tendencies, religion "never had any particular influence." [24] This generalization would find little support among social scientists today; for, no matter what objective validity one may grant to a particular religion or religious teaching, there can be little doubt of the powerful influence exerted by it throughout life. The inability of the authors to grasp the subjective effect of religious beliefs upon the Polish peasant is all the more amazing because they must have been fully aware of the brutal persecutions which he endured down through history in order to maintain his beliefs intact.

It is possible that this failure to grasp the subjective effect of religious belief on the individual accounts for a certain misconception of the role of the parish in the immigrant's life. The authors are correct in calling the parish the "most important Polish-American institution" and in pointing out that "the Polish-American parish is much more than a religious association for common worship under the leadership of a priest." [25] However, they betray their inability to take into account the subjective aspect of religion and its strength in shaping the attitudes of the individual by insisting on the merely external control which the parish as an institution is able to exert. Considered in this way, the parish is "simply the old primary community, reorganized and concentrated." Hence, since it is obvious that the Polish-American parish "does not control the life of its members as efficiently as did the old community," the authors concluded that it would not be powerful enough to overcome the disintegrating forces undermining the institution of marriage.[26]

Final Appraisal of This Important Study

In the light of the preceding analysis, the following conclusions concerning the work of Thomas and Znaniecki would seem to be permissible. First, they failed in their prediction about the future marital condition of the Polish-American because they assumed certain laws of social change which led them to accept the cases in the records of the Legal Aid Society as typical, without seeking statistical verification of their representativeness.

Second, although they rightly insisted on the necessity of considering the subjective factors in social change, they oversimplified reality by not recognizing the manifold "values" forming an "attitude" and by underestimating the possibility of a conflict of "attitudes" resulting in an ambivalence which rendered prediction well-nigh impossible. With his usual discernment, Blumer succinctly summarizes this point in the form of a dilemma: "On the one hand, an inescapable need of including the subjective element of human experience, but, on the other hand, an enormous, and so far, unsurmounted, difficulty in securing devices that will catch this element of human experience in the way that is customary for usable data in ordinary scientific procedure in other fields." [27]

This critical analysis of one theory on the influence of religion in social life indicates where further work must be centered if a better understanding of social change is to be attained. The uncritical accumulation of statistical data on attitudes can only produce a pseudo-scientific knowledge of social life. Research methods must be fashioned to get at the deep, inner core of the human person, so that the wellsprings of action are laid bare. Only then will research yield knowledge which can be used in the prediction of social action.

We have presented this rather detailed analysis of Thomas and Znaniecki's theory because their position is rather typical of the approach used by all those who see in religion only another institution achieving conformity by external pressure rather than by the force of internalized values. As we shall have occasion to point out again and again, the precise point of tension for the Catholic as a representative of a religious minority is the conflict which arises between his internalized values and the institutions, customs, and practices of a secular culture which does not implement these values. If religion operated only as an organized external force, the chances of the Catholic minority surviving for any length of time would be slight indeed.

MIXED AND CONVERT MARRIAGES

Since the acceptance of a specific set of religious beliefs may be assumed to affect the attitudes and actions of an individual in marriage, a comparison of the mixed and nonmixed marriages appearing before the chancery separation court should reveal some of the consequences of valid mixed marriages on marital adjustment. We have indicated that there is no basis in the data for assuming that valid mixed marriages are more unstable than other valid marriages although we have admitted that the study may include too few mixed marriages in which the husband was the Catholic party. The majority of petitioners in the court were women, and there is the possibility that a non-Catholic spouse would not have recourse to the court as readily as a Catholic one if trouble arose. Hence, it may be admitted that the cases upon which the present study is based are underrepresented in mixed marriages in which the wife is non-Catholic.

Further, it should be emphasized that we are dealing only with those valid mixed marriages which had recourse to the chancery court when trouble arose. There is evidence that mixed marriages tend to weaken the faith of the Catholic party so that a good number may ignore Church regulations and have recourse directly to the civil divorce courts. Nevertheless, we feel that the data contain sufficient interesting and valuable information to justify detailed treatment here. Information on convert marriages has been added. There is some indication that convert marriages which experienced maladjustment displayed a distinct pattern in courtship and marriage relationships.

The chancery records supplied data on five types of marriage: marriages in which both partners were Catholic (75.9 per cent), mixed marriages in which the husband was the non-Catholic party (12.7 per cent), mixed marriages in which the wife was the non-Catholic party (4.5 per cent), marriages in which the husband had been converted at marriage (3.4 per cent), and marriages in which the wife had been converted at marriage (3.4 per cent). Marriages in which both partners were Catholic, because they represented such a large proportion of the cases, naturally displayed traits in conformity with the general average for most categories. However, in comparison with the other four types, these cases revealed a higher proportion of marriages breaking up because of drink and a lower proportion because of adultery. Further, they included significantly lower percentages for war marriages, "forced" marriages, and marriages in which children were excluded.

Mixed Marriages in Which the Husband Was the Non-Catholic Party

Mixed unions in which the husband was non-Catholic present some distinct characteristics. Polish and Italian males were scarcely represented here, Irish males were underrepresented while the German and other nationals were overrepresented. This was not true for the nationality of the wife. German and Irish wives were overrepresented and only Polish wives were greatly underrepresented since they revealed only half the expected number of cases. There was a significantly high percentage of these cases in which marriage took place after less than one year's acquaintance.

Wives in these marriages tended to marry at a later age and there were relatively higher percentages who were the same age or older than their husbands. There were proportionately more childless and one-child families and less having four or more children than when both parties were Catholic. Only about half the expected proportion broke up because of drink, but almost one-third more than expected because of adultery. As we would expect, religion ranked third among the factors in the breakdown. War marriages, "forced" marriages, and the exclusion of childen were overrepresented.

Mixed Marriages in Which the Wife Was the Non-Catholic Party

In the third type, the wife was the non-Catholic partner. There were few Irish, Polish, and Italian wives involved in this type. Cases in which marriage took place after a brief acquaintance and in which there was a short or no engagement period were highly overrepresented. Both partners tended to be relatively young at marriage. There were double the expected number of cases falling in the lower white-collar occupational class. Childless and one-child families were overrepresented, and families with three or more children were relatively few. Maladjustment asserted itself early in this type. More than double the expected amount broke up within six months and considerably more than expected within the first five years. As in all mixed marriage cases in the records, drink was underrepresented as a factor in the breakdown, and adultery was overrepresented. Infidelity on the part of the wife appeared about five times more frequently than expected, although it is impossible to ascertain whether this disproportion relative to the husband in such marriages may be due to the nature of our data; that is, it is possible that when the Catholic husband is unfaithful, the non-Catholic wife may take her cause directly to the civil divorce court.

Marriages in Which the Husband Was Converted at Marriage

The fourth type involves marriages in which the husband was converted at the time of marriage. As we would expect, Irish, Polish, and Italian husbands are underrepresented in this type. Marriage tended to take place after a relatively pro-

longed acquaintance and engagement period. Both partners
were somewhat older at marriage than the average. Convert
husbands were overrepresented in the unskilled occupational
class.

This fourth type is similar to those mixed marriages in which
the husband was non-Catholic in the relatively high percentages of childless and one-child families. Maladjustment appeared early in these unions. One out of five broke up within
the first year and over half did not survive the first five years.
Drink ranked only fourth as a disintegrating factor, but there
was a higher percentage involving adultery than in any other
type.

Marriages in Which the Wife Was Converted at Marriage

In the fifth type, the wife was the convert at marriage. No
Polish or Italian wives were involved in these cases. There was
some tendency for these marriages to take place after a relatively brief acquaintance, and the convert wives were overrepresented in youthful marriages. Husbands were overrepresented in the lower white-collar occupational class. There
were less than the expected number breaking up because of
drink and approximately the expected number involving adultery, although when this category is analyzed according to the
sex of the offender, cases in which the wife appeared as the
offender were overrepresented.

From this brief description of the various religious types of
marriage cases, several interesting patterns have emerged. We
have indicated the principal deviations from the general average and feel that they justify the following conclusions. First,
the study of religious outgroup marriage must consider sexual
differences. Marriages involving a non-Catholic husband differed from those involving a non-Catholic wife, and the same
pattern was apparent in convert marriages. Second, religious
differences in marriage represent factors in the breakdown not
primarily as quarrels over religious practice or the education
of the children. They are more likely to be manifested in disagreement over the nature and purposes of marriage itself.

MALADJUSTMENT AND THE FAMILY CYCLE

The chancery court records reveal that distinct problems are associated with specific periods in the family cycle. By dividing the cases according to their duration, it is possible to point out what areas of maladjustment lead to marriage breakdown during the various stages. This knowledge is valuable for two reasons. First, studies of marriage adjustment based on cases which have endured ten or twenty years will necessarily be biased through the elimination of those cases which break up quickly, and it is important to point out what type of problem tends to disintegrate the union in the early years of marriage. Second, marriage preparation instructions tend to concentrate on areas of tension occurring in the early years of marriage. The consideration of unstabilizing factors which make their appearance only later in the family cycle can add more realism to marriage preparation courses.

A study of divorce rates in the past few decades indicates that there was a precipitous rise in the probabilities of divorce for the first three years of married life and a gradual decline after the fourth year. Currently, about two-fifths of all divorces and annulments are granted to couples married less than five years, and one-fourth to those married from five to nine years.[28] It may reasonably be supposed that causes of tension and conflict which break up a union of short duration differ from those which cause separation or divorce after years of married life. For example, in an interesting research on female attitudes, Ciocco states that the women in his study differed in their complaints according to age groups.[29] Conflicts involving temperamental maladjustments were more commonly reported by younger women, while the husband's infidelity was found most frequently among the oldest.

It is obvious that factors leading to serious conflict early in marriage are not likely to be found in older groups. A large number of cases so afflicted will be eliminated by separation or divorce in the early years of marriage. For this reason, a study of the duration of broken marriages and the factors in-

volved in their breakdown should throw some light on how
the various factors leading to dissolution affect the marriage.
Indeed, it might be possible to construct a chart showing the
possible danger zones for the different periods of married
life. Further, such a study will help to counterbalance the
present tendency of devoting proportionately too much time
to the problems of adjustment in the early years of marriage
with consequent neglect of the maladjustments which make
their appearance or can arise later in life.

Period When Catholic Marriages Broke Down

The duration pattern of the marriage cases appearing before the chancery separation court differs only slightly from
that of cases found in the civil divorce courts.[30] However, when
the cases which were classified as atypical are considered separately, marked differences in duration become readily apparent. Table 27 presents the percentages for the various atypical

TABLE 27

DISTRIBUTION OF CASES IN THE VARIOUS TYPES ACCORDING TO DURATION

Types of Marriage	Less than 1 Year	1-5	6-10	11-15	16-20	21 and Over
War marriages	32.6	54.9	12.4	.0	.0	.0
Bride pregnant	18.1	38.1	20.0	12.4	6.7	4.8
Children excluded	20.7	46.0	21.4	7.5	3.7	.7
Widowed	32.3	35.3	16.1	6.4	3.2	6.4
All others	10.7	24.4	23.8	17.6	11.4	11.9

Number of Years

categories and for the remaining "typical" cases. As we have
pointed out, most of the atypical cases tend to be of short
duration and on this score alone would merit separate treatment. At this point, we are primarily interested in the duration
pattern of the typical marriage cases. Table 27 shows that
approximately 11 per cent broke up in less than one year,
one-fourth in the next four years, almost one-fourth more in
the sixth to the tenth year, and the remaining 41 per cent
thereafter. Couples who separated during the first eleven
months of marriage can scarcely be credited with giving their

marriage an opportunity to succeed. In general, the first five years of marriage eliminated most of the initially unstable unions, although it may be assumed that the couples separating during this period gave their marriage an honest try and made more earnest attempts at adjustment than those who failed within the first few months.

An analysis of the data reveals that marriages breaking up between the first and fifth year differ from those which failed within the first year to the extent that the added time-span gave certain disintegrating factors such as drink and adultery an opportunity to become manifest. It is reasonable to expect, therefore, that the cases which lasted longer than five years will reveal different disintegrating characteristics, for most of the initially unstable unions will have been culled in the first five years. By classifying our cases according to duration and then analyzing the factors which entered into the breakdown of the marriages included in each duration category, we can uncover the principal tension areas which develop during the various stages of the family cycle.

Factors Involved in the Breakdown at Various Duration Periods

Table 28 shows the incidence of the various factors which have entered into the breakdown of the marriages classified

TABLE 28

DISTRIBUTION OF CASES ACCORDING TO DURATION AND FACTORS
WHICH ENTERED INTO THE BREAKDOWN

Number of Years

Factors	Less than 1 Year	Less than 5 Years	6-10	11-15	16-20	21 and Over
Drink	8.9	17.7	30.9	35.5	41.1	43.3
Adultery	12.5	19.0	27.7	34.4	23.3	23.5
Temperaments	14.9	12.5	12.0	8.2	10.6	17.6
Irresponsibility	15.5	17.4	12.5	8.9	11.7	4.3
Sex	14.9	8.9	3.7	3.2	4.4	2.1
In-laws	19.0	13.9	4.8	2.5	4.4	1.6
Religion	4.8	3.8	4.0	2.5	.0	1.1
Mental	3.0	3.1	2.9	2.5	2.2	4.3
Money	1.8	.7	.5	.4	1.7	1.6
Unclassified	4.8	3.1	.8	1.8	.6	.5

according to different duration periods. It is evident from this table that the elements of disintegration which affected marriages of short duration differed considerably from those affecting marriages which failed later. For example, among the marriages which failed during the first year, in-law trouble was the disintegrating factor in approximately one out of each five cases (19.0 per cent) but accounted for less than 5 per cent of the cases breaking up after the first five years. Problems connected with sexual relations appeared early in marriage (14.9 per cent) and then decreased rapidly in the longer duration categories. On the other hand, the incidence of drink and adultery was relatively low (8.9 and 12.5 per cent respectively) among the marriages breaking up within the first year. Since the second duration category includes all the marriages which failed during the first five years, it reveals much the same pattern as the first, which included only those failing during the first year. However, the incidence of drink and adultery increased considerably (17.7 and 19.0 per cent respectively), while that of sex and in-laws decreased (8.9 and 13.9 per cent respectively).

In the remaining duration categories, drink looms as the most important factor in the breakdown, accounting for approximately one out of each three cases among those marriages enduring from six to fifteen years and for over 40 per cent in the remaining categories. Adultery appeared as the second most important factor, accounting for more than one out of each three cases in the 11-15 year category and for approximately one out of each five in the others. The incidence of irresponsibility was highest among marriages breaking up early where it accounted for one out of each six cases. However, it remained relatively prominent even in the later duration categories where it manifested itself primarily through desertion. Clash of temperaments appeared as an important unstabilizing factor during most periods, although it should be noted that this term includes a rather wide variety of traits frequently difficult to classify.

One may well ask: How significant are these findings? After all, one would expect unstable marriages to be eliminated early, with the disintegrating factors for the various duration periods revealing considerable differences. Is this important? A moment's reflection shows that this knowledge is important, and the percentage differences which have been revealed are pertinent to our understanding of the family.

The Threat of Alcohol

In the first place, given the importance of drink as a disintegrating factor in marriage, is it not strange that marriage preparation courses seldom refer to the danger of drink? The assumption seems to be that if individuals are happily married they will not drink, at least, not to the extent that this might harm family relationships and endanger the union. The overwhelming testimony of the present study throws serious doubt on this assumption.

Whatever may be the reason why men drink, serious frustration in marriage does not appear to play a major role. After interviewing the interested parties, the counselor was seldom left with the impression that the origin of the drinking habit was to be traced to serious maladjustment in marriage. Rather, the habit was acquired gradually and had started disrupting smooth family relationships before its full seriousness was recognized. By that time, the individual found himself enmeshed in a whole web of relationships—on the job, at home, during weekends, after the day's work having a "few" with the "boys"—so that he found it impossible to break with the habit. Rather than admit this to himself or especially, to his spouse, he claimed he was master of the habit and insisted nobody had the right to tell him how to drink.

The sequel depended on the patience of the spouse. Frequently, she deteriorated under the humiliation, abuse, and lack of companionship with the result that her reaction merely increased the propensity of her husband to seek refuge in drink. By the time the case reached the separation court, the whole gamut of family relationships had been undermined and disrupted so that reconciliation appeared hopeless, short of an extended period of rehabilitation for both partners.

In the light of these facts, is it not astonishing that so little is said about the dangers of alcohol in studies on marriage and in premarital counseling? Here is a habit which strikes at the very heart of well-established family relationships through its concomitant evils of nonsupport, cruelty and abuse, infidelity, lack of companionship, and loss of prestige. Yet, we are to assume that it does not exist, or if it does receive mention, it is to be considered only as a "symptom" of marital failure— almost as if the wife and children were receiving a just reward for not making the marriage less frustrating for the drinker.

One might suggest two reasons why the danger of drink receives so little attention in contemporary society. There are some who act on the principle that individuals are so conditioned by their environment that their actions can be wholly "explained" away in terms of their life history. These are the cultural determinists. Among other difficulties related to their position is the problem of explaining why two individuals subjected to what appears to be the same environmental conditioning turn out quite differently.

Secondly, there are those who seem overly impressed by the failure of the poorly enforced and much disliked Prohibition Law of the twenties. They have no inclination to give comfort to the proponents of such legislation. Perhaps one of the most far-reaching deleterious effects of the Prohibition Era is that it has hindered Americans from taking an unbiased and unemotional view of the problem of drink so that most attacks on the problem appear old-fashioned and ridiculous to them.

Whatever may be the reasons for the past neglect of the problem, it is time that Americans make a reappraisal of their position and start to look upon drinking as a widespread *social* problem having radically disastrous effects on the basic unit in society. Tolstoy, in one of his plays, portrays Satan contemplating the most effective way to destroy the Russian peasantry. He finally arrived at a very simple solution: teach the peasants how to make alcohol from grain, and all the other evils he desired for them would follow. One does not have to be a "Prohibitionist" to feel that the devil had something there.

The Threat of Infidelity

A second observation based on Table 28 is the high prevalence of infidelity. It will be noticed that for the marriages failing in the first fifteen years, adultery presented as great a threat to the union as did drink. Although the percentages are not shown in Table 28, the duration patterns of cases involving adultery differed, depending on whether the husband or the wife was the offender. When the wife was the offender (roughly, one out of each five cases), nearly 40 per cent of the marriages broke up within the first five years, one-third in the 6-10 year period, and the remainder thereafter. When the husband was the offender, approximately 24 per cent failed within the first five years, 25 per cent in the 6-10 year period, and the remainder thereafter.

This difference in the duration suggests that cases involving infidelity on the part of the wife may constitute a group quite distinct from the cases in which the husband was the offender. A check on the various characteristics of the two groups revealed significant differences in age at marriage, age differences between the spouses, number of children in the family, occupational class, and so forth. It follows that any meaningful analysis of the factor of adultery in marital breakdown must heed these differences.

Remaining Factors in the Breakdown

It is interesting to note that the much-discussed problem of in-laws was a major factor in marital breakdown only in the early years of marriage. More than 28 per cent of these marriages disintegrated within the first year and more than two-thirds within the first five years. In other words, the type of in-law trouble which leads to separation makes its appearance soon after the honeymoon. It would seem that the newlyweds either work out some satisfactory form of in-law relationships very early or the marriage fails. Marriage cases involving in-law problems of a serious nature have little that is humorous about them so that it would appear that the frictions which form the basis for most mother-in-law "jokes" are not the type which cause the disintegration of the marriage.

The remaining factors need little comment. It is to be expected that when there are marked sexual difficulties the marriages will break up quickly. Table 28 shows that about 15 per cent of all the marriages seeking separation in the first year fell in this category. A detailed study of these cases reveals that when the difficulty arises on the part of the wife, over one-third break up in the first year and two-thirds within the first five years. The category labeled "clash of temperaments" accounted for relatively uniform percentages of marriages in all duration periods. However, if these cases are considered by themselves, it develops that the majority broke up only after the first five years. The cases involving irresponsibility did not present a uniform pattern. Nearly 55 per cent broke up within the first five years, another 23 per cent in the 6-10 year period, and the remainder thereafter. In most of these cases the irresponsibility was indicated from the outset, but recourse was not had to the chancery court until after the husband had secured his "poor man's" divorce by desertion.

Material for Premarital Instructions

Finally, this consideration of the duration patterns of broken marriages raises the question of the material for premarital instructions. It appears that much of the stress in textbooks and conferences is on the early months of marriage. It is evidently assumed that if proper adjustments and required adaptations are made then, all will be well with the marriage throughout the family cycle.

One may well question this assumption. There is no doubt that securing satisfactory husband-wife relationships early in marriage is desirable and offers some guarantee of the future stability of the family. On the other hand, there are many problems which arise as the couple pass through various stages of the family cycle. What may appear as excellent adjustment at one stage may prove to be a poor foundation for the next. Particularly if the couple fail to grow in intimacy and shared experience, the unfolding of the family cycle may find the partners living in separate worlds. She, who was the "angel of the house," has become the "devil in the kitchen," and he, who was the head of the family, has been reduced to the role of breadwinner. Further, there are some very real external hazards to marital success such as drink and adultery. These can create serious threats even to apparently well-established marriages.

It seems somewhat unrealistic and consequently, somewhat unfair to fail to stress these dangers when preparing couples for marriage. Of course, it is easy cavalierly to dismiss drink and adultery as mere symptoms of frustration in marriage, but anyone who has ever had to deal with broken marriages knows that even well-founded families are not immune to their insidious attack. Unless couples possess the prudence which avoids unnecessary exposure to danger and the humility which counsels caution, they have no guarantee that "it can't happen here!"

SUMMARY

This chapter has summarized the data on ethnic groups, mixed and convert marriages, and the duration patterns of maladjusted Catholic families. Owing to the influence and prestige of Thomas and Znaniecki's monumental study of *The Polish Peasant*, we devoted considerable space to demonstrating not only that their marriage predictions concerning Polish marriages have fortunately not been realized, but also that the conceptual framework of their study was inadequate. They misunderstood the function of religion both in the individual's life and in the life of the community. Since the present study of Catholic families is primarily interested in the function of religion and religious ideals, we felt that a thorough analysis of some aspects of *The Polish Peasant* would help toward a better understanding of our work.

Finally, we discussed the factors of maladjustment in terms of the family cycle. It was possible to demonstrate that some factors are primarily associated with early breakdown, while others make their appearance much later in the family cycle.

This suggests that preparation for marriage should include some instruction on the factors which may threaten marital success in later years. Concentration on the more obvious problems of early marital adjustment can readily obscure more basic causes of failure which may have their origin early in marriage, but are unrecognized because their significance can be grasped only by studying the maladjustment patterns of later years.

CHAPTER TEN

The Nontypical Cases

In this chapter we shall consider marriage breakdown among several special types of marriages which have been judged atypical. Such unions appear unstable either because of unusual factors related to the circumstances accompanying the marriage or because of conditions placed in the contract which imply that marriage adjustment may prove difficult. We have classified as atypical war marriages, "forced" marriages, marriages in which children were positively excluded by one or both partners, and marriages of the widowed. These cases have been given separate treatment for two reasons. First, some of them, such as war and "forced" marriages, are of special interest in themselves. And second, their inclusion in the typical cases would have biased many of the findings. The atypical cases constitute a little over 20 per cent of all the cases studied. Of this number, war marriages account for a little over one-third, "forced" marriages for almost one-fifth, marriages excluding offspring, approximately one-third, and marriages involving the widowed, only about 7 per cent.

WAR MARRIAGES

The first atypical category to be treated will be war marriages. The term *war marriages* is used here to include all those marriages which were contracted during or just prior to World War II, and in which separation occasioned by military service prevented the establishment of normal married life. This use of the term is rather broad. Ordinarily, war marriages signify those marriages contracted during the first five or six months of the war.[1] The exceptional instability of war marriages was noted after World War I. According to Hall, the marriages contracted during the war years were very unstable, although, as he demonstrates, those contracted immediately after the war were even more so.[2]

Cuber excellently summarizes the problems of war marriages under five headings: (1) the hurried nature of many of these marriages which occurred between two persons not emotionally quite ready for marriage; (2) the effects of the prolonged separation; (3) the problems of a quasi "home"; (4) the subtle and important influence of the ever-potential third party in this kind of marriage; and (5) the wartime nuptial pregnancy.[3] Waller devoted considerable study to the problems of war marriages and predicted "a thumping increase in the divorce rate as one of the costs of the war."[4] Bossard asks a very pertinent question concerning such marriages: Are they worth saving?[5] Of course, for Catholics, who maintain that all consummated valid marriages are indissoluble, the answer is in the affirmative, but this does not discount the basic instability of such unions.

Catholic War Marriages

There are no available data on how many war marriages there were among Catholics, but by placing all the cases before the chancery court in a separate category, it will be possible to learn something about the characteristics of those that failed. Hence, we cannot answer the question: How did the war marriages turn out? but we do know something about a representative group that failed. A study of their records should throw some light on the major unstabilizing factors in such unions.

Our cases included only valid Catholic marriages. Apparently these couples accepted the Church's teaching that marriage is "for life." We have no reason to believe that on that happy wedding day when the marriage vows were exchanged, they had any thought but that theirs was to be a joyous life together "until death do us part." Yet several of these unions did not last three weeks, one out of six broke up within six months, and in 90 per cent of the cases, the partners had gone their separate ways within five years. What evil force had penetrated the intimacy of this new-found union, smashing all hope of wedded happiness?

For two out of three couples it was the same monotonous history: infidelity and desertion. To be sure, the variations on this motif were numberless. No two cases were alike, and yet, in a sense, they were all alike. The war had separated the newlyweds before they were able to establish durable marriage relationships. Shared experiences were too few. The common feelings, attitudes, and ideals essential to enduring unity had not been given time to form. The couples were too immature and knew too little of each other to foster mutual understanding and sympathy through the difficult medium of letters during the long months of forced separation. Hence, the familiar sequence: first, frequent, fervent letters, mutual protestations of enduring love and longing; then, as each acquired new experiences, experiences which they were incapable of communicating to each other, the letters slackened, the messages grew monotonous and dull, a forfeit of duty rather than an act of devoted love.

It was at this juncture that the third party frequently entered the scene. There is a common assumption that it was always the husband who failed. In our study it was the wife at the ratio of three to two who found fidelity too burdensome. In many cases the implications of the new attachment were not faced until the war had ended and "Johnny came marching home again." Marching home again to what? Normally, it would be to resume the routine family relationships so rudely disrupted by the war. But the waiting bride had not always waited. At times, Johnny had formed new attachments during the separation. Then the march home continued right on to the separation court and one more war tragedy was recorded.

This was the story of those who made no attempt to resume marital life after the war. They represent nearly 70 per cent of the cases studied. The remaining 30 per cent did try to establish normal family life after the war. These couples had cherished real hopes of making a success of their ill-fated marriages. In many cases, however, the reunion proved disillusioning for one or both the partners.

In some instances, the husband was nursing a bad case of "nerves"—like the ex-bomber pilot of whom one of the counselors remarked: "This poor fellow made sixty trips over Germany and hasn't come to earth yet." In many cases the couples found that their unshared experiences had so changed them that they were comparative strangers. They had been granted so little time to know each other as husband and wife, and during the long months of separation they had built up in their dream-world such unrealistic images of their beloved that the actual experience of living together proved seriously upsetting.

They were facing the post-honeymoon adjustment without the honeymoon. The impulsive, romantic mood inspired by the atmosphere of war had subsided. "Johnny" looked less impressive without his uniform and stripped of the aura of the soldier about to do or die for his country. And the starry-eyed bride? Frequently enough, she was starry-eyed no longer. Her former hero-worship seemed a little outmoded in the postwar fatigue and let-down. Perhaps she had been holding a job and was now self-reliant and matured by the experience. Or, as was true in nearly 50 per cent of the cases, she had become a mother, going through the enriching but trying period of young motherhood alone.

It was natural for her to look for cooperation, sympathy, affection, and understanding in her new role, and she was

deeply hurt when her returning husband showed little eager-
ness or enthusiasm to assume his obligations as father. It is not
surprising that these couples found the postwar adjustment
very difficult; so difficult in fact, that a considerable number
sought escape in separation or divorce. All circumstances considered, perhaps we should be surprised at the number that
achieved success.

Some Characteristics Indicative of Instability

Up to this point we have been considering only the outcome
of these ill-fated marriages. We have indicated some of the
patterns which they followed and some of the obvious obstacles which the more enduring ones had to face. Is it possible
that by analyzing some of the characteristics of these unions
one could safely predict a high rate of failure? Some of our
findings suggest that these war marriages entailed unusual
risks.

In the first place, the mixed marriage rate for the group was
almost twice as high as for the area from which the cases
were drawn. Our research indicated that there was some increase in mixed marriages during the war but not to the extent
represented here, so that we can conclude that mixed marriages classified as war marriages are particularly unstable.
The reason why such marriages may be highly unstable is that
they were contracted hurriedly with little thought of the difficulties necessarily involved in such unions. Further, lack of
agreement on such basic marital issues as the use of contraceptives, fidelity, and indissolubility are bound to appear in
a specially acute manner during the disturbing circumstances
of war.

Many of these cases revealed all the signs of haste and immaturity usually associated with war marriages. Over 50 per
cent of the couples whose marriages ended with infidelity and
desertion had been acquainted for less than one year prior to
marriage. In general, the couples appeared younger than average. Among the brides, more than one out of each five had
married at age eighteen or younger and over 50 per cent were

age twenty or under. The husbands presented a similar pattern. Nearly one out of five was twenty or younger and approximately 50 per cent were age 22 or under at marriage.

Finally, the high percentage of childless couples appearing among these cases leads one to suspect that they had not accepted, at least in practice, the Church's teaching on the primary end of marriage. Among those cases in which the wife was unfaithful and had deserted, approximately 70 per cent of the unions were childless; when the husband had been the offender, 63 per cent were childless. It may be significant that among the couples who tried to make a success of their marriage after the war, nearly 50 per cent had one child or more.

To conclude, therefore, the war marriages studied presented specific indications of instability for the following reasons. First, the impulsive and immature tended to rush into them. This was shown by the high percentage of mixed marriages, the relatively brief period of acquaintance prior to marriage, the early age at marriage of the spouses, and finally, the thoughtless entrance into a contract with the desire of obtaining its privileges while making no provisions to fulfill its obligations as evidenced in the high percentage of childless marriages.

Second, the very circumstances of war were seen to have placed tremendous strains on these unions. There was the inevitable separation preventing the sharing of experience and mutual growth in marital unity. This factor was especially harmful. It frequently came soon after marriage and hung as a threat over the youthful union, causing the couple to postpone obligations and avoid necessary adjustments. Further, there was the ever-present threat or suspicion of the existence of a third party. Finally, there was the disillusionment and emotional letdown that usually follow periods of tension and high enthusiasm. To the manifold readjustments and adaptations necessarily involved in the return to civilian life were added the many difficulties of establishing a home and adjusting to the intimate, restricting personal demands of life with another in the relatively new and confining roles of husband and father.

"FORCED" MARRIAGES

"Forced" marriages have been classified separately, since, as their name suggests, they represent marriages which would not have been contracted, at least at the time when they were, unless the bride had become pregnant.[6] In this connection, it should be noted that contemporary dating, courtship, and engagement practices give rise to a host of serious problems for which society offers no ready solution. Modern man has removed the taboo upon sex discussion, together with most of the traditional restraints governing relationship between the sexes, but he has substituted no acceptable set of rules or modes of conduct in their place.[7]

To be sure, moral agencies in society still strongly condemn premarital intercourse and set a premium on premarital continence. At the same time, however, as soon as boys and girls reach sexual maturity they are permitted to engage in extensive physical intimacies which render the preservation of these moral standards highly improbable. During the dating and courtship periods, which generally last for several years, young people are unsupervised and unchaperoned. They are left free to engage in intensive sexual stimulation under circumstances which place a severe strain on their moral resources. It is a distressing commentary on the confusion dominating the thinking of contemporary parents that they permit and even encourage their immature offspring to engage in activities which they would consider highly dangerous for their own moral life.

Size of the Problem

To what extent young people fail to guard their moral integrity in this matter is difficult to say. Under the circumstances, however, it will come as a shock only to the superficial to learn that research uncovers a good deal of failure. A question which immediately suggests itself is what effect this failure may have on later success in marriage. There are many possibilities. Intimacies may take place only with others than the future spouse, or only with the future spouse, or with both.[8] These intimacies may have no overt social consequences, or they may result in pregnancy. This latter contingency is our concern in this chapter.

When premarital pregnancy occurs, recourse may be had to three possible modes of action. The couple may contract marriage, thus legitimizing the offspring; the mother may remain unmarried and give birth to an illegitimate child; or she may seek an abortion. There is sufficient evidence to show that all three methods are being employed to a considerable degree in present-day society. Since only therapeutic abortions are legal, there are no reliable data on the number of "criminal" abortions which take place. Estimates range from half a million to well over a million annually. Although the majority of illegal abortions are induced by married women (the consensus is that they account for between 85 and 90 per cent), this still leaves an appalling number of abortions which are induced by unwed mothers.[9]

The social stigma placed upon the unmarried mother and her illegitimate child varies with social class, race, and region. Nowhere in our society, however, is illegitimacy viewed with approval, so that its relatively high frequency should occasion some surprise. More than 100,000 illegitimate babies have been born each year since 1944, and in 1947, the estimated number rose to 131,900. It is reported that in the ten-year period 1938–47 an estimated 657,200 illegitimate babies were born.[10]

The third solution to the problem of premarital pregnancy is marriage. From the very nature of the case, it is impossible to know the exact number of times this solution is followed. Christensen has investigated the problem in two widely separated groups—1,670 couples in Utah County, Utah, and 1,531 families in Tippecanoe County, Indiana—and has found that a little more than 20 per cent of the firstborn were premaritally conceived.[11]

He found that premarital pregnancy was higher during the depression years of 1929–31 than for either 1919–21 or 1939–41. It was higher than average for parents who married young, had a civil or secular ceremony, and were classified occupationally as laborers. The majority of the couples had married

about two or three months after the time of conception, that
is, soon after the pregnancy condition had become definitely
known to them.[12] Christensen points out that we have no way
of judging the applicability of his findings to the rest of the
United States but suggests that there would be considerable
regional differences. His general conclusion, however, seems
acceptable: "From all available research, one might judge premarital pregnancy to be a rather common phenomenon in
most societies." [13]

On this point our research among Catholic couples covers
only a small sample of 130 marriages. The data were obtained
from cases entering the obstetrical department of two hospitals during a brief period. It was found that in approximately
10 per cent of the cases, the firstborn had been premaritally
conceived. This sample, too small to justify any generalizations, does point up the fact that the problem we are considering is not uncommon, but because of the sample's size, we shall
make no further use of the data here.

As we have shown, the high rate of abortion, illegitimacy,
and premarital conception offers a thought-provoking commentary on contemporary dating and courtship practices. It
appears that the cultural ideal of premarital chastity is increasingly ineffective. The evidence would seem to justify
a re-examination either of the cultural ideal or of the dating
and courtship practices. Since Catholics hold that premarital
chastity is a necessary corollary to their integral concept of
chastity, that is, to the rationally ordered use of their reproductive faculties, the direction which their thinking must take
is clear.

Should Marriage Be Advised?

One of the serious problems which arises when failure to
observe premarital chastity results in pregnancy is whether
the couple should be encouraged to marry. Marriage is apparently the easiest and simplest solution to a socially embarrassing situation. If pregnancy results from something more than
a mere casual relationship, this is probably the solution which

is most frequently suggested. There are many reasons. Abortions are costly, illegal, dangerous, and immoral. Illegitimacy bears a social stigma for mother and child—the lot of the bastard has been rough down through the ages.[14] The reputation of the girl and her family are thus preserved, for by a kind of social fiction, society accepts the *post factum* legitimizing of the relationship with no stronger censure than a knowing smile.

On the other hand, "two wrongs do not make a right." Marriage is a holy state, based on a sacramental contract freely entered into by two competent persons. It would seem to partake of the nature of a sacrilege, therefore, to use marriage as a facile cover-up for an embarrassing failure. The possible life-long consequences of dragooning an unprepared and unsuited young couple into marriage should give pause to all who must deal with such cases.

Unfortunately, the social pressure on both the couple and their families is so great that mature judgment is rarely exercised in making the decision. The parents love their children and value their future happiness, but they are embarrassed, irritated, and secretly conscious of their own neglect. They find it easy to rationalize their short-term view by telling themselves all will turn out well. The couple are usually frightened and bewildered when their previous conduct is exposed. Sensing the condemnation of society and of their immediate families, their first impulse is to seek escape. Since this is seldom possible, they are willing to do anything to end the matter and forget.

A fair evaluation of the situation demands that neither the pleas of the parents nor the loving protestations of the couple be given undue weight. The problem will be to judge whether the prospective union offers some guarantees of happiness and stability to the parties, since matrimony was never meant to be a punishment for previous indiscretions. The following considerations will necessarily enter into the final judgment deciding whether the couple should marry or not.

A "forced" marriage is one which by definition would not be contracted at this time except for the condition of the bride.

In this case, marriage is being sought as the easiest way out of a socially embarrassing situation. No doubt, considerable pressure is being brought on the young man by one or both of the interested families; his sense of duty and responsibility is being appealed to; in general, he is being made to feel that "this is the right thing to do." As a result, he may be entering marriage emotionally unprepared, and his bride likewise. Both may eventually feel resentment because marriage was contracted under pressure. Both parties may find relations with their in-laws strained and tense, at least in the beginning.

Further, when conflicts arise in married life, as they are bound to do, the whole sordid past may be cast up by one or both of the partners, and what started as a minor quarrel may soon assume the proportions of a bitter duel in mutual recrimination. Is it not possible that this sad state of affairs may continue until one or the other can endure it no longer and decides to break the union, or else seeks refuge outside the home?

"Forced" Marriages and Marital Success

Are such marriages successful? Obviously, if the estimates on premarital pregnancy are correct, a good number of them appear to work out all right. On the other hand, in a study of divorced and of happily married couples, Locke found marriages forced by pregnancy were very prevalent among his divorced couples.[15] In a study of elopements, Popenoe found that two-thirds of the marriages ended in failure when the elopement was motivated by pregnancy.[16] Christensen, reporting on his Indiana study, stated that the premarital pregnancy group had the highest divorce rate of any of the couples studied.[17] These findings receive some corroboration from the studies which have been made on the relationship between premarital intercourse and success or failure in marriage.[18] In general, they support the conclusion that couples with no experience of premarital intercourse have the higher probability of marital success, while couples in which husband or wife had premarital relationships with spouse and/or with others have a lower probability.

"Forced" Marriages Involving Catholics

Although we do not know what percentage of "forced" marriages eventually fail, it is possible that an analysis of the cases which appeared before the chancery court will reveal some factors predictive of instability. All the cases studied were "forced" marriages in the sense that the bride was pregnant at the time of marriage. The term *forced* as used here does not imply that the marriage would not have taken place eventually if the pregnancy had not occurred; it does imply that the pregnancy was the immediate occasion for the contract.

Causes of Failure. What factors had entered into the breakdown of these unions? Adultery had occurred in 41.9 per cent of the cases (30.5 per cent on the part of the husband; 11.4 per cent on the part of the wife). Marked irresponsibility or immaturity was displayed by one or both parties in 22 per cent of the cases. Clash of temperaments characterized by constant bickering and quarreling, accounted for approximately 19 per cent, and hostility and interference on the part of the in-laws for the remaining 18 per cent of the couples. Hence, the areas in which forced marriages found adjustment most difficult were fidelity, responsibility, temperaments, and in-laws.

Duration of the Marriage. How long did these couples remain together? Approximately one out of each six separated within the first year, and over 56 per cent within the first five years of marriage. Of the remainder, 20 per cent broke up during the five to ten year period, and the rest sometime after the first ten years. Some may question the pertinence of the premarital pregnancy factor in the disintegration of those unions which lasted for more than ten years, but the couples themselves considered it a real factor. In explaining their marriage problems, they usually introduced some remark to the effect that "our marriage started wrong in the first place."

Number of Children. Did these couples have many children? There is a prevalent assumption that children are a stabilizing factor in marriage, but it should be pointed out that a child who is the product of a forced marriage may well have the opposite effect on the marriage. There is some support for this contention in the fact that 51.5 per cent of the families had but one child, who was, presumably, the cause of the marriage. However, since well over half of these unions lasted less than five years, we would expect the number of children per family to be low. For this reason, it is impossible, except in individual cases, to state what role the unplanned child played in the marriage breakdown. At any rate, it was apparent that we cannot assume that children are always a stabilizing factor in marriage. To complete our figures for the remaining couples: 21.9 per cent had two children; 17.2 had three or more; and 9.5 per cent had no living children at the time of the separation.

Husband's Occupation. From what occupational class did these couples come? Data on illegitimacy indicate that the majority of unwed mothers come from the lower socioeconomic classes. Our data reveal that the majority of husbands in the cases studied came from the laboring classes. For example, 57.1 per cent were classified as either unskilled or semiskilled; 29.5 per cent were skilled, and only 13.3 per cent were from the white-collar classes.

Type of Marriage. These cases were overrepresented in mixed marriages. Approximately one out of each four was mixed, indicating that interfaith marriages under these circumstances were particularly hazardous. It is obvious that the great danger of mixed marriages under conditions implying force is that the non-Catholic party, who does not hold that marriage is indissoluble, may readily use marriage as a facile means of escaping a difficult situation since a subsequent divorce is always possible.

Courtship Characteristics. The data on length of acquaintance and of engagement revealed considerable precipitation. One out of five forced marriages was contracted after an acquaintance of less than six months, and nearly two-thirds, after an acquaintance of less than one year. Approximately 70 per cent of the couples had not been engaged, and the majority of those who were had been engaged for less than six months. It is scarcely necessary to remark that the engagement of a couple serves several purposes in our society. It is a clear declaration by two people that they are in love and intend to marry in due season.

Further, it is a period when the prospective mates can come to know each other's character a little better and also can have some time to make definite plans for the future. Since 70 per cent of the couples had no engagement period, we can assume that many of them had entered marriage before they had reached that stage in their friendship at which they were ready to make their mutual affection public by the act of becoming engaged. Further, they would be handicapped in their marriage by not having a sufficient knowledge of each other's personality. Finally, they would probably have been plunged into the difficult task of founding a home without having made adequate plans and preparations.

The Couple's Age. One of the most significant factors in the cases studied is the age of the parties at marriage. Maturity is not necessarily related to age, and it is well known that age at marriage varies according to culture, race, and social class. Nevertheless, any marked deviation from prevalent standards of a given group is evidence of uncustomary behavior and is likely to result in serious maladjustment. This is particularly true if the deviation consists in a high percentage of early marriages. In any cultural group, youth is brought to maturity and prepared to fulfill its obligations in life only at a specific age. Circumstances forcing an individual to embrace a mature status in the group prematurely are likely to produce a situation which will find him unprepared for his role.

The age at marriage data for the forced marriages studied are so striking as to need little comment. One out of ten husbands was married before reaching age 19; one out of five, before 20, and well over half at 21 or younger. Similar data for the brides are even more revealing. One out of five was married before 18; more than two out of five before 19; well over half before they were 20, and approximately two-thirds were less than 21.

Summary. Hence, it appears that there are several predictive factors which are significant in counseling couples contemplating a forced marriage. Factors to watch are difference in religion, length of acquaintance and engagement, and age at marriage. In other words, when the proposed marriage will be mixed, or when the prospective marriage mates have known each other only a relatively short time, or when they have not been engaged, or when one or both are relatively young (the girl under 20, the boy under 23), we have a clear warning that it is hazardous indeed to allow the couple to choose marriage as the way out of their predicament.

Particular attention should be called to a combination of these factors, for example, mixed marriage and youthfulness or brief acquaintance. In such cases, it appears that marriage would be an unreasonable risk. In general, therefore, our study shows that it will not be prudent to maintain any a priori position which on general principles either excludes or recommends marriage as a solution in all cases. Each case must be studied separately, and it is hoped that the factors which have been shown to have predictive value will help the counselor reach a prudent decision when he is asked for an opinion.

In conclusion, it should be emphasized that the problem of forced marriages should be dealt with at two levels. First, at the cultural level, those dating and courtship practices which are opposed to the Christian ideal of chastity must be modified so that we do not tolerate conditions which render the violation of that ideal highly probable. This is a long-range policy requiring the cooperation of parents and religious forces. Second, since premarital pregnancy will continue to occur until these cultural changes are effected, prudent norms for handling such cases must be established lest an unrealistic, a priori rule of either excluding or recommending marriage under all circumstances should greatly multiply the harm which has been done.

MARRIAGES IN WHICH CHILDREN WERE EXCLUDED

Marriages in which offspring were prohibited have been classified as a third category of atypical unions. The intention of one or both the partners to exclude children is a predisposing condition making for great marital instability. Catholics who are taught that the primary end of marriage is the procreation of children and yet, with malice aforethought knowingly exclude the possibility of having them, cannot enter wholeheartedly into the marriage contract.

It is not merely the absence of children which renders such unions unstable, but rather it is the intention of accepting only part of the responsibilities and obligations associated with the marriage contract. This represents, as it were, a partial consent, an attempt to establish a union short of marriage, a selfish withholding of that total surrender which marital love is generally assumed to imply. Hence, the essential weakness of these unions consists in the restricted nature of the contract and the limited quality of the consent. We repeat, it is not the existence or nonexistence of children which is regarded as peculiarly unstabilizing in these marriages, but rather, the sentiments which the will to exclude children betrays.

Furthermore, it is possible that not all the cases in which children were absolutely excluded from the marriage have been detected and placed in this category. Indeed, the high percentage of childless marriages (35 per cent) among the couples appearing before the chancery separation court leads one to suspect that there were additional cases in which children were implicitly excluded. However, this fact was not uncovered in the interviews, signifying that the exclusion of children had not become a subject of disagreement between the partners.

In other words, the cases classified under this heading represent marriages in which the explicit intention of excluding offspring was recognized as a disintegrating factor in the mar-

riage. Marital disintegration followed two broad patterns
among these cases. In the first, one of the partners constantly
refused to permit offspring, and this refusal became a subject
of contention and disagreement for the couple. In the second,
both had agreed to exclude children, but when the union had
started to disintegrate, either one or both had come to recognize that their marriage had been started under false pretenses.

Factors in Maladjustment

What were the immediate factors which entered into the
breakdown of these unions? In approximately 45 per cent of
the cases, adultery appeared as the major disintegrating factor.
The husband appeared as the offender in two out of three
cases. In-law trouble was alleged in about 15 per cent of the
cases. The remaining 40 per cent broke up because of constant
quarreling and fighting. Maladjustment among this latter
group appeared to follow on the refusal of one or both partners
to make any concessions. In general, these cases evidenced a
selfish individualism which readily claimed privileges but
recognized few obligations. It is possible that we are dealing
here with a basic type of immaturity.

Pertinent Characteristics of These Couples

The nationality groups exhibited some differences worthy
of notice. Cases involving husbands and/or wives of Italian
descent were highly overrepresented. Irish and Polish husbands were underrepresented. German husbands were slightly
overrepresented, whereas German, Irish, and Polish wives
tended to follow the average. Husbands and wives of the
other national groups were underrepresented. It is difficult
to interpret the significance of these ethnic differences. For
example, those of Italian descent may be overrepresented in
this category either because they are more likely to be involved in marriages in which children are excluded or because
when such exclusion does take place, the marriage does not
survive.

Mixed and convert marriages were overrepresented in this
category. This was true especially among those cases in which

the marriage was broken because of infidelity, where only 56 per cent were both Catholic, 28 per cent were mixed, and 16 per cent were convert marriages. The acquaintance, engagement, and age at marriage characteristics of this group showed slight deviations from expectancy. On the other hand, the data on age difference between the spouses were revealing. Cases which ended in adultery were overrepresented in unions involving spouses of the same age, and where age differences existed, they were all found in the 1-5 year class. Among the remaining cases there were almost no marriages in which the spouses were the same age; a high percentage of wives were older than their husbands; and in those cases where the husband was older, he tended to be six or more years older. It is primarily among this group that age difference between the spouses appeared as a significant factor in the maladjustment.

The white-collar occupational classes tended to be overrepresented in this category. As was to be expected, most of these cases were childless. However, in about one out of every seven cases there was one child. The interviews revealed that this child was undesired by one or both the partners, and in many cases, its arrival was the occasion for the separation of the couple. This was particularly true in those cases in which the wife refused to submit to an abortion at the request of the husband. Most of these unions broke up relatively early. Only one-third endured for more than five years and less than 12 per cent lasted more than ten years.

This brief description of the broken marriages in which children were excluded confirms the hypothesis that such cases are atypical and should be studied separately. They constitute one species of what has been called the "companionate" or "arrested" family.[19] Participants in this type are characterized primarily by their intent to avoid offspring and all possible social responsibilities. This approach to marriage has been made possible by the widespread acceptance and dissemination of fairly reliable contraceptive techniques. Couples now have it within their power to enjoy marital relations without accepting any of their social consequences. Although it is conceivable that a given couple may advance rather cogent reasons such as health, income, or peculiar circumstances for postponing or limiting their offspring, the absolute exclusion of children motivated by the desire to escape all social responsibilities of the marriage contract reflects a selfish attitude scarcely compatible with successful marital adjustment. It was the appearance of precisely this attitude which caused us to place these cases in a separate category. In other words, couples who enter marriage with this attitude are not likely to make the adjustments and adaptations which life together implies.

MARRIAGES INVOLVING THE WIDOWED

Marriage cases involving the widowed were placed in a separate category not because such marriages were considered particularly unstable but because they were characterized by distinctive traits meriting separate study. It is not known how many Catholics were involved in such unions, but an investigation of the marriage licenses issued in the area reveals that between 6 and 7 per cent of all individuals seeking a license were widowed. Although our study includes a relatively small number of cases, a brief description of their characteristics will indicate some of the problems of adjustment which occur in such unions.

In over 80 per cent of the cases, the maladjustment leading to the breakdown of the marriage was caused by the presence of children from a previous marriage. The difficulty arose in a variety of ways. In some cases the children refused to accept the new parent or were hostile through fear of losing some of their inheritance. In other cases, there were accusations of partiality and favoritism. This was particularly evident when both parties came to the marriage with children from a previous union. The small remaining percentage of cases broke up for a variety of reasons ranging from drink to problems of sexual adjustment.

In most of these cases both spouses were Catholic. They had married after an acquaintance of one year or less. Approximately 94 per cent of the husbands were 30 years and over at marriage, and the same percentage of wives were 27 years and over. As might be expected, the age differences between the spouses were marked. Over 40 per cent of the husbands were six years or more older than their wives. Over 75 per cent of the unions were childless; one out of six had one child, and a few cases had two children. These marriages were of short duration. One-third broke up within the first year; two-thirds within the first five years, and the majority of the remainder shortly thereafter.

From this brief description it can be seen that marriage cases involving the widowed represent a distinct category. The problems of adjustment facing these unions are unique, and although the participants have the benefit of experience and maturity, it is evident that some are not capable of making the necessary adaptations. As the records reveal, insecurity, loneliness, and economic necessity were the principal motives for contracting the new marriage. It would be interesting to know how many marriages contracted with these motives actually produce the happiness of the parties. It is apparent that the "marriage expectations" of these couples differ from those expressed by individuals involved in the more youthful first marriages, but there is no reason to believe that they do not result in considerable happiness and satisfaction. All the present study has accomplished is to indicate some of the possible tension areas in such alliances.

GENERAL SUMMARY

This concludes our study of broken Catholic marriages. We have seen that for the average Catholic studied, the institution of matrimony is something very serious, imposing obligations and duties binding in conscience. Only the failure to fulfill one of the essential roles of a marriage partner was sufficient to break up the marriage in the majority of cases. The records reveal that one of the parties, at least, had endured a great deal before turning to the chancery court for permission to live apart from the spouse. This was particularly true in the cases which involved drink.

This willingness to endure hardships in the marriage state

shows that for the majority of well-instructed Catholics marriage is very definitely something more than a contract. Their actions indicated that they recognized the sacramental nature of the union even though they may not have been capable of giving a clear theological explanation of their beliefs. The indissoluble nature of the marriage bond was impressed deeply on all of them, and they exhibited a sufficient understanding of its implications in their own case. No doubt this conviction lent considerable force to their desire to make a success of their marriage.

In the final analysis, no matter what one may hold concerning the causes of maladjustment in marriage, it is obvious that success in marriage depends largely on the desire of the marriage partners to make a success of their union. Every marriage demands cooperation, mutual adjustment, and forbearance. Success in marriage is not based on the lack of temperamental differences, "incompatibilities," and disagreements, but rather, on how these are resolved in each individual case. And the will to resolve these differences in a dynamic union is the essence of successful marriage.

Now it seems obvious that if the two parties to the union are firmly convinced that the contract is indissoluble and therefore, if they are to find happiness in marriage, it must be found in *this* marriage, their will to make adjustments will be strengthened. For this reason, the cliché, so prevalent in some writings on divorce, that divorce never broke up a marriage, since the union was already broken and the divorce was only the final closing act of the marital tragedy, strikes one as extremely shallow and as obviously not based on actual experience in dealing with marriage cases.

Further, it should be remarked that in Catholic marriage, at least, the factors which lead to some unhappiness and dissatisfaction do not necessarily lead to the breakdown of the marriage. This point must be emphasized. Some of the studies on happiness in marriage leave the impression that the factors leading to unhappiness in marriage and the factors leading to complete breakdown of the union are identical. For the cases studied this was not true. As we have indicated, only failure to fulfill an essential role as a marriage partner leads to the complete breakdown of the union in the majority of cases. When marriage partners have a serious view of their obligations, they are willing to endure a great deal from the mate both for the sake of their ideals and the assumed good of their children. Many who have serious complaints against the partner and have engaged in rather violent quarrels do not think of these things in terms of separation or divorce. These are accepted as the necessary concomitants of the marriage state. There is little thought of escaping them through breaking up the union.

On the other hand, certain actions such as adultery and drink create situations which readily become intolerable. They are quickly identified in the minds of most married people with the breakdown of marriage. This is particularly true of adultery. Drink has the same ultimate effect, but since it does not imply direct violation of the marriage vows, experience shows that much more patience and toleration are exercised in its regard. However, it still remains a factor closely identified with the breakdown of marriage.

Finally, too much emphasis is sometimes placed on the initial adjustments required in marriage to the neglect of pointing out that marriage is a dynamic union requiring constant adjustment along constantly changing lines. There appears to be a rather general impression that a marriage which starts out well will endure. This is not the impression which emerges from the study of our data. It is very possible that early adjustments are readily managed and the marriage gets off to a good start, but this is no guarantee in itself that the union will not be broken. The coming of children, sudden changes in economic or social status, the influence of outside acquaintances, all these and a variety of other factors demand constant adjustment in the marriage cycle. A successful marriage is something that is constantly being made. There is no more tragic figure in all the court records than the individual who has taken his or her marriage for granted only to discover after five, ten, or even twenty years, that the ties of affection which bound them together at the start of marriage have withered away from inanition.

PART V

Programs for Survival

CHAPTER ELEVEN

Minority Values and Cultural Support

Up to this point our study of the American Catholic Family has been primarily descriptive. First, we have aimed at presenting the "frame of reference" within which the typical Catholic views marriage and the family. Developing the hypothesis that Catholic families constitute a distinct subsystem in American society, we have shown how they must "define the situation" in terms of their basic ideology and derivative institutional norms. In other words, the Catholic approach implies the existence of a set of absolute value premises which serve as unchanging points of departure in establishing practical programs for living. It was necessary to define these concepts clearly since it is precisely the focus of this study to investigate how Catholic families can realize these values in American society.

Second, we have asked who and where the Catholic families are. Summarizing the available data, we found that the Catholic minority numbers roughly 30 million, it is primarily urban, and tends to be regionally concentrated in the industrial areas of the East and Great Lakes region. Owing to its immigrant origin, it is far from unified. Ethnic differences still persist, and descendants of the Old and New Immigration have reached different stages in the acculturation process. Rated on the basis of formal schooling, occupational class, and income, members of the Catholic minority are found chiefly in the middle and lower classes. Their social class rating varies in different sections of the country since in some regions besides the three factors enumerated above, ethnic background and religion enter as discriminating factors in the appraisal of social status.

It was necessary to present these descriptive data concerning Catholic families because members of a minority encounter the dominant culture where and as they are. If the minority is relatively isolated and group members display strong solidarity, cultural differences are seen as group rather than personal differences. However, if group members mix freely with outgroup members, cultural differences are felt as personal problems, and there is a persistent tendency to conform to majority standards. Further, even when group solidarity is at a minimum, the proportion of group members in the community tempers the effect of the dominant culture. In other words, the dominant culture impinges differently on the relatively isolated Catholic family of the South and West than it does on the Catholic family in Boston or Brooklyn. Finally, the family's relative position in the social system will determine its contacts with various aspects of the dominant culture. Particularly in an industrialized urban environment, lower-middle and lower class families will be highly conscious of economic insecurity. On the other hand, it is generally conceded that both the lower and upper class families feel the "strain for consistency" much less than do the mobile middle class families. It is among these latter that the desire to conform may create serious obstacles to the realization of the Catholic family ideal.

Third, we have described some contemporary Catholic marriage patterns. One of the obvious threats to minority group survival is outgroup marriage. Considered from the viewpoint of religion, such unions may be either valid or invalid. Invalid marriage represents complete defection, temporary or permanent, from the group. Valid mixed marriage involves serious dangers to the faith of the group member and the possible offspring. Although there are no adequate data on invalid marriages, we presented indications that the number was relatively large and represented a serious avenue of "leakage" from the Catholic minority. Roughly one-fourth of all valid marriages were mixed. There is reason to believe that this proportion will increase as ethnic solidarity diminishes in the major urban centers.

Finally, we discussed some of the factors involved in the breakdown of Catholic marriages. After carefully distinguishing between what might be called typical marriages and those which were contracted under circumstances hardly predictive of success, we analyzed the major disintegrating factors which are operative in marital failure. It was apparent that marriage was viewed as a serious obligation by at least one of the partners with the result that considerable sacrifice had been made to maintain the union in most cases. This description of extreme cases of maladjustment served to outline the major tension areas in contemporary family life. Although separation is not an index of all marriage failure, it does indicate basic trouble spots. We need to know these if we are to make a realistic appraisal of the obstacles to success which the modern family must overcome in its effort to actualize its religious ideals.

FAMILY VALUES AND THEIR CULTURAL CONTEXT

Before we can come to grips with the real problems challenging the successful implementation of Catholic marriage values, we must outline briefly the pertinent characteristics of contemporary American society. This is necessary for two reasons. First, Catholic families do not operate in a social vacuum nor are they isolated from the normal influences exerted by society on the family unit. Second, Catholics must implement their marriage goals in the context of modern society. Abstract values and ideals mean very little until they are translated into definite social relationships. This process of translation or implementation will necessarily be conditioned by the social milieu within which it takes place.

Values Must Be Distinguished from Their Cultural Implementation

Unfortunately, this relationship between abstract values and their cultural implementation has frequently been ignored in the past. Men tend to identify specific cultural implementations of a value with the value itself. Under these conditions, when changed circumstances arise requiring a different implementation of the value, experience shows that men frequently cling vainly to outmoded patterns or reject both the value and its implementation since they have identified the two.

For example, consider the abstract value or principle represented by the private ownership of property. As a value to be maintained, this principle requires that individuals own and manage property because this is the best way that the goods of the earth can be brought into the service of the common good for which they were intended by their Creator. The implementation of this principle through specific social relationships may take on many forms such as feudalism, small individual holdings, or huge corporations. Each of these may represent fairly adequate implementations of the value under given circumstances. However, history reveals that in actual practice, the cultural implementation tended to be identified with the value so that when conditions changed, some clung vainly to outmoded forms and others rejected both the established social relationships and the value they had once implemented. As a result, some looked back with nostalgia to various types of an *ancien régime*; others rejected the principle of private property altogether; and still others embraced a new principle which, in reality, divorced private ownership from its intrinsic relationship to the common good. Only those who recognized the value as an absolute and its cultural implementations as relative could work effectively for its realization in a changing society.

Returning now to the family, what we are saying is that when one studies a given family system such as that represented by the Catholic family in Italy, Germany, Ireland, or the United States, one is studying what may be called a "cultural approximation" of the Catholic ideal. In other words, we are viewing the more or less adequate attempt of Catholics in these various cultures to implement the family values and goals which they hold in common. These cultural approximations will differ, for though they represent the translation of similar ultimate values into concrete social relationships, this occurs under dissimilar circumstances. They are called approximations because their very relatedness to a given social milieu limits them to being but one expression of the ideal. They are subject to modification inasmuch as changes in the total social system may render ineffective some established patterns and call for the substitution of others.

Values Are Related, Not Relative, to a Culture

Consequently, we do not expect to find that the American Catholic family has the same characteristics as the European Catholic family, nor do we suppose that the Catholic family of the future will be identical with that of the past. These statements do not imply cultural relativity of ultimate family values but cultural "relatedness" of values. The unchanging, absolute element is the marital society of male and female based on a sacramental contract and established for the fitting procreation and education of offspring, mutual service, companionship, and so forth. The changing, "related" elements are associated with differing concepts of the status and roles of male and female, parents and offspring, nuclear family and extended kinship groups, and family unit and society. These in turn are conditioned by the economic, political, and social structures within which the family and its members operate. An adequate understanding of both the static and dynamic elements in family systems will obviate some common misapprehensions found in discussions of family trends.

Limitations of an A Priori Approach

In the first place, an analysis of the characteristics of male and female and of the nature of conjugal society will yield only a limited knowledge of the family as a going concern in a specific society. This a priori approach will reveal basic purposes and goals, the essential structure of the family unit, and certain requisite functions. These are the unchanging, absolute elements in the family. However, this approach will not tell us how these purposes are to be fulfilled, what the actual structure of the family is in a given social setting, nor how the requisite functions are to be achieved.

For example, we can determine that the basic purpose of marriage is the procreation and education of offspring; we cannot a priori determine how many children a couple should produce nor what type of education they should give them. We can conclude that the husband is the head of the family, but we cannot from an analysis either of the characteristics of the male or of his status of husbandhood determine how this headship is to be fulfilled. We can conclude that the family unit must have a stable economic basis, but we cannot a priori determine either what this is to be nor how the means used to achieve it will affect all other relationships in the family unit. In other words, we cannot formulate programs for the practical implementation of Catholic family ideals and values without studying the total social environment in which it is to be achieved. There has been some tendency either to rest content with the reiteration of general family ideals and values as if this were sufficient to insure their implementation in a given social milieu, or, what is more distressing, to attempt to formulate specific means for their achievement without considering the conditions under which they would be effective. Both approaches lose sight of the dynamic character of a family system.

Applicability of Alien Solutions

Second, since an operating Catholic family system must represent the attempt to realize a specific set of family ideals and goals in a given social environment, examples of successful family life drawn from former or alien cultures will have limited value. One may consider adequate and efficient the family systems of Ireland, Germany, Italy, or nineteenth-century rural America; it does not follow that they would be desirable in our industrialized urban environment. In a rapidly changing society, each generation faces the problem of working out the adequate implementation of traditional family ideals and goals in a modified social milieu. Patterns of husband and wife and parent and child relationships which formerly functioned satisfactorily in a rural environment or in an alien culture may prove frustrating and inadequate today.

What is involved is much more than a problem of adaptation which all too frequently implies some sacrifice of values; what is required is a reinterpretation and a retranslation of traditional goals and values in terms of the modified social situation. This implies, as we have indicated, a clear distinction between values and their cultural implementation, but what is even more important, it necessitates a profound rethinking of the significance and implications of family goals and values in themselves. This can be illustrated by selecting just one example from the contemporary scene.

Changes in the status and roles of women as well as modification of the family structure have operated to place the wife in a position of equality with the husband. Does this signify that the husband is no longer the head of the family, or if he is still considered to be the head, does the wife cease to have equality? Obviously, this problem would not arise in a society which considered males to be naturally superior nor is it likely to occur in a rural environment where the economic functions of the domestic unit clearly specify the different tasks of family members in a common enterprise. Modern changes, however, need not require the rejection of the husband's headship; they do demand a rethinking of what it means.

In terms of Catholic teaching this will reveal that husband and wife are equal as persons; they enjoy equal rights in what pertains to the marriage contract. However, inasmuch as they are constituted by nature to fulfill different roles in the reproduction of the species, they will have different statuses and roles in the procreative society which they have formed. These differences are functional; that is, they are oriented in terms of reproduction. They do not imply inequality since they are not strictly comparable. The husband's headship, consequently, is functional; that is, it must be defined in terms of exigencies of the family unit. This does not imply the wife's domination by the husband but indicates that both husband and wife have united to form a unique society in which their sexual complementarity specifies different roles. The husband's headship, therefore, flows from and is limited by his role as protector and provider of the reproductive unit.[1]

Stable Values in a Transitional Culture

In the third place, it is necessary to distinguish between the static and dynamic aspects of an integrated family system lest we come to regard family values as wholly relative. In cataloguing the changes which the family has undergone in its transfer from a rural to an urban environment, the tendency is to declare that new family values must be substituted for the old if maladjustment is to be avoided. This implies that there is nothing static in a family system. The error in this approach is to confuse a specific cultural implementation of family values with the values themselves. Changed situations may require modifications in traditional family relationships; they do not necessitate new ultimate family values.

It appears that much of this confused thinking about changes in the family has arisen because, as a matter of fact, the family's transfer from a rural to an urban environment in America created a situation in which the changes which had previously taken place in traditional family values became clearly revealed. As long as the family remained in a small town or rural environment, traditional behavioral patterns persisted unchallenged, and it was easy to believe that traditional family values had remained unchanged. What had actually taken place, however, was a gradual dilution of the content of Christian ideology which had formerly furnished the basic premises from which men's thinking on marriage and the family was derived.

Consequently, only when traditional behavioral patterns were challenged under the impact of an industrialized urban environment did it become apparent that the value premises underlying the traditional family system were no longer operative. The full significance of this loss of ideology is apparent today. As we have indicated, there is little consensus on behavioral patterns and family norms because men no longer agree on ultimate value premises. In analyzing the situation, however, it is an error to assume that it was the process of urbanization which destroyed the value system; the truth of the matter is that this process merely offered the occasion for the realization that the traditional ideology had ceased to be operative.

This is not a mere forensic problem. Many people assume that traditional family values are no longer attainable or desirable in our urban environment. This assumption appears to be based on the historical fact that the American family's adjustments and adaptations to its urban environment have been made in terms of new family values. Further, it is obvious that changes in the social system require a repatterning of family relationships. Since a clear distinction is not made between values and their cultural implementation, it is concluded that the entire family system is relative and subject to change. Now if this were true, our present study of the Catholic family would represent little more than the description of a colossal cultural lag. Sooner or later, Catholic families would have to come to terms with their urban environment by modifying their value premises. On the other hand, since an integrated family system possesses both a static and a dynamic aspect, adaptations to changed social situations can be made without sacrificing essential family values. Even as a minority group, Catholic families can preserve their ideals and achieve their goals providing they make their adjustments in terms of their own value system rather than that of the dominant culture.

CHANGING STRUCTURAL CONTEXT OF
AMERICAN SOCIETY

This close relationship between family values and their social implementation necessitates some understanding of the social organization within which Catholic families must operate. What are the changes in American society which have caused family problems to become particularly acute in our day? For purposes of analysis these changes may be considered under two headings: structural and ideological. Structural changes are the objective changes which have taken place in those complexes of patterned relationships which constitute our juridical, political, economic, educational, and other social institutions. Ideological changes are changes which have taken place in those doctrines on the nature and purposes of man and of society which influence the form and functioning of the social order. In other words, to understand contemporary family problems it is necessary to know not only what changes have occurred in the social order but also what changes have taken place in the way people in general look upon social institutions and their functions. Although structure and ideology reciprocally influence each other, they constitute distinct elements and should be studied separately.

Transition from a Rural to an Urban Way of Life

One of the most interesting revolutions which has occurred in the past century is the shift of population from the farm to the city. In 1790, approximately 5 per cent of the population lived in cities of 2,500 or over. In 1950, close to 60 per cent were city dwellers. The principal factors in this continued increase of urban population are the rapid growth of industry which creates constant demand for industrial workers; a rising standard of living opening up new jobs in the service trades; better opportunities for advance and for acquiring a higher standard of living in an urban environment; the low prestige value of rural occupations in an industrial society; and the advent of the Industrial Revolution on the farm with the result that many less workers are required to supply the agricultural needs of the population.[2]

It is not easy to assess the social significance of this rapid urbanization of the American people. Undoubtedly, the city offers many advantages to the individual and the family. Churches, schools, hospitals, and cultural organizations are more readily accessible. There is a better choice of food, clothing, and housing for those with money. There are more jobs and avenues of social mobility open to those with energy and ambition. On the other hand, when people with varied personal traits, occupations, and culture dwell in close proximity, social stratification and spatial segregation are unfavorably accentuated. Kinship groups and the local community exercise less control over the conduct of the individual since people do not know each other very well, and interpersonal relationships tend to be segmented and impersonal. The individual's sense of belonging and of meaningful participation in the group among whom he lives is seriously weakened.[3]

Furthermore, an urban environment tends to blur moral standards. Working relationships must be established with such a vast variety of personalities, cultural differences, and value systems that the individual acquires a confused toleration even for moral differences. There is an over-all tendency to regulate conduct according to external group controls rather than by inner personal restraint. Paradoxically, in spite of the heterogeneity found in the urban center, the movement toward increasing homogeneity in interests, styles, intellectual outlook, and standards of conduct appears almost inevitable. The mass production of goods and services is geared to standards which will appeal to the greatest number so that a certain mediocre uniformity is gradually established in education, the press, the radio, movies, television, and so forth.

Urbanization has had far-reaching effects upon the family. In the traditional rural society, cooking, canning, sewing, the preparation of meals, the family garden, and the farm made the domestic unit relatively independent of outside economic institutions. Members of the rural family worked together as a close-knit, more or less isolated unit with the result that a strong family spirit was easily developed. This family spirit was characterized by the recognition of strong family bonds, the assumption that family property was held in common and consequently, was to be used for the maintenance and support of all the family members, and deep concern for the continued prosperity of the family group. Aged members were provided for and the young were assisted in establishing a new domestic unit. Many factors contribute to the weakening of this family spirit in an urban environment. The domestic unit is no longer a common economic enterprise, inadequate housing frequently makes it impossible for the family to take care of its aged and incapacitated members, and the increased mobility, both vertical and horizontal, characteristic of an urban society, widens the distance between family members and generations.[4]

This weakening of the family spirit leaves many individuals relatively isolated, thus increasing their feeling of insecurity. At the same time, although the city offers wider opportunities for higher standards of living, it makes the economic existence of many families more precarious. City people tend to live very near to the margins of their budgets. No doubt, they are more exposed to the exploitation of clever advertisers. Under the constant attack of high-pressure salesmanship, the distinction between necessities and nonnecessities is easily blurred. In like manner, the desire to "keep up with the Joneses," or to satisfy the complaint that "everybody in the block has one," leads many families to spend to the limit of their budget. The result is constant worry over money and a feeling of basic insecurity. The slightest drain on the family finance through sickness, accident, and so forth, can create an economic crisis.

Rapid Industrialization

Other changes in American society have added to the economic insecurity at least of the working-class family. The rapid industrialization of the economy has given America tremendous productive capacity and a high rate of employment. However, an ever-increasing percentage of the population no longer possesses productive property but is wholly dependent on the contents of pay envelopes for economic subsistence. Approximately 45 million of the 52 million people employed in manufacture, trade, transportation, finance, and government are wage and salary earners.

The fact that the large majority of workers do not own productive property from which they can draw revenue, particularly after retirement, necessarily affects family life. People worry about the time when they can no longer hold their jobs. They fear unemployment occasioned by technological changes, the migration of industries, or another depression. They are anxious about saving money, although under the circumstances in which many find themselves, the saving of substantial sums is impossible. Hence, American society presents the paradoxical picture of great wealth and relatively high standards of living for all, together with a feeling of essential insecurity impelling the individual to seek assurance in organized groups or the state rather than in the traditional family system.

Changes in the Family System

Closely associated with the industrialization of American society is the shift from a consanguine to a conjugal family type. The conjugal family is constituted by the community of husband, wife, and immature offspring. Major emphasis is placed on the husband-wife-child relationship or the immediate conjugal group, and although the relatives of both husband and wife are recognized, they exert little influence on the individual family unit.

The consanguine family type emphasizes blood relationship while the basic unit of the family is the group of blood relatives. The individual family unit is only part of the extended kinship group, and group members are structurally related to each other. In other words, the system sets definite patterns of social rights and responsibilities for all members during childhood, manhood, and old age. One never ceases to be a member of the family group. Individuals and conjugal units may come and go, but the family group persists. The consanguine family requires stability, restraint, and discipline, but it offers considerable individual security in return.[5]

The shift toward the conjugal family type in American society has significant social implications. Family members and family generations tend to become separated. Since the primary obligation of the individual is to his immediate conjugal unit, the orphaned, the sick, the incompetent, and the aged must be taken care of by society rather than by the family group. Each conjugal unit is autonomous but isolated, forced to encounter its problems and its crises alone. Individual domestic units must be established and maintained by young couples forced to rely upon only their own limited resources and experience.[6] Increased freedom, as always, implies increasing personal responsibility. Although the shift toward the conjugal family type has been accompanied by increasing individualism, it is worth noting that the primary factor involved is the powerful influence of economic institutions on other social units. The modern industrial organization demands worker mobility. The worker follows the job and industry hands out its awards on the basis of personal achievement rather than on status in a kinship group. Under these conditions, prestige and success go to those who have been trained from youth to be independent and to think in terms of personal not group promotion.

Finally, industrialization tends to modify the status and roles of family members. Since the father is compelled to spend much of his time away from the domestic unit, his control and influence over the children has been considerably modified. The wife has tended to assume more influence in the home and in the training of children. At the same time, industry offers the female many opportunities for work outside the home so that she is less dependent upon marriage and the male for her security. Most women are employed for some time before marriage. This experience increases their self-assurance while extending their interests beyond the domestic unit.[7] Children in a modern industrialized urban environment lose much of their economic utility. The period of adolescence is prolonged, and the school is used both for education and as a stop-gap until they are old enough to enter industry. As a result, there are serious discontinuities in the preparation of youth. Neither the domestic unit nor the school offers gradual stages of introduction to their life work in an industrial environment. They remain children too long and are forced to assume the responsibilities of men too quickly.

IDEOLOGICAL CONTEXT OF THE AMERICAN FAMILY

Although regional, social class, ethnic, and religious differences characterize American families, they all operate in a broad ideological context possessing specifically American features. We need to know something about this context if we desire to understand the conditions within which the Catholic family as a distinct subsystem must operate in realizing its goals. To be sure, the manner and force with which various features of the dominant culture impinge upon the individual family will vary according to location and social position, nevertheless, to the extent that Catholic families are not isolated, they will all experience the "strain for consistency" set up in every culture. This persistent pressure to conform, to be like others, to meet their problems as others meet them, can be the source of considerable strain for Catholics since all too frequently their frame of reference will not coincide with that of the dominant group.

It would be a serious error, however, to conclude that the cultural context is wholly or primarily inimical to Catholic family ideals. Owing to its complex, changing character, the culture tends directly neither to support nor oppose the realization of Catholic family goals. In general, it provides a relatively tolerant, permissive climate within which various subsystems are free to work out their destiny. It follows that the burden of elaborating the specific cultural implementation of a given value system rests with members of the group embracing this system. Furthermore, it is left to the subgroup to insure an adequate knowledge of its values, the identification of group members with these values, and the support and reinforcement of all members in their realization. It is this constant necessity of formulating and vitalizing its practical program in a neutral or nonsupportive culture which renders the understanding of the broad ideological context imperative when studying the conditions for minority survival.

American Culture Is Complex

Every society possesses broad cultural goals and through its norms, customs, and behavioral patterns defines, regulates, and controls the acceptable modes of attaining these goals. Cultures differ widely, however, in the clarity with which they define their goals, the degrees of integration existing among their various goals, and the extent to which institutional norms and behavioral patterns implement their goals. In a simple, well-integrated society, cultural goals are clearly defined and hierarchically ordered. At the same time, institutional norms and behavioral patterns are established to secure their general achievement. A complex, loosely integrated society, on the other hand, is characterized by its rather vaguely defined cultural goals, its toleration of variant cultural subsystems, and its acceptance of divergent behavioral patterns. Hence, a complex society requires only a limited degree of consensus; that is, its members must cooperate in the achievement of its temporal goals, and they must accept the general juridical, political, and economic framework within which society achieves these goals. Beyond this, they are free to organize their activities and work out their personal destinies in accordance with their respective philosophies of life.

American society presents all these characteristics of complexity. Indeed, we find it difficult to define just what we do mean by the "American way of life." It is relatively easy to outline broadly our political, economic, and social institutions, but over and above these, we feel there is much more. We think of respect for the individual, personal freedom, initiative, equality of opportunity, and the right to strive for happiness at the physical, intellectual, and spiritual levels of our being.

These are positive qualities; not easily defined nor measurable, but nevertheless real and highly prized in our culture.

Unfortunately, it is frequently forgotten that their full realization places heavy demands upon the individual—such freedom has a price. When a society does not clearly define behavioral patterns or institutional norms and leaves its cultural goals loosely integrated and somewhat nebulous, it is left to the individual to formulate his own "design for living" by wisely choosing among the various patterns society offers him. That many find the burden of personal choice too difficult is suggested by recent warnings that American youth are "conventional and gregarious," and their elders have acquired a "group think" mentality. The danger in this is not that people choose the expedient of conformity, for this has always been a tendency in organized groups. The present danger arises from the fact that when a group lacks a consistent ideology, group values are regarded not only as expedient—doubtless, a human failing—but as right and morally good. Self-determination implies a clearly defined value system, an internalized set of ultimate value premises from which practical programs of action are derived. Most individuals appear incapable of formulating their own consistent set of values and of selecting suitable behavior patterns to implement them so that if the culture does not provide these, they by-pass moral decisions and follow the standards of their immediate groups.[8]

Family Values in a Complex Culture

In analyzing the cultural context of the family we ask these questions. First, what is the structure of the family, and how is it integrated in the social system? We have answered by indicating the pertinent features of our modern industrialized urban society. Second, how do people look upon the family and the relationship associated with family life? In other words, what meaning do people give to sex, marriage, and the family institution? We shall attempt to answer that question in the paragraphs which follow. Considering the complexity of American culture, it is obvious that only the salient traits can be outlined, but this will prove sufficient to clarify the principal problems which the Catholic subsystem must face.

One of the most imperative drives which every society must regulate among its members is that which is concerned with the reproduction of the species. As we have indicated, the exercise of this function may be considered either a moral act—and consequently, its regulation will fall under the general norms specifying the morality of all human acts—or merely an act fraught with serious social consequences—and consequently, its regulation will be governed solely by the needs of the group. American society, since it supports a culture originally based on Christian traditions, follows in theory the first type of regulation: the exercise of the reproductive function is a moral act, and stable, monogamous marriage is the social institution established to channel its legitimate use.

However, in a complex culture lacking ideological consensus, individuals and groups embrace widely different concepts concerning the origin, nature, and destiny of man. It follows that they will advocate different systems for the regulation of the sexual drive. Unfortunately, ideological differences are seldom brought out into the open so that divergent behavioral patterns are tolerated or promoted with apparently slight awareness that they contradict traditional values. The result is that conventional standards and rules persist in the culture, while the life-conception or ideology which gives these patterns of behavior their value and meaning is no longer accepted by many.

Two practical consequences follow from this condition. In the first place, American society can reach little agreement on the regulation of the sexual drive. Since there is no unified thinking on premises, there can be none on practical programs. Open exploitation of the drive, with obvious detrimental social consequences, is tolerated in advertising, entertainment, art, and literature. Second, the process by which one set of norms and behavioral patterns is strongly advocated in theory and a different set is tolerated and promoted in practice gives rise to serious personal contradictions and tensions with the result that the subject of "sex" has come to preoccupy people's minds excessively and assumes a position out of all proportion to its importance in stable social life.

"Sex" Becomes a Problem

"Sex" has come to preoccupy the American mind not merely because the so-called Puritan and Victorian taboos have been discarded. Many of these were outmoded, unrealistic, and of doubtful social utility. What has happened is the toleration of every form of "sex-tease" in a society which is incapable of developing uniform norms and behavioral patterns culturally channeling the legitimate expression of the reproductive drive. It is this combination of stimulation and confusion which has made the problem acute. In the final analysis, the loss of a common ideology paralyzes democratic action for there exists no common premises on the basis of which practical programs can be established.

The family encounters the problem in many ways. Parents feel the serious need to instruct and prepare their children in sexual matters but have few precedents to rely on in their own childhood training. Hence, some rest content with the repetition of traditional warnings, while others gladly confide the task to an outside organization such as the school. Further, because biological maturity is reached several years before the accepted age for marriage and because society permits intimate and unsupervised relationships between the unmarried of both sexes, modern youth are subjected to tension, uncertainty, and frustration in patterning their activities. They are the prime victims of the contradiction between theory and practice which we have indicated above. At a period when they have not yet had time to develop adequate habits of control and a consistent personal attitude toward their own sexual drive and that of others, they are expected to display a reserve under excitation which their elders would probably be incapable of exercising.

The family is further affected by the present tendency to emphasize only the physical aspects of the reproductive drive.

Contrary to what the sex-tease experts appear to believe, the exercise of sex is an act of the person implying more than physical participation if it is to prove normally satisfying. The mere seeking of physical gratification results in nothing less than sexual exploitation, a totally different process from marital union in which the partners give themselves to each other as a culminating act of love. Unfortunately, the prevalent emphasis on the physical aspects of sex have led many to seek nothing more than this gratification even in marriage. Some marriage preparation manuals have contributed to this error by stressing only the physical techniques of sexual excitation as if they were dealing not with persons but some segmented phenomenon lending itself to detached manipulation.

Another disastrous effect of this undue emphasis on the physical aspects of sex is that marriage partners tend to regard each other as sexual objects rather than as persons. Hence, the mutual development and fulfillment which should be one of the chief personal fruits of marriage is never achieved. It is possible that this loss was less pernicious in former times when the institution of marriage offered other compensating benefits, but today when the isolated nuclear family places such stress on companionship and the affectional bonds between the partners, it may have serious consequences. It seems almost trite to suggest that in marriage as in all other institutions, it is the nonachievement of "expectations" or aspirational goals which is the primary factor in frustration.

Finally, this failure to develop an integral view of the personal and social functions of the reproductive drive gives rise to a series of discontinuities in the training and maturing process of American youth. By this we mean that the concept of sex which is stressed before marriage, since it emphasizes primarily the sex-tease and physical aspects of the drive, does not adequately prepare young people to take a mature view of sex in marriage. As a matter of fact, the reproductive drive in male and female *is* related to reproduction. The vast majority of people who marry *do* want one or more children. However, the prevalent segmental view of sex dissociates this normal purpose of the drive from its other aspects. Consequently, there is little training and preparation for the roles of parenthood. This might be stated in other words by saying that the emphasis is placed on marriage, not the family. American attitudes in this respect resemble the Hollywood script in which "getting married" is the final act rather than the first scene, as in real life experience.

This segmented, piecemeal thinking occurs whenever people lose sight of the normal purpose of an activity. American society offers many examples. Consider the present plight of college athletics. Sports were introduced into college life on the hypothesis that a sound mind in a sound body was desirable. Furthermore, competitive sports were tolerated presumably on the basis that teamwork and cooperation were traits that would prove valuable for later life in society. The college curriculum was obviously not designed as a preparation for gladiators. However, what was meant to be a means has been elevated into an ultimate purpose. Little attention is paid to the physical fitness of the average student. Huge expenditures of time and money are devoted to a handful of "special students" whose essential role in the college is to man the teams. The purpose of sports in an academic setting is forgotten. Somewhat the same process has occurred in regard to the function of the reproductive drive. In the training of youth, the essentially meaningful purpose of sex is unstressed so that their premarital experience, while perhaps making them masters at the techniques of the "pursuit," leaves them unprepared both in attitude and actual training for their integral roles as partners in the reproductive unit.

Contraceptives Become Institutionalized

Closely related to the disagreement concerning the function of sex is the variety of attitudes manifested toward the use of contraceptives. Catholics and some Protestant bodies consider their use to be morally objectionable. At the opposite pole are those who deny all moral content to the exercise of sex so that the use of contraceptives is held to be an amoral, individual affair. Between these polar positions appear various shades of thought distinguished primarily by the type of justifying cause they postulate for legitimizing the practice. In spite of these conceptual differences, however, it appears that some form of artificial family limitation is widespread. Herein lies the significance of the practice for the family.

What is the real significance of this general and socially accepted practice of birth control? It represents modern society's solution of the difficult problem of population control. The practical consequences for both the individual and the social system are manifold. Once the practice has become established (institutionalized), it is integrated or fitted into the total social structure, thus conditioning the aspirational goals of marriage partners and affecting the relationships of the family to other institutions. In other words, equilibrium or balance among various social relationships is worked out in terms of this practice. The patterned expectancies of individuals presuppose it, so that it serves a necessary function in coordinating major life goals.

A few examples will suffice to illustrate this point. Prescinding from the effect the practice may have on premarital chastity as well as on the quantity and quality of the population, let us consider some contemporary behavioral patterns which are obviously closely related to it. Americans tend to marry younger than members of most other Western nations. In practice this means that the period during which the female is exposed to pregnancy is lengthened. Hence, unless some type of birth control is employed, early age at marriage will normally be closely associated with a high birthrate. Further, the present tendency is to bunch the desired pregnancies in the early years of marriage. This planning implies some form of eliminating pregnancies in the later years of marriage since nature has endowed the female with a relatively long reproductive span.

Finally, in an industrialized urban setting, children tend to become an economic liability seriously competing with the material symbols so highly prized in that environment. Consequently, the acquisition and maintenance of a desired standard of living may conflict with nature so that some form of birth control is presupposed in formulating the normal expectancies of the average couple. It should be noted that the problem of control has acquired added significance owing to the splendid advances which have been made in the medical care of infants. In recent times, infant mortality has been reduced to a probable minimum, with the result that family planning no longer has to take into account the inevitable loss of offspring which characterized former periods.

Drawing our examples from a wider social context, we could point out that modern housing, both in design and size, reflects the practice of limiting offspring. In more subtle ways, wages, spending habits, formal educational patterns, advertising, entertainment, and the approved recreational patterns of the spouses during the various periods of the family cycle are geared for a society in which birth control is presumably practiced. This is part of the reciprocal adjustment and adaptation which occurs in the social system when the family, as the basic unit of society, is oriented to new values. In practice, the interactional process is difficult to analyze since cause and effect are obscured by the variety of reciprocal influences at work.

Lastly, the widespread dissemination and use of scientific contraceptive methods to control reproduction has profoundly affected the status and roles of women in American society. Until the discovery and social acceptance of easy and fairly reliable methods, the majority of women found themselves inevitably associated with the role of motherhood. Granted that there was considerable talk and agitation for "liberating" women from the "burdens" of motherhood and the "servitude" of the home, most women wanted to marry, and marriage meant children. At present, they can dissociate marriage from parenthood or, if they desire children, can specify when and how many with fair reliability. The significance of this "rationalization" of the reproductive process is that modern woman can follow her natural impulses for companionship and security in marriage and still avoid or limit her role as mother. Liberation from the burdens of motherhood and the servitude of the home need no longer be idle talk. She has it in her power to choose being a "homemaker," a "career" woman, or some combination of both.

It is pertinent to observe that institutionalizing contraceptive birth control has widened the area of choice and planning in marriage and the family. Moral and wider social considerations aside, what significance does this hold for successful family life? At first glance, it would appear to offer an excellent opportunity for solving many of the stresses and pressures which modern living conditions impose upon the family. Assuming early age at marriage, the prevalent insistence on physical union as the expression of the growing need for companionship and affection in the isolated nuclear type family which is developing, and the increased health care assuring the survival of most offspring, the control and planning of pregnancies would seem to be called for in the average marriage.

On the other hand, the widespread acceptance and use of contraceptive methods of control raise serious questions seldom faced in discussions of the problem. Considering the economic and social pressures brought to bear on the young couple, together with their obvious immaturity, how capable are they of making an intelligent choice in family planning? An intelligent choice in this matter implies some understanding of the meaning of children throughout the family cycle. Is it not possible that present pressures will blind the couple to their own best interests? Children, we are told, are hostages to the future. The choice not to have them is also a pledge to the future. How will this choice appear to the couple when they are forty or fifty? The point we are making is not that reproduction should be considered an irrational act. As a human act it implies right order and consequently, control and choice. But the introduction of relatively facile methods of control increases the responsibility of making an intelligent choice. There is little in the prevalent segmented, piecemeal thinking on the function of sex which indicates an awareness of the full implications of this fact.

Further, how does the contrived dissociation of physical union from reproduction affect the meaning of this union to the marriage partners? Under these conditions can physical union represent more than mutual gratification? Does it differ in quality from the unifying, mutually completing gift of the spouses' entire reproductive potential to each other? We cannot simply assume that physical union restricted to mutual gratification produces the same stabilizing and unifying effects as normal intercourse. Here again we are dealing with a pledge —on the one hand, to mutual gratification; on the other, to mutual completion in the reproductive unit.

These examples of the far-reaching effects of contraceptive birth control methods in society suggest that those who reject these methods will be faced with serious problems of adjustment and adaptation of their own. Since the practice has been institutionalized in the dominant culture, both the aspirational goals and the patterned relationships of the dissenting minority will be affected by the strain of conformity. In this case, what the dominant culture considers "normal" is pathological judged from the viewpoint of the minority. We shall treat this problem of the normalcy of the pathological in a later chapter when we discuss the basis for minority survival.

Divorce and the Family System

A further indication of cultural complexity—and confusion— is the American institution of divorce. Catholics regard a valid, consummated marriage as indissoluble. Cessation of cohabitation or separation "from bed and board" is allowed either temporarily or permanently when cohabitation would prove physically or spiritually harmful to one or both the partners or to the children. Although civil divorce legislation varies from state to state, the right to dissolve valid marriages is maintained by all states. Unless a divorce is contested, and only a small percentage are, the legal grounds on the basis of which the decree is granted are not significant, since it is an open secret that the great majority of such suits involve collusion. This distressing situation has arisen because of the disparity between accepted behavioral patterns and established legal norms. Divorce legislation is based on the assumption that marriage is a socially significant institution and that the public interest requires some control over its formation and dissolution. Divorce is granted only to the "innocent" partner on proof that the "guilty" spouse has committed one of the offenses (legal grounds) specified by the law. Public opinion, on the other hand, tends to regard marriage as a private affair. Common law marriages are still recognized in a number of states. Few regulations governing the entrance into marriage are tolerated, and the courts have been forced to acquiesce in the popular demand for the equivalent of divorce by mutual consent.

The contemporary evaluation of the social significance of this attitude toward divorce has been characterized by remarkable shallowness. We are told that divorce in itself is not significant since it is merely the public act which legally dissolves a marital union already broken. Some even argue that the high divorce rate is an indication of the great esteem in which the marriage state is held since couples refuse to remain in a union which does not fulfill their lofty expectations. To understand the real significance of divorce we must consider it as an institutionalized practice, not as an individual act. It is true that an individual divorce may be merely the legal dissolution of a previously disintegrated union, but divorce as an institutionalized practice is something different. It implies that the accepted family system is based on conditional stability. Hence, couples may enter the marriage state thoughtlessly and easily, for the union can be dissolved if it does not meet their expectations. During marriage the spouses may shirk their mutual responsibilities or refuse to make the normal adjustments and adaptations required for successful family life inasmuch as an escape through divorce is open to them. Furthermore, the mutual fidelity required by stable monogamous marriage is seriously threatened when the possibility of marital dissolution and the formation of a new union is rendered socially acceptable.

It follows that the social significance of divorce lies in its effect on the stability of the family system. Once the practice is institutionalized other social relationships are geared to it with the result that the entire family system is transformed. The process tends to have a cumulative effect. When divorce becomes common, marriages are contracted carelessly, marital adjustment loses some of its motivation, mutual fidelity is rendered more difficult, and more spouses come to find their union intolerable. Although we are not interested here in defending the indissolubility of marriage or in refuting the doctrine of divorce, it is consonant with our present purposes to point out that the core of the modern confusion concerning divorce is found in the pseudo-opposition which has been assumed to exist between the individual and his social institutions. Self-realization and the full development of personality are considered apart from society. Hence, institutional restraints, such as the marriage bond, represent limitations of individual freedom to be endured only as the individual sees fit.

But this dichotomy between the individual and his social institutions is based on untenable premises. In reality, social institutions are essential prerequisites for self-realization and the fullest development of personality. Individual and institution are not opposed but mutually supportive. Consequently, institutional regulations are not limitations of developmental freedom but represent the necessary channeling of human social activity along lines in conformity with the fullest self-realization of the individual.

Normless Striving

Finally, the ideology offers no standards or stable measures of success. This is a consequence of our "open class" system which recognizes no clearly defined class divisions separating people into closed categories defining and limiting their expectations and aspirations. We are proud of our system. In theory, anyone who is willing to work can climb the ladder of success. We are encouraged and free to mount to a higher socioeconomic position than that of our parents. Our standard of living is limited not by our social class but by our ability to earn in a competitive economy. The requisite to success—education—is open to all. This is the "American way" and we like it.

On the other hand, the system has its shortcomings. As we have indicated, it offers no meaningful standards by which to judge success. When is a man a success? When has he "arrived"? Theoretically, the "sky is the limit" and one advance merely sets the stage for another in a feverish, competitive climb to a "top" which is not defined. In such a system the only recognized symbols of success are material—the make of car you drive, the size of the home you own, the quality of the clothes you wear, the vacation trips you can afford, the grade of liquor you serve, indeed, even the size of the screen on your television set. It matters not whether these things increase your comfort or your happiness. They are external symbols by which you prove to yourself and to your neighbor that you are a success. If you do not have them, you are unhappy because the "Joneses" have them and, surely, "we are just as good as they are!"

We may well ask, as many observers have, "What makes them work so hard?" Or, in the words of the novelist, "What makes Sammy run?" The answer is our competitive, open-class system with only its material symbols as guarantees of success. This normless striving is reflected in family relationships. Some couples are so busy trying to keep up with or to get ahead of their neighbors that they neglect the possibilities for happiness in their own family. Marriage is regarded merely as the conventional basis of operation in the competitive struggle. Children are regarded as competitive pawns or as burdens limiting freedom and restricting the material symbols the couples can buy. Wives abet the prevalent competitive spirit by subtly urging their husbands to strive for more rapid advancement even at the cost of health and the sacrifice of human values. Husbands rationalize their neglect of wife and children as a necessary consequence of their absorption in business.

A major psychological effect of this striving is that it encourages only shallow relationships with others. We are compelled to interact with many different people during the course of the day but our competitive position prevents us from learning much about any of them. Relationships are partial and segmented—sufficient for the purpose but precluding any deep attachment. Indeed, the individual soon learns it is better to mind his own business and not to show too much interest in those with whom he has to deal. In a competitive society, "business is business," and one weakens his position if he allows himself to become emotionally involved. It is better to repress your feelings and to look upon people as things to be manipulated rather than as persons—one gets hurt less often and the wounds are more quickly healed.

This shallowness in social life may carry over into marriage. Some spouses never achieve profound mutual understanding. Indeed, some appear never to have tried to do so, either because they took their marriage for granted, or they were psychologically unprepared for deep insights and profound emotional relationships. We see them go through the regular dating, courtship, engagement, and wedding routines and then all progress in knowledge seems to stop as if the honeymoon were the culmination of intimacy in marriage, not its first fumbling initiation. Consequently, there is no progressive growth in knowledge leading to ever deeper emotional attachments and ever profounder insights into the many-faceted treasures of their partner's personality.

They are not "two-in-one-flesh," growing together through their mutually experienced joys and sorrows. Rather, they are two closed personalities dwelling in the same household. He turns to his business interests and his friends; she finds an emotional outlet in her children. Very often they do not realize how completely they have grown apart until the children leave home. The "empty nest" finds them facing each other as cohabiting strangers with little to talk about and less to do together. Strange as it may appear, through all these years they have progressed to little more than carnal knowledge of each other. The union ordained for their mutual development and support has remained an empty promise. They have paid their tribute to the species and to society and now they face the future in barren isolation.

SUMMARY

This chapter has presented a brief outline of the major structural and ideological social patterns pertinent to the American family system. Although the rapid transition from a rural to an industrialized urban environment has been well documented, the significance of this change for the family has led to various interpretations. Because family values have not been clearly distinguished from their specific cultural implementations, the inevitability of social change has led some to conclude that family values are necessarily relative to the social organization within which they are found. It is obvious that the social means employed to achieve family goals must be repatterned in a changing society; it does not follow that the goals themselves must be modified. Historically, the American family system underwent changes in both structure and goals because accompanying the shift from a rural to an urban way of life was a profound, though frequently unperceived, modification of the popular concepts concerning the origin, nature, and destiny of man.

As a result, the original American family system was deprived of its traditional ideological foundation. The industrialized urban environment necessitated numerous adjustments and adaptations, but there was no consensus on the ultimate premises in terms of which practical programs could be formulated. We have indicated the confusion which has arisen concerning the function of sex, the use of contraceptives, and the practice of divorce. In each area lip-service is still paid to traditional values, though new behavioral patterns have been developed on other premises. The over-all effect has been to create "problems" in the fields of sex, personality, and marriage which can only be solved by a straightforward reintegration of values, norms, and behavioral patterns. Unfortunately, a schizoid culture which refuses to make explicit its value premises offers no favorable opening for the application of such logic.

Finally, we have pointed out some of the family implications of a competitive, open-class, secular society. It is a society which places great value on success, and success is measured primarily in terms of material symbols. This normless striving tends to relegate family values to a secondary position inasmuch as even marital success is evaluated in terms of material acquisitions. At the same time, the qualities which prepare the individual for success in a competitive society frequently limit his ability to enter adequate relationships in the family. The over-all result is a certain lessening of esteem for the values which can be achieved only in family life.

CHAPTER TWELVE

Family Standards and Group Conformity

In a society characterized by competing value systems and rapid change, divergent subgroups can expect little direct support for their distinctive institutional norms and behavioral patterns from the dominant culture. Under these conditions, the minority faces the difficult problem of securing the conformity of group members to its standards. Conformity produces conformity in an integrated culture. That is to say, where there exists high consensus on norms and standards of conduct, a whole series of social mechanisms operate to encourage and enforce conformity. Minor deviations merit group disapproval and loss of esteem, while serious nonconformity is subjected to concrete sanctions. Human respect and acquired habits of acting tend to keep individual behavior consonant with group expectations. However, in a pluralistic culture embracing competing value systems, the operation of these social mechanisms is greatly restricted, and they are effective only to the degree that the individual values solidarity with his group.

Hence the practical problem facing the Catholic minority in American culture is how conformity to approved family standards can be secured. We have shown that Catholic families constitute a distinct cultural subsystem in American society. The essential elements of this subsystem as well as the ideological doctrines upon which it is based have been explained so that we now understand how it differs from the dominant family system. These differences on the level of theory are easily demonstrated, but they are pertinent only to the degree that they appear in practice. Discrepancies between family theory and practice manifest themselves even in well-integrated cultures, and, considering the lofty ideals of the Catholic system, only the inexperienced will be shocked to learn that in no period of the Church's history has perfect conformity by all members been achieved. However, the situation of the Church in America presents many unique aspects. Catholics exist as a more or less united minority in a predominantly non-Catholic culture.

Our next step, therefore, is to investigate the conditions requisite to securing conformity to Catholic family standards in a minority situation. Generally speaking, three conditions are necessary for conformity. First, group members must possess an adequate knowledge of the approved standards. Second, they must be sufficiently motivated to observe them. Third, they must be assisted and encouraged by other members of the group. We shall examine each of these conditions in some detail and then point out to what degree the Catholic minority is capable of meeting them. This approach will clarify some of the basic problems Catholics encounter in maintaining their family ideals.

CONFORMITY REQUIRES ADEQUATE KNOWLEDGE

First, group members must have an adequate knowledge of the approved family standards. The requirements of this condition appear obvious since there can be no more than chance conformity where the norms regulating conduct are not known. However, a minority group faces special problems in maintaining adequate knowledge of family standards among its members. Difficulties arise both in formulating the specific contents of the standards and in their dissemination throughout the group. In this connection, it should be noted that the Catholic family system, as we have explained it, involves a complete philosophy of life. Particular family norms and practices are intelligible only in terms of this philosophy.

Formulation of Family Standards

What are the special difficulties that a minority encounters in formulating the specific contents of its family standards? Briefly, although Catholic family values are considered absolute and unchanging, the social means used to implement them in a given culture are subject to modification. One need only recall the changes in family structure occasioned by the transition from a rural to an industrialized urban way of life to understand the point we are making. The contents of the marriage contract have remained the same; husbands are still husbands, wives are still wives, parents and children are still parents and children, but the intimate web of family relationships has undergone gradual change. In short, through a complex and often unconscious process, the statuses and roles of family members have been variously redefined. Although the definition of statuses and roles constitutes an integral part of the contents of family standards, from the viewpoint of the minority it is often difficult to judge which redefinitions are compatible with its value system. The implications and unanticipated consequences of some redefinitions are not always immediately apparent.

It follows that there will remain a degree of indecisiveness in the formulation of family standards. Basic doctrinal points and obvious practical applications will be clearly stated, but the minority's position on problems which arise at what may be termed the "growing edge" of family theory will be formulated rather slowly. To cite a few examples: What are a couple's obligations to have children? How many must they have? The use of periodic continence has introduced these problems in an acute fashion for the first time. Should married women seek employment outside the home in other than cases of dire necessity? Changes in the economic system, the status of women, and the anticipated standards of living have brought this difficult problem to the fore. Until adequate solutions are developed, minority members will maintain various positions on these issues, although there will be a tendency to conform to the standards of the dominant culture.

Dissemination of Knowledge

What are the difficulties which a minority encounters in disseminating adequate knowledge of its family standards? A consideration of the social vehicles used to inculcate cultural values indicates the principal ones. The family unit, of course, serves as the primary transmission belt for these values. It is in the family unit that the culture first and most enduringly impinges on the new member of society. In the second place, the school, particularly in American society, plays a large role in the dissemination of knowledge and the formation of attitudes. Next, the Church stands as the constant teacher and interpreter of the moral law and its applications. Through instruction, ritual, and symbol, it exercises a powerful influence on the character and outlook of the faithful. Finally, in the wider society there are peer groups, acquaintances, organizations, and the popular channels of information and entertainment. In an integrated culture, these forces would support and supplement each other in the transmission of accepted family standards. This is frequently not the case in a society where there exists a plurality of subsystems.

It follows that a minority must rely primarily on the family, the Church, and its private schools for the dissemination of its family doctrine. The public schools must, of necessity, refrain from teaching distinct subsystem values in a pluralistic society. Unless the minority remains isolated, contacts in the wider society offer conflicting and contradictory standards so that the added difficulty of refuting and counterbalancing these influences is imposed on the minority. In this connection, it is pertinent to recall the shift from the extended or consanguine family to the conjugal type which we have pointed out as characteristic of the American family system. The extended family system tends to satisfy the individual's need for emotional security and approval much more adequately than the conjugal type. Hence, as a result of the shift, the individual tends more and more to seek assurance and approval from the group and consequently, he more readily accepts their values and symbols of success.

The maintenance of what might be termed doctrinal balance is a further problem which a minority faces. In reacting to outgroup threats to its family standards, there is danger that great stress will be placed primarily on those specific doctrinal points under attack. With the passage of time, this can lead to warping and distortion of the integral doctrine as it is perceived by group members. Marriage standards come to be regarded primarily as prohibitions, while continued emphasis on fragmented or partial aspects may produce veritable caricatures of the original doctrine. For example, the prevalence of divorce leads to emphasis on the indissolubility of marriage and frequent neglect of the more positive qualities of the contract. The decadence of sexual morality may produce disgust with all physical manifestations of sex as well as unbalanced stress on the merely negative aspects of chastity. In practice, as minority standards come to differ more markedly from those of the dominant culture, it becomes more difficult for group members to maintain proper doctrinal balance.

The Catholic Minority and the Formulation of Family Standards

We have examined the difficulties involved in the formulation and dissemination of knowledge which a minority group may be expected to encounter. How well is the Catholic minority meeting these in American society? In regard to the formulation of marriage standards, the Catholic minority presents several unique characteristics. In the first place, Catholic belief in an authoritative teaching Church assures the universality, uniformity, and continuity of essential family doctrine and practice. The broad framework of life-values within which Catholics view the family also remains basically unchanged. Down through the centuries, theologians have carefully formulated the pertinent dogma, canon lawyers have developed a comprehensive juridical framework to guarantee its fulfillment, moralists have worked out its practical applications in minute detail, and the hierarchy have spelled out timely directives as the occasion demanded.

Consequently, the Catholic minority possesses a substantial body of morally sanctioned knowledge concerning marriage and the family. This teaching is clear, consistent, and readily intelligible in terms of ultimate Catholic premises so that the formulation of standards creates no problems in this area. Nevertheless, since adequate knowledge involves an understanding of the social means used to implement these standards in the practical order, the situation of the Catholic minority is not without its difficulties. These arise from two sources, and their importance merits detailed consideration.

In the first place, American society is characterized by complexity and rapid change. It follows that the Catholic family must repattern its family relationships to meet the new situations which constantly arise. Caholics find little precedent in their past nor can they rely wholly on the solutions offered by the dominant culture. As a result there is a degree of confusion, disagreement and indecisiveness in some areas. We have mentioned the problem of rhythm and the employment of women outside the home. There are others. For example, Catholic standards maintain that the husband is the head of the family. Precisely what does family headship imply under modern urban conditions? Premarital chastity involves the avoidance of all willful libidinous excitation. In a culture which specifies that mate selection is primarily the obligation of the individual, what dating and courtship practices are compatible with chastity? Parents are obliged to instruct, guide, supervise, and protect their adolescent offspring. What does this obligation imply and what means must parents employ to fulfill it in modern society? Little consensus has developed on these important points. Changes have come so quickly and the influence of the dominant culture has been so pervasive that Catholics have worked out no widely accepted solutions.

Second, the relatively large, highly cohesive ethnic groups within the Catholic minority have displayed considerable variety in their application of basic Catholic family standards. As we have indicated, these ethnic groups arrived with their own "cultural approximation" of the Catholic ideal, and their assimilation has been gradual and unequal. Consequently, the Catholic minority presents varied patterns of family relationships. The process of adjusting to new situations has not been uniform nor has it benefited from total group solidarity. There can be little doubt that this lack of solidarity has been an important factor in the failure to achieve consensus on the important issues which we have previously indicated.

The Catholic Minority and the Dissemination of Knowledge

Granting that there is a substantial body of family values and norms upon which Catholics can readily agree, how well are they prepared to meet the difficulties that a minority must encounter in disseminating it? As we have pointed out, three basic needs must be met by the minority in this regard. It must succeed in communicating adequate knowledge of its family standards to all group members. It must answer satisfactorily the objections to its doctrines advanced by outgroup members. It must maintain doctrinal balance. The principal social vehicles that it can use are the family, the Church, and the private school. The other sources of knowledge normally available to the individual will be either neutral or confusing and positively dysfunctional. How well do these vehicles serve their educative purpose for the Catholic minority? We shall consider them separately, although in practice they are mutually supportive and complementary.

The American Catholic family, like all other families, plays a fundamental role in the communication of knowledge. Social scientists are unanimous in stressing that the early family environment of the child is the most powerful influence in the development of his personality. For the infant, the family circle is the world. The intimate relationships established there may vary in intensity during later life, they are never obliterated. In a very real sense the individual is the "product" of his family. The aims and life goals he sets for himself have been largely shaped by his family. The emotional attachments he has formed through long years of intimate relationship with the members of his family color all his later relations.[1]

The supreme importance of the family becomes readily apparent if we consider the ways through which the child is affected by actions in the family circle. The child is subjected to interaction within the family in all the ways that it is possible to receive communication. First, on the sensory level, as an infant he is capable of noticing the sound of the voice, the look, the gesture, the caress, the act of rejection or punishment. On the emotional level, the child can sense the feelings of those around him. He reacts to love, fear, joy, hate, and tension. Finally, as he develops, the child learns to speak and understand language. There is communication of ideas, sentiments, evaluations, and judgments. Hence, it is apparent that the family starts the interactive process as soon as the child is born. The child is being trained, is learning from those around him, long before it is possible to communicate ideas through language.[2]

What are the particular difficulties that the American Catholic family encounters in communicating knowledge of its family standards? In the first place, it has followed the general trend of delegating its formal teaching function primarily to an outside institution, the school.[3] However, as a minority group possessing a distinct set of values, Catholics have attempted to establish their own private school system for the education of their children. These private schools include religious instruction as a regular part of their curriculum, with the result that Catholic families have tended to entrust the entire formal religious training of their children to the school.[4] In a study of over 16,000 parochial school children entering first grade, we discovered that only a little over one-half knew how to make the Sign of the Cross, one-third could recite the "Hail Mary," and less than one-fourth could recite the "Our Father." Knowledge of religious dogma was likewise deficient, for only approximately one-third had some idea of the Christmas story, the meaning of the Crucifix, and the special presence of Jesus in church. As one of the first-grade teachers remarked, "In regard to religious training, we have to start right from the beginning. It seems that modern parents are too busy to instruct their little ones." [5]

Specifically, the failure of Catholic families to give their children adequate knowledge of family standards is reflected in the widespread demand for and introduction of marriage preparation courses in Catholic colleges and high schools. The amazing rise of such movements as Pre-Cana, marriage preparation forums, lecture series for engaged couples, and correspondence courses in marriage preparation indicates the same deficiency. Furthermore, when the movement to introduce "sex instructions" in the schools was met by the traditional Catholic objection that this was primarily and properly the obligation of parents, it was discovered that parents were either incapable or unwilling to supply these instructions. Consequently, considerable effort has been made to instruct and motivate parents in this neglected function.

A further difficulty affecting the Catholic minority in its transmission of family standards is that over one-fourth of all Catholic marriages are mixed. Even prescinding from the ever present possibility of overt religious conflict, it seems reasonable to conclude that parents involved in these marriages will be less likely to instruct their children adequately in Catholic family standards. Since the educational role of the mother is dominant in the modern family, mixed marriages in which the wife is the non-Catholic partner will probably encounter the greatest difficulty in this regard. At the same time, children from mixed marriages are less likely to attend Catholic schools so that no remedy for the family's failure to give adequate religious instruction is available. In this connection, it should be noted that whether the family gives formal religious instruction or not, it always remains a basic molder of attitudes concerning religion. In delegating religious instruction primarily to the school, or in tacitly by-passing it as is often required in mixed marriages, parents are bound to convey the impression that religion is something to be learned or picked up as one grows older rather than a profound, formative influence permeating all human activity.

Finally, that sizable portion of the Catholic minority which represents members of what we have called the New Immigration and their descendants encounters special difficulties in transmitting its family standards. The assimilation process tends to separate first- and second-generation ethnics from their parents. This is particularly true when the group is bilingual. Parental concepts of marriage and the family differ in some respects from those their children acquire in the new culture. When the language barrier operates to slow down the acculturation of the parents, children may come to feel that their parents are old-fashioned and do not understand the changed situation. As a consequence, the teaching function of the parents is severely limited and their anxious attempts to inculcate their own "cultural approximation" of the Catholic family may lead their children to reject the entire value system. Fortunately, the national parish, through its school and numerous organizations, has generally served as a brake on rapid acculturation, thus narrowing the gap between generations and smoothing the transition to a new culture.

The role of the private school in disseminating knowledge of family standards has already been indicated. Through religious instruction classes and especially through formal courses on marriage and the family at the high school and college levels, the school system transmits traditional Catholic doctrine and its approved applications, while implicitly or explicitly answering objections to the Catholic family system. Nevertheless, the tendency to delegate all religious instruction to the school involves several serious weaknesses which become particularly noticeable in regard to communicating adequate knowledge of family standards. First, it is not the function of the school to give "sex instructions." This is a parental obligation which by its very nature cannot be delegated to an institution. Instruction in the schools covers broad general principles and is geared to meet the average needs of the class. Adequate sex instructions imply a personal approach patterned to the specific needs of the gradually maturing adolescent and developing in time according to his growth. To confide this task entirely to the school is to burden the school and the teachers with an obligation which they cannot fulfill adequately. Teachers may assist parents in this task, but effective instruction must be supplemented and supported by home training. After all, the child is in the school only a relatively short time each week, and the environment of the school is not highly conducive to the intimate, personal instructions required by the nature of the subject.

Further, to confine this training primarily to the school leads to a dangerous confusion of school and life-values which can produce fatal results once the child leaves school. The child can easily come to identify religious precepts concerning sex with the rules and regulations of the school. Just as he falls into the habit of attending Mass, and so on, only because it is demanded by the school or because the whole group does it, he can look upon moral precepts as something associated not with life but with the school. Indeed, it is not uncommon for children to acquire a positive distaste for regimentation in the school and where this is associated with religion, they tend subsequently to transfer their dislike to the practice of religion itself. This is not a reflection on the school for it has been burdened with obligations which it cannot adequately meet. It is a commentary on serious parental failure.

Finally, parental failure to communicate adequate knowledge of family standards takes on added significance when we realize that large numbers of Catholic children do not attend Church schools or attend them for only brief periods. Various factors enter into this situation. In some cases, schools are not available or are already overcrowded. Some parents are indifferent, dislike the added expense which may be involved, or deliberately choose the public school in the belief that their child will make better "contacts" there. Several of the ethnic groups of the New Immigration have been slow to build schools either because they were little interested in education or because there was no precedent for such schools in their homeland.

The third basic vehicle of instruction is the Church. The Church has unique significance for the Catholic minority in this regard. On matters of faith and morals, its teaching is held to be infallible. Through ritual and symbol, its sacramental system functions as a powerful teaching instrument. The sacrament of matrimony has always received particular attention.

Canon law supplies a detailed juridical framework and clearly specifies that prospective partners receive adequate instruction in the nature, rights, and obligations conferred by the sacramental contract. The family holds a prominent place in sermons, retreats, parish missions, and encyclical letters. Various family movements such as Cana, the Christian Family Movement, and so forth, have been either initiated or strongly supported by the Church. Furthermore, the Church has placed serious sanctions on deviations from its family standards. Its stand on divorce, contraceptives, and abortion are known to every Catholic.

What are the special problems which the Church encounters in disseminating its family doctrine in America? We are here considering the Church as a social institution exercising its teaching function through its hierarchy and clerics and operating through the territorial units of the diocese and parish. As the religious institution of a minority group, the Church must promote adequate knowledge of its doctrines among its members, it must answer attacks against that doctrine, and it must maintain doctrinal balance in doing so. One of the chief difficulties involved in the Church's teaching function stems from the need to promulgate integral family doctrine. By this we mean that it no longer suffices to teach immediate family norms and their practical applications. Ultimate value premises must be made clear so that the faithful understand the connection between approved practice and ultimate premises. In other words, when a nonisolated minority group maintains a distinct family subsystem, "adequate knowledge" of family standards implies an understanding of the entire value system. There are several reasons why this is so. First, a family program represents conclusions based upon ultimate premises of value as well as upon observable facts. Hence, family standards can be understood only in terms of these premises. Second, when a minority is not isolated, group members are constantly exposed to family norms and practices which challenge their own and which are enhanced by the approval of the dominant culture. If group members do not understand the premises upon which their family program is based, they will tend to adopt the standards of the dominant culture.

Perhaps the pertinence of this observation will appear more clearly if we reflect that when a minority remains relatively segregated or quasi-autonomous, interaction with the dominant culture leads to conflict of group standards; when the minority moves to closer integration with the dominant culture, however, these conflicts tend to become individual or intrapersonal. Members of the minority meet the challenge, not as group members but as individuals. They tend to make their choice not on the basis of group solidarity but in terms of their own philosophy of life. Obviously, this requires knowledge of ultimate premises and of their relation to challenged practices.

Why should this constitute a teaching problem for the Church? In the first place, it is not easy to communicate adequate knowledge of premises and practices to group members. The faithful tend to be satisfied with practical conclusions until these are seriously challenged in their interaction with the outgroup. It may be objected that the faithful accept on faith the teachings of the Church and consequently, there is little need for them to understand the relationship between practice and premise. This is to forget that one of the principal premises implicitly being challenged is the authoritative teaching power of the Church. It follows that unless group members are taught to think in terms of an integrated philosophy of life rather than in terms of segmented norms and practices, they will not sense the full implications of the outgroup challenge. When this happens, it is easy to fall back on some rationalization such as, "They (the clergy) don't understand the problems of married people in the modern world."

Second, this constitutes a teaching problem for the Church since the clergy themselves have not always recognized the need for an integral approach. In this connection it should be noted that a large percentage of the Catholic immigrants to this country came from simple rural backgrounds where the faith was taken for granted. They tended to settle in large, relatively isolated groups where their first interest was to earn a living and preserve their traditional beliefs. Under these conditions, the chief teaching function of the clergy was to stress basic dogma and the practice of Christian virtues. There was little need to expand on the teaching authority of the Church, nor was it necessary to clarify ultimate value premises and their necessary relationship to specific norms and behavioral patterns. In the minds of the faithful, the cleric represented the legitimate interpreter of Catholic family standards. His authority was accepted both because he stood for the Church which they cherished, and he was well educated while they were not.

However, this approach is inadequate when group solidarity is weakened and minority members are exposed to norms and behavioral patterns established on different value premises. The teaching function of the clergy remains the same, but the requisites for fulfilling that function become increasingly more difficult as the problems confronting the faithful become more complex. In other words, effective teaching now requires intimate knowledge of the changing social situation, clear understanding of the pertinent value premises, and lucid exposition of the practical program to be followed. This latter is nothing more than the logical application of pertinent value premises to concrete social situations, but it calls for careful rethinking and restatement of the meaning of life in terms of Catholic values and contemporary living conditions. For example, in developing the Church's stand on contraceptives, effective teaching requires more than insistence on the moral evils of the practice. The relationship between cherished values and this practice, between the vocation of parenthood and personal development, between a socially and individually pertinent hierarchy of values and man's purpose in life, must be reformulated in a way that group members can readily understand.[6]

What we are saying is that the clergy must recognize that they are pastors of a minority group maintaining a distinct family subsystem in a culture tending to be established on different premises. Consequently, they must not only make clear the premises upon which their teaching is based, but they must make explicit the implicit premises from which are derived the objectionable practices in the dominant culture. This is much more than was required in the past. Briefly,

there must be a thorough knowledge of the cultural orientations of the society within which the minority lives since
individual Catholics will necessarily be affected by these.
There must be the willingness and ability to undertake a
positive and integrated approach to some moral areas such
as sexual activity. In former times, these could be treated
negatively. The Church's teaching was not challenged, and
individuals, particularly adolescents, were not exposed to the
calculated exploitation of their sexual drive.

CONFORMITY REQUIRES MOTIVATION

However, adequate knowledge of family standards does not
suffice to assure conformity; minority members must be satisfactorily motivated to pattern their conduct according to
these standards. Even in a well-integrated society, individual
conformity does not automatically follow normative consensus,
but various social mechanisms operate to channel behavior
according to approved standards. In a pluralistic culture,
the existence of distinct institutional subsystems such as the
family is constantly threatened by widespread deviation from
standards and loss of motivation because the mechanisms for
securing conformity available to the minority are necessarily
limited. Our problem, therefore, is to investigate how the
Catholic minority maintains adequate motivation in regard
to its family standards and what special difficulties this process
encounters in American society.

A preliminary observation is in order. Catholic family standards impose difficult and exacting obligations on the individual. Indeed, when Our Lord promulgated His teaching
on the indissolubility of marriage, his startled apostles replied:
"If the case of a man with his wife be so, it is not expedient
to marry." (Matt. 19:3-10; Mark 10:2-12.) Furthermore, the
control of the sexual drive in any society is not easy. The
reason is that inner unity and order in man is not simply a
static, given reality—it is a dynamic state to be achieved and
arduously maintained. The human person exists in a state of
tension through a necessity inherent in its very structure.

This point was developed in Chapter Two when the Catholic position on chastity was being discussed. It is sufficient here to recall that Catholics harbor no illusions concerning the difficulties involved in maintaining their family standards. One of the effects of original sin was the loss of integrity. This is to say, man now encounters difficulties in imposing right order on his faculties. To be sure, the sacramental system, through which the individual participates in the fruits of the Passion, offers special assistance in this regard. However, unless man uses his common sense in avoiding the occasions of sin, and as a social being, cooperates with others in maintaining a social system which supports his ideals, there is little likelihood that virtue will long prevail.

Positive Motivating Factors

What are the principal factors which motivate the individual to conform to Catholic family standards? In the first place, the average Catholic has been trained from his youth to identify with them. He is accustomed to view self-realization and happiness in terms of their specifications. He sees eternal salvation related to conformity inasmuch as deviations are judged sinful. Hence, nonconformity is accompanied by personal guilt; that is, he considers he has sinned by acting contrary to God's law and his own personal obligations. This threatened loss of divine friendship, plus the frustration of his internalized ideals, acts as a powerful motive in maintaining conformity. It would be a serious error to underestimate its force. Even in those instances when violations of standards occur, it operates as a strong stimulus to return to conformity. This can be seen, for example, among Catholics who have contracted invalid marriages. A good number either separate or seek convalidation of their union by the Church.

Hence, internalized religious ideals offer a complex set of factors which orient the individual toward conformity. They not only represent his inner, personalized goals, but deviations from them are associated with acute tension and anxiety owing to the deprivation of God's friendship, fear of divine punishment, and loss of self-esteem. Two extremes should be avoided in assessing the efficacy of these factors for assuring conformity. First, some social scientists have seriously underestimated their motivating force because they have been overimpressed by the seemingly determinative pressure exerted on the individual by the group, whether it be the extended family or the community. As we have taken pains to point out in an earlier chapter when evaluating Thomas and Znanieki's predictions in *The Polish Peasant,* the fact that kinship group and community may exert strong pressure for conformity on the individual does not rule out the motivating force of spiritual ideals. It was precisely because these latter remained operative that the Polish family in America did not disintegrate as predicted.

Second, some spiritual writers and philosophers appear to regard the individual as a "closed" atom or some type of free-floating nomad, implying that spiritual ideals are the primary determining factor in securing conformity. This is to forget that the individual's actions only partially derive from the activity of spiritual motive-forces. As a social being and as a composite of body and soul, the individual is affected by people and things physiologically and psychologically, in the conscious and the nonconscious. It follows that his reaction to a concrete situation is a complex process built up of all these factors. The efficacy of spiritual motives depends upon the individual's ability to transcend these factors and follow his ideals.

A further motive for conformity appears in the very serious sanctions which the Church imposes on specific deviations from Catholic family standards. Invalid marriage attempted before a Protestant minister, for example, entails excommunication for the Catholic parties. This means that they are cut off from the communion of the faithful, forbidden access to the sacraments, and refused Catholic burial at death. In other words, the deviant is not only conscious of an inner conflict, but his prohibited action involves an overt, enduring deprivation of religious participation which acts as a constant reminder of his failure to conform. The effect of this powerful sanction on the instructed, practicing Catholic should not be underestimated. It operates both in maintaining conformity and in securing the return to religious participation of those who have deviated.

It should be noted that an organized teaching church performs a twofold function in the dynamics of ideas. Through its authoritative teaching it keeps reminding the faithful of their religious value system, and in countless ways, it spells out for them the relationships between these values and acceptable behavioral patterns. This counteracts the normal tendency of men to ignore embarrassing conflicts between theory and practice and to seek spurious peace of conscience by means of various convenient rationalizations. Particularly in modern society, where people are so preoccupied with the business of living, the teaching function of the Church is of paramount importance in removing both simple and opportune ignorance. Further, through the rigid enforcement of its religious sanctions it stands as a public witness to the importance and sacredness of its family ideals. Whether he chooses to conform or not, the instructed Catholic harbors no uncertainty concerning how he is expected to act.

Factors Leading to Loss of Motivation

What factors in society tend to weaken the motive-force of Catholic family ideals? In this connection it should be recalled that we have characterized the Catholic minority as a group moving from relative isolation toward closer integration with the dominant culture. As such, its members will necessarily be affected by the cultural value orientations and ideals of the society in which they live. Few would challenge this statement, but it is important to point out its implications for the individual Catholic. In the first place, as Catholics move into more intimate contact with competing behavioral patterns, many of which represent obvious deviations from traditional Catholic norms, their own family standards may appear problematical for the first time. Unless they possess adequate knowledge, apathy and loss of conviction may result, and if conformity to group standards imposes considerable sacrifice, they will follow the dominant culture.

Second, the movement toward closer integration with the dominant culture may involve the adoption of certain practices and goals not obviously inimical to Catholic standards. However, the implications and unanticipated consequences of some of these adoptions may seriously increase the burden of conformity to Catholic standards. One has only to recall the strain on premarital chastity created by some modern dating and courtship practices to understand how this situation may arise. Adolescents who do not follow the Catholic teaching on chastity may find some escape from the strains and frustrations associated with the free and unsupervised contacts between the sexes, permitted for such long periods before marriage, by developing various techniques of "petting," that is, methods of mutual sexual arousal calculated to stop short of intercourse and designed as a substitute for it. Catholic adolescents, however, since they believe that it is sinful to deliberately arouse or give consent to venereal pleasure under these conditions, necessarily find the burden of maintaining chastity extremely difficult. It is not unrealistic to suppose that some of them will consider the burden too great and will seek some convenient rationalization for their behavior. Even when Catholic standards are not rejected outright, there is likely to result a loss of conviction and a feeling that one is being penalized for one's religious beliefs.

Hence, the difficulties associated with securing adequate motivation for maintaining Catholic family standards stem from two sources. In the first place, as the Catholic minority is drawn into closer integration with the dominant culture, Catholic family standards may appear problematical to many Catholics for the first time. This condition results not only from the fact that increasing numbers of the Catholic minority are becoming socially mobile, but traditional minority segregation with its accompanying insulation of group values has become difficult to maintain in American society. Modern mass communication, with its fund of conflicting facts, judgments, beliefs, and values, has invaded even the most isolated localities. At the same time, the basically interdependent character, particularly of modern economic and political institutions, creates numerous situations in which individuals possessing different or conflicting values necessarily interact or become aware of each other.[7]

In the second place, as the dominant family system adapts to its rapidly changing urban environment, its deviations from Catholic standards become more sharply accentuated. Hence, modern Catholics will encounter more value conflicts than did their fathers. More important, many of the adjustments worked out in the dominant culture are of such nature as to place serious strain on those who attempt to maintain minority family standards. We have mentioned dating and courtship practices as a specific example of this. Less obvious, but perhaps equally effective in engendering loss of conviction and what the psychologists call "withdrawal of affect," is the total climate of popular opinion expressed through daily conversation and the routine avenues of mass communication. Although Catholic family standards may not be explicitly attacked, they are frequently treated as questionable or inapplicable to modern conditions with the result that the motivation of minority members is subjected to a process of slow attrition. This combination of social situations leading to strain and of popular opinion which produces loss of conviction goes far to explain why some mobile Catholics come to regard Catholic family standards with apathy.

CONFORMITY REQUIRES MUTUAL SUPPORT

A third requisite for achieving conformity to group standards is some degree of mutual support and reinforcement at least from group members. Individuals may possess adequate knowledge and may be personally attached to a given set of family standards, but unless these standards gain some group support and are reinforced by other values in society, enduring conformity is not likely to be achieved. This statement represents an application to family values of the general process governing the realization and maintenance of all cultural goals in society. Let us analyze this process in some detail so that its present application will be evident.

Every stable society embodies systems of norms regulating

the conduct of its members. The seriously obligatory norms usually center around major social needs and represent the basic structure by which group behavior is patterned and given order and unity. This means that in every stable society there are established certain behavioral forms which are particularly valued by its members. In a sense, these represent their ideals. Hence, those who fulfill these acquire status in the community, and the qualities which made them successful are esteemed by the group. The social position of those who are successful is considered highly desirable, representing a goal worth striving for by members of society. Further, this cherished status receives awards symbolically represented to members of the group by prestige, privileges, and/or possessions. Practically speaking, these awards furnish the actual goals for which people strive. Young people in the society are urged to acquire those virtues which lead to success as defined by the group, and in successful members they have concrete examples of the awards which may be theirs if they develop the necessary virtues.[8]

The obvious working of this principle can be seen in modern society where social success is defined in terms of income. Those who have acquired wealth enjoy prestige and power while the qualities which are thought to have contributed to their success are highly esteemed. Consequently, youth are trained to show independence, initiative, aggressiveness, and the capacity to survive competition. One is taught to play according to the rules of the game, but there is never any doubt that the object of the game is to win.

If we apply this principle to the realization and maintenance of Catholic family standards, it must be apparent that enduring conformity becomes probable only if those who practice their ideals successfully are shown prestige and respect, while the virtues associated with their success are esteemed and considered worthy of imitation. Under these conditions, youth are taught reverence for sex, respect for self-control, and concepts of life-success which are consonant with Christian parenthood. In a complex society characterized by competing value systems, this support and reinforcement of family standards must come primarily from group members. Unless they show respect for success as defined by these standards and esteem the virtues which make this success possible, enduring group conformity becomes highly improbable. "Virtue hath its own reward," to be sure, but the concept of virtue itself tends to be profoundly influenced by group attitudes in all but the strongest characters.

Factors Providing Positive Support

In determining the factors which positively support and reinforce Catholic family standards, a distinction must be made between outgroup and ingroup forces. Let us first consider the former. Although we have indicated that the dominant culture tolerates or promotes many values and behavioral patterns scarcely compatible with Catholic family standards, nevertheless, explicitly and at least in theory, such values as premarital chastity, marital fidelity, and stable marriage still represent desirable cultural goals. Particularly among the members of the large non-Catholic religious groups, traditional family values are esteemed. Compromises have been made concerning divorce and the use of contraceptives, but in most cases, divorce is still regarded as an unfortunate failure, and the adoption of contraceptive practices is rationalized as an application of modern scientific discoveries to the service of the family.

Second, in spite of the traditional American reluctance to tolerate state "interference" in regard to family affairs, recent social legislation has made some effort to support and supplement the economic and protective functions of the family. Social legislation since the depression of the thirties has shown a growing awareness of the importance of the family unit in society.[9] It is not necessary to subscribe to all the details of these various programs nor is it implied that such areas as health, housing, and family allowances have received the consideration they deserve, but in contrast to the past, it must be admitted there are encouraging signs that the public has developed some understanding of the profound significance of the family for a stable social order.

Finally, the changing status of women in modern society

contains many features which support and reinforce Catholic family standards.[10] Considering the confusion, exaggerations, and deviations which have characterized the modern feminist movement, this statement may appear somewhat of a paradox. However, if one contrasts the present status of women with their position in the post-Reformation past, particularly under Blackstonian legislation and the Napoleonic Code, it becomes apparent that many benefits have resulted. Our position in this controversial matter can be summarized by stating that modern women are offered more opportunities than their post-Reformation sisters for fulfilling the divine command to develop their personalities by being co-partners with males in the important and personally meaningful function of propagating the species.

In this connection it should be noted that according to Catholic doctrine, marriage should provide a context within which the personality of the partners can be developed. People develop through association. Consciously or otherwise, this is what people are looking for when they marry. They desire to give expression to themselves, their innermost drives and potencies. This is not a selfish urge but the natural flowering out of the personality, vaguely conscious of its own incompleteness and reaching out in love and security for its existential fulfillment. In marriage, this means that the partners aid each other to develop by supplying a proper milieu within which male and female can work out their mutual complementarity.

In the Catholic value system, marriage is not meant to be a sacrifice of virgins to the inexorable demands of the species, nor is it the holocaust of the female on the altar of male passion. God said: "It is not good for man to be alone." Male and female were made to be companions—helpmates. Marriage, as the institutionalizing of this companionship, therefore, provides the social framework within which individuals are to aid each other in developing that fullness of their nature which God ordained. It seems scarcely necessary to add that this divine ideal like so many others, has been obscured and rendered difficult by the effects of original sin. The pagan glorification of the male, which was in effect little more than the glorification of male passion, infiltrated even Christian practice, limiting the restoration of the divine ideal of marriage effected by Christ. To be sure, modern woman may continue one of the errors of the feminists by mistaking equality for identity with the male, but it is our contention that her present status offers her increasing opportunities for personal development through companionship with the male in marriage.

The ingroup forces offering support and reinforcement to Catholic family standards require little comment. To the extent that minority members identify with the group, they sense the approbation or condemnation with which other members regard their conduct. The church, school, and kinship group function as powerful instruments for the reinforcement of Catholic ideals. The effect of the family is especially noteworthy in this regard. It encompasses the individual with strong emotional bonds, and deviation from approved family standards is generally accompanied with some degree of alienation.

The effectiveness of group support will vary according to group solidarity. Among strongly cohesive ethnic minorities, for example, approved family standards are closely identified with group values so that deviations are accompanied with loss of esteem and frequently, practical ostracism. As solidarity breaks down, however, group reaction loses much of its effectiveness, and only the church and family remain as operative forces in supporting conformity. Our study of Catholic ethnic minorities indicates that these have maintained their solidarity only to the extent that they have clustered around the national parish. Many of these centers are threatened by the rapid shifts in population which characterize most of our urban centers. Consequently, unless a new basis for solidarity is found, the Catholic minority, considered as a distinct ingroup, will lend decreasing support to Catholic family standards. By this we mean that individual Catholics will be less conscious of group approval or condemnation of their actions. This loss of group support must be compensated for by a clearer understanding of the integral Catholic value system and a deepened sense of personal responsibility if conformity is to be achieved.

Factors Implying Lack of Support

In previous sections we have indicated some of the norms and behavioral patterns incompatible with Catholic family standards. There is no need to review these here, but their significance for the Catholic minority must be discussed. From the Catholic viewpoint, these norms and behavioral patterns represent deviations from approved family standards. Nevertheless, the dominant culture apparently bestows equal respect on those who follow these alternate standards of conduct. The divorcee, the birth controller, and the unfaithful seemingly suffer little loss of prestige. Although lip-service is still paid to traditional values, marked deviations are openly tolerated and implicitly approved. It is not surprising, therefore, that daily contact with such divergent standards of conduct dulls the keenness of moral perception and leads to guilt-soothing rationalizations of behavior clearly contradictory to Catholic ideals.

However, the failure of the dominant culture to support Catholic family standards may affect the minority in more subtle ways. Let us consider, for example, the failure of the culture to lend juridical support to family stability. For all practical purposes, marriage is considered a personal affair. One can enter a marriage contract or break it pretty much as one pleases. It is generally admitted that in most states divorce can be obtained by mutual consent since the average divorce proceeding is characterized by collusion. This travesty of the law need not concern us here except that it creates a social climate in which the sacredness of the marriage contract disappears, and laws are looked upon as obstacles to be circumvented by collusion.

To be sure, no instructed Catholic is likely to trust the efficacy of the civil law to dissolve his marriage, but he can be affected in other ways. Specifically, this lack of juridical support can color his views on the sacredness of marriage and on his vocation in the family. Catholic couples may forget that there is more to the Church's teaching on the marriage contract than that it is indissoluble. They may forget that it is a holy vocation calling for cohabitation and the mutual sacrifices required to make this possible. The readiness of some Catholic couples to seek "separation" as a solution to their marital problems is a clear indication that they have been affected by the secular attitudes of the dominant culture. According to Catholic teaching, marriage is a vocation, a life task, a total dedication of self, a way of life within which salvation must be achieved, and because of the peculiar nature of marriage, a vocation within which salvation is mutually achieved. As one judge of a diocesan separation court remarked, "Ninety per cent of the couples coming here for separation apparently have forgotten that the marriage contract obliges them to cohabitation and mutual support. The only portion of Catholic doctrine they have retained is that they cannot divorce and remarry."

Further, in contemporary society the lack of cultural support has even deeper significance for the Catholic minority. The transition from a rural to an industrialized urban environment has subjected the traditional family system to new conditions calling for numerous adjustments and adaptations. The resulting behavioral patterns are not the work of one individual or of one family. They evolve gradually out of the general social process in which individual familes develop broadly similar patterns for meeting similar needs. Consciously or otherwise, this development tends to proceed in terms of the dominant value system. Of course, behavioral patterns and values mutually affect each other in the process, but the pertinent point for the present discussion is that final solutions are worked out in terms of the dominant value system.

It follows that the Catholic minority, since it embraces a system of unchanging ultimate family values, may find little support from the dominant culture in working out its solutions to new situations. In practice this means that the minority must develop solutions of its own or otherwise minority members will tend to accept those of the dominant culture with possible serious repercussions on Catholic moral standards. A case in point is our modern dating and courtship system. Catholics tend to follow the dominant culture here with the result that Catholic youth are subjected to serious strain. Catholic parents imitate others in tolerating or promoting years of unsupervised contact between adolescents of both sexes, yet Catholic youth are forbidden premarital intercourse or its culturally devised substitute, the practice of petting.

A more instructive example might be found in considering modern attempts to define the marriage role of male and female. In this case, there is rather general confusion. What does the culture tell us, for example, about the role of women in marriage? What are the characteristics of the ideal wife? Fidelity? Companionship? Motherhood? Co-breadwinner? Career-woman? There is no general consensus. Researchers are busily working on their questionnaires to show that no matter what traditional ideals the public may voice, their practice belies their words. And the male, what of his role in marriage? Obviously, he is a bit confused concerning the meaning of "head of the family" when marriage unites him in a competitive struggle with the "new woman."

How does this confusion affect Catholic families? As members of a minority group, their task is a difficult one. In the first place, they cannot look to the past for ready solutions. It is now recognized that partial and even false views of sex have colored much immediate past thinking on the subject, and furthermore, social institutions have undergone such profound changes in recent times that the structure of the family itself has undergone considerable modification calling for a new definition of roles and new attitudes. Second, many modern changes affecting the family are not simply good or simply evil. They must be carefully evaluated in the light of Catholic principles and made use of accordingly. For example, the broad statement that "woman's place is in the home" is only a half-truth. Increased education, the acquisition of political rights, the organization of modern housekeeping granting her more freedom from "homemaking" once the children have reached school age, earlier age at marriage and increased longevity, all cooperate to broaden her interests and her activities beyond the traditional kitchen, children, and church trilogy.

Third, some modern conditions seriously affecting marriage roles must simply be accepted as part of the social order. In these cases, marriage partners must work out adjustments and seek compensatory ways of achieving their ideals. Night work, working in split shifts, jobs which take the husband away from the home for long periods, the separation occasioned by military service, financial crises forcing the wife to seek employment outside the home, and so forth, might be cited as examples.

This confusion about roles in marriage shows up clearly in the preparation and education of youth for family life. For all practical purposes, girls receive the same training as boys and are even taught to compete with them for jobs. More important, girls are not trained in their families for their role as mothers. There is no clearer example of what we have called partial or segmented thinking than that displayed by so many parents who work and worry for years to secure a "good" marriage for their daughters, yet do nothing to prepare their children for the roles which successful marriage implies. It appears that their thinking never gets past the wedding day—and only part of that—since they make little effort to prepare their daughters for the wedding night!

Although examples demonstrating lack of support for Catholic family standards could be multiplied, we have deemed it more useful for present purposes to indicate the principal types of nonsupport and to concentrate on the consequences of this lack for Catholic families. In a permissive, complex society, the survival of a cultural subsystem is threatened not so much by direct attack or outright opposition as by the steady, often unrecognized "pull" of the total culture away from subsystem standards. Minority members experience this "pull" not only by exposure to the general "climate of ideas and valuations" existing in the culture, but also through participation in social, economic, and political activities. At the same time, the lack of cultural support renders the achievement of their own family standards more difficult, with the result that the temptation to find a *modus vivendi* through some compromise of their ideals becomes very strong.

SUMMARY

In this chapter we investigated the conditions requisite for securing conformity to Catholic family standards in a minority situation. The first condition is adequate knowledge. This includes both the clear formulation of standards and their efficient dissemination among group members. Since the Catholic minority follows an organized, teaching church, the formulation of family standards is relatively easy although there is some indecisiveness in the application of ultimate principles to changing situations. The primary vehicles for the dissemination of knowledge are the family, the church, and the school. These institutions ordinarily complement each other in the teaching function. However, there is some indication that the family is abdicating its role as religious teacher in favor of the school. The chief teaching problems of a minority church are the maintenance of doctrinal balance in its practical exposition of dogma and the necessity of explaining the relationships between ideology, family norms, and behavioral patterns. This latter problem becomes more acute as minority members move toward closer integration with the dominant culture.

The second requisite for conformity is satisfactory motivation. Catholic family standards impose difficult and exacting obligations on group members. A powerful factor motivating Catholics to follow Catholic family standards is the fact that deviations are defined as sins. Further, these standards form a part of the total philosophy of life which has been developed in the normal Catholic from youth. Finally, the Church enforces serious sanctions in the case of some deviations. These serve as a constant reminder of the standards and exert considerable pressure on the deviant to return to conformity. Several factors tend to weaken motivation in our culture.

As the minority moves toward closer integration with a pluralistic culture, minority family standards are challenged and may appear problematical for the first time to minority members. Second, the adoption of some current behavioral patterns may increase the difficulties associated with the achievement of Catholic family standards to a degree which renders them unduly burdensome. Finally, loss of conviction may develop through daily contact with individuals and groups who do not accept the minority's family standards.

The third requisite for conformity is support and reinforcement from others. This is necessary for both the acquisition and achievement of group standards. Members of the dominant culture lend some support to Catholic family standards, and there is a growing consciousness of the importance of the family evidenced in public opinion and social legislation. Furthermore, the changing status of women in modern society, despite obvious shortcomings, offers women the opportunity to fulfill their role in marriage in a manner more in conformity with Catholic standards. Lack of support appears in the failure of society to reward conformity and to withdraw esteem from deviants. At the same time, minority members receive little support from the dominant culture in working out solutions to new situations which the family must encounter in a changing society.

CHAPTER THIRTEEN

An Effective Family Program

In previous chapters we have outlined the characteristics of the Catholic family system and the ideology upon which it is based. We have described the Catholic minority, their immigrant origins, their present social position, and the family problems which they encounter. We have pointed out those factors in American society which render the achievement of Catholic standards difficult and have indicated that in some important respects the dominant family system is moving toward more sharply defined contrasts with these standards. Finally, the chief requisites for securing conformity to Catholic family standards have been presented so that the fundamental problems involved in minority survival could be clearly understood in their cultural context. There remains to investigate the program which must be followed if the minority is to maintain its family ideals intact and operative in the practical order.

For purposes of study, the problem of outlining a program can best be approached at two levels. First, from the viewpoint of the minority considered as a more or less solidary group, we can investigate the essential factors involved in the formulation of group policy. This approach is concerned with what might be termed long-range programs and pertains primarily to group leaders and the policies of group movements. Second, we can study the immediate, more direct programs which must be formulated to meet the practical needs of minority members at the present time. Although these two approaches actually represent only two phases of the same problem, it is useful to consider them separately. Minority members tend to view differences in behavioral patterns and family standards in a restricted, practical context, thus losing sight of the total system and the ultimate value conflicts involved. Hence, they attempt to solve problems without considering the total social context within which these problems developed. Many current practices which constitute "problems" for Catholic families represent adjustments and adaptations developed to meet new family needs in a changing environment. Consequently, a practical program devised merely to build up resistance to a specific cultural solution will have little long-range efficacy since the original need remains unmet. What is required is a Catholic solution to replace the objectionable one current in the culture.

PREREQUISITES OF A LONG-RANGE PROGRAM

An adequate treatment of the basic issues confronting the Catholic minority in their attempt to maintain approved family standards implies some understanding of several general propositions which merit explicit statement at this point. We have called them the prerequisites of a long-range program because they represent the factors which necessarily condition the minority's policies. Although some of them have been mentioned in other connections, it is desirable to restate them here so that their significant bearing on group survival can be clearly demonstrated. No exhaustive treatment of these propositions will be attempted, nor is it necessary. Our primary concern is to call attention to those factors which must be taken into consideration by the Catholic minority in formulating its family programs.[1]

The Catholic Family System Must Be Viewed as an Integral System

This proposition is significant because in a culture characterized by complexity, permissiveness, and relative tolerance,
the profound implications of religious minority status may
easily be overlooked.[2] When religious differences or conflicts
arise, people tend to forget that what may be ultimately
involved is a clash of value systems. In daily life, religious
differences are usually viewed as segmented, separate problems rather than as practical manifestations of diverse doctrinal systems. People say, "Catholics can't get a divorce," or
"Catholics can't practice birth control," as if these were authoritarian edicts associated with Church membership rather
than specific applications in the practical order of essential
Catholic dogma. In other words, when religious differences
arise, both Catholic and non-Catholic tend to consider them
apart from their context in an integral system of religious
beliefs.

This failure to evaluate specific Catholic standards and
practices in terms of a total religious complex of values has
particularly serious implications for the maintenance of the
Catholic family system. In this connection, for example, it is
not the fact that Catholics may differ from others in their
attitudes toward divorce and contraceptives which is important. The significant point is that these attitudes form an
essential part of an integrated system of values, norms, and
behavioral patterns springing from a thoroughly developed
body of religious truths common to all Catholics and constituting their basic philosophy of life. It follows that it is meaningless to discuss Catholics' attitudes toward divorce or
contraceptives apart from their philosophy of life, just as it
is unlikely that these attitudes will be preserved if Catholics
lose sight of their total value system.

This first proposition takes on added significance when considered in the light of two facts which have been previously
established. First, members of the Catholic minority are moving toward closer integration with the dominant culture.

Second, in several important respects, the standards and behavioral patterns current in this culture reveal increasingly wide departures from the Catholic system. In the last chapter we noted that as long as Catholics remained a relatively isolated minority, their characteristic family standards and behavioral patterns were viewed primarily as *group* differences. Since group differences clash chiefly at the level of group interaction, individual Catholics could maintain their religious ideals intact to the extent that they retained solidarity with their group. In the past, this solidarity was facilitated by similarity of immigrant background, consequent ethnic cohesiveness, and current outgroup animosity.

However, as Catholics become socially mobile and start mingling freely in the wider society, differences in family ideals and practices are perceived primarily as intrapersonal rather than as group problems. The individual rather than the group feels the impact of alien cultural traits. Under these conditions, the problems of religious minority survival is set in an entirely new context. Briefly, individual Catholics must be prepared to face the issues themselves. This implies that they understand thoroughly the "reasons for the faith that is in them." A vague feeling of religious solidarity may still strengthen their loyalty; it can no longer compensate for their intellects.

What are the implications of this shift from relative segregation to fuller integration in an increasingly alien culture? On the practical level, many Catholics will be forced to make choices among competing family norms and practices for which their previous training may have given them little preparation. In other words, when moral issues arise, the individual must be prepared to evaluate them in terms of a personally assimilated philosophy of life. In these circumstances, it will not suffice to say, "I am a Catholic, and *we* hold that this is right." Rather the argument must run, "I know that this is the right thing to do because this action represents a logical application of the basic premises which constitute my system of life values as a Catholic. I know these are true because I believe that Christ founded a visible church with infallible teaching authority in matters of faith and morals." Experience shows that members of a minority seeking integration in a complex, rapidly changing society will continue to conform to group standards primarily to the degree that they understand how these standards are related to the total religious value system which they profess.

Why are many American Catholics poorly prepared to meet new or conflicting family norms and practices? First, when a religious group is either dominant or exists as a relatively segregated minority, there is less immediate need to clarify ultimate value premises and to demonstrate their necessary relationship to specific family norms and behavioral patterns. Ultimate premises tend to be assumed as commonly accepted, and primary emphasis is placed on specific norms and practices. To use an illustration from a related field, until the rise of totalitarian governments in Europe, Americans paid little attention to the ultimate premises upon which their democratic system was founded. Major stress was placed on securing more equitable distribution of the fruits of democracy for all citizens, and it was only when these practices were challenged by totalitarian philosophies that Americans began to think seriously about ultimate premises and their relationships to the American way of life.

Now the not too distant ancestors of a large percentage of American Catholics came from societies in which Catholicism was either dominant or highly segregated. Further, circumstances placed them in a relatively isolated minority position in this country until very recently. Consequently, their tradition inclines them to assume ultimate premises and to stress specific practical applications. As we have indicated, this approach proves inadequate when group solidarity is weakened and minority members are exposed to norms and behavioral patterns established on different value premises. Under these conditions, minority members are faced with a choice, and given the "strain for conformity" which is felt in every society, they will tend to accept the standards of the dominant group unless they are made keenly aware of their ultimate religious value premises and the practical implications of these in their daily lives.

Second, the majority of Catholic immigrants came from

rural peasant backgrounds and entered American society at the bottom of the socioeconomic ladder. Under these conditions, the amount of formal education among the laity tended to be limited, with the result that their well-educated religious leaders enjoyed great prestige, and a pattern of more or less authoritarian leadership was widely accepted. This pattern has persisted even though the educational level of the laity has continued to rise steadily. One of the undesirable features of this tradition is that it tends to foster a nonintellectual attitude toward religion and morality. Popular Catholic thought tends to be satisfied with practical conclusions and applications so that there is little interest concerning ultimate premises and the logical relationships between these and approved practices. Some Catholics can give no better explanation of "fish on Friday" than that "Catholics don't eat meat on Friday." The same nonintellectual approach is maintained toward chastity, divorce, contraceptives, and so forth.

How can this intellectual apathy be remedied? The first step is a serious revaluation of traditional methods of religious indoctrination. Whether through historical accident or unreflecting intent, much of Catholic religious education, preaching, and writing has emphasized specific norms and behavioral patterns without clearly relating these to the Catholic ideology; that is, to the ultimate value premises upon which they are based. As a result, it appears that the majority of Catholics tend to view obligatory practices in terms of authority rather than in terms of absolute principles and their logical applications to the practical order. Catholic family values and practices are then seen as a collection of disparate rules and regulations (no divorce, no birth control, and so on) and not as an integrated system. As we have indicated, once the Catholic minority starts moving toward closer integration with an increasingly alien culture, this segmented approach to Catholic family standards proves quite inadequate.

Hence, in formulating any long-range program the Catholic family system must be viewed as a distinct cultural subsystem maintained by a minority with its own peculiar characteristics. This approach forces us to think in terms of the basic elements of integral cultural systems rather than in terms of specific norms and practices. Hence, we are made aware of the necessary relationships between ideology, family objectives, and approved behavioral patterns. As we have suggested, when conflicting family values are encountered in the culture, there is a tendency to discuss and evaluate them apart from the total system of which they form only a portion. Deprived of their ultimate value referents, many Catholic family norms appear meaningless or as the arbitrary impositions of religious authority rather than the practical implementations of accepted dogma.

The Catholic Family System Has Functional Requisites

Every institutional system has certain general organizational features which are requisite to its continuation as a going concern.[3] For example, no family system can endure unless men and women are willing to subordinate their personal interests to the demands of the marriage state. If they refuse to bind themselves to a more or less stable union, there can be no family. What we are saying is that there is a requisite functional relationship between marital stability and a family system. If relationships between the sexes were ephemeral and promiscuous as among some animals, there could be no family system. Hence, we use the term *functional requisite* to express the idea that specific cultural solutions in one institution or social area require specific solutions in other related institutions or social areas.[4]

Applied to the family, therefore, the concept of functional requisite implies that a given family system, because of the values which it seeks to realize, requires the existence of other distinctive elements in the culture. A family system is not a closed unit; it exists *in* society and consequently, it affects and is affected by other institutions upon which it depends for the fulfillment of its purposes. Inasmuch as the Catholic family system maintains distinctive values, it requires special qualities in other institutions. An obvious illustration can be drawn from Catholic marriage doctrine. Since marital fidelity is one of the qualities of marriage, it follows that all the relationships between the sexes must be so regulated that fidelity becomes possible. This requisite functional relationship can be stated in another manner: if a group holds that marital fidelity is a desirable quality of marriage, simple logic will impel them to pattern all the relationships between the sexes in a manner conducive to the achievement of fidelity. In other words, when one quality (marital fidelity) appears in society, it must be accompanied by the other (regulation of the relationships between the sexes).

It is precisely because the Catholic family system has definite functional requisites that its existence as a subsystem is beset with special problems. On the one hand, if Catholic family values are to be operative, they must be translated into specific social relationships and these relationships, in turn, must be supported or at least not hindered by the customs, practices, and institutions within which they operate. On the other hand, the social implementations of these values entails the establishment of a whole series of practices which may be at variance with the practices promoted or tolerated by members of the dominant culture. For example, the implementation of the Catholic ideal of premarital chastity requires adequate instruction of the young; habits of self-control in thought, word, and action; dating and courtship practices which do not unduly expose the participants to temptation, and so forth. Such a program is likely to find little favor with those who deny the moral significance of sexual activity and consequently, consider the acquisition of sexual experience a necessary part of the maturing process.

Special significance attaches to the concept of functional requisites from the fact that Catholics are attempting to maintain their family system in a culture characterized by rapid and constant change. New social situations arise for which the past offers no solutions. Members of the dominant culture tend to work out suitable adjustments and adaptations in terms of their own value system. The Catholic minority may accept these only to the extent that they are consistent with its essential family standards. An example would be the situation which arises from the increased opportunities open to women for employment outside the domestic unit. The higher standard of living made possible by the employment of the wife is an obvious gain. However, if this is achieved by the postponement or limitation of children through contraceptive practices, or if it interferes seriously with woman's roles as wife and mother, it is obvious that the Catholic minority will have to work out its own behavioral patterns in this respect.

Hence, knowledge concerning the functional requisites of the Catholic family system has a twofold value. First, it indicates what cultural elements and social relationships must be established and maintained if Catholic family ideals are to be achieved. Second, it enables us to understand the special problems which a family subsystem encounters in a society characterized by competing value systems and rapid change. In other words, an understanding of this concept prevents a minority from formulating its family program in terms of mere declarations of "principles" which never leave the realm of theory. Such declarations can be little more than deceptive, pious clichés which satisfy only those who pronounce them. It is shallow thinking to hold up the family as the basic unit of society and then to refuse support to programs for decent housing and a living family wage. It betrays a naive lack of realism to praise the Christian ideal of chastity and to do nothing about the conditions and practices which render the achievement of that ideal well-nigh impossible. It is a little shortsighted to insist—very justly—that parents and not the schools should give sex instructions to children, and yet to make no effort to train parents for this task when there is ample evidence that they are not prepared to do so.

These are rather obvious examples of failure to consider the functional exigencies of approved principles. In practice, the formulation of any effective family program requires detailed knowledge of the social system and how it works. You cannot pretend to desire the ideal unless you also desire the conditions which make it possible. This is merely restating the old scholastic principle that you cannot say you really desire an end or goal unless you also desire the means which are necessary for the attainment of that goal.

Change Is Inherent in the Social System

This proposition appears self-evident, at least when applied to modern society. Nevertheless, the significance of change is not so readily understood. People tend to evaluate each invention or institutional change in itself without considering its effect on the total system. For example, the invention and widespread use of the automobile has greatly facilitated transportation; it has created a massive new industry offering employment to numerous workers and opening the market to many new products; it has facilitated the growth of suburbs; it has modified the pattern of American vacations and social life; but it has also vastly increased the incidence of accidental death and injury, decreased the significance of the local community, and seriously modified parental control and supervision of youth, to say nothing of what it has done to many family budgets. Our present purpose does not require an extensive treatment of change in general. It suffices to point out the obvious fact that in a complex, technologically advanced society such as our own, all institutions are highly interdependent so that a change in one calls for adaptations and adjustment in others.

Changes in the social system affect a family system primarily in two ways. First, they may result in alterations of basic family relationships, particularly those between husband and wife, parents and children, and nuclear family and its kinship group. Second, they may lead to modifications of the meaning these relationships have to the participants. Indeed, analysis reveals that any change in family structure leads to some modification in the meaning of the affected relationships. Reciprocally, a change in meaning leads to a repatterning of the relationships concerned. For example, the shift from a rural to an urban way of life led to the employment of the husband in an enterprise distinct from the domestic unit, thus modifying the role of the husband and father in the family and depriving the wife of partnership with him in a common economic enterprise. In the adjustment worked out to meet this new situation, not only the pattern of relationships was altered, but the meaning of these to the participants was redefined. Increasing value came to be placed on companionship as expressed in the mutual satisfaction of the emotional and affectional needs of the spouses since it was primarily in this area that the sense of domestic community and mutual participation remained possible.[5] The over-all result has been an unprecedented insistence on compatibility as expressed in emotional and affectional response.

In a complex society characterized by rapid change the difficulties of formulating an adequate family program for a cultural subgroup are greatly magnified. Minority members participate in the social system, and their family relationships will necessarily be affected by changes in the system. The possible consequences of these changes and their pertinence to Catholic family standards must be carefully weighed. This implies a clear understanding of what we have called the functional exigencies of the Catholic family system. In other words, one must know what that system requires if it is to function adequately, and in the light of this knowledge, the effects of current changes can be gauged. Once these effects are known, the family program can be adjusted accordingly. The characteristics of that program will be treated later; the point we are making here is that the fact of change and its possible repercussions on the Catholic family be taken into consideration.

It would not be necessary to insist on the significance of change if it were not so frequently forgotten in practice. There appears an inherent tendency in men to cling to past solutions and patterns long after they cease to be pertinent to new situations. This can be especially deleterious in regard to family problems. As the basic unit in society, the family is sensitive to all changes which occur. Its basic needs are immediate and not to be postponed. Hence, impractical solutions are exposed at once. Family members cannot permit themselves the luxury of mere speculation. They must work out solutions to their needs at once so that it helps them very little to think about the "good old days" when family life was supposedly easier and less complex.

In practice, therefore, a minority's adjustment to changes

affecting its family system involves a clear distinction between basic family standards and their practical implementation, or what we have called their cultural approximation. Basic family standards and the obligations they imply remain unchanged; the way they are achieved will vary according to the possibilities inherent in the actual situation. In other words, *what* must be done remains unaltered; *how* it can be done is subject to change. For example, we pointed out that marital fidelity requires the regulation of the relationships between the sexes in society; how this is done will vary among different Christian cultures.

To recapitulate, an understanding of the distinction between what must be done (function) and how it can be done (structure) enables us to evaluate changes in the family system. One of the perennial failings of mankind has been to confuse function and structure. This confusion may have the following serious consequences. First, men may attempt to preserve traditional structures or sets of relationships long after they have ceased to fulfill the functions for which they were originally established. Second, if a specific structure becomes outmoded because of changes in the social order, men may reject both the structure and the function. Third, when function and structure are confused, there is a tendency to overstress structure as a value in itself and to forget the function it is supposed to fulfill. For example, in some cultures the father's headship of the family has been translated into a set of domineering relationships which are stressed as values in themselves, forgetting that the function of headship is the preservation of the common good of the family and not the protection of arbitrary male prerogatives.

In general then, the work of formulating a family program is the same as that which Christians have been attempting to do from the beginning and which they will have to continue doing until the end in all areas of living: translate principles into practice in an ever-changing social situation. This task is never finished since society represents not only a dynamic process giving rise to new institutions and new social relationships, but also a complex of interdependent units so that a change in one area necessitates modifications in all others. It follows that the need to "Christianize" society, that is, to regulate it according to Christian principles, is continuous. Just as there is no such thing as a really static society, there is no such thing as a static Christian order for society. Christian principles are "static," that is, unchanging and absolute, but their application is relative to the social situation within which they operate. One of the most persistent and dangerous errors of the past has been the tendency to defend a given social order as the Christian ideal and to forget that only Christian principles are absolutes.

It Is Primarily the Dominant Group Which Regulates Change

It is not necessary for our purpose to advance any comprehensive theory of social causality and social change. The present proposition merely calls attention to the obvious fact that a cultural subgroup such as the Catholic minority is not in a position to channel or orient social change in terms of its value system. In other words, prescinding from the difficult problem of ascertaining how social change originates, the proposition maintains that the complex social process by which institutions and behavioral patterns undergo change is a product of the dominant group in society.[6] This means that Catholics will be faced with institutional patterns, practices, and customs affecting the family, over which they have no direct control.

Hence, in formulating its family program, the minority must realize not only that some change is inevitable, but also that the family adjustments and adaptations occasioned by changes in other areas of the social system will be worked out in terms of the value system of the dominant group. Since Catholics embrace family standards differing in many important respects from those effectively maintained by the dominant culture, there is every possibility that many of these adjustments will prove unacceptable to them. When this difficulty arises, the task of the minority is twofold. First, group members must be made fully aware of the conflict between the socially accepted practice and the minority's value system. This is necessary because, as we have seen, people tend to take a partial, segmented view of problems, thus missing their logical relationship to the ultimate values which they hold. Here again, adequate knowledge of the functional requisites of the Catholic family system is imperative since some commonly accepted behavioral patterns will appear objectionable only when appraised in terms of these requisites. For example, the custom of initiating the "dating" experience at an increasingly early age must be evaluated in terms of Catholic standards of premarital chastity.

Second, substitute or compensatory practices must be devised since simple rejection frequently results in unfulfilled needs. It must be emphasized that rejected solutions, no matter how objectionable, generally represent attempts to solve real 'problems. They are adjustments worked out to meet a present need. Consequently, simple rejection of the objectionable practice does not solve the problem. An effective program must either advance an acceptable solution or, at least, attack the conditions which have created the need. For example, the dominant culture has sanctioned the use of contraceptives for purposes of family limitation. Obviously, this is a situation over which the Catholic minority has no direct control. Since the use of contraceptives is a practice clearly inimical to Catholic family standards, it has been necessary first, to alert the members of the Church to the conflict, and second, to attack those factors in society which tend to make numerous children a burden for the modern family. Hence, programs have been proposed for better housing facilities, more adequate family wages, and various types of insurance, and there has been increased emphasis on social legislation to aid the family.

Problems May Arise from Failure to Adjust or
from Conflict in Values

In a complex society undergoing rapid change, disorganization and conflict may arise either from the failure to adjust some institutions or behavioral patterns to modifications in others (cultural lag), or from the introduction of changes based on a shift in basic value premises. This fifth proposition stresses the importance of distinguishing between these two sources of possible conflict. Since innovations and changes affecting the realization of Catholic family standards appear inevitable, the minority must be prepared to make necessary adjustments and adaptations. This simple statement of the situation is deceptively clear inasmuch as it tacitly assumes careful discrimination in the acceptance of change. A religious minority's position in this situation is complicated by many factors. First, it tends to view with suspicion innovations and changes introduced by the outgroup, particularly where these appear to touch upon moral values. For example, the adoption of smoking, bobbed hair, lipstick, and slacks by the modern female has at one time or another been attacked as contrary to womanly virtue. Although one may advance aesthetic, hygienic, or other objections to these practices, in themselves they do not represent morally objectionable acts.

Second, some fashions and customs are objectionable at the time of their introduction either in themselves, by reason of their novelty, or because of those who employ them. With the passage of time, many of these objectionable features may disappear, thus making the change acceptable. This places the minority in the embarrassing position of first rejecting and then accepting changes. When such cases arise, there is always the implication either that the minority's first position was wrong or that it has since compromised under pressure. Examples could be cited from fashions in dress, dancing, and recreation. In this connection it should be noted that although at times it is possible that what is traditional has been confused with what is moral, nevertheless, generally where there has been a change in the Catholic minority's position, this has resulted either from a modification of the initially objectionable features in the practice, or widespread usage has rendered it morally innocuous. Custom plays an interesting role here. As the moralists say: "What is customary does not affect us." [7]

Third, in matters touching on intimate family relationships, tradition normally tends to conflict with change because each generation evaluates these relationships in terms of their own experience. For example, parents usually attempt to raise their children as they themselves were raised, especially if they themselves had a happy childhood. This would appear to be a common sense approach, but it can lead to conflict and even serious disorganization in a changing society. The new generation must adjust to a different social situation. They are exposed to different social pressures and at an earlier age so that they require more instruction and guidance than did their parents. At the same time, many additional forms of parental control are no longer possible. As a result, unless parents seek new ways of educating, guiding, and supervising their children, serious difficulties may arise. The parental problem, of course, is not simply one of clinging to traditions. Many parents are ill prepared to meet the demands placed upon them by the needs of their children. Guidance and supervision become increasingly more difficult as outside forces beyond parental control are multiplied. Since society has worked out no solution to this problem but has assumed a vague, *laissez-faire* attitude toward youth, it is not surprising that many Catholic parents make few adjustments to new conditions.

Finally, the minority's task of exercising careful discrimination in the acceptance of change is rendered more difficult by the complexity of change in itself. By this we mean that many innovations and behavioral patterns which are introduced have unforeseen implications and unanticipated consequences for Catholic family standards. Since they appear inevitable and more or less harmless, they are casually adopted without making adequate provision to counteract their possible deleterious effects. This situation usually arises when the wide acceptance of the change represents an unperceived shift in value premises. To cite an obvious example, in contemporary society, young people are primarily responsible for the wise selection of their marriage partners. Inasmuch as wise selection implies knowledge, sufficient opportunities for becoming acquainted must be offered to adolescents of both sexes. Out of this need have developed contemporary dating and courtship practices. They appear inevitable under the circumstances, relatively unobjectionable, and consequently acceptable.

However, the situation has implications which experience has not been slow to reveal. The prolonged, unsupervised, relatively intimate contact between adolescents of both sexes results in no minor degree of sexual stimulation. Because pre-marital intercourse is not accepted in most social circles, various forms of "necking" and "petting" have been developed as substitutes. Obviously, Catholics find this solution morally objectionable, but their difficulties are not settled by merely rejecting the practice in theory. Further, they cannot radically change the general pattern of dating and courtship in society. Hence, they must face the fact that their children need special guidance and instruction, intelligent supervision, and sympathetic counseling. At the same time, Catholics must realize that many others do not have the same problem. A change of value premises has occurred, and others may no longer regard willful libidinous excitation and the enjoyment of venereal pleasure outside of marriage as immoral.

ELEMENTS OF A LONG-RANGE PROGRAM

The five propositions which we have been considering constitute the basic prerequisites for the formulation of an adequate family program by the Catholic minority in America. In substance they have done little more than call attention to the fact that the translation of religious dogmas and principles into practical social norms must always be made with reference to the changing complex of social traditions and cultural institutions into which they are incorporated. The specific social applications of a religion depend not only on the inner logic of its moral doctrine but on the type of culture in which they are made.[8] Hence, we have emphasized the minority position of the Catholic group, the complexity, cultural pluralism, and rapid change which characterize American society, and the consequences of these for the realization and maintenance of Catholic family standards. We are now prepared to consider the basic elements of a minority's family program. What alternatives does a minority have? If it chooses integration, how can it survive? Why are a minority's problems so complex?

The Minority Must Make a Choice

When a minority constitutes a distinct subculture, it can attempt to maintain its system either by isolating itself from the influence of the dominant culture, or it can attempt limited integration. Complete isolation is not easily achieved in modern society, although a few small groups, such as some of the Mennonites in the United States and the Doukhobors in Canada, appear to have had considerable success.[9] Most ethnic and racial minorities maintained or endured practical isolation during their early years in America. As we have indicated, some ethnic groups of the Catholic minority established strong solidarity around their national parishes and constructed relatively effective cultural "fences" to hedge their members off from outgroup influence. These served to slow down the process of integration, but at best they could only partially shield group members from the effects of social change taking place in the dominant culture. At present, descendants of the Old Immigration have ceased to be identifiable as ethnic minorities, and the descendants of the New are rapidly following their lead in moving toward limited integration.

By limited integration we mean that the members of the minority mix freely in society and follow general cultural orientations and behavioral patterns except when these openly conflict with the realization of their value system. This is roughly the position of the majority of Catholics in American society. It follows that their family program must be formulated in terms of integration rather than isolation. For better or worse, the Catholic minority is being gradually assimilated. Catholic families today are subjected to the same influences and pressures as are all other families in American society.

Under these circumstances, the Catholic minority's family program must reflect the following qualities. First, the system established to implement its ideals must be flexible enough to integrate needed modifications required by the changing social structure. Second, it must distinguish clearly between these necessary adaptations and those innovations based on premises opposed to its own and rendering the realization of its own values either improbable or impossible. Third, when a current social practice must be rejected, the minority must take positive steps to meet the need which the rejected practice was designed to fulfill. Although the import of these qualities should now be clear, it will be worth while to treat them in some detail so that their full significance may be clearly understood.

The Program Must Be Flexible

The pattern of pertinent social relationships which the minority has established for the implementation of its family values must be flexible enough to absorb or integrate those modifications or repatternings required by changes in the social structure. This involves making a clear distinction between abstract value premises and the concrete social relationships developed to implement them in a given cultural situation. We have pointed out the inevitability of change in the social system and have suggested that the institution of the family, as the primary unit of society, is highly sensitive to whatever changes occur in other institutions. These changes tend to affect the relationships between the nuclear family and the kinship (extended family), as well as the statuses and roles of husband, wife, and children. It follows that Catholic families must be prepared to make numerous adjustments and adaptations if their family system is to function smoothly and achieve its essential purposes.

Let us consider, for example, the isolation of the individual family unit brought about by the change in the way men make a living. An industrial society tends to foster the growth of the conjugal family type, that is, the independent family unit composed of husband, wife, and immature offspring. In other words, it weakens and even renders inoperative the influence and assistance of the wider, "extended" family group. This means that the modern young couple starting out in marriage must frequently rely only on their own resources. They are isolated from their kinship groups—their relatives—at least to the extent that they can make no claims upon them. Each unit must stand on its own feet and meet its own problems singlehanded. Relatives may help; they are not obliged to do so, and frequently are not in a position to do so.

The extended family system does not fare well in an industrial society for many reasons. Modern industrial organization demands considerable mobility. Consequently, one frequently does not live near one's relatives but near one's job. Further, promotion in such a society tends not to be based on family name or prestige but on the individual's qualifications in a highly competitive atmosphere. Both these factors, in turn, tend to build up a spirit of independence and individualism which resents "interference" from the extended kinship group and acknowledges few obligations toward them.

The consequences of this shift in family systems are apparent in contemporary society. The family no longer takes care of its orphaned minors, its incapacitated and sick, its aged. We have accepted the principle that "society"—that is, the state—must take care of them. It is well to remind ourselves that the problem of the aged is not merely the result of increased longevity. It is a clear indication of the isolation of the conjugal type which must turn not to relatives—the extended family—but to society for help in times of need. The current demand for baby-sitters is another indication of family isolation. Grandparents, maiden aunts, and younger sisters are no longer available.

What is the significance of this trend for the Catholic family program? Clearly, it is not realistic to pass over piously the serious strain that numerous children place upon the isolated young mother. One must not underestimate the modern family's justifiable fear of sickness, accidents, and unemployment. We will not dismiss the drive for greater companionship between husband and wife in marriage as a romantic whim, but see that it is needed to offset their loss of wider family ties. Finally, it is apparent that intimate relationships within the family are now supporting a heavier emotional load since they are the principal bonds which remain, and consequently, when friction occurs, it is now more intense and destructive.

This is only one example of how change in the social system affects the family. One could continue this approach and point out the need for adjustment occasioned by the increase of leisure time, the modification of family roles in an industrialized urban environment, the growth of outside forces competing with the parents in the formation and control of children. The point to be stressed, however, is that Catholic families must maintain a clear distinction between essential family values and their concrete implementation. If they fail to make this distinction, there is grave danger that when the cultural situation requires adjustment, they will attempt to defend both their family value system and its cultural implementation as unchanging absolutes which must be retained at all costs. The result can only be failure to achieve their family ideals. What is required, therefore, is a clear understanding of essential family values and a willingness to make whatever adjustments and adaptations are required for their realization. If traditional means prove ineffective, then new means must be devised. The essential purposes of the family remain unchanged. Unless means are found to realize these purposes in a manner compatible with Catholic standards, others will be adopted. Family needs are immediate and cannot readily be postponed.

The Program Must Be Selective in Accepting Change

The second quality of an effective family program is the possession of sufficient insight to distinguish clearly between necessary adaptations and those innovations which would render the realization of Catholic family standards either improbable or impossible. American society embraces several conflicting value systems, so that certain attitudes, customs, and practices may gain widespread social acceptance although they are incompatible with the Catholic value system. Because they are part of the over-all pattern of change, it is possible for members of the minority to confuse them with necessary changes and overlook the fact that they are based on unacceptable premises. We have already discussed how difficult it may be to make this distinction in practice. The significance of some behavioral patterns can be understood only through studying their effects in a given social context.

The point to be emphasized here is that Catholic families in a pluralistic culture may never be simply "conformists." They may not indiscriminately follow the family adjustments and adaptations worked out in that society. This statement is obvious when applied to such practices as contraception, sterilization, abortion, divorce, premarital or extramarital intercourse, and so forth. It applies likewise to some dating and courtship practices, fashions in female dress, forms of recreation involving the two sexes, conversation, reading, and entertainment. It is pertinent also to the hierarchy of cultural goals. Physical comfort, avoidance of pain, pursuit of "happiness," accumulation of the material symbols of success, social prominence and acceptance are goals which hold a subordinate position in the Catholic system of values. Hence, Catholics who blindly "follow the crowd" and still attempt to maintain their family standards demonstrate a distressing lack of logic. It is not surprising that they find Catholic ideals "unrealistic" and unattainable in modern society.

The Program Must Be Positive

The third quality of an effective family program requires that when a prevalent cultural practice must be rejected by the minority, positive steps be taken to meet the need which the rejected practice was fulfilling. The mere recognition and rejection of an objectionable practice constitute only the first steps which a minority must take in protecting its value system. The rejected practice had obviously been introduced to meet a need in society. Further, once it was introduced and accepted (institutionalized), other institutions were modified in terms of it with the result that a new social equilibrium or balance of relationships and mutual expectations was established. Hence, to reject the practice is to disturb the equilibrium. This places such serious strain on minority group members that unless positive steps are taken to establish a new equilibrium based on acceptable practices, many of the minority will simply follow the rejected practice.

For example, once the use of contraceptives for purposes of family limitation has gained widespread social acceptance, a series of changes will take place in those relationships associated with or affected by the practice. Wages, standard of living, housing facilities, and spending habits will be geared to the small family. Couples may marry with the expectation that both partners will maintain their job and thus increase the family income. Early age at marriage, which would normally increase the exposure-to-pregnancy period, need no longer be a factor in family size. Pregnancies may be "bunched" in the early years of marriage, thus shortening the span during which the wife must be confined primarily to the home and freeing her for extrafamilial activities while she is still relatively young. In general, the whole complex of family expectations and practices undergoes modification because the number and spacing of children can be "planned."

Now consider the position of minority members who reject contraceptive practices because they conflict with Catholic family standards. They participate in a social system which has achieved equilibrium in terms of this practice. Hence, rejection places them under a considerable strain. If they follow the prevalent custom of marrying young, they may normally expect numerous offspring. Wages make no allowance for the size of the family. The standard of living of their socioeconomic class, which presumably they will attempt to maintain, is formulated in terms of a small family. If the couple do not own their own home, the search for living quarters suitable to a large family can be both expensive and humiliating. The "bunching" of planned pregnancies in the early years of marriage is normally more difficult so that the wife must look forward to a longer span of childbearing and childrearing. In addition there are the psychological burdens of lack of understanding and sympathy, criticism, and even sophisticated pity.

It follows that the mere reiteration of the moral evils involved in the use of contraceptives will not answer the problems of minority members. A positive program is required, and this must take two approaches. First, on the spiritual level, there must be a careful restatement of the meaning of life in terms of the Catholic value system and contemporary living conditions. The relationships between accepted value premises and practical conduct, between the vocation of parenthood and personal development, between an individually and socially pertinent hierarchy of values and man's purpose in life must be reformulated in a way that group members can readily understand. This spiritual approach is necessary not only because the culture no longer supplies it, but also because traditional definitions were formulated in a different social context and consequently, lack realism and cogency.

Second, on the practical level, steps must be taken to enable group members to achieve social equilibrium in a pattern of relationships which does not include the use of contraceptives as a solution to their problems. This calls for a serious reappraisal of many accepted customs and practices as well as an intelligent revitalizing of the virtue of social charity. Girls must be prepared not only for marriage but motherhood. Young men must acquire the virtues of prudent saving and responsibility. Heavily burdened households must be aided by relatives, or in their absence, by members of the community or parish. Workable programs for slum clearance, adequate housing, health insurance, and so forth, must be initiated and supported. In brief, a spiritual and social climate must be produced within which group members come to recognize and practically express their religious solidarity.

The crux of the problem which the Catholic minority encounters in maintaining its family standards grows out of the very nature of the social system. First, in any given system, values, norms, and behavioral patterns tend to be integrated. In practice, this means that people's actions imply certain implicit or explicit norms, and these norms, in turn, presuppose certain values. For instance, when a couple seek to get a divorce, this implies that they believe that the marriage bond can be dissolved by a civil court. This in turn presupposes that marriage is not founded on a sacramental contract but on a private agreement subject to state regulation. Second, in a going system, institutions are interrelated. A change in one has widespread repercussions leading to readjustments in others. Consequently, when change occurs, it is gradually "geared into" the entire system. Aspirational goals and social relationships are modified in terms of it. In fact, it gradually becomes "institutionalized."

Hence, the minority's problem is not concerned with individual, objectionable acts, but with a morally pathological system. From the Catholic viewpoint, such culturally "normal," institutionalized practices as divorce and contraceptive birth control are morally pathological. It is this normalcy of the pathological in the system which makes the achievement of Catholic family standards so difficult. In other words, Catholics must participate in a system geared to goals they cannot accept, and which has achieved some type of working balance or equilibrium by institutionalizing practices which they consider pathological. It is for this reason that we have stressed the need for a positive program which will realistically clarify Catholic family goals and through the restoration of some form of group solidarity will enable Catholic families to maintain their balance.

SUMMARY

In this chapter we have studied the characteristics of an effective family program. How can American Catholics maintain their family standards in a society which does not accept these standards and consequently establishes institutions and practices which either oppose or fail to support them? It was pointed out that Catholics embrace a distinct set of family values. These require the support of related institutions and practices if they are to be adequately achieved. Since American society is undergoing rapid change, these values must be realized in a constantly changing social situation. This calls for a clear distinction between values and the specific means used to implement them in a given social order. Inasmuch as change in our society is not under the control of the Catholic minority, customs and practices may arise which prove inimical to the Catholic family system.

In this latter case, mere negative rejection will not be sufficient to insure minority survival. A positive program using both a spiritual and a social approach must be initiated if minority members are to meet the strain of nonconformity with the dominant culture. The fundamental problem of the minority arises from the fact that Catholics must participate in a social system which regards the morally pathological as normal.

CHAPTER FOURTEEN

Restorations and Developments

In the last chapter we saw that the fundamental problem of Catholics consisted in realistically defining their family goals and in providing the institutional means required for their realization *as a minority*. In a pluralistic society, the Catholic minority's aspirations tend to conflict with the socially structured means available for the realization of these aspirations. It is the dominant group which develops these socially structured means. They are designed for the realization of the dominant group's, not the minority's, aspirations. A consideration of immediate Catholic family needs, therefore, must take this fact into account. Although it may prove difficult, a minority which desires to survive may never assume a mere "group-think" mentality and simply "follow the crowd."

On the theoretical level, this represents a minor danger for Catholics since they are members of an authoritative teaching church which clearly defines Catholic family standards and carefully evaluates the morality of related behavioral patterns. In practice, however, the influence of the dominant culture appears inevitable. What is more important perhaps, the reaction to this influence may result in exaggeration, misplaced emphasis, and the segmentation of essential Catholic principles. The maintenance of basic doctrinal balance is assured by the teaching Church, but this does not imply that individual Catholics or groups of Catholics will always understand and apply these principles intelligently. It follows that there will be need for "restorations"—that is, for rethinking and revaluating specific applications and practices in terms of first principles and the doctrinal whole. This would be necessary even in societies which were predominantly Catholic; it has special significance when Catholics constitute only a minority.

The present chapter, therefore, is concerned with the immediate needs of the Catholic family system. What positive steps must be taken to strengthen the contemporary Catholic family? What "restorations" must be made in order to bring practice into line with principles? Ultimate premises are assumed so that the argument will run: *If* you hold these principles, *then* you must act as follows. We do not wish to imply that the Catholic family system has fared miserably in the past nor do we suggest that present Catholic families are hopelessly inadequate. Rather, in the light of what we have learned about the Catholic population, the characteristics of American society, and the exigencies of Catholic family standards, we desire to point out weaknesses and suggest remedies appropriate for the times.

Assuming the role of a critic involves its hazards. There is always the danger that one will appear to be casting blame where none is due. For this reason it may be well to state our position in this matter clearly from the beginning. We feel that there have been failures in the past, and we maintain that there are weaknesses in the family system at present. For the most part, these are the result either of failure to make adequate adjustment to change in the social system, or of inability to counteract the unanticipated consequences of certain necessary programs, or of using inept means to achieve desirable goals. Hence, our criticism does not imply blame; rather, it is a realistic taking stock of where we are in order to outline a more effective program for the future. Once it is considered beyond criticism, a social institution, like an individual, must be treated either as infallible—or dead.

SOME RESTORATIONS

Strictly speaking, the term *restoration* implies the replacing of something which was originally present but has since disappeared. Although we desire to retain this connotation of the term, we are not interested here in historical reconstructions. The question of whether family systems of the past were more adequate than the present can be left to family historians. As used here, restoration denotes the replacing of something which is considered lacking in terms of an ideal. This is to say, assuming the actualization of Catholic family standards as an ideal goal, a study of the present family system reveals certain lacks or deficiencies which should be met. Lest the deficiencies which will be indicated appear to be based on hasty generalizations, it should be noted at once that they do not represent "all or none," but rather, "more or less" propositions. In other words, it is maintained that these lacks are more or less general and to the extent that they exist, they must be remedied.

The Restoration of Parental Roles

A commonplace in contemporary literature on the family is the statement that changes in the social system have caused the family to lose many of its traditional functions, with the result that the institution of the family has lost much of its meaning. Although it is obvious that some of the activities formerly carried on in the home have been taken over by outside institutions, and all family functions have undergone some modification, the essential roles of parenthood remain the same. If they are not being fulfilled today, this is due to the inability or voluntary demission of parents and not to changes in the social system or the inevitable encroachments of outside institutions. According to Catholic doctrine, the primary purpose of the family is to provide for the fitting procreation and education of offspring. Parental roles receive their specification from this purpose. Consequently, inherent in the very nature of the family is the parental obligation to provide that type of training required by the child for his development into the status of Christian manhood. Among Catholics there can be no disagreement on this goal, but the question arises: How is this to be achieved?

In Chapter Twelve, we pointed out that the Catholic parent suffers from the same inferiority complex in regard to education as does the average American parent. Professional educators and child psychologists have painted such a distressing picture of parental mistakes that parents are afraid to act. Further, some argue that the preschool child is too young to receive any formal instruction and once school begins, he is thought to be in capable hands. Others contend that in spite of shorter hours of work and the addition of many labor-saving devices in the home, modern parents are too busy about other things to have time to instruct their children.

All these explanations may carry some weight, but there appears an additional reason why Catholic parents may gradually have come to neglect their duties in this regard. It may very well be one of the unanticipated consequences of the parochial school system. By this we mean it is possible that the strong, persistent, and courageous emphasis on the parochial school has led Catholics to neglect or undervalue a cardinal tenet of family doctrine: that the primary, natural, and ordinarily irreplaceable school of religion and the moral virtues is the home; that the principal and only adequate agents of religious and moral training are the parents; that the parochial school and the religious teacher can at best serve only as aids, not as substitutes for the home and the parent in the religious formation of the child.

We would not be misunderstood here. This is not an attack on the parochial school! When we have written in this vein in the past, superficial adversaries of the parochial school system have seized upon our words as if they now had ammunition, made in Rome, against the parochial school. This is patently absurd. What we are saying is that the parochial school is necessary; in fact, given the seemingly unavoidable "neutrality" of our contemporary public school system, it is absolutely indispensable. Paradoxically, it is the very acuteness of the need for parochial schools that has created the problem under discussion.

It has often been said that one of the glories of American Catholicism is the parochial school system. No competent observer would deny this. The achievement is all the more outstanding inasmuch as many of the Catholic immigrants came from countries in which church and school were given financial support by the state. Nevertheless, at great personal sacrifice, American Catholics have built their parochial school system, while at the same time, they have supported through taxes one of the most expensive public school systems in the world. This unique achievement has not come without effort. Its success reflects equal credit on the foresight of the hierarchy, the courage and ingenuity of pastors, the self-sacrifice of teaching sisters, brothers, and priests, and the generosity of the faithful. Further, the parochial system is not self-sustaining. Besides the ever constant financial burden, there is the competition of the nonparochial school system and the steady inroads of indifference and secularism upon Catholic families.

Consequently, in order to establish, maintain, and enlarge the Catholic parochial school system, the clergy must not only plan and labor unceasingly, they must constantly encourage and exhort their parishioners to support the schools. In their sermons they must frequently stress the value of a Catholic education and the serious obligations of parents to provide this for their children. Catholic parents who support the schools must be praised. They must be made to feel that one of the finest heritages they can bestow on their children is the gift of a Catholic education.

This constant emphasis on Catholic education is needed if the system is to endure. On the other hand, it may well be asked whether this preoccupation with maintaining the system has not resulted in some neglect of Catholic doctrine concerning the personal role of parents in the education of their children. Is it possible that steady emphasis on the Catholic school, without equal emphasis on the role of the family, has left the average Catholic parent with the impression that his essential obligations in the religious training of the child are fulfilled if only he sees to it that the child attends the parochial school? Is one source of the parental neglect which we have indicated above traceable to this false impression?

What we are talking about here may be viewed as an unanticipated consequence of a necessary mode of action. It is well known to students of society that some social programs which are good in themselves may have indirect and unanticipated consequences which turn out to be very harmful. This does not mean that the program must be abandoned. Rather, it demands that the harmful, unanticipated consequences should be recognized and effective remedies developed to meet them.

Hence, under present conditions in American society, it is absolutely necessary to emphasize the obligations of parents to support a separate school system and to send their children to Catholic schools. On the other hand, there is evidence that this emphasis has resulted in some parents unfortunately getting the impression that their essential obligations in the religious training of their children were fulfilled as long as they supported the parochial school and saw to it that their children attended. Indeed, some parents seem to imply that they are doing the "Church" a favor when they entrust their uninstructed youngsters to the parish school.

Therefore, it seems necessary to insist that, along with the emphasis on the need for Catholic education, there should be equal emphasis on the personal obligation of parents to instruct and train their children. This training, in the words of Pius XII, "must start with the cradle." Parents should be instructed to see in the school an indispensable aid, but only an aid, in carrying out their primary obligation of developing the future "citizens of two worlds."

The argument is sometimes raised that the school is eminently fitted to handle the entire religious training of children. After all, the sisters, brothers, and priests are much more skilled in teaching than is the average parent, so why not entrust the schools with the entire religious training of children? Just as the family relies on the schools to instruct the children in reading, writing, and arithmetic, why may it not trust the schools to give them their religious training?

This is utterly to misconceive the meaning of religion in life.

Religion is something more than knowledge; it is knowledge plus habit and practice. It is understanding life and living life in terms of the supernatural. This is an hourly task not confined to the classroom. This is a basic orientation of life not to be postponed until the child reaches first grade. To confine religion to the classroom is to segmentalize and "compartmentalize" it from life, thus laying the foundations for the false philosophy that "business is business" and moral precepts apply only in specific areas of living or on Sundays.

To be specific, the schools cannot be entrusted with the entire religious training and instruction of the child for the following reasons. First, the religious training of children is a sacred parental obligation and privilege which cannot be entirely delegated to others, even to sisters and priests. To be sure, the pastor and the parochial school teacher are aids to the parents, they should not and cannot replace them.

Second, the child is deprived of religious influences in his most formative years if we wait until he is sent to school in order to start religious training. The child starts learning as soon as it is born. At no time is this learning process more active and more long-lasting than in the early, formative years of life. The child continues to learn every day, and it is important that the idea of God and the truths of the faith enter into the understanding of his little world from the very beginning of the learning process.

In the third place, we burden the school and the teachers with a task which they cannot fulfill adequately without the aid of the parents if we hand over the religious training of the child entirely to the school. The school should be a continuation of and aid to the religious training in the home. School training must build on previous training in the home and on training going on in the home every day. The child is in the school only a relatively short time each week. Unless the school can rely on the constant collaboration of the parents, it cannot succeed in its all important task of helping to mould the character of the child along religious lines.

Finally, the danger of confusing school and religion, a confusion which can produce fatal results once the child leaves the environment of the school, is ever present if religious training is confined primarily to the classroom and the school. The child easily identifies the precepts of religion with the rules and regulations of the school. He readily falls into the habit of attending Mass and fulfilling other religious obligations only because it is demanded by the school or because the whole group does it. It is a well known fact that some children acquire a positive distaste for this regimentation and refuse to carry on faithfully once they are away from school. Others learn to take a very superficial view of religion and religious practices since religious sanctions are imposed not by their parents, whom they love and admire, but by outsiders, whose motives they may misunderstand and sometimes distrust. This all adds up to saying that the school can succeed only if it has the active cooperation of the parents.

Even more cogent reasons why parents should personally initiate and continue the religious instruction and training of their offspring flow from the very nature of parent-child relationships in the family. The whole problem of parental control is involved here. Judges, social workers, and sociologists have constantly pointed out that the contemporary family is no longer supplying the type of guidance, training, and discipline that children need in the modern world. Their observation is not limited to the families of juvenile delinquents; in many other families, children are growing up with little guidance or discipline.

For their part, modern parents complain they no longer have the control over their children which they need if they would perform this task successfully. They point out that their children refuse to obey them. "They simply won't listen to what we tell them! Every time we try to guide them or supervise their actions, they call us 'old-fashioned' and point to the 'modern parents' of their companions who don't have any of the same 'narrow' ideas." This is an amazing admission indeed!

How can a general situation arise in which children refuse to follow the guidance of their parents? Surely, in no previous age have children ever been in such need of protection and guidance, yet those who stand in a natural position to furnish this, maintain they are unable to do so. Of course, we are well aware of the enormous increase in the number and variety of influences playing upon young people today. This forms a great contrast with the situation thirty years ago when there were few movies, no radio programs, no television sets, few magazines, no tabloids, and only a very limited number of organized recreational centers taking young people from the home and away from parental supervision. However, these are external agencies. They do not account for the breakdown of parental control; they merely make guidance more difficult and more necessary.

Why have some parents lost control over their children? Our hypothesis is that they do not have control over their children during the all-important period of adolescence because they have not laid the foundations for that control from the child's earliest years. Parents cannot step into the role of moral protector and guide for their child at puberty if they have not fulfilled that role in the child's life from the cradle. On the other hand, few children will reject parental control during the difficult and confusing years of the early teens if they have been accustomed to turn to their parents for help and guidance from the beginning. Parent-child relationships have to be worked at. They do not spring up spontaneously through the development of some mysterious kind of instinct. If the ten-year-old or fifteen-year-old child thinks of his parents as those who know best, or, at least, as those who should be obeyed, it will be because they have played this role in his life from infancy. Parents will be accepted as the moral directors and guides of their children only if it is they who have introduced the child to God, have taught him his first prayers, have showed him what is right and wrong, have day by day, lovingly yet firmly, taught him to distinguish good from evil.

Restoration of the Catholic Concept of Sex

Always and everywhere the phenomenon of sex has appeared as something unique, and people are still puzzling over the problem of reconciling the need for control with the need for expression. Human reaction has run the gamut from complete rejection to worship. Mankind has always been somewhat ill at ease in dealing with it. Some have tried giving it the "silent treatment," only to discover that it has an uncomfortable way of asserting itself, especially when it is most ignored. Lately, there has been an attempt to study the phenomenon "scientifically," but this approach has produced little more than a caricature of reality. At all times, the unprincipled in art, literature, and entertainment have regarded it as a kind of enduring, providential seven-year-itch to be exploited for profit.

The Catholic concept of sex developed in Chapter Two is founded on an ideology which takes into consideration the origin, nature, destiny—and history—of man. In other words, it determines the proper function of sex by studying its nature and purpose in terms of human nature integrally conceived. This person-centered approach avoids the error of conceiving sex as something merely physical, a kind of unfortunate, extrinsic property, as it were, attached to the individual but not really constituting an essential part of him. Rather, it insists that human nature is expressed bisexually: "Male and female He created them." Consequently, the function of sex can never be dissociated from the human person; its conscious exercise is always a human act; and its proper use constitutes an enrichment of the individual's personality. Furthermore, the essence of the marriage contract is the conferring of the mutual, exclusive, and perpetual right both to acts which are of their very nature proper for begetting offspring and to the sharing of life together. The sacrament of matrimony is founded on the phenomenon of sex.

Unfortunately, one of the accompanying effects of original sin was the loss of the special grace through which man was able to impose right order on his appetites. Because of this loss, the control of his "passions" has presented man with a constant struggle. Since the reproductive drive is at times so easily stimulated, and when aroused, so imperative in its demands for fulfillment, he has come to look upon it as one of his major personal problems. Experience has taught the Christian that the exercise of chastity is possible only with the help of God's grace and the intelligent avoidance of prohibited sexual stimulus. Hence, the virtuous man attempts to avoid everything which is likely to excite venereal pleasure contrary to right order either in himself or others. He does this, not because he considers venereal pleasure to be evil in itself. However, experience has taught him that once it is aroused, there is danger that he may consent to it contrary to right reason, thus sinning against chastity. The truly modest person is neither puritanical nor prudish. He is a realist who works on the principle: If you wish to avoid unchastity, you had better avoid actions which arouse venereal pleasure since experience teaches that this passion, once aroused, frequently entices consent.

This Catholic concept of sex is so comprehensive, balanced, and consistent with experience that Catholics should have little difficulty in maintaining sane attitudes towards sexual phenomena. Unfortunately, this is not the case, and one must only conclude that there is something unique about sex. This is not the place to trace the history of attitudes toward sex, intriguing as such a work might prove. Our present concern is to indicate some contemporary aberrations and to point out their deleterious consequences for the achievement of Catholic family standards. Because the phenomenon of sex is so profoundly involved in the development of personality and the stability of the family, even slight divergence from the Catholic concept has far-reaching effects.

One of the basic current aberrations stems from a confusion between sins of unchastity and physical manifestations of the reproductive drive. The mistake has been made of extending the character of sinfulness from the prohibited act to the physical phenomenon. This is to say, because the conscious, deliberate consent to venereal pleasure under circumstances when this is prohibited constitutes sin, the error has been made of attributing the quality of sinfulness to the venereal pleasure itself and to the physical organs which give rise to it. As a result, there is a tendency to look upon the physical manifestations of the reproductive drive as sinful and to lose sight of the fact that the sinfulness of unchaste acts is a quality of the act of consent not of the venereal pleasure involved.

This extension of sinfulness to the physical manifestations of sex has serious theoretical consequences. In the first place, it perverts the Catholic doctrine of sin and leaves the door wide open to the heresy of Manichaeism, the belief that there is something inherently evil in the physical. According to Catholic teaching, sin consists in the conscious, deliberate choice to act contrary to God's will as the individual knows it. Contrary to Manichaean doctrine, the physical world is not evil, although it may be used for evil purposes. Hence, when the quality of sinfulness is attributed to the physical manifestations of sex, Catholic doctrine concerning sins against chastity is perverted and the essentially un-Catholic attitude that bodily or physical phenomena are evil is promoted.

In the second place, this confusion has led to a distorted concept of chastity. The chaste person is conceived of as some type of asexual or sexless creature. He is one who never feels the physical manifestations of sex rather than one who always uses his sexual powers in accordance with God's will. As a result, mere physical integrity comes to be regarded as a value in itself. There is the implicit, though unexpressed, attitude that the virtue of chastity applies primarily to the unmarried. That this is contrary to basic Catholic doctrine needs no comment, but the fact that this attitude exists is one more indication that where sex is concerned, the logical application of ultimate premises to known facts has not characterized much popular thinking on the subject.

Third, this confusion is based on a nonexistent separation between the physical or corporal and the spiritual in man. Sexual acts are considered "carnal," "animal," or manifestations of man's "lower nature." As we saw in Chapter Two, the individual is a unity composed of two co-principles, body and soul. Hence, human acts cannot be merely "carnal," or "animal," or of man's "lower nature." It is the human person that acts in all cases. To speak of sexual acts as other than human acts is to deprive them of their meaning and dignity by implying an unreal divorce between the two co-principles in human nature. No doubt, this unconscious "smear campaign" was initiated to dissuade people from performing acts against chastity and to strengthen their control over their sexual drives. Paradoxically, it has resulted in weakening that control, for it has deprived the sexual drive of none of its force, yet it has separated the sexual act from its meaning and dignity. At the same time, this emphasis on the physical aspects of the sexual act reveals little essential differences from the contemporary secular view. The frame of reference is different, but the thing in itself is viewed in the same way.

Further, this confusion has resulted in an unbalanced stressing of what might be termed the negative aspects of the virtue of chastity. Emphasis is placed on what not to do. Especially among adolescents, the concept of chastity may be summarized as a series of "don'ts." This negative approach is characteristically partial and segmented. The relationships between chastity and modesty are not clearly indicated, so that some actions are arbitrarily judged sinful rather than the possible occasions of sin. Specific manifestations of sex are treated separately, with the result that an integrated, positive view of the nature and function of sex is seldom presented. This makes everything connected with sex rather vague, indefinite, a source of worry and anxiety, if not of actual disgust. However, since one does not eliminate the positive assertion of sex in the individual's life by merely ignoring it or by taking a negative approach, people develop a whole series of rationalizations, subterfuges, and disguises for dealing with it. The whole matter of sex is made to appear as a kind of "open secret," to be talked about in whispers or behind closed doors, but never to be brought out into the open and appraised in accordance with right reason and Catholic doctrine.

Finally, this confusion has led to a devaluation of the nature of sex itself. By this we mean that the inherent qualities of maleness and femaleness which the possession of "sex" denotes tend to be ignored or passed over in silence, if not suppressed, while thinking centers on the physical aspects of the reproductive drive. According to Genesis, God created male and female as companions and helpmates. Hence, each possesses characteristic complementary qualities which must be actualized if the personality of each is to be fully developed in marriage. Although these qualities are ultimately oriented around the different reproductive roles of male and female, their significance extends far beyond the act of physical union. They are the physical, emotional, psychic, and spiritual qual-

ities of sex enabling male and female to complete each other
as companions and co-partners in the procreation and education of the child and the full development of their personalities. It follows that the identification of sex with the physical
manifestations of the reproductive drive loses sight of the integral meaning of sex. Its complementary qualities are under-
valued so that in marriage there is frequently competition
rather than cooperation, and cohabitation without companionship.

The theoretical consequences of this first aberration have
been listed in some detail since they often pass unperceived.
The practical consequences are more obvious. First, because
sex has come to be looked upon as something sinful, or, at
least as something "dirty," "nasty," and peculiarly "unladylike," parents find it difficult to instruct their children in the
necessary facts of sex and to aid them in developing the integral virtue of chastity. As a result, children are driven to
questionable sources in the legitimate quest for knowledge,
parental attitudes leave the impression that sex is something
which cannot be dealt with intelligently, the virtue of chastity
is reduced to a series of "don'ts," the physical manifestations
of sex are not related to the sublime privilege of procreation,
and the puzzling, persistent, gradually developing assertion
of sexual potency appears as a source of worry and anxiety.
Adolescents are confused by its novelty and power and per-
plexed by the need for its control.

There is no necessity to dwell further on the existence of this
problem inasmuch as numerous youth surveys, teachers, retreat masters, and parents have revealed its extent. However,
we shall add a few observations to clarify the point. First, parents must not believe that because they say nothing directly
about sex to their children, they are thereby not teaching.
Their silence, attitudes in refusing to answer questions, and
chance comments on the subject teach the child more clearly
than words that there is something strange, improper, or sinful about sex. Of course, the same impression can be given by
the worried parent who, on a given day, takes the child aside
and grimly tells him "all." Such parents should realize that
instruction and training in any virtue must be geared to the

experience and development of the child. Particularly in regard to sex, elders tend to project their feelings into the child's world so that a simple, innocent question is greeted either with consternation or an abbreviated version of the Kinsey reports.

Second, adequate training of youth in the virtue of chastity does not require that the parents be skilled in anatomy and have the technical names of all the organs on the tip of their tongues. This approach lends a certain air of sophistication to the instructions; it has little to do with the interpretation of experience and the formation of attitudes. Obviously, some knowledge of a few essential organs is required. One may as well use the technical terms for these as the ridiculous euphemisms frequently coined in the nursery. However, the important point is the formation of sane, healthy attitudes toward sex. This involves the acceptance of sex and its consequences for the balanced development of personality. It involves some knowledge of the manifestations of sex in the individual, of how the physical and psychical mechanisms function, and of the stimuli which initiate the whole sequence of sexual response.

Further, it involves an integral approach to sexual phenomena; that is, the specific manifestations of the reproductive drive in the growing youth must be related to the procreative function so that he can grasp their meaning. For example, it makes a great deal of difference in the development of a balanced personality whether the growing girl views the onset of menstruation as "the curse," or as nature's warning that she is approaching biological maturity and the capacity for full womanhood. It matters whether the growing boy views nocturnal emissions as "pollution," or as the indication that he is approaching biological maturity with its added powers and responsibilities. Finally, the development of sound attitudes toward sex involves taking cognizance of current false attitudes and misinformation. As Artemus Ward once remarked in another connection, "It ain't so much the things we don't know that get us in troubles. It's the things we know that ain't so." Parents must be aware that their children are exposed to a great deal of popular knowledge about sex that "ain't so" and must take steps to correct it, although in the long run, the best corrective is the positive approach recommended above.

A second practical consequence of this failure to understand the Catholic concept of sex is revealed in parental attitudes toward dating and courtship. Because they refuse to face openly and intelligently the phenomenon of sex and its significance, many Catholic parents act as if their growing adolescents were sexless creatures, or at least, quite above "such things." Hence, added to the failure to train and instruct positively in the virtue of chastity is parental toleration or promotion of premarital relationship patterns between the sexes which are normally calculated to induce considerable sexual arousal with possible danger of consent. Children are encouraged to start the dating process at very early ages. Since they feel socially insecure in this process, young people tend to start "going steady." It obviates the problem of getting "dates" and of widening the circle of their acquaintances—a painful problem for the young who lack experience and self-confidence. Yet even the most shallow parents must realize the sexual difficulties involved in going steady long years before marriage becomes a social possibility. Of course, such parents rationalize their position by ignoring sex, and besides, "My child is not that type!"

Apart from neglecting the problem of "going steady" at early ages, many parents exercise little supervision over the social life of their children. Whom are they with? Where do they go? What do they do? Many parents are proud because their child is so "popular." They insist on regarding adolescents as mature persons and are insulted by the suggestion that their children require guidance and supervision. Their attitudes are all part of the "open secret" approach to sex. They are quite aware that their daughter has "sex appeal," and many are adept at promoting this even to the extent of tolerating considerable "sex-tease" in dress. They are aware from personal experience that attraction between the sexes is not platonic. On the other hand, because they have never faced the fact of sex squarely in their own lives, they persistently ignore it in their children. Nevertheless, neither in philosophy nor in practical life does one destroy reality by refusing to admit it exists.

A third practical consequence of this segmented concept of sex is related to marriage. Two points must be considered here. First, a negative approach to sex hinders intelligent preparation for marriage. Since the primary purpose of marriage is the procreation and education of children, it would appear logical to conclude that adequate training for marriage would involve some preparation for the fulfillment of this function. However, since girls are not taught to view their femaleness in terms of motherhood, and boys, their maleness in terms of fatherhood, they enter marriage with slight consideration for the implications of parenthood. Under these circumstances, pregnancy may be regarded as a necessary misfortune rather than a normal fulfillment of womanhood. Children are viewed as competitors rather than as one of the "goods" of marriage. Their care becomes unnecessarily burdensome because parents are prepared neither in attitudes nor practical techniques for their responsibilities. What we are saying is that there is a "discontinuity" in the training of youth for marriage. Great stress is placed on dates, popularity, and getting married, but little on the normal implications of the marriage state, since the integral meaning of sex has been ignored by parents and youth alike.

Second, this negative approach to chastity and sex has repercussions in marriage itself. Females who have been trained to regard the physical manifestation of the reproductive drive as "animal" or "unladylike," are not inclined to change this view by merely going through the marriage ceremony or receiving a few "instructions" before marriage. Males who grow up with the idea that "sex" is primarily a masculine attribute designed for their physical pleasure are likely to maintain this attitude in marriage. As a result, physical union in marriage is not seen as the culminating act of domestic love, an act into which each partner enters freely, entirely, and unselfishly, with the immediate purpose of giving pleasure to the other. Physical union in marriage does not promote the consciousness of "two in one flesh" when it is regarded merely as an obligation by one and a right by the other.

Another result closely related to this last point is that the female grows up to believe, or at least to act as if she believes, that woman has slight need for physical union, and in contrast to her husband, easily rises "above" such desires. Hence, even when she dutifully accedes to her husband's request, her obedient rather than spontaneous response humiliates him with its implication that she is not as "carnal" as he and would willingly forego the whole affair. One can only speculate on the number of husbands who suffer frustration because of this misconceived "angelism" in their wives. At any rate, this attitude deprives physical union in marriage of its true dignity as a unifying act leading to an increase of mutual love and an enrichment of personality.

Finally, this negative and implicitly derogatory view of sex hinders mutual understanding in marriage. Spouses find it difficult to express or discuss their sexual feelings, needs, or desires. Since adjustments and adaptations are normally required in order to secure mutually satisfactory physical union, this inability to communicate becomes an obstacle to success. At the same time, it contributes to misunderstanding. The character of the sexual drive differs between the sexes, between individuals of the same sex, periodically, and during various stages of the life cycle. These differences should be understood by the spouses, but they are not normally learned by some type of intuition. If the spouses are capable of intelligent communication in this area of their relationships, instances when one or the other desires abstinence will not be misinterpreted as refusal. At the same time, when circumstances require continence, both partners will understand the needs of the other and will be prepared to forestall undesired sexual arousal.

To recapitulate, therefore, the failure to distinguish clearly between sins of unchastity and the physical manifestations of the reproductive drive has serious consequences. On the theoretical level, it perverts the Catholic doctrine of sin and leaves the door wide open to the heresy of Manichaeism; it distorts the concept of chastity; it deprives the sexual act of its meaning and dignity; it leads to an unbalanced stress on the negative aspects of the virtue of chastity; and it devaluates the nature of sex itself. On the practical level, it has inhibited parents from taking a positive approach toward the development of chastity in their children; it has caused them to ignore the hazards to chastity involved in modern dating and courtship practices; it has contributed to lack of adequate preparation for marriage; it has distorted the meaning of physical union in marriage; and it has rendered marital adjustment more difficult by inhibiting communication between the spouses.

Although the present state of knowledge does not permit a judgment as to how extensive this departure from the integral Catholic concept of sex may be, few would deny that many of its consequences are apparent and widespread. Fortunately, an increasing number of Catholic couples are demonstrating adequate knowledge of the integral concept. As we shall point out in the next chapter, much of the enthusiasm and vital drive of contemporary Catholic family movements stems from the realization that the integral Catholic concept of sex must be restored since only on this basis can Christian family life be stabilized in an alien culture. We have treated this aberration and its consequences in some detail while prescinding from estimating its prevalence. To the extent that it exists, it should be corrected.

SOME DEVELOPMENTS

This summary of the immediate needs of the Catholic family program would not be complete without some consideration of several contemporary developments closely related to the actualization of Catholic family standards. We use the term *development* to denote a gradually emerging trend which bids fair to prove helpful to Catholic family life. In other words, a start has already been made, and this beginning should be expanded and promoted. Space permits the treatment of only a few developments here. These have been selected not because of their prominence, but because they have been judged most necessary for the support of the Catholic family under present circumstances.

The Reappraisal of Womanhood

The extensive economic, political, and social changes which have characterized the history of the West during the past two centuries have profoundly modified the formal rights of women and the roles they are expected to play in society. Large numbers of married and unmarried women are now employed outside the home, and although they seldom compete directly with men, they have entered many traditionally male occupations. They share equal educational opportunities with men, enjoy relatively equal freedom in recreational pursuits, and are granted considerable initiative in the dating and courtship process. At the same time, numerous legal restrictions have been lifted so that women now enjoy the right to vote, to participate in politics, and to retain their legal personality even in marriage. Many factors have contributed to the development of these changes, and opinions still differ widely concerning the significance and long-range consequences of what has happened.

However, more important from the viewpoint of the family, is the reappraisal of womanhood which has been associated with these changes. What degree of honor and esteem do women enjoy? It must be obvious that the mere acquisition of formal legal rights and the adoption of traditional masculine roles may indicate slight gain for women as any female Russian factory worker can attest; hence, the significance of knowing how society evaluates womanhood. Are the expected roles and social position of women clearly defined? In other words, do women know the part they are expected to play in society, or has their new freedom merely endowed them with conflicting, if not contradictory, aspirations and difficult choices? "Home-maker," "career woman," or "glamour girl," which shall it be? Or should she attempt to combine them?

The movies and popular magazines promote the "glamour girl" ideal. But nature is not always cooperative and besides, time shortly makes it a losing battle. Though she may never consent to grow old gracefully but fights every step of the way, a culture which places such a high premium on youth has weighted the scales against her. The "career woman" ideal appeals to some girls in their studies, but experience teaches them that the prestige of the spinster is low in our society. Shall they be "home-makers"? Though little in their past training has prepared them for it, the vast majority will try it. But marriage may fail to meet the aspirations they have fostered. They feel out of the run of things and miss their old associates at work. Some find nothing to do in the home because they do not know what to do. Others want to feel needed; want to make some "worth-while" contribution. It is all very well to tell them on Mother's Day that they are doing a wonderful job, performing the most important work in society. They really aren't convinced and are not at all sure that others are either. Granted that this picture may be somewhat overdrawn, nevertheless, it indicates modern woman's dilemma. She has increased freedom, but she does not always know what to do with it since feminine roles are so poorly defined in our society.

This problem exists not merely because in a pluralistic culture there is no agreement on ultimate values and premises. Rather, the source of the problem is the attempt to define feminine roles in themselves without considering the essential, reciprocal relationship of the female to the male. Neither male nor female basic roles in society can be defined independently of each other. Since human nature is manifested bisexually, this complementary quality of maleness and femaleness cannot be ignored in considering the essential roles of the sexes. Historically, modern feminism represents a reaction to an old error. It was the male sex which was equated with human nature so that the aspirations, rights, and roles of the female were formulated in terms of the male. In other words, instead of viewing male and female as equal though different expressions of human nature, the female was always viewed in terms of the male but seldom vice versa. Modern feminism reacted to this error, but in doing so, made the mistake of attempting to evaluate woman only in terms of herself. Neither position gives adequate attention to the bisexual quality of human nature.

This brief outline of the feminine problem suffices to indi-

date the significance of the "development" under discussion.
Roughly speaking, the condition of modern woman is something like that of the hobo in the classic description of Robert
Park, "He [the hobo] has gained his freedom, but he has lost
his directions." [1] Neither the traditional view, which was predi-
cated on the natural superiority of the male, nor the feminist
approach, which implicitly denied the mutual complementarity of the sexes, can give woman "directions" in the modern
world. What is needed is a profound reappraisal of womanhood. Increased freedom and enlarged opportunities are meaningless unless women understand what constitutes the full
development of their personality as women.

Pius XII, who has spoken more often on this subject than his
four predecessors combined, has concisely outlined the problem and pointed out the direction which its solution must
take.[2] Briefly, the problem regarding woman hinges entirely
on the question of how to maintain and strengthen under
modern circumstances that dignity which woman has from
God. What is this dignity which woman has from God? The
Pope defines the problem in its proper context: "Put the question to human nature as formed by God and elevated and
redeemed in the Blood of Christ." [3] Hence, the solution will
be found not by considering the male or the female separately,
but by analyzing human nature as it is manifested bisexually.
How much past and present confusion would have been
avoided had this approach always been followed.

The Pope goes on to analyze the nature of woman's dignity
and we shall quote in full since his statement represents a land-
mark in Christian thinking on the subject and furnishes the
basis for all future development of this difficult problem.

> In their personal dignity as children of God a man and
> woman are absolutely equal, as they are in relation to the last
> end of human life, which is everlasting union with God in
> the happiness of heaven. It is the undying glory of the Church
> that she has put these truths in their proper light and honor-
> able place and that she has freed woman from degrading, un-
> natural slavery.
>
> But a man and woman cannot maintain and perfect this
> equal dignity of theirs, unless by respecting and activating

characteristic qualities which nature has given each of them, physical and spiritual qualities which cannot be eliminated, which cannot be reversed without nature itself stepping in to restore the balance. These charactisteristic qualities which divide the two sexes are so obvious to all that only willful blindness or a no less disastrous utopian doctrinaire attitude could overlook or practically ignore their significance in social relations.

The two sexes, by the very qualities that distinguish them, are mutually complementary to such an extent that their co-ordination makes itself felt in every phase of man's social life.[4]

It follows that from the viewpoint of the family the woman's problem cannot be considered apart from the man's problem. Wifehood and husbandhood, motherhood and fatherhood involve reciprocal, interdependent, complementary family statuses and roles. It is significant, therefore, that modern Catholic thought as expressed in writing, sermons, discussion groups, and extensive family movements has tackled realistically these mutual statuses and roles. The work has only begun; in fact, as we have indicated, the application of basic premises to changing social facts must be continuous, but a sound beginning has been made. It is an encouraging "development."

The Sociology of the Parish

Our development of the Catholic concept of marriage has shown the close relationship which exists between the maintenance of Catholic family standards and the practice of religion. It is fundamental to Catholic belief that the actualization of these standards requires divine assistance which is obtained primarily through prayer and the sacraments. Since Christ founded the Church to dispense the sacraments, He reaches and sanctifies the faithful through the Church. Hence, in considering the history of Christianity it is customary to use the dichotomy, the Church and the World. The Church, that is, the Church Militant headed by the hierarchy under the guidance of the Holy Spirit, are striving as one vast army in the dual struggle to save their own souls and to win the world to Christ.

This is a true picture, to be sure, but if we would study the actual line of battle, we must look at the parish as the basic unit, the fundamental point of contact between the Church and the individual in the world. As Archbishop Cushing has eloquently phrased it:

> The Catholic parish, with its pastor and priests, its altar and confessionals, its pulpit and its schools, its good works, its sinners, its saints—the Catholic parish so constituted is a microcosm, it is the whole church in miniature, and through the parish, Christ does for a limited group what He founded the universal church to do for the whole world.[5]

It follows that the parish plays a basic role in the sanctification of the faithful and consequently, in the preservation of Catholic family life.

The legal nature of the parish is defined in Canon Law as follows:

> The territory of every diocese is to be divided into distinct territorial units; and each unit is to have a special church with a designated people, and a special rector is to be given charge over it as its proper pastor for the necessary cure of souls. . . . Such units are parishes.[6]

This is a static view of the parish, and need not concern us here, but it should be pointed out that in the United States there are a large number of "national" parishes superimposed upon the "territorial" parishes. These "national" parishes were originally established because of the language differences of various immigrant groups. A "national" parish usually has vaguely defined territorial limits since it either services all the members of one ethnic group in the surrounding area, or at least, draws its parishioners from several territorial parishes.

If the parish is considered in action, that is, under its dynamic aspects, it will be seen as a socioreligious group embracing a series of important relationships: pastor and parishioners, pastor and potential parishioners, parishioners and parishioners, parishioners and nonparishioners. Functioning within the framework of these relationships, the parish, in its dynamic aspect, emerges as a complex unit of interacting personalities. As such, the parish takes on many of the characteristics of the personalities which compose it. Consequently, it is not very meaningful to speak of parishes *in abstracto*. A rural parish differs from a city parish; city parishes differ from each other according to the socioeconomic class of their constituents; ethnic parishes differ from each other and from "mixed" parishes; and finally, parishes relatively isolated in non-Catholic communities differ from those located in areas predominantly Catholic. These observations are elementary, but they need to be kept in mind if one is to arrive at any profound understanding of the problems confronting the parish in modern society.

These remarks take on added meaning when we recall some of the characteristics of the American Catholic population. First, Catholics are a minority group. Second, the rapid growth of the Church in this country has been brought about primarily by the influx of huge waves of Catholic immigrants. Third, the majority of Catholics dwells in the industrial urban centers or in the surrounding metropolitan areas. Their parishes are city parishes. Finally, the Catholic population is not evenly distributed throughout the country.

It has been suggested that every parish is, in a sense, a mission.[7] This follows not only because within its territory are found many who are not of the faith, but also because even among the "faithful" there are many who have abandoned all or almost all religious practices. Common and accepted opinion has it that approximately 20 per cent of the Catholic population do not practice their religion. That is, they do not frequent the sacraments and have cut themselves off from active participation in parish life. How well is the modern parish fulfilling its mission? It should be noted that parochial organization is an historical product. Its institutional structure must be adjusted to meet changing circumstances. What does adjustment imply and in what areas must it take place?

Although many questions concerning the structure and function of American Catholic parishes cannot be answered in the present state of knowledge, important beginnings have been made. In the past few decades there has been a growing awareness that the modern urban parish is encountering considerable difficulties. The rapid turnover of parishioners, the unwieldy size of some parishes, the loss of membership owing to shifts in population, and the modern exodus to the suburbs have all contributed to break down parish solidarity. Pastors find it difficult to know their parishioners. Families in the parish frequently recognize no common bond of parochial unity. Parish churches are filled on Sundays and feast days, but experienced pastors have the uneasy conviction that many of the faithful become indifferent and are lost in the urban shuffle. They require the personal attention of a pastor, but how is this possible when they are frequently unknown, and numerous other duties claim his immediate attention?

Various aspects of this problem have been studied in some localities, and a few attempts have been made to analyze the parish as a functioning social unit.[8] These are only beginnings, but they are encouraging. Such studies can supply the indispensable data required for the formulation of an effective parish program. What is more important, perhaps, is that the present parochial organization is no longer taken for granted. Pastors and parishioners alike are coming to realize that parish solidarity, that is, the parochial community, fulfills a vital need in modern Catholic life which can be met only by the active cooperation of all. This development may come slowly, but through the aid of the liturgical movement, Catholic action groups, and various family life programs, a new type of parish solidarity can be created. By this we mean the restoration of a Christian sense of community so that Catholic families will mutually aid each other in meeting their common problems, and it can once more be said of them, "See how they love one another."

Wider Community Responsibility

Since Catholic families are members of a minority group, many of the social problems which they encounter can be solved only through cooperation with others in their community. The realization of wider community responsibility has advanced slowly among some Catholic groups both because of their relative socioeconomic status and their tendency to maintain ethnic solidarity. However, as they move from relative separation to closer integration with the dominant culture, the necessity of cooperation with all men of good will in the community becomes obvious. In addition to civic and political obligations, such problems as juvenile delinquency, housing, slum clearance, public health, race relations, and so forth, can be dealt with only through united community action.

All Christians are under obligation to mold contemporary institutions and behavioral patterns according to the laws of God. In a pluralistic, changing culture this is no easy task. Unless all Christians cooperate in the broad, communal aspects of this work, important problems will remain unsolved and the social system will be permitted to drift without direction. This is no minor threat in a democratic society which must rely on group consensus for action. In those areas where no consensus is forthcoming, no community action is taken and problems grow apace.

Cooperation on practical community programs by various religious groups implies considerable understanding and tact. More important, however, it may also demand some compromise, on the principle that half a loaf is better than none. Nevertheless, a great deal could be accomplished in the problem areas mentioned above if Christian groups, consistent with their beliefs, made a cooperative effort to restore all things in Christ. Of course, this is an obvious statement, but it is worth pointing out that Christians in America are only beginning to perceive it. It is worthy of note, therefore, that Catholics are entering into more active cooperation with others. This is a development which should be continued.

SUMMARY

This chapter has called attention to some of the immediate needs which must be met by an adequate Catholic family program. Under the term *restoration* we summarized those areas in which the rethinking and revaluation of specific applications and practices in terms of first principles and the doctrinal whole are required. The first restoration is concerned with parental roles. Catholic families have tended to hand over the entire formal religious training of their children to the schools. This has burdened the schools with a task which they cannot adequately perform; it has lessened the meaning of religion for the child; and it has diminished parental control at a time when it is most needed.

The second restoration dealt with the Catholic concept of sex. Here we developed the theoretical and practical consequences of extending the character of sinfulness to the physical manifestations of the reproductive drive. In general, this has led to a negative, if not derogatory, view of the nature and function of sex with the result that the Catholic concept of the virtue of chastity has been distorted, and the act of physical union in marriage has been separated from its dignity and meaning.

Under the term *development* those emerging trends in contemporary society which bid fair to prove helpful to Catholic family life were discussed. The first was the reappraisal of womanhood. Neither traditional views nor modern feminism have paid adequate attention to the bisexual character of human nature in appraising womanhood. Male and female are complementary, and the essential roles of neither can be defined without considering the other. The second development was renewed interest in the sociology of the parish. The maintenance of Catholic family standards is closely related to the practice of religion so that the efficient functioning of the parochial organization is important for the family. Recent studies have pointed out some of the problems and supplied some of the data requisite for their solution. Finally, attention was called to the growing sense of community responsibility manifested in many Catholic circles. Since many family problems require community support for their solution, this trend is of considerable importance to Catholic families.

CHAPTER FIFTEEN

Contemporary Family Programs

Previous chapters have outlined the characteristics of the Catholic minority and described the principal problems which Catholics face in maintaining approved family standards. Their task is a formidable one. In 1949, the American Hierarchy pointed out what they characterized as "a calculated attack upon family life" in the modern world. They warned Americans that this attack on the family constitutes "a present danger, more fearsome than the atom bomb."[1] The Catholic family must not only make the difficult adjustments involved in the transition from a rural to an industrialized urban environment, but it must achieve balance and stability in a culture which regards the pathological as normal. This normalcy of the pathological in the dominant society presents particularly acute problems to a minority seeking closer cultural integration. Differences in family standards and behavioral patterns become more sharply defined. Institutions related to family life lend little support to the minority's ideals for they are geared to other values. It follows that Catholics must rely

411

heavily on their own resources in actualizing their family standards.

Under these circumstances, it should occasion no surprise that a considerable number of Catholics have compromised their family ideals, while others have experienced severe strain in living up to them. What is more pertinent for the present study, however, is the vital, enthusiastic renewal of Catholic family life throughout the country. This is more than the awakening to a threat; it is very close to a renaissance. The significance and practical implications of the sacramental nature of marriage is receiving special consideration. Through study, discussion, and meditation, both married and unmarried are deepening their understanding of marriage as a vocation, a way of life, a source of mutual perfection and sanctification. This probing of the spiritual values in marriage has resulted in a keener appreciation of male and female differences. The traditional stress on the objective, "institutional" purposes of marriage has been extended to its subjective, personal goals, thus emphasizing the dignity of the human person and restoring a doctrinal balance too often neglected in practice.

The purpose of this chapter is to review some of this activity in the area of the family. There is such a variety of programs and movements that some selection is imperative. Consequently, this treatment makes no pretense at being inclusive. Since every archdiocese and diocese in the country fosters activities related to the family, it would be impractical to attempt to deal with all of them separately. Further, there are numerous organizations which support some type of family program although this is not their primary purpose. Indeed, almost every form of "Catholic action" directly or indirectly touches the family because this institution is basic in both Church and society. The present aim, therefore, is to offer a more or less composite picture of family life activities in general and a treatment of two contemporary programs, Cana and the Christian Family Movement, in some detail.

THE GENERAL PICTURE

Official Catholic action in the United States falls under the general direction of the National Catholic Welfare Conference. The Conference is not a council or legislative assembly, but acts as a clearing-house of information regarding activities of Catholic men and women throughout the country. The purpose of the bishops in establishing the Conference was to unify, coordinate, and organize the Catholic people of the United States in works of education, social welfare, immigrant aid, and other related activities. As the bishops stated in their joint pastoral letter: "We have grouped together, under the NCWC, the various agencies by which the cause of religion is furthered. Each of these, continuing its own special work in its chosen field, will now derive additional support through general co-operation." Hence, the Conference does not create new organizations. Its aim is to assist and unify those that already exist.

The Family Life Bureau

It is not necessary for present purposes to explain the complex and highly specialized structure of the Conference. Eight "departments" are included in its organization. Each of these is subdivided into "bureaus" which deal with various specialized work. The Family Life Bureau of NCWC represents one activity of the Department of Social Action. The Bureau is under the guidance of a special director,[2] and its activities cover an extensive field. The National Catholic Conference on Family Life, which sponsors annual meetings in various cities to stimulate discussion of Catholic family affairs, serves as a cooperating agency of the Family Life Bureau. The National Council of Catholic Women and, more recently, the National Council of Catholic Men have been influential in publicizing the work of the Bureau in the various dioceses throughout the country.

Some estimate of the Bureau's work can be gathered from the following summary of its specific projects and the methods it uses in promoting them: (1) the study and dissemination of Christian marriage principles with special emphasis on the encyclical of Pius XI concerning Christian Marriage; (2) the promotion of parent education as advocated in the encyclical of Pius XI on the Christian Education of Youth; (3) the development of a popular literature on marriage and the family, and on parent education; [3] (4) the encouragement of the formation of maternity guilds; (5) the assistance of study clubs dealing with family topics, and the promotion of individual reading and study of family literature in the home; (6) the cooperation with other Catholic agencies and organizations at home and abroad in their efforts to strengthen the home; (7) the development of Catholic leaders in the field, particularly by urging due provision in schools and colleges for courses on Christian marriage, the family, and parent education, and by stimulating the formation of voluntary study clubs in Catholic educational institutions; (8) the promotion of interest in family study among Catholic youth outside the school system through such means as sodalities or similar organizations; (9) the fostering of interest in the Association of the Holy Family; and (10) the promotion of fitting celebration of the Feast of the Holy Family.

Since the work of the Bureau has been so varied and extensive it is difficult to evaluate its over-all effect on Catholic family life throughout the country. However, it is safe to maintain that it has unified, coordinated, and promoted family life activities in the United States and has definitely stimulated and fostered interest in the plight of the modern family. The Bureau is not designed to replace diocesan initiative and activity nor to launch specific types of family movements. Its aim is to assist, stimulate, and coordinate all family life activities throughout the nation.

Diocesan Activities

The basic unit of the Church's activity in family life is the diocese. In this field, as in all others related to religious practice, it is the bishop who has both the authority and the responsibility to initiate activity within the diocese. American bishops have been energetic and farseeing in their promotion of family life activity, but the problems which individual bishops face are so varied that it is difficult to present an adequate picture of their accomplishments. It is obvious that bishops in charge of rural dioceses will have different problems from those in urban areas. Further, regional differences play an important role inasmuch as the distribution of the Catholic population is not uniform, and some sections of the country have particular ethnic or racial problems which require specialized programs. Finally, some bishops have limited manpower resources with which to work. Recent population shifts have created a demand for new parishes and consequently, for more pastors, so that it is frequently impossible to free many priests for specialized activities within the diocese.

Owing to this considerable diversity among dioceses, any generalizations concerning activities within the field of marriage and the family are extremely hazardous. Approximately one hundred bishops have established family life bureaus under the supervision of a trained director. Some employ existing organizations to achieve the same purpose. The schools and various youth organizations are rather generally used to teach and disseminate an adequate understanding of Catholic family standards. Most of the major dioceses now have some type of premarital preparation program for engaged couples. Several, such as Buffalo and Philadelphia, attempt to assist newlyweds in the first year of marriage by mailing them a series of short letters which are designed to review Catholic family values and to suggest ways of dealing with possible problems. Parent education is promoted either through parent-teacher associations, discussion and study clubs, lectures, or more specialized programs.[4]

To summarize, therefore, the multiplicity and extent of diocesan activities concerning family life reflect the interest, and we might add, the anxiety of the American hierarchy. They make their position clear in their 1949 statement on "The Christian Family."

> The family needs to gather again around its hearths and rekindle there the fires of religious fervor. The home must

again become a shrine of fidelity, a place where God is the unseen Host. We commend the program of the Catholic Family Life Conference as one means of meeting the evident present need for better and happier homes. Family retreats, Cana conferences, courses on family life in schools and colleges, and study groups concerned with preparation for family life, should be widely encouraged and zealously promoted throughout our country. The press, radio, motion pictures and all agencies of public opinion should give constant aid in emphasizing the ideals of worthy family life. These powerful forces should be an unfailing support for the virtues which safeguard the home and give nobility to the nation.[5]

Various Organizations Aiding Catholic Family Life

Many organizations supply considerable direct or indirect assistance to Catholic family life. Although they cannot receive detailed treatment here, the general picture would not be complete unless we called attention to at least a few.

Catholic Charities is the agency of a diocese which plans, coordinates, interprets, and finances social work under Catholic auspices. At present there are approximately 275 diocesan and branch agencies which represent the official interests of 109 dioceses in organized Catholic Charities. Child welfare services, family welfare services, recreational services for youth, health services, and care for the aged are the principal fields of activity in which these agencies are engaged. An estimate of the services offered can be gained from the following figures: 332 institutions for dependent children care for 36,528 children; 26 institutions are maintained for the physically handicapped, and 14 for the mentally handicapped; 177 protective institutions provide for the needs of 20,418; 21,479 children receive care under Catholic auspices in foster homes; psychiatric and counseling services are available in some dioceses; 80 settlements and 120 day-care centers are maintained throughout the country; and 290 homes for the aged care for 25,224 persons.

The National Catholic Rural Life Conference was founded to strengthen Catholicity in the rural areas and to promote the general welfare of the rural population. One of the major aims of the Conference is to encourage the development of strong family life upon the land and in rural areas, where there is easier access to space, light, and air, and to ownership of productive property. The Conference cooperates with diocesan directors of rural life, organizes and sponsors rural institutes and schools, furnishes study club material to seminaries, schools, and lay groups, provides speakers for meetings on rural life, and supplies literature on land settlement, homesteading, and other rural items.

The Society of St. Vincent de Paul is an association of Catholic laymen devoted to personal service of the poor through the spiritual and corporal works of mercy. The activities of the society include: spiritual and material comfort for inmates of hospitals and institutions, care of poor and neglected children, religious instruction of public school students, country vacations for the underprivileged, the purchase of books for the poor attending parochial schools, providing Christian burial for the poor and friendless, furnishing food and shelter for homeless transients, and so forth. There are approximately 3,200 units of the society in the United States with a membership, active and honorary, of 35,000. During the past 33 years about $78,750,000 have been distributed to the poor. According to the society's report, for the year ended 1952, more than 400,000 visits were made to the poor and more than $3,350,000 were expended. The society was instrumental in having 1,173 marriages validated; 2,806 baptisms arranged; and 3,993 individuals return to their religious duties.

Other activities which can only be mentioned are the Catholic maternity guilds which operate in 35 dioceses, the Family Rosary Crusade directed by Fr. Patrick J. Peyton, C.S.C., the Christopher Movement founded in 1945 by Fr. James G. Keller, M.M., the Grailville School at Loveland, Ohio, which trains young Catholic leaders for the active apostolate, and the Family Communion Crusade which promotes family group communion at least once a month, veneration and imitation of the Holy Family, and the establishment of the Feast of the Holy Family as "Family Day." Further, many universities and colleges annually sponsor conferences or institutes dealing with marriage preparation and Catholic family life.

MAJOR FAMILY MOVEMENTS

The publication in 1930 of Pius XI's encyclical letter on Christian marriage stimulated renewed interest in the plight of the family throughout the Christian world. After reviewing the traditional Catholic concept of marriage and indicating the factors in society which threaten the realization of this ideal, the letter broadly outlined a program designed to meet present-day family needs. In the light of later developments, the most stimulating passage in the encyclical was its analysis of domestic love. The passage merits quoting in full for it supplies an understanding of the inspiration and enthusiasm displayed in contemporary Catholic family movements.

> This conjugal faith, however, which is most aptly called by St. Augustine the "faith of chastity" blooms more freely, the more beautifully, and more nobly when it is rooted in that more excellent soil, the love of husband and wife which pervades all the duties of married life and holds pride of place in Christian marriage. For matrimonial faith demands that husband and wife be joined in an especially holy and pure love, not as adulterers love each other, but as Christ loved the Church. This precept the Apostle (St. Paul) laid down when he said: "Husbands, love your wives as Christ also loved the Church," which of a truth He embraced with a boundless love, not for the sake of His own advantage, but seeking only the good of His spouse.
>
> The love, then, of which we are speaking is not that based on the passing lust of the moment nor does it consist in pleasing words only, but in the deep attachment of the heart which is expressed in action, since love is proved by deeds. This outward expression of love in the home demands not only mutual help but must go further, indeed must have its primary purpose that man and wife help each other day by day in forming and perfecting themselves in the interior life; so that through their partnership in life they may advance ever more and more in virtue, and above all that they may grow in true love towards God and their neighbor, on which indeed "dependeth the whole law and the prophets." For all men, of every condition and in whatever honorable walk of

life they may be, can and ought to imitate that most perfect example of holiness, placed before man by God, namely, Christ Our Lord, and by God's grace to arrive at the summit of perfection, as is proved by the example of many saints.

This mutual inward moulding of husband and wife, this determined effort to perfect each other, can in a very real sense, as the Roman Catechism teaches, be said to be the chief reason and purpose of matrimony, provided matrimony be looked at not in the restricted sense as instituted for the proper conception and education of the child, but more widely as the blending of life as a whole and the mutual interchange and sharing thereof.

By this same love it is necessary that all the other rights and duties of the marriage state be regulated so that the words of the Apostle, "Let the husband render the debt to the wife, and the wife also in like manner to the husband," express not only a law of justice but a norm of charity.[6]

This emphasis on the role of love in marriage and family relationships meets an acute modern need. The increase of the relatively isolated, conjugal family type, together with the development of the "cult of personality" in courtship and marriage, has intensified the modern couple's aspirations for "oneness" and heightened their sensitivity to intimate family relationships.[7] More specifically, Catholic couples are anxious to convert their increased marital companionship and "oneness" into a meaningful process of mutual sanctification. As the practical implications of their subsystem position in American society become more clearly defined, Catholic families are eagerly seeking the means "to arrive at the summit of perfection" in their vocation. In a sense, their interest reflects the general awakening to the importance of marriage and the family for the happiness of the individual and the full development of personality. As Catholics, however, they view "happiness" and the "development of personality" in an integral Christian context. This is to say, their personal goal is sanctification, to be achieved by imitating the example of Christ in their daily lives. They want family life to serve this purpose. They know that in the economy of salvation "grace builds upon nature." Hence, their personal sanctification must be realized primarily within the framework of their marriage relationships.

It follows that Catholics see no necessary conflict between the institutional and personal purposes of marriage. Man is a social being. If an individual chooses to enrich his personality through the exercise of his reproductive faculties, that is, if he chooses the vocation of marriage, his personality will be developed in accord with the institutional demands of the marriage state. In other words, the exercise of one's reproductive power by its very nature can lead to a meaningful enrichment of personality only through cohabitation in a stable procreative union. Emphasis may shift from the institutional to the personal aspects of marriage, but the assumption that there is an inherent conflict between these purposes implies a denial of the social character of man and ignores the bisexual quality of human nature.

It should be noted that in the passage of the encyclical which was cited, Pius XI pointed out both the institutional and the personal aspects of marriage. Regarded as a specific institution, marriage is established to provide for "the proper conception and education of the child." However, it can be looked at "more widely as the blending of life as a whole and the mutual interchange and sharing thereof." This latter may be termed the personal aspect of marriage. It is, as the Roman Catechism teaches, one of the principal reasons why people enter matrimony. Considered under this aspect, marriage is a community, a unique society in which husband and wife mutually assist each other in striving for perfection. Owing to the development of individualism, the changing status of women, and the drive for greater companionship in marriage, this personal aspect needed to be stressed. The encyclical treatment restated a doctrinal position which apparently had been neglected in popular presentation. The response was immediate. Catholic thinking and writing [8] reflected this new orientation as did the various family movements which appeared a few years later.

The Cana Conference Movement

One of the major contemporary family movements is the Cana Conference. As Cardinal Stritch has succinctly defined it, "The Cana Conference is an effort to help married people and those preparing for marriage to realize in full the graces and the fruits of the graces which come to them in marriage." [9] The center of the movement is the conference. This is an all-day or half-day meeting held annually or semi-annually in many cities throughout the country. In these meetings, married couples come to hear instructions on how to make their marriage and family life a success. The conferences consider the basic principles of family life, the sacramental nature of marriage, the statuses and roles of husband and wife, the physical, psychological, and spiritual aspects of marriage relationships, parent education, family economics, and other related subjects. During the conference, couples are given an opportunity to discuss their problems and to pool their experiences. The concluding feature of the typical Cana Day is the renewal of marriage vows before or during Benediction of the Blessed Sacrament.

Briefly, then, Cana may be described as a movement to supply inspiration, motivation, formation, and practical helps to make a happy and full Christian married life.[10] It aims to teach the asceticism of married life. A perceptive Cana director has described the movement as follows. "Cana Conferences might be called a Christian marital adjustment movement in the restricted sense of their being an attempt to adjust modern couples to the Christian plan of marriage and family life as drawn by God in the natural law and transformed by Christ." [11] Clemens notes that "the Cana Movement is a spontaneous and informal attempt to exploit more fully the Church's potential for the reconstruction of Christian family living. By informal discussions, reflections and prayer it hopes to improve the internal religious milieu of the modern home." [12]

Although the Cana Movement is essentially an American product, its origin may be traced to France.[13] During the thirties, young French couples who had graduated from the youth organizations established the Family Renewal Association with the purpose of promoting weekend meetings in which couples and priests could discuss the spiritual aspects of marriage. Fr. John Delaney, S.J., became acquainted with the work of the Association during a stay in Europe and ini-

tiated a similar movement in the United States under the title
of "Family Renewal Days." Between 1943 and 1945, he conducted approximately forty "retreats" for five distinct groups
who became affiliated in a Family Renewal Association. In
1944, the idea was taken up by Fr. Edward Dowling, S.J., and
a group of couples in St. Louis. It was here that the meetings
took on the character of a conference rather than a retreat.
As Fr. Dowling described the meetings, they were to consider "not so much spiritual things, as things spiritually." It
was he who coined the term "Cana Conferences," the name
they have retained ever since.

The spread of the movement has been spontaneous and
rapid. Married couples and priests from all sections of the
country have enthusiastically cooperated in promoting conferences, and the hierarchy have been quick to grasp the significant pastoral value of the movement. At present, Cana programs exist in over ninety dioceses in the United States. Although considered as a social movement, Cana is nationwide,
there are no national headquarters. The movement's specific
programs are organized on a diocesan basis. However, regional meetings of interested groups are held from time to
time, and an annual study week for Cana directors was orig-
inated in 1947. During the past few years these meetings have
wisely been broadened to include the active participation of
married couples. As a result, the study weeks are gradually
taking on the character of meetings representative of the
movement rather than as specialized training periods for the
directors. In other words, it is possible that the study week
may evolve into an annual meeting of the movement. This
would seem to be a logical step in the development of Cana
as a nationwide family movement.

At present, the Cana Movement includes several additional
programs which merit consideration. In some sections the conferences have led to the development of "Cana Clubs." These
are small groups of couples which meet monthly or oftener
under the direction of a chaplain in order to discuss and study
in greater detail the implications of Catholic marriage ideals.
In a few cities, the conferences have resulted in the establishment of Cana Retreats. These are two- or three-day retreats for

married couples who desire to deepen their spiritual life by means of the special techniques employed in retreats.[14]

Finally, there is the important Pre-Cana conference. As the Cana movement developed, it soon became evident that much of the instruction which Catholic married couples were seeking should have been available to them before marriage. The Pre-Cana conference, therefore, was introduced to prepare young engaged couples for Catholic family life in the modern world. Although the premarital program differs in various dioceses, it usually consists of three or four conferences given on several days by skilled directors from pertinent backgrounds. For example, one of the more common combinations includes a priest director, a doctor or nurse, and an experienced married couple. In some dioceses the program is so organized that engaged couples have relatively easy access to a conference almost the year around. In others, conferences are offered at definite periods each year, and couples contemplating marriage can generally be accommodated. Many parishes sponsor a series of lectures on courtship and marriage during the six Sundays of Lent. These marriage preparation conferences have acquired great popularity in a short time so that they are now considered a significant part of the Cana Movement.

How many couples has the Cana Movement reached? Adequate statistics are lacking, but some indication of the progress of the Movement may be gathered from a consideration of the published report of one active center. With no intention of stimulating invidious comparisons, we shall present the achievements of the Cana Conference of Chicago since these were conveniently summarized in a progress report released on the occasion of its 10th anniversary, November 5, 1954. In evaluating this report it should be recalled that the Cana Conference of Chicago has benefited from a happy combination of circumstances. His Eminence Samuel Cardinal Stritch has given it his constant and energetic support. The chancery officials and the priests of the archdiocese have cooperated with remarkable initiative and zeal. Under the capable guidance of its full-time director, Fr. John J. Egan, the Conference has enlisted the enthusiastic assistance of married couples and successfully tapped the latent resources of the lay apostolate.[15]

For the ten-year period of its existence, the Conference listed the following achievements: 23,250 married couples have voluntarily attended Cana Conferences; 22,940 engaged couples have voluntarily attended the Pre-Cana series (during the 1954–1955 season, Pre-Cana was expected to reach one-half of the Catholic couples being married in Chicago); 12,420 young people have attended "Courtship and Marriage" lectures given on the six Sundays of Lent. A staff of 25 priests, 41 doctors, and 46 couples give the Pre-Cana conferences. An additional 25 couples work in organization and in areas of planning. Cana Conferences were originally held on a regional basis. At present they are parish-sponsored and organized with the aim of eventually making a Cana Conference available annually in each parish. Thirty-three priests conduct these conferences and 24 couples aid the parishes in organizing the day. During this period the Conference also published *The Couplet,* a four-page "news letter" which reprinted pertinent items and kept Cana members informed of significant developments in the diocese and throughout the movement.

This brief description of the purposes and accomplishments of the Cana Movement tells us what it aims to do and how it attempts to function; it does not tell us what it represents as a social movement. Further analysis reveals several important features. First, it is what may be termed a lay movement, that is, it represents a movement of persons who are seeking perfection in the marriage vocation. To be sure, the assistance of pastors and priest directors is required by the very nature of the movement, but as Msgr. Edward A. Burke has stated with keen insight:

> Even this amount of interest, however, would be of no great avail without the efforts of our husbands and wives in the field, for Cana is essentially a lay movement. In embracing it as their responsibility, in devoting themselves to making it possible for growing numbers of couples to receive instruction and inspiration, they have truly become instruments of the Holy Ghost. Their work, their generous giving of time and energy is what made The Cana Conference a reality and what will make it endure.[16]

This feature requires emphasis, for it is an essential characteristic which may be easily overlooked. The Cana Movement has grown and will continue to spread not only because Catholic couples desire instruction and inspiration and are willing to contribute time and energy to the project. What is more essential is that the very nature of the problems which these couples face requires a movement which represents the cooperative approach of priest and laity. There are two reasons for this. First, every practical program is a conclusion based upon value premises as well as upon social facts. Consequently, a practical family program must be developed from the pooled experience of couples (social facts) and the careful application of value premises (the work of the priest). Not that the couples do not understand the value premises, nor the priest, the pertinent social facts, but many of the problems now facing the Catholic family are so complex and novel that their solution calls for the cooperation of "experts" if a workable program is to be developed. The couples are sensitive to the social facts as they experience them; the priest is trained in the application of moral and ascetical principles. Together they can work out a program which is meaningful in terms of the current situation.

There is a second reason why the essentially lay character of the Movement must not be overlooked. One of the elements which couples have found in Cana is the inspiration and stimulation which comes from group participation and a "consciousness of kind" that develops in the atmosphere of informality pervading the typical conference. Sermons, parish missions, and retreats can supply both information and inspiration to married couples, but one of the unique features of the Movement is that it brings together couples with common aspirations and similar problems. Members of a subsystem in a secular culture experience an increase of solidarity and mutual support in the Conferences which goes far to explain the enthusiasm that Cana has aroused.

The next feature which an analysis of the Movement reveals is that the needs which it attempts to meet, such as information, inspiration, and motivation, are constant, universal, yet apparently new. By this we mean that Catholic couples have always been more or less eager for perfection in their married vocation, and consequently, they have always stood in need both of further understanding the Catholic ideal and of being constantly motivated to achieve it. Does the rapid spread of Cana indicate that modern couples are more spiritually inclined or more idealistic than their parents? There seems little evidence to substantiate this. What we can conclude, however, is that modern couples have come to realize that new developments in society have given rise to family problems which they are little prepared to solve and that their religious minority position has left them spiritually isolated in a secular culture. Hence, their basic family goals are old, but their practical needs are new.

It follows that the third feature of the Movement which analysis reveals is that it is a response to profound changes in society and the family system. For example, the "couple-centered" emphasis of Cana reflects changes in the family structure. The shift from the extended to the conjugal type, the growth of individualism, and the changing status of women have led to new aspirations in marriage. Catholic couples have accepted the accent on companionship and personal values in marriage, but they feel the need to develop an adequate concept of sanctity in terms of it. Further, since the family system of the dominant culture is oriented around a different set of values, Catholic couples must work out their own adaptations to changes affecting family relationships, and for this, group action appears most effective. Finally, Catholic couples are necessarily impressed by the prevailing anxiety concerning contemporary family disorganization. Engaged couples worry about the future, newlyweds wonder whether they are "adequate," and parents are solicitous less they fail. This mass anxiety motivates many couples to seek all possible guarantees of success in a venture which their forefathers took pretty much for granted.

Hence, the Cana Conference Movement, like every social movement, is ultimately based on felt social needs. As more and more members of society come to recognize their needs, the more energetic among them tend to organize in order to do something about satisfying them. This is the ultimate origin of Cana. Under the impact of rapid change in a complex society, Catholic couples come to recognize the need for a profound rethinking of their marriage vocation in terms of basic Catholic principles and their present social situation. Inspired by the encyclical on Christian Marriage to strive for "the summit of perfection," they feel the need for a deeper understanding of married life and its relationship to personal sanctification. They seek workable answers to the everyday, practical problems which they face because they are in earnest about their vocation and recognize a personal responsibility to do something about it.

In conclusion, the Movement arose as a response to a need. It has grown because it has come to grips with an existing problem. It will endure as long as it represents an authentic organization flexible enough to realistically approach contemporary family issues. It must remain, therefore, essentially a lay movement. Its leaders must constantly revaluate both their methods and the problems they are attempting to meet. With the passage of time, social movements tend to harden into a bureaucratic structure dominated by "vested interests." Under these conditions, the organization tends to become an end in itself so that its perpetuation becomes more important than the needs which it was originally established to meet. The Cana Movement can avoid this fate if it continues to absorb new members into its leadership ranks and if it courageously re-examines its working premises, its methods of attack, and the relative importance of the needs which it aims to fulfill. Cana is a new movement. It will succeed to the extent that it remains geared to the current family situation and continues flexible enough to integrate the pertinent contributions of theology, philosophy, and science.

The Christian Family Movement

The enthusiasm and zeal which has characterized the rapid growth of the Christian Family Movement is indicative of the perennial vitality of Catholic laymen in response to recognized needs. This is the genius of Christianity. By upholding the elevated goal and personal dignity of each individual, it automatically confirms his right and obligation to strive for perfection in his chosen vocation. This sense of personal responsibility constitutes an enduring stimulus to action in every Christian. At the same time, as a social being privileged to hold membershp in the Mystical Body of Christ through the sacrament of baptism, the Christian necessarily views his personal responsibility within the framework of his social relationships. He is his brother's keeper, and though his responsibility is personal, its expression will be social. Hence, the apparently spontaneous development of movements such as CFM should be expected within the Christian community once needs arise which are recognized as calling for group action.

The activity which led to the development of CFM goes back to 1942 when a group of eight men from different sections of Chicago started meeting in order to learn what contribution they could make to the parish apostolate. They discovered that the chief concern they had in common was family life, and they concluded that this should be their field of apostolic activity. Selecting some approved techniques of Catholic Action, they worked out a simple formula for their meetings: some gospel and liturgy study to provide inspiration, and the "social inquiry" method (observing, judging, acting) to lead to action. Their wives formed similar groups and it soon became evident that the problems of the family could be met most effectively if they were tackled by couples rather than by husband and wife working separately. Consequently, in 1947, under the guidance of Msgr. Reynold Hillenbrand, the original groups combined and reorganized along parish lines.[17]

Meanwhile, similar groups had been developing in New York and South Bend, Indiana. By 1949, when a national meeting was held for the purpose of exchanging ideas and techniques, delegates representing twenty-five groups from ten different cities were present. Since that time, the movement has spread to almost all sections of the country so that it now includes approximately eleven thousand couples. An annual convention is held each summer, and besides various booklets and manuals, the movement publishes *Act,* a monthly news letter giving current information on CFM and its work.

Briefly stated, the purpose of the movement is to restore Christian ideals in family life by working on the environment in which families live. According to Msgr. Hillenbrand, one of the pioneer chaplains of the movement, four particular items characterize CFM. First, it is based on small groups of couples (four to eight), so that each member can actively participate. Second, it uses the "inquiry" method, a process of observing one's surroundings, judging what is wrong in the light of Christian principles, and acting together to correct the wrong. Third, the chaplain, characterized as "an outsider but indispensable" brings to the group the riches of the Church. Fourth, the movement aims at the formation of the complete apostle. "Our Lord wants His redemptive influence to get into economic life, civic life, international life—and obviously domestic life and parochial life." [18]

The structure of the movement is not complex. The original group in a parish is called a section and is composed of from five to seven couples. After the group has been meeting for some time, each couple organizes an action group of the same size. Unity is achieved through having the leaders of the action groups continue with the section meeting every two weeks. Several times each year parishes in which the movement is well organized hold general meetings to which all interested couples in the parish are invited. Cities or dioceses in which the movement has developed on the parish level will establish a federation. Each section will be represented in the federation and several meetings will be held monthly for the purpose of coordinating activities and sponsoring joint action.[19] Each year, the Coordinating Committee of the movement, acting on the suggestions submitted from the various section committees throughout the country, prepares an "annual inquiry booklet" which furnishes material for the bi-weekly meetings throughout the year. Emphasis is placed on a different subject each year, for example, social responsibility and education, community, and so forth.

It should be noted that the movement represents something

more than a unique organization of study clubs designed to discuss family problems. The bi-weekly meetings of the groups are meant to prepare the couples for immediate action. They provide a training school in which the members, through discussion and thought, clarify their understanding of basic Christian principles and focus attention on their immediate environment with the purpose of personally carrying out the practical application of these principles in their own neighborhoods. It is this note of specificity and immediacy which stimulates interest and prevents the meetings from evolving into sterile discussions. In a sense, the couples learn by doing. They are made aware that the values which they cherish have consequences. By gradually developing the habit of thinking in terms of basic principles and their specific applications, they acquire a practical Christian outlook on life geared to their personal horizon. This approach breaks through what the social scientists call the routinized "cake" of custom and enables the participants to see their parish, community, and family in a new perspective.

The purposes, structure, and growth of CFM can be easily discovered, but what is its significance as a social movement? Obviously, it is essentially a lay movement. Its primary focus is on the family within the framework of the parish community. It is "democratic" and *à la mode* in its insistence on small groups and personal participation. It may be considered typically American in its accent on immediate, practical action. Its couple-centered emphasis conforms to the increased desire for companionship in marriage. However, none of these characteristics fully explain its development as a vital social movement. To understand it, we must pass beyond these obvious features and ascertain what needs it is fulfilling for contemporary Catholic families.

Analysis reveals that it is responding to many of the same needs as the Cana Movement, but its orientation and techniques are somewhat different. It would be repetitious to restate these needs here so we shall concentrate on what is distinctive in the CFM's approach. In its small-group structure and its frequent meetings, the movement reflects the response to two basic needs. The first is the need for solidarity. Within the traditional framework of the parish, Catholic families experience a sense of spiritual isolation from their non-Catholic neighbors and a lack of real union with fellow parishioners. Frequent meetings in small groups restore this sense of solidarity, not merely because couples are brought together for discussion or recreation, but because they pool their talents, experience, and efforts in a tangible apostolate inspired by a shared faith.

It is precisely because CFM supplies a social vehicle through which Catholic couples can think, pray, and work together in an uninhibited atmosphere of common understandings that the movement produces such a refreshing, personal experience of group solidarity. Members of the Catholic minority can never feel quite "at home" when mixing in an alien, secular culture. They are consciously or unconsciously inhibited by lack of mutual understanding and shared beliefs. There tends to be an incompleteness or fragmenting of personality in their secular contacts since communication develops only in those areas in which there are common values. On the other hand, in the intimacy of small group meetings among themselves, minority members feel "at home." They have the exhilarating experience of recapturing their integrity as uninhibited followers of Christ.

The second need is closely related to the first. As members of a distinct subculture, Catholics must work out their own adjustments and adaptations to social changes affecting the family system. Families can best do this by pooling their mutual experiences and techniques and, when workable solutions are developed, by presenting a united front. In this way, individual families will not feel that they are bearing the impact of an alien culture alone. They will be aided in their plan of action by knowing what other families, sharing the same ideals, are doing. At the same time, they will be encouraged by the thought that others are facing the same difficulties as themselves.

Through CFM, this mutual support of families, not only on a group basis, but on a parish basis as well, can go far to restore that social equilibrium which Catholics necessarily lose in rejecting pertinent institutionalized behavioral patterns of the dominant culture. We have pointed out that Catholics face the problem of the normalcy of the pathological in our society. Consequently, their move toward integration involves definite reservations and limitations which prevents them from simply "following the crowd." Nevertheless, if they do not experience some personal expression of solidarity as minority group members, the pervading tendency to conform will induce many to follow the behavioral patterns set by the majority. The essential function of CFM and other family movements, therefore, is not merely to instruct and inspire. To the extent that they are vital social movements, they respond to the minority's acute need to have some appropriate vehicle for the expression and promotion of group solidarity. The superficial, who regard them as merely an additional means for securing instruction, completely ignore their significance as social movements.

Since CFM has such a short history, it is premature to predict what course its development will follow. However, a few observations may not be out of place even at this early stage. First, the movement must penetrate all ranks of society. In their beginnings, both CFM and Cana have naturally drawn heavily on college graduates and professional people, but since the bulk of the Catholic population is not found in these classes, they must continue to make serious efforts to penetrate all classes. This is necessary not only because all have need for such movements, but more important in the long run, the character and orientation of the movements must be all-inclusive rather than class-centered. These are democratic, lay movements, so that the character of the participants will necessarily color the purposes and methods which gradually emerge. Unless they make every effort to secure broad participation, they run the danger of being oriented toward one stratum of society.

Second, the stress on what we have called the personal or personalist purposes of marriage must be carefully evaluated. Realism requires that the prosaic institutional aspects of marriage and family life be duly stressed since they constitute the indispensable framework of every durable family system. Further, the aspiration for companionship and "two-in-oneness" in marriage must take into account individual differences as well as the indisputable fact that the human person is by definition incommunicable. The unity and "togetherness" of spouses possible in marriage is both relative and limited. The emphasis on "couple-centeredness" must not be carried to the point of excluding appropriate expressions of individuality. It is possible that the novelty of the concept in our industrialized urban society has led to some exaggeration. It is important to proceed slowly and realistically when formulating marriage ideals in this area.

CONCLUSION

The programs and family movements which we have considered have been designed to meet the needs of the Catholic minority in a complex, changing society. It would be premature to pass judgment on their adequacy or efficiency since, for the most part, they are still in the early stages of development. Previous chapters have outlined the Catholic concept of marriage, the characteristics of the Catholic population, the major problems which Catholic families encounter, and the requisite conditions for religious minority survival in our society. Throughout this work we have attempted to emphasize the relationships between ultimate value premises, derivative institutional goals, and approved behavioral patterns. The specific problems of a religious minority can be understood only within this framework.

Catholic families are subjecetd to the same pressures as all others in an industrialized urban environment, but they must work out their adjustments in a distinct and clearly defined frame of reference. Especially as differences in family standards and related behavioral patterns become more sharply defined, the Catholic minority must take positive steps to insure conformity to its family ideals. The maintenance of this conformity requires adequate knowledge, motivation, and group support.

Furthermore, in adjusting to its changing environment, the Catholic family system must be flexible enough to adopt new methods in achieving its essential purposes, sufficiently discerning to reject practices incompatible with its ideals, and realistically constructive in meeting genuine needs. Finally, as a minority group, Catholics face the constant threat of gradual disintegration through outgroup marriage. Although the mixed marriage rate has shown only slight increase in the past, there are indications that mixed marriages will appear more significant as ethnic solidarity breaks down and the social mobility of Catholics becomes more extensive. At the same time, invalid marriages are involving increasing numbers of the faithful. There is little likelihood that this trend will be arrested.

The American hierarchy have clearly indicated the serious challenge which the Catholic family system faces in contemporary society. It would be illusory to deny that Catholics have been affected by the culture within which they live. Realism prompts the admission that there is evidence of considerable apathy, compromise, and defection. On the other hand, the extensive and enthusiastic response to various forms of family programs and movements manifests an enduring vitality in the Catholic minority which bids fair for the future of its family system. Particularly significant is the participation of the laity in all these activities. If their interest and cooperation continues to grow, the future will reveal not a mere reaction to a threat, but a veritable renaissance of Christian family life.

Footnotes

CHAPTER ONE

[1] George P. Murdock, *Social Structure* (New York: The Macmillan Company, 1949), pp. 1-40.

[2] Robert K. Merton, *Social Theory and Social Structure* (Glencoe, Ill.: The Free Press, 1949), pp. 126-29.

[3] See the statement of the United States Hierarchy, "On Secularism," *The Catholic Mind*, XLVI (January, 1948), 1-8.

[4] John Sirjamaki, "Culture Configurations in the American Family," *American Journal of Sociology*, LIII (May, 1948), 464-70.

[5] Arthur W. Calhoun, *A Social History of the American Family*, 3 Vols. (New York: Barnes & Noble, 1945); Willystine Goodsell, *A History of Marriage and the Family* (New York: The Macmillan Company, 1934).

[6] See any of the standard sociological texts on marriage and the family.

[7] See George E. Howard, *A History of Matrimonial Institutions*, 3 Vols. (Chicago: The University of Chicago Press, 1904); Carle C. Zimmerman, *Family and Civilization* (New York: Harper and Brothers, 1947).

CHAPTER TWO

[1] Ellsworth Faris, *The Nature of Human Nature* (New York: McGraw-Hill Book Company, Inc., 1937), pp. 7-18.

[2] See M. M. Philipon, *The Sacraments in the Christian Life* (Westminster, Md.: Newman Press, 1954).

[3] For a fuller treatment of this subject, see John L. Thomas, "Sex and Society," *Social Order*, IV (June, 1954), 242-48; Murdock, *Social Structure*, p. 261-62.

4 Pius XII, "Sports and Gymnastics," *The Catholic Mind*, LI (September, 1953), 571-72.

5 St. Thomas, *De Anima*, 8, ad 7.

6 St. Thomas, *Summa Theologica*, II, II, 141, 2, 2.

7 *Ibid.*, II, II, 153, 3.

8 This use of the term *reason* has none of the connotations of the *ratio* of the Enlightenment. Following St. Thomas, we use the term to signify man's power to grasp reality. Man grasps reality not only in natural cognition but also by faith in the revelation of God. "The order of reason," therefore, is the order which corresponds to the reality made evident to man through faith and knowledge. See Josef Pieper, *Fortitude and Temperance*, trans. Daniel F. Coogan (New York: Pantheon Books, 1954), pp. 56-60.

9 Pieper, *op. cit.*, p. 60.

10 Henry Davis, *Moral and Pastoral Theology*, 3 Vols. (New York: Sheed and Ward, 1941), II, p. 200.

11 The term *virtue* as used here signifies an "operative habit that gives both the power and the impulse to do readily that which befits rational nature so as to achieve true happiness." See Davis, *op. cit.*, I, p. 253.

12 Davis, *op. cit.*, II, p. 200.

13 It should be noted that this is a specific application of the virtue of modesty which is traditionally defined as that virtue which moderates "the external manner, in style of dress, comportment, conversation, so as to order all things by reasonable decorum, having regard to place, time and person." See Davis, *op. cit.*, I, p. 268.

14 The internal will or disposition to avoid all that would excite venereal pleasure contrary to right order is not relative.

15 E. Hocédez, "Pour la Modestie Chrétienne," *Nouvelle Revue Théologique*, LII, (Juillet, 1925), 396-413; John L. Thomas, "Clothes, Culture and Modesty," *Social Order*, IV (November, 1954), 386-94.

16 J. Creusen, "La Chasteté," *Nouvelle Revue Théologique*, LXV, (Février, 1938), 180-94.

17 Pieper, *op. cit.*, p. 54.

18 John L. Thomas, " 'Forced' Marriages," *Social Order*, IV (March, 1954), 99-104.

19 For the official Catholic position on periodic continence and the motives which justify its use, see Pius XII, "Apostolate of the Midwife," *The Catholic Mind*, L (January, 1952), 49-64.

20 A. Snoeck, "Morale Catholique et Devoir de Fécondité," *Nouvelle Revue Théologique*, LXXV (Novembre, 1953), 897-911.

21 Pius XI, *Christian Marriage* (Casti Connubi), 5th ed. (New York: The America Press, 1943), p. 17.

22 *Ibid.*

23 "Sanctitatem sine nuptiarum damnatione novimus et sectemur et praeferimus, non ut malo bonum, sed ut bono melius." Tertullian, *Adv. Marcion.*, I, xxix, P.L., t.ii, col. 280. For the latest official document on the subject, see Pius XII, "On Holy Virginity," *The Catholic Mind*, LII (August, 1954), 491-512.

24 Matt. 19:17-21.

25 Pieper, *op. cit.*, p. 84.

26 St. Augustine, *De Virginitate*, 8.

27 St. Thomas, *Summa Theologica*, II, II, 152, 3; 152, 3 ad 1; 152, 5.

28 "Counsels," *The Catholic Encyclopaedia*, IV, 435-36.

29 "De Benedictione et Consecratione Virginum" (Concerning the Blessing and Consecration of Virgins), *Pontificale Romanum,* Pars Prima (Ratisbonae, Neo Eboraci et Cincinnatii: Frederick Pustet, 1888), see the prayer for the Preface, pp. 157-58.

30 See Ernest C. Messenger, *Two In One Flesh,* I, *An Introduction to Sex and Marriage* (Westminster, Maryland: The Newman Press, 1948), for an extended treatment of this subject.

CHAPTER THREE

1 *Dictionnaire de Théologie Catholique,* T. 9e, 2e partie (Paris: Librairie Letouzey et Ane, 1927), col. 2109.

2 It should be noted that St. Augustine used the term *sacramentum* to signify a mystery. This is what the term means in the Greek language and in the Scriptures. Centuries later the term was given a specific theological connotation in the sense of a sacrament. However, the fact that Augustine and early Christian writers did not use the term *sacramentum* to signify sacrament does not mean that they did not believe that marriage was a sacrament! As we have indicated, all the essential notes of marriage as a sacrament were taught by the Church Fathers. They merely used a different terminology.

3 Roland H. Bainton, "Christianity and Sex, An Historical Survey," in *Sex and Religion Today,* ed. Simon Doniger (New York: Association Press, 1953), p.18.

4 Davis, *Moral and Pastoral Theology,* Vol. II, p. 53. For a good treatment of the Catholic concept of marriage, see Bakewell Morrison, *God Is Its Founder* (Milwaukee: The Bruce Publishing Company, 1946).

5 Pius XI, *Christian Marriage,* pp. 2-3.

6 *Catechism of the Council of Trent,* II, 8, 13.

7 Pius XI, *op. cit.,* p. 8. For an excellent review of the past and present theological writing of Catholic authors on the purposes of marriage, see Francis W. Carney, *The Purposes of Christian Marriage* (Washington: The Catholic University of America Press, 1950).

8 Pius XII, "Apostolate of the Midwife," 56-7.

9 "The Church is not unaware of these problems; she is not indifferent to their agonizing aspects, as is proven by the documents recently coming from the Holy See concerning family life, national economy and the relationships between peoples, some of whom find themselves abundantly provided with wealth while others remain in tragic conditions." Pope Pius XII, "Population Problems: Address to Catholic Delegates to the World Congress on Population, September 9, 1954," *The Catholic Mind,* LIII (April, 1955), 256.

10 See Fairfield Osborn, *Our Plundered Planet* (Boston: Little, Brown & Company, 1948); William Vogt, *Road to Survival* (New York: William Sloane, Associates, 1948); Guy I. Burch and Elmer Pendell, *Human Breeding and Survival* (New York: Penguin Books, 1947); etc. The entire question of overpopulation was excellently summarized in an article which appeared in the November 8, 1948 issue of *Time,* entitled "Eat Hearty," pp. 27-31.

11 See Kingsley Davis, "Small Families Are Still the Fashion," *The New York Times Magazine* (July 11, 1954), pp. 17, 35.

12 See John F. Cronin, S.S., "Social Economics of Pope Pius XII," *The Catholic Mind,* XLIX (October, 1951), 683.

13 See John L. Thomas, "Alleged 'Good Sense' of Small Families," *America,* XCI (September 11, 1954), 563-64; Harvey Leibenstein, *A Theory of Eco-*

nomic-Demographic Development (Princeton, N. J.: Princeton University Press, 1954), pp. 171ff.

14 Leo XIII, "Christian Marriage," in *Social Wellsprings*, ed. Joseph Husslein, I (Milwaukee: The Bruce Publishing Co., 1940), 35-36; Code, 1012.

15 Council of Trent, Session 24.

16 Leo XIII, "Christian Marriage," *op. cit.*, pp. 28-30.

17 Pius XI, *op. cit.*, p. 13.

18 Canon law is codified in the *Codex Canonici Juris*, which went into force on May 19, 1918. The *Codex* contains 2,414 canons, grouped under 107 titles, in 5 books.

19 For commentaries in English, see: T. Lincoln Bouscaren and Adam C. Ellis, *Canon Law: A Text and Commentary*, rev. ed. (Milwaukee: The Bruce Publishing Co., 1951); Stanislaus Woywod and Callistus Smith, *Practical Commentary on the Code of Canon Law* (New York: J. F. Wagner, 1952). All decisions of the Rota are published in *Sanctae Romanae Rotae Decisiones seu Sententiae* after a lapse of ten years from the date of judgment. Decisions of immediate public interest are reported promptly in *Acta Apostolicae Sedis*. Both series, published in Latin, are available in any diocesan chancellery or theological seminary.

20 For a more detailed explanation see Clement S. Mihanovich, Gerald J. Schnepp, and John L. Thomas, *Marriage and the Family* (Milwaukee: The Bruce Publishing Company, 1952), pp. 159-93.

21 Fowler V. Harper, *Problems of the Family* (Indianapolis: The Bobbs-Merrill Company, Inc., 1952), pp. 172-73.

22 See Mihanovich, Schnepp, and Thomas, *op. cit.*, pp. 179-81.

23 Canon 1094.

24 "Divorce," *The Catholic Encyclopaedia*, V, 54-69.

25 Canon 1118.

26 The consummation of marriage is effected by the conjugal act. This act must be complete and in accordance with nature. If the married couple have lived together, it is presumed that they have consummated their marriage. See Bouscaren and Ellis, *op. cit.*, p. 545.

27 St. Paul, I Cor. 7:2 sqq.

28 See "Instruction to Be Observed by Diocesan Tribunals in Handling Cases of Nullity of Marriages," issued by the Sacred Congregation of the Sacraments (August 15, 1936), reprinted in *The Canon Law Digest*, II, by T. Lincoln Bouscaren (Milwaukee: The Bruce Publishing Company, 1943), pp. 471-529. The *Acta Apostolica Sedis*, XXVIII (September, 1936), 312-370, gives the text in Latin.

29 Canon 1908.

30 Canon 1909.

31 *Marriage Laws of the Catholic Church* (Chicago: Christian Family Movement, 1953), p. 17.

32 Canons 1914-1916.

33 *Acta Apostolica Sedis*, XXXXV (May, 1953), 329-68.

34 Canon 1129.

35 Canon 1131.

36 Third Council of Baltimore (1884), Decree 126.

37 *Ibid.*, Decree 124.

CHAPTER FOUR

[1] Thus Carroll, attempting the first complete enumeration, classification, and description of the religious forces of the United States on the basis of census returns from 1890, 1900, and 1910, speaks of the "miracle growth" of the Catholic Church. See H. K. Carroll, *The Religious Forces of the United States* (New York: Charles Scribner's Sons, 1912), p. lxxi.

[2] For the history of American immigration see: Henry P. Fairchild, *Immigration*, rev. ed. (New York: The Macmillan Co., 1925); George M. Stephenson, *A History of American Immigration, 1820–1924* (Boston: Ginn and Co., 1926); Maurice R. Davie, *World Immigration* (New York: The Macmillan Co., 1936).

[3] See Maurice R. Davie, *Refugees in America* (New York: Harper and Brothers, 1947), for the most detailed study of their provenance, numbers, and adjustment.

[4] Oscar Handlin, *The Uprooted* (Boston: Little, Brown and Company, 1951), p. 3.

[5] See Ray Allen Billington, *The Protestant Crusade 1800–1860* (New York: Rinehart & Company, Inc., 1938), for the most comprehensive study of the origins of American nativism. An excellent historical treatment of anti-Catholic feeling in America may be found in Michael Williams, *The Shadow of the Pope* (New York: McGraw-Hill Book Co., Inc., 1932).

[6] Stephenson, *op. cit.*, pp. 145-147; Carl Wittke, *We Who Built America* (Copyright, 1951, by Carl Wittke), pp. 498-505; Joseph L. Cross, "The American Protective Association," *The American Catholic Sociological Review*, X (October, 1949), 172-87.

[7] See Wittke, *op. cit.*, pp. 505-509; Donald Young, *American Minority Peoples* (New York: Harper & Brothers, 1932), pp. 257-261.

[8] Davie, *World Immigration*, p. 184.

[9] Willard Johnson, "Religion and Minority Peoples," in *One America*, 3rd ed., eds. Francis J. Brown and Joseph S. Roucek (New York: Prentice-Hall, Inc., 1952), p. 526.

[10] *The American Character* (New York: Alfred A. Knopf, 1944), p. 98.

[11] Israel Zangwill, *The Melting Pot*, rev. ed. (New York: The Macmillan Company, 1923), pp. 184-85.

[12] "Such words and phrases as 'good patriotic American,' 'Americanism,' 'civic loyalty,' 'old fashioned American ideals,' 'patriotism,' etc., were used very freely by the advocates of Americanization, yet seldom did they define terms." Edward G. Hartmann, *The Movement to Americanize the Immigrant* (New York: Columbia University Press, 1948), p. 269.

[13] Constantine M. Panunzio, *Immigration Crossroads* (New York: The Macmillan Company, 1927), p. 254.

[14] Quoted by Allen Burns in "Organic Americanization," *Proceedings of the National Conference of Social Work* (Chicago: N.C.S.W., 1919), p. 729.

[15] "That was the essence of practical Puritanism—the restriction of others." Marcus L. Hansen, *The Immigrant in American History* (Cambridge: Harvard University Press, 1948), p. 105.

[16] "Conform in many large and fundamental ways the immigrant must, if he is to survive. That is as a matter of course. But that he should become a Protestant, vote the majority ticket, 'root' for the home team, celebrate Mother's day, eat corn flakes, live beyond his income, divorce his wife, and speculate

in city lots would not seem to exhaust the nobler opportunities that America holds for him." Arthur E. Woods, *Community Problems* (New York: Century, 1928), p. 430.

[17] Franklin K. Lane as quoted by William C. Smith in *Americans in the Making* (New York: Appleton-Century-Crofts, Inc., 1939), p. 116.

[18] Smith, *Americans in the Making*, p. 303; Wittke, *op. cit.*, p. 409.

[19] "While America has always insisted that her immigrant population should become Americanized she has never made, as a nation, a single intelligent effort to aid them in a process which, even under favorable circumstances, can be very difficult." Angelo M. Pellegrini, *Immigrant's Return* (New York: The Macmillan Company, 1951), p. 71.

[20] A critical issue facing many ethnic leaders today is to decide when the active promotion of solidarity ceases to work for the best interests of the group. It is at least conceivable that the continued promotion of group cohesion will impede the social and economic mobility of group members.

[21] The term *ethnic* as used here refers to those organized groups of immigrants and their progeny who exhibit characteristics of social organization and culture more or less at variance with those of American society. See Leo Srole, "Ethnic Groups and American Society" (Ph.D. thesis, University of Chicago, 1940), pp. 6-7.

[22] Gerald Shaughnessy, *Has the Immigrant Kept the Faith?* (New York: The Macmillan Company, 1925), p. 189.

[23] In this connection it should be pointed out that reliable data on the religious affiliation of the population are lacking for the years studied. Further, immigration statistics are admittedly incomplete and misleading on national origins. On this subject, see the excellent study of Brinley Thomas, *Migration and Economic Growth* (Cambridge: At the University Press, 1954), pp. 42-50; and Marian R. Davis, "Critique of Official United States Immigration Statistics," App. II of *International Migrations*, Vol. II, ed. Walter F. Willcos (New York: National Bureau of Economic Research, 1931), 647-48.

[24] The following national groups are usually included among the old immigrants: British, Irish, Norwegian, Swedish, Danish, Dutch, Belgian, French, German, and Swiss; among the new are the nationals from Russia, Poland, Czechoslovakia, Jugoslavia, Italy, Portugal, Spain, Greece, and the Balkan nations. See Brown and Roucek, *One America*, pp. 13-14; Edward C. McDonagh and Eugene S. Richards, *Ethnic Relations in the United States* (New York: Appleton-Century-Crofts, Inc., 1953), pp. 288-89.

[25] For a scholarly treatment of this whole problem, see Colman J. Barry, *The Catholic Church and German Americans* (Washington: The Catholic University of America Press, 1953); also, Emmet H. Rothan, *The German Catholic Immigrant in the United States (1830–1860)* (Washington: The Catholic University of America Press, 1946); and John A. Hawgood, *The Tragedy of German-America* (New York: G. P. Putnam's Sons, 1940).

[26] In 1923, Archbishop Joseph Schrembs estimated that Catholics of German descent numbered about four million. This appears to be a rather generous estimate. See Rt. Rev. Joseph Schrembs, "The Catholic German Immigrant's Contribution," in *Catholic Builders of the Nation*, ed. C. E. McGuire (Boston: Continental Press, Inc., 1925), p. 63.

[27] Major concentrations are: Greater New York (650,000), Chicago (600,-000), Detroit (350,000), Buffalo (200,000), Milwaukee (180,000), Cleveland (175,000). See Arthur L. Waldo, "Poles in the United States," *American-Polish Participation* (New York: New York's World Fair Publication, 1939).

[28] Estimates on the membership of this sect vary from 180,000 to 250,000. See Theodore Andrews, *The Polish National Church in America* (London: Society for Promoting Christian Knowledge, 1953).

[29] *Rocznik Polonii,* Year Book and Directory of Poles Abroad (London: Taurus, Ltd., 1952).

[30] William I. Thomas and Florian Znaniecki, *The Polish Peasant in Europe and America,* 2nd ed. (New York: Alfred A. Knopf, 1927), II, 1704-6, 1751-52.

[31] John L. Thomas, "Marriage Prediction in *The Polish Peasant,*" *The American Journal of Sociology,* LV (May, 1950), 572-78.

[32] The heavy immigration from the North of Italy occurred several decades earlier and settled primarily in South America. See the excellent treatise by Robert F. Foerster, *The Italian Immigration of Our Times* (Cambridge: The Harvard University Press, 1919).

[33] For example, in 1940 there were 1,095,000 Italian Americans living in New York City. See Brown and Roucek, *op. cit.,* pp. 262-65.

[34] See Henry J. Browne, "The 'Italian Problem' in the Catholic Church of the United States, 1880–1900," *Historical Records and Studies, United States Catholic Historical Society,* XXXV, (1946), 46-75.

[35] See evidence offered by Foerster, *op. cit.,* pp. 397-98; Bernard J. Lynch, "The Italians in New York," *The Catholic World,* XLVII (April, 1888), 69ff.; Lawrence Franklin, "Italians in America," *The Catholic World,* LXXI (April, 1900), 67 ff.

[36] See John V. Tolino, "Solving the Italian Problem," *The American Ecclesiastical Review,* IC (September, 1938), 246-56; "The Church in America and the Italian Problem," *Ibid.,* C. (January, 1939), 22-32; "The Future of the Italian-American Problem," *Ibid.,* CI (September, 1939), 221-32.

[37] The conservative estimate is made by Brown and Roucek, *op. cit.,* p. 215; Richard A. Schermerhorn, *These Our People* (Boston: D. C. Heath and Company, 1949), p. 330, maintains the higher estimate is closer to the truth.

[38] See Casimir P. Sirvaitis, *Religious Folkways in Lithuania and Their Conservation Among the Lithuanian Immigrants in the United States* (Washington: The Catholic University of America Press, 1952), p. 39.

[39] See Wasyl Halich, *Ukranians in the United States* (Chicago: The University of Chicago Press, 1937).

[40] The term *national parish* is used here in a broad sense to include all those parish communities which are composed primarily of one national group and in which the various parish activities accentuate national characteristics. Strictly speaking, a distinction should be made between juridical and nonjuridical national parishes. The former have been established by ecclesiastical authorities to answer the needs of a distinct language or racial group and exercise jurisdiction over all the members of that group living within the surrounding area. The nonjuridical national parish is a traditional territorial parish in which the majority of members happen to possess a similar national background. See Thomas J. Harte, "Racial and National Parishes in the United States," in *The Sociology of the Parish,* eds. C. J. Nuesse and T. J. Harte (Milwaukee: The Bruce Publishing Company, 1951), pp. 154-77; Joseph E. Ciesluk, *National Parishes in the United States* (Washington: The Catholic University of America Press, 1944).

[41] For evidence of their retarding influence, see Robert E. Park and Herbert A. Miller, *Old World Traits Transplanted* (Chicago: Society for Social Research, University of Chicago, 1925), pp. 97-98, 232-34.

[42] For example, a study of all the marriages performed in a diocesan urban

parish located outside the area of minority group settlement revealed that in the seventeen years from 1936–1952 inclusive there were 1,276 marriages. Of this number, 416, or approximately one-third (32.6 per cent), involved members of one ethnic group. An analysis of these 416 marriages showed that in only one-third (34.14 per cent) of the cases had ingroup marriage taken place; in the remaining two-thirds (65.86 per cent), the mate had been selected from outside the ethnic group. These data are all the more striking since the ethnic group in question revealed an outgroup marriage rate of only 10 per cent in its national parishes.

[43] For example, in the Archdiocese of Chicago as of 1953 there were 144 territorial diocesan parishes, 136 juridical national parishes, and 4 Negro parishes. Although some of these national parishes served mixed groups, the majority were strictly national in character.

[44] An analysis of the leadership in many of these organizations reveals that their militant nationalism came, not from the typical peasant immigrant, but from a small, middle-class group composed mostly of political refugees and journalists. It is unfortunate that these leaders did not make greater use of their talent and position to promote the adjustment of their peasant nationals in their new environment.

[45] See John L. Thomas, "The Factor of Religion in the Selection of Marriage Mates," *American Sociological Review,* XVI (August, 1951), 487-91; and "Out-Group Marriage Patterns of Some Selected Ethnic Groups," *The American Catholic Sociological Review,* XV (March, 1954), 9-18.

[46] See Thorsten V. Kalijarvi, "French Canadians in the United States," *The Annals of the American Academy of Political and Social Science,* CCXXIII (September, 1942), 1932-33.

[47] Just how hazardous predictions of cultural survival can be may be gained by considering the position of the Louisiana French. Generation after generation, they have maintained their language, culture, religion, and mode of life intact. Furthermore, they have displayed a remarkable capacity for absorbing extraneous elements such as Germans, Dutch, Irish, and "Americans." As a cultural group they number about 565,000, or 44 per cent of Louisiana's native white population. See T. Lynn Smith and Homer L. Hitt, *The People of Louisiana* (Baton Rouge: Louisiana State University Press, 1952), pp. 47-49.

[48] See McDonagh and Richards, *op. cit.,* pp. 174-200; Charles F. Marden, *Minorities in American Society* (New York: American Book Company, 1952), pp. 131-33.

[49] See Pauline R. Kibbe, *Latin Americans in Texas* (Albuquerque: University of New Mexico Press, 1946); for a sensitive study of a Mexican community in California, see Ruth Tuck, *Not with the Fist* (New York: Harcourt, Brace and Company, Inc., 1947); for exploitation of workers, see Robert C. Jones, *Mexican War Workers in the United States* (Washington: Pan American Union, 1945); Raymond Bernard, "Run-Around for Migrants," *Social Order,* I (October, 1951), pp. 353-60; for basic material, see *Migrant Labor, a Human Problem,* and *Migratory Labor in American Agriculture,* Report of the President's Commission on Migratory Labor (Washington: 1951).

[50] See C. Wright Mills, Clarence Senior, and Rose K. Goldsen, *The Puerto Rican Journey* (New York: Harper and Brothers, 1950).

[51] See *The Present Housing Emergency in New York City* (New York: Welfare and Health Council of New York City, 1953).

CHAPTER FIVE

[1] Joseph H. Fichter, "The Profile of Catholic Religious Life," *The American Journal of Sociology*, LVIII (September, 1952), 149.

[2] *Ibid.*, 147-48.

[3] George Kelly, *Catholics and the Practice of the Faith* (Washington: The Catholic University of America Press, 1946), p. 197.

[4] Confirmation for this statement appears in several foreign studies. See, for example, Aldo Leoni, *Sociologia e Geografia Religiosa di una Diocesi* (Romae: Apud Aedes Universitatis Gregorianae, 1952); Gabriel Le Bras, *Introduction a l'histoire de la pratique religieuse en France* (Paris: Presse Universitaire de France, Vol. I, 1942; Vol. II, 1945).

[5] See the careful study by Robert F. Cissell, "A Statistical Analysis of Catholic Population Data" (Mimeographed, Xavier University, Cincinnati, 1951). A sharp and, no doubt, just criticism of *The Directory's* population statistics in the past can be found in Shaughnessy, *Has the Immigrant Kept the Faith?*, p. 201.

[6] *The Official Catholic Directory* (New York: P. J. Kenedy & Sons, 1954).

[7] According to the census definition in use in 1940, rural-farm population includes all persons living on farms in rural areas. A farm consists of all the land operated by one person, provided it includes three acres or more or provided it produced a total of agricultural products valued at $250 or more during the year in question. Rural-nonfarm population includes all persons dwelling in rural areas who are not living on farms.

[8] See *A Survey of Catholic Weakness* (Des Moines: National Catholic Rural Life Conference, 1948), pp. 10-11.

[9] *Ibid.*, pp. 12-13.

[10] Howard W. Odum, *Southern Regions of the United States* (Chapel Hill: University of North Carolina Press, 1936), pp. 5-7.

[11] Hadley Cantril, "Educational and Economic Composition of Religious Groups," *American Journal of Sociology*, XLVII (March, 1943), 574-79.

[12] A "voting" poll is interested in ascertaining the opinion of those who can vote, consequently, southern Negroes are under-represented. In a "social" poll, Negroes usually comprise 9 or 10 per cent of the sample. However, even most "social" polls are far from satisfactory in describing religion and class patterns. Usually the ascription of class is made by the interviewer on more or less subjective indexes. Further, the samples seldom reflect the regional distribution of religious bodies or their proportional representation of the total religious membership.

[13] This study is reported in *Information Service* (New York), May 15, 1948, pp. 1-5. See the review of this study and that of Cantril's by Liston Pope, "Religion and the Class Structure," *Annals of the American Academy of Political and Social Science*, CCLVI (March, 1948), 84-91.

[14] Starting in November, 1952, the *Catholic Digest* published a series of articles based on this survey. Mr. Ben Gaffin has generously made available the data used here.

[15] Carson McGuire, "Family Life in Lower and Middle Class Homes," *Marriage and Family Living*, XIV (February, 1952), 1-6.

[16] Warner and Srole, *The Social Systems of American Ethnic Groups* (New Haven, Conn.: The Yale University Press, 1946), pp. 67-102; W. Lloyd Warner, Marchia Meeker, and Kenneth Eells, *Social Class in America* (Chicago:

Science Research Associates, Inc., 1949), pp. 186-99; Talcott Parsons, "A Revised Analytical Approach to the Theory of Social Stratification," in *Class, Status and Power*, eds. Reinhard Bendix and Seymour M. Lipset (Glencoe, Ill.: The Free Press, 1953), pp. 118-19.

[17] Warner, Meeker, and Eells, *op. cit.*, p. 96.

[18] James West, *Plainville, U.S.A.* (New York: Columbia University Press, 1945), p. 145.

[19] Robert S. and Helen M. Lynd, *Middletown* (New York: Harcourt, Brace and Company, 1929), p. 332.

[20] Robert S. and Helen M. Lynd, *Middletown in Transition* (New York: Harcourt, Brace and Company, 1938), p. 313.

[21] W. Lloyd Warner, *Democracy in Jonesville* (New York: Harper and Brothers, 1949), p. 153.

[22] Warner and Srole, *op. cit.*, pp. 67-102.

[23] Samuel A. Stouffer, "Trends in the Fertility of Catholics and non-Catholics," *The American Journal of Sociology*, XLI (September, 1935), 143-66.

[24] Frank W. Notestein, "Class Differences in Fertility," *The Annals of the American Academy of Political and Social Science*, CLXXXVIII (November, 1936), 33.

[25] P. K. Whelpton and Clyde V. Kiser, "Social and Psychological Factors Affecting Fertility," *The Milbank Memorial Fund Quarterly*, XXI (July, 1943), 221-80.

[26] *Ibid.*, 271-72.

[27] Evelyn M. Kitagawa, "Differential Fertility in Chicago, 1920–40," *The American Journal of Sociology*, LVIII (March, 1953), 481-92; Clyde V. Kiser, "Fertility Trends and Differentials in the United States," *Journal of the American Statistical Association*, XLVII (March, 1952).

[28] Smith and Hitt, *The People of Louisiana*, pp. 153-57.

[29] Calhoun, *A Social History of the American Family*, Vol. 2, pp. 9-148; Vol. 3, pp. 65-130; Goodsell, *A History of Marriage and the Family*, pp. 457-80; Howard, *A History of Matrimonial Institutions*, Vol. 2, pp. 388-497; Vol. 3, pp. 3-160.

[30] Everett C. Hughes, *French Canada in Transition* (Chicago: University of Chicago Press, 1943), pp. 4-9.

[31] Tuck, *Not with the Fist*, p. 123.

CHAPTER SIX

[1] Legislation was needed only for women since in that man's world, the wife followed the religion of her husband.

[2] *Christian Marriage*, p. 26.

[3] *The Progress and Problems of the American Church* (New York: The America Press, 1939), p. 15.

[4] According to Canon Law, only those mixed marriages which are sanctioned by Catholic nuptials are valid. All other mixed marriages involving a Catholic are invalid according to the law of the Church.

[5] Bishop's Committee on Mixed Marriage, *A Factual Study of Mixed Marriages* (Washington: National Catholic Welfare Conference, 1943), p. 5.

[6] August B. Hollingshead, "Cultural Factors in the Selection of Marriage Mates," *American Sociological Review*, XV (October, 1950), 619-27; Ruby Jo Reeves Kennedy, "Single or Triple Melting Pot? Intermarriage Trends in

New Haven, 1870-1940," *American Journal of Sociology,* XXXIX (January, 1944), 331-39.

[7] John L. Thomas, "The Factor of Religion in the Selection of Marriage Mates," 487-91; "Some Observations on Mixed Marriage in the United States," *Lumen Vitae,* VI (January, 1951), 173-86; "The Pattern of Marriage Among Catholics," in *Marriage Education and Counselling,* ed. A. Clemens (Washington: The Catholic University of America Press, 1951), pp. 43-60.

[8] Whelpton and Kiser, *The Milbank Memorial Fund Quarterly,* XXI, 227-28.

[9] Gerald J. Schnepp, *Leakage from a Catholic Parish* (Washington: The Catholic University of America Press, 1942), p. 88.

[10] Joseph H. Fichter, *Dynamics of a City Parish* (Chicago: The University of Chicago Press, 1951), p. 107.

[11] A diocese is a district presided over by a bishop, and is generally named after the city in which his residence is located. Very few dioceses cross state lines, but there may be several dioceses within the same state.

[12] Gerald J. Schnepp, "Three Mixed Marriage Questions Answered," *Catholic World,* CLVI (November, 1942), 203-207.

[13] Judson T. and Mary G. Landis, *Building a Successful Marriage,* 2nd ed. (New York: Prentice-Hall, Inc., 1953), p. 152.

[14] *Ibid.,* pp. 152-54.

[15] H. Ashley Weeks, "Differential Divorce Rates by Occupation," *Social Forces,* XXI (March, 1943), p. 336.

[16] Howard M. Bell, *Youth Tell Their Story* (Washington: American Council on Education, 1938), p. 21.

[17] In the parish which he studied thoroughly, Schnepp found that the chances were twice as great for the breakup of mixed as for Catholic marriages. However, his sample was small and parishes vary greatly in this respect. See *Leakage from a Catholic Parish,* p. 130.

[18] Judson T. Landis, "Marriages of Mixed and Non-Mixed Religious Faith," *American Sociological Review* XIV (June, 1949), p. 405.

[19] Ray Baber, "A Study of 325 Mixed Marriages," *American Sociological Review,* II (October, 1937), 705-716.

[20] Murray Leiffer, "Interfaith Marriages and Their Effects on the Religious Training of Children," *Lumen Vitae,* IV (July-September, 1949), 445-47; John L. Thomas, "Mixed Marriages—So What?" *Social Order,* II (April, 1952), 155-59.

[21] Fichter, *Dynamics of a City Parish,* pp. 107-108.

[22] Schnepp, *Leakage from a Catholic Parish,* p. 91.

[23] Thomas F. Coakley, "Some Revelations of a Recent Parish Census," *Ecclesiastical Review,* LXXXI (March, 1930), 312-14; "New Light on Mixed Marriages," *Ibid.* (April, 1930), 412-17; "Revelation of a Parish Census," *Ibid.,* XC (May, 1934), 525-31; "Leakage in Peter's Barque," *Information,* LXIII (April, 1949), 145-50.

[24] *A Factual Study of Mixed Marriages,* p. 8.

[25] Kelly, *Catholics and the Practice of the Faith,* pp. 53-87.

[26] Prescinding from death-bed conversions, we would place the over-all rate of conversions in mixed marriage at about 5 per cent. There are a considerable number of conversions before marriage or with marriage to a Catholic in view. It is somewhat hazardous to venture estimates of conversions from mixed marriage since individual dioceses and parishes differ a great deal in this regard.

[27] Leiffer, "Interfaith Marriages," 447.

²⁸ Leiffer, *The Christian Century*, January 26, 1949, p. 107; Landis and Landis, *op. cit.*, pp. 156-157.
²⁹ Leiffer, "Interfaith Marriages," 447.
³⁰ "Leakage in Peter's Barque," 147.

CHAPTER SEVEN

¹ Statement of the American Hierarchy, "The Christian Family," *The Catholic Mind*, XLVIII (February, 1950), 125.
² For example, see Katherine B. Davis, *Factors in the Sex Life of Twenty-two Hundred Women* (New York: Harper and Brothers, 1929); Gilbert V. Hamilton, *A Research in Marriage* (New York: A. and C. Boni, 1929); Robert L. Dickinson and Laura Beam, *A Thousand Marriages, A Medical Study of Sex Adjustment* (Baltimore: Wilkins & Wilkins, 1933); Ernest W. Burgess and Leonard S. Cottrell, *Predicting Success or Failure in Marriage* (New York: Prentice-Hall, Inc., 1939); Lewis M. Terman, *Psychological Factors in Marital Happiness* (New York: McGraw-Hill Book Company, Inc., 1938); Ernest W. Burgess and Paul Wallin, *Engagement and Marriage* (Philadelphia: J. B. Lippincott Company, 1953). However, a representative sample of Indiana Protestant couples was used by Harvey J. Locke, *Predicting Adjustment in Marriage* (New York: Henry Holt and Company, 1951).
³ Jessie Bernard, "Factors in the Distribution of Success in Marriage," *American Journal of Sociology*, XL (July, 1934), 52.
⁴ Kingsley Davis, "Changing Modes of Marriage," in *Marriage and the Family*, eds. Howard Becker and Reuben Hill (Boston: D. C. Heath & Company, 1942), p. 108.
⁵ Willard Waller, *The Family*, rev. ed. Reuben Hill (New York: The Dryden Press, Inc., 1951), p. 9.
⁶ William L. Kolb, "Sociologically Established Family Norms and Democratic Values," *Social Forces*, XXVI (May, 1948), 451-56.
⁷ Clifford Kirkpatrick, *What Science Says About Happiness in Marriage* (Minneapolis: Burgess Publishing Company, 1947).
⁸ See Albert Ellis, "The Value of Marriage Prediction Tests," *The American Sociological Review*, XIII (December, 1948), 710-18, and the rejoinder by Lewis M. Terman and Paul Wallin, "The Validity of Marriage Prediction and Marital Adjustment Tests," *The American Sociological Review*, XIV (August, 1949), 497-505.
⁹ Ernest W. Burgess, "The Value and Limitations of Marriage Prediction Tests," *Marriage and Family Living*, XII (Spring, 1950), 55.
¹⁰ Hill rightly stresses the need to consider personality development in evaluating marital success, but he offers no criteria for judging development. Self-expression to be developmental must be considered in relation to a definition of self. See Hill, *The Family*, pp. 343-71.
¹¹ Ernest Burgess in Leland F. Wood and John W. Mullen, *What the American Family Faces* (Chicago: The Eugene Hugh Publishers, Inc., 1943), pp. 6-10. In this connection, Kinsey makes the following shrewd observation. "A preliminary examination of the six thousand marital histories in the present study, and of nearly three thousand divorce histories, suggests that there may be nothing more important in a marriage than a determination that it shall persist. With such a determination, individuals force themselves to adjust and to accept situations which would seem sufficient grounds for a break-up, if

the continuation of the marriage were not the prime objective." Alfred C. Kinsey, Wardell B. Pomeroy, and Clyde E. Martin, *Sexual Behavior in the Human Male* (Philadelphia: W. B. Saunders Co., 1948), p. 544. See also, Alfred C. Kinsey, Wardell B. Pomeroy, Clyde E. Martin, and Paul H. Gebhard, *Sexual Behavior in the Human Female* (Philadelphia: W. B. Saunders Co., 1953), pp. 11-12.

[12] Although separation or divorce are a criterion of marital adjustment, their absence does not necessarily signify marital happiness and success. In spite of the fact that divorce has become a socially acceptable means of dissolving an unhappy union, religious and cultural values are still effective in keeping some unhappy unions out of the divorce court.

[13] This method for securing a representative sample of data arranged alphabetically was suggested by Philip Hauser of the University of Chicago.

[14] United States Bureau of the Census, *Population—Second Series, Characteristics of the Population of Illinois, Sixteenth Census of the United States* (Washington: Government Printing Office, 1942), pp. 146ff.

[15] *Statistical Abstract of the United States, 1947* (Washington: U. S. Dept. of Commerce, Government Printing Office, 1947), pp. 39ff.

[16] All percentages in the following tables are recorded with one decimal and are correct to the nearest tenth of one per cent. The procedure used in rounding percentages is that recommended by Frederick E. Croxton and Dudley J. Cowden, *Applied General Statistics*, 2nd ed. (New York: Prentice-Hall, Inc., 1955), pp. 139-40.

[17] A study of the records of a marriage counseling center in the same area, which handles approximately two thousand cases each year, revealed that Polish wives here also outnumbered Polish husbands two to one in outgroup marriage. This suggests that females of Polish descent have considerable difficulty in adjusting to such unions.

[18] It will be recalled that Landis discovered only 6.7 per cent of this mixed marriage type were divorced. See Landis and Landis, *Building a Successful Marriage*, p. 143.

[19] Ernest Burgess and Harvey J. Locke, *The Family* (New York: The American Book Co., 1945), p. 462.

[20] Burgess and Cottrell, *op. cit.*, pp. 164-66, 357.

[21] Paul Popenoe, "Length of Engagement and Marital Adjustment," *Social Forces*, XVI (May, 1938), 552-55.

[22] Terman, *op. cit.*, pp. 370-71.

[23] *Ibid.*, pp. 197-98.

[24] Locke, *op. cit.*, pp. 89-90.

[25] *Ibid.*, p. 90.

[26] Terman, *op. cit.*, p. 198.

[27] *Ibid.*, p. 368; pp. 198-200.

[28] Burgess and Cottrell, *op. cit.*, pp. 167-68.

[29] Popenoe, "Length of Engagement and Marital Adjustment," 554-55.

[30] Locke, *op. cit.*, pp. 93-94. It is not clear from the examples which he presents precisely what Locke understands by the term *engagement*. It involves no external rite and seemingly precedes the formal proposal to marry.

[31] United States Bureau of the Census, *Population, Special Reports, Series P-45, No. 7* (Washington: Government Printing Office, May 28, 1945). In regard to data on age at marriage, Monahan has maintained that "nearly all studies of the subject of marriage age, including those of the U. S. Bureau of

the Census, were unsound." Thomas P. Monahan, *The Pattern of Age at Marriage in the United States* (Philadelphia: Stephenson Brothers, 1951), Vol. I, iii.

32 Louis I. Dublin, *The Facts of Life* (New York: The Macmillan Company, 1951), p. 42.

33 See Frank W. Notestein, "Differential Age at Marriage According to Social Class," *The American Journal of Sociology*, XXXVII (July, 1931), 22-45; W. Lloyd Warner and Paul S. Lunt, *The Social Life of a Modern Community* (New Haven: Yale University Press, 1941), p. 252; James H. S. Bossard, "The Age Factor in Marriage: A Philadelphia Study, 1931," *The American Journal of Sociology*, XXXVIII (March, 1933), 536-49; Otis D. Duncan, "The Factor of Age in Marriage," *The American Journal of Sociology*, XXXIX (January, 1934), 469-82.

34 Gilbert V. Hamilton and Kenneth McGowan, *What Is Wrong with Marriage* (New York: A. & C. Boni, 1929), p. 25.

35 Katherine B. Davis, *op. cit.*, pp. 50-52.

36 See Hornell and Ella B. Hart, *Personality and the Family*, rev. ed. (Boston: D. C. Heath and Company, 1941), pp. 123-28; Burgess and Cottrell, *op. cit.*, p. 116; Terman, *op. cit.*, p. 181; Paul Popenoe, "Should College Students Marry?" *Parents Magazine*, XIII (July, 1938), 18-19; Ethel Rogers, "One Hundred Juvenile Marriages," *Social Forces*, XIII (March, 1935), 400-409; Locke, *op. cit.*, pp. 100-103; Landis and Landis, *op. cit.*, pp. 108-13.

37 Terman, *op. cit.*, p. 370.

38 Duncan, "The Factor of Age at Marriage," 469-82.

39 Bossard, "The Age Factor in Marriage," 536-49.

40 Weeks, "Differential Divorce Rates by Occupations," 336.

41 William F. Ogburn, "Marital Separations," *American Journal of Sociology*, IL (February, 1944), 316-23; and "Education, Income, and Family Unity," *American Journal of Sociology*, LIII (May, 1948), 474-76.

42 Terman, *op. cit.*, p. 370.

43 Judge A. Sbarbaro, *Marriage Is on Trial* (New York: The Macmillan Co., 1947), pp. 28-29.

44 Terman, *op. cit.*, pp. 171-73; Burgess and Cottrell, *op. cit.*, pp. 258-61; Bernard, "Factors in the Distribution of Success in Marriage," p. 51; Landis and Landis, *op. cit.*, p. 434; Locke, *op. cit.*, pp. 163-66.

45 Meyer F. Nimkoff, *Marriage and the Family* (Boston: Houghton Mifflin Co., 1947), pp. 494-96, 630-31.

46 Alfred Cahen, *Statistical Analysis of American Divorce* (New York: Columbia University Press, 1932), p. 112.

47 Paul H. Jacobson, "Differentials in Divorce by Duration of Marriage and Size of Family," *American Sociological Review*, XV (April, 1950), 235-44.

48 *Ibid.*, 242.

49 Dublin, *op. cit.*, p. 69.

CHAPTER EIGHT

1 *Plutarch's Lives*, The Loeb Classical Library, trans. Bernadette Perrin (Cambridge, Mass.: Harvard University Press, 1918), VI, pp. 365-67.

2 That the average marriage demands adaptations not bargained for in courtship is rather cynically stated by Erasmus: ". . . what man would be so silly as to run his head into the collar of a matrimonial noose if (as wise men

are wont to do) he had beforehand duly considered the inconveniences of a wedded life? Or indeed, what woman would open her arms to receive the embraces of a husband, if she did but forecast the pangs of child-birth and the plague of being a nurse?" Desiderius Erasmus, *In Praise of Folly* (London: George Allen & Unwin Ltd., 1925), p. 14.

3 After studying families in crises, Hill states: "Perhaps the most overpowering impression of our study is the tremendous variety in family organization, living conditions, family objectives, interpretations of what's important and what's not important in life, and ways of reacting to family-shattering crises." Reuben Hill, *Families Under Stress* (New York: Harper and Brothers, 1949), p. 313.

4 Robert Straus, "Excessive Drinking and its Relationship to Marriage," *Marriage and Family Living*, XII (Summer, 1950), 79-83; John L. Thomas, "Marriage Breakdown," *Social Order*, II (December, 1952), 445-50.

5 "Sexual incompatibility is often said to be the major *cause* of divorce or of the failure of marriages as judged by other criteria of marital success. It can be stated quite categorically that there is no convincing scientific evidence in support of this assertion. There is evidence indicating that successful marriage and sexual adjustment tend to go together, but the evidence does not reveal which is cause and which is effect." Burgess and Wallin, *Engagement and Marriage*, p. 676.

6 These studies are reported in Landis and Landis, *Building a Successful Marriage*, pp. 302-303.

7 Burgess and Wallin, *Engagement and Marriage*, pp. 598-99.

8 See John L. Thomas, "In-laws or Outlaws?" *Social Order*, III (December, 1953), 435-40.

9 For opposing positions on whether it is more difficult for the husband or for the wife to achieve emancipation from parents, see Mirra Komarovsky, "Functional Analysis of Sex Roles," *American Sociological Review*, XV (August, 1950), 508-16; and Robert F. Winch, *The Modern Family* (New York: Henry Holt and Company, Inc., 1952), pp. 296-303.

10 See Evelyn Millis Duvall, *In-Laws: Pro & Con* (New York: Association Press, 1954), for a popular discussion of various in-law relationships.

CHAPTER NINE

1 Park and Miller, *Old World Traits Transplanted*, pp. 146-59.

2 Caroline F. Ware, *Greenwich Village, 1920–1930* (Boston: Houghton Mifflin Co., 1935), pp. 404-20.

3 Warner and Srole, *The Social Systems of American Ethnic Groups*, p. 108.

4 Ware, *op. cit.*, p. 399.

5 Park and Miller, *op. cit.*, pp. 232-34.

6 *Ibid.*, pp. 97-98.

7 Thomas and Znaniecki, *The Polish Peasant in Europe and America*. See Thomas, "Marriage Prediction in *The Polish Peasant*," *op. cit.*, 572-77.

8 Thomas and Znaniecki, *op. cit.*, II, pp. 1751-52.

9 *Ibid.*, II, p. 1704.

10 *Ibid.*, II, p. 1706.

11 U. S. Bureau of the Census, *Sixteenth Census of the United States: Population*, Second Series: *Characteristics of the Population of Illinois* (Washington: Government Printing Office, 1942), pp. 146ff.

[12] Herbert Blumer, *An Appraisal of Thomas and Znaniecki's "The Polish Peasant in Europe and America"* (New York: Social Science Research Council, Bulletin 44, 1939), p. 70.

[13] *Ibid.*, p. 71.

[14] *Ibid.*, p. 83.

[15] *Ibid.*, p. 84.

[16] *Ibid.*, p. 86.

[17] Thomas and Znaniecki, *op. cit.*, II, p. 1653.

[18] *Ibid.*, pp. 1738-39.

[19] *Ibid.*, pp. 2099-2153.

[20] *Ibid.*, pp. 1511-74.

[21] *Ibid.*, pp. 1703-1706.

[22] *Ibid.*, p. 1706.

[23] *Ibid.*, p. 1516.

[24] *Ibid.*, p. 1738.

[25] *Ibid.*, p. 1523.

[26] *Ibid.*, p. 1524.

[27] Blumer, *op. cit.*, p. 111.

[28] Dublin, *The Facts of Life*, p. 68.

[29] Antonio Ciocco, "On Human Social Biology, Disruptive and Cohesive Factors in the Marital Group," *Human Biology*, X (December, 1938), 452-53.

[30] John L. Thomas, "Marital Failure and Duration," *Social Order*, III (January, 1953), 24-29.

CHAPTER TEN

[1] William F. Ogburn, "Marriages, Births and Divorces," *The Annals of the American Academy of Political and Social Science*, CCXXIX (September, 1943), 2-29.

[2] Calvin Hall, "The Instability of Post-War Marriages," *Journal of Social Psychology*, V (November, 1934), 523-530.

[3] John F. Cuber, "Changing Courtship and Marriage Customs," *The Annals of the American Academy of Political and Social Science*, CCXXIX (September, 1943), 30-47.

[4] Willard Waller, *The Veteran Comes Back* (New York: The Dryden Press, 1944), p. 286.

[5] James H. S. Bossard, "Family Problems in Wartime," *Psychiatry*, VII (February, 1944), 156.

[6] Thomas, "Forced Marriages," 99-104; "The Prediction of Success or Failure in Forced Marriages," *Theological Studies*, XIII (March, 1952), 101-108.

[7] Contemporary society, while violently rejecting traditional "Victorian" restraints, has been unable to substitute others, thus leaving sexual behavior without adequate social regulation and appropriate institutional supports. See Thomas, "Sex and Society," 242-48.

[8] For an extended treatment of these possibilities and their effects on the marital success of middle-class, urban, non-Catholic couples, see Burgess and Wallin, *Engagement and Marriage*, pp. 319-90.

[9] See Mihanovich, Schnepp, and Thomas, *Marriage and the Family*, pp. 351-54.

[10] "Illegitimate Births, 1938–47," *Vital Statistics—Special Reports*, 33, 5

(Washington: National Office of Vital Statistics, Federal Security Agency, February 15, 1950), pp. 72, 73, and 84.

11 Harold T. Christensen, *Marriage Analysis* (New York: Ronald Press, 1952), p. 153; and "Studies in Child Spacing: I. Premarital Pregnancy as Measured by the Spacing of the First Birth from Marriage," *American Sociological Review*, XVIII (February, 1953), 53-59.

12 Christensen, "Studies in Child Spacing," p. 58.

13 *Ibid.* For studies of the problem in England, see John Fitzsimmons, *Woman Today* (New York: Sheed and Ward, 1952), pp. 66-7; for four Czechoslovakian provinces, Louis Henry, "Etude Statistique de l'Espacement des Naissance," *Population*, VI (July–September, 1951), 423-44; for Finland and the Scandinavian countries, Sydney H. Croog, "Premarital Pregnancies in Scandinavia and Finland," *American Journal of Sociology*, LVII (January, 1952), 358-65. In the countries studied, premarital pregnancy rates ran uniformly higher than those found by Christensen in the United States.

14 Horace H. Robins and Francis Deak, "The Familial Property Rights of Illegitimate Children: A Comparative Study," in *Selected Essays on Family Law* (Brooklyn, N. Y.: Foundation Press, 1950), pp. 728-48.

15 Locke, *Predicting Adjustment in Marriage*, p. 92.

16 Paul Popenoe, *Modern Marriage* (New York: The Macmillan Company, 1940), p. 225.

17 Harold T. Christensen and Hanna H. Meissner, "Studies in Child Spacing: III. Premarital Pregnancy as a Factor in Divorce," *American Sociological Review*, XVIII (December, 1953), 641-44.

18 See Davis, *Factors in the Sex Life of 2,200 Women*, p. 59; Hamilton, *A Research in Marriage*, pp. 393-95; Terman, *Psychological Factors in Marital Happiness*, pp. 324-25; Burgess and Wallin, *Engagement and Marriage*, pp. 368-71.

19 Ernest R. and Gladys H. Groves, *The Contemporary American Family* (Philadelphia: J. B. Lippincott Company, 1947), pp. 38-98.

CHAPTER ELEVEN

1 Jacques Leclercq, *Marriage and the Family*, trans. T. R. Hanley (New York: Frederick Pustet Co., 1949), pp. 314-18.

2 See "Making a Living," in Leo C. Brown et al., *Social Orientations* (Chicago: Loyola University Press, 1954), pp. 105-216.

3 Louis Wirth, "Urbanism as a Way of Life," *American Journal of Sociology*, XLIV (July, 1938), 1-24.

4 Margaret Park Redfield, "The American Family: Consensus and Freedom," *American Journal of Sociology*, LII (November, 1946), 179-81.

5 See Ralph Linton, "The Natural History of the Family," in Ruth Anshen (ed.), *The Family* (New York: Harper and Brothers, 1949), pp. 18-38.

6 For a good structural description of the American kinship system, see Talcott Parsons, "The Kinship System of the Contemporary United States," *American Anthropologist*, XLV (January–March, 1943), 22-38; also, "Age and Sex in the Social Structure of the United States," *American Sociological Review*, VII (October, 1942), 604-16.

7 Paul C. Glick, "The Life Cycle of the Family," *Marriage and Family Living*, XVII (February, 1955), 3-9.

8 See William F. Whyte, "Groupthink," *Fortune*, XXV (March, 1952), 114-17, 142-46; David Riesman, *The Lonely Crowd* (New Haven: Yale Univer-

sity Press, 1950), and *Individualism Reconsidered* (Glencoe, Ill.: The Free Press, 1954); Francis J. Corley, "Individualism Reconsidered," *Social Order,* IV (November, 1954), 409-14.

CHAPTER TWELVE

[1] Brown *et al., Social Orientations,* pp. 11-24.

[2] Mihanovich, Schnepp and Thomas, *Marriage and the Family,* pp. 283-303.

[3] William Ogburn and Clark Tibbitts, "The Family and Its Functions," in *Recent Social Trends in the United States: Report of the President's Research Committee on Social Trends* (New York: McGraw-Hill Book Co., Inc., 1933), p. 674.

[4] John L. Thomas, "Religion and the Child," *Social Order,* I (May, 1951), 205-10; "Religious Training in the Roman Catholic Family," *American Journal of Sociology,* LVII (September, 1951), 178-83.

[5] This study was based on first-grade children attending parochial schools. There is no reason to believe, indeed, there is some evidence to the contrary, that Catholic parents who do not send their children to the parochial school are more solicitous about their children's religious instruction.

[6] See John L. Thomas, "The Catholic Family in a Complex Society: II A Cultural Subsystem," *Social Order,* V (February, 1955), 69-76.

[7] See Robin M. Williams, Jr., *American Society* (New York: Alfred A. Knopf, 1951), pp. 386-87.

[8] See Walter Goldschmidt, "Values and the Field of Comparative Sociology," *American Sociological Review,* XVIII (June, 1953), 287-93.

[9] See Section IV, "Social Security," in *Social Orientations,* pp. 329-408; John L. Thomas, "Some Aspects of Family-State Relationships in the United States," *Politeia,* V (1953), 182-94.

[10] See William B. Faherty, *The Destiny of Modern Woman* (Westminster, Md.: The Newman Press, 1950).

CHAPTER THIRTEEN

[1] John L. Thomas, "The Catholic Family in a Complex Society," *Social Order,* IV (December, 1954), 451-57.

[2] Thomas, "The Catholic Family in a Complex Society: II A Cultural Subsystem," 69-76.

[3] D. F. Aberle, A. K. Cohen, A. K. Davis, M. L. Levy, Jr., and F. X. Sutton, "The Functional Prerequisites of a Society," *Ethics,* LX (October, 1949), 100-11.

[4] Walter Goldschmidt, "Ethics and the Structure of Society: An Ethnological Contribution to the Sociology of Knowledge," *American Anthropologist,* LIII (October–December, 1951), 506-24; "Values and the Field of Comparative Sociology," *American Sociological Review,* XVIII (June, 1953), 287-93.

[5] This example, of course, abstracts from the many other factors operative in producing the change, but it serves to illustrate the reciprocal interplay of structure and meaning in a given instance.

[6] "It is the majority, in short, which sets the culture pattern and sustains it, which is in fact responsible for whatever pattern or configuration there is in a culture." Robert Bierstedt, "The Sociology of Majorities," *American Sociological Review,* XIII (December, 1948), 709.

⁷ For the development of this principle, see: Thomas, "Clothes, Culture and Modesty," 386-94.

⁸ Christopher Dawson, *Medieval Essays* (New York: Sheed and Ward, 1954), p. 55.

⁹ W. M. Kollmorgen, "The Agricultural Stability of the Old Order Amish and the Old Order Mennonites of Lancaster County, Pennsylvania," *American Journal of Sociology*, XLIX (November, 1943), 233-41; W. G. Foster, "Canadian Communist: The Doukobors Experiment," *American Journal of Sociology*, XLI (November, 1935), 327-40.

CHAPTER FOURTEEN

¹ Robert Park, "The City," *American Journal of Sociology*, XX (March, 1915), 579-83.

² See the excellent analysis of Pius XII's contribution by William B. Faherty, *The Destiny of Modern Woman*, pp. 109-66.

³ Pius XII, *Woman's Duties in Social and Political Life* (New York: The Paulist Press, 1945), p. 4.

⁴ *Ibid.*, pp. 4-5.

⁵ Quoted by John D. Donovan in "The Sociologist Looks at the Parish," *American Catholic Sociological Review*, XI (June, 1950), 68-69, from *The Boston Morning Globe*, Boston, Mass., December 29, 1947.

⁶ Canon 215, 1-3.

⁷ See Abbé Michonneau, *Revolution in a City Parish* (Westminster, Md.: The Newman Press, 1949). The original French edition appeared as *La Paroisse, Communauté Missionnaire* (Paris: Les Editions Cerf, 1946). See also, John L. Thomas, "Family and Parish," *Social Order*, I (September, 1951), 291-96.

⁸ For a good summary of the progress in this field, see *The Sociology of the Parish*, eds. C. J. Neusse and T. J. Harte (Milwaukee: The Bruce Publishing Company, 1951). Two recent works reporting the results of an intensive study of one parish are *Dynamics of a City Parish* (Chicago: The University of Chicago Press, 1951), and *Social Relations in an Urban Parish* (Chicago: The University of Chicago Press, 1954), by Joseph H. Fichter.

CHAPTER FIFTEEN

¹ Statement of the American Hierarchy, "The Christian Family," pp. 121-25.

² Rev. Edgar Schmiedeler, O.S.B., well-known authority on the Catholic family; see in particular *Marriage and the Family* (New York: McGraw-Hill Book Company, Inc., 1946); *An Introductory Study of the Family*, rev. ed. (New York: Appleton-Century-Crofts, Inc., 1947).

³ For a convenient summary of the Bureau's publications, see Mihanovich, Schnepp, and Thomas, *A Guide to Catholic Marriage*, pp. 311-14.

⁴ For example, in the diocese of Buffalo and in the archdiocese of Philadelphia, the bishop's Committee for Christian Home and Family furnishes mothers with a series of pamphlets on the religious training of their children. A member of the Committee visits each mother at intervals of three months during the first three years of a child's life and gives her a pamphlet appropriate for the age of the child. The Confraternity of Christian Doctrine renders a somewhat similar service in many dioceses.

⁵ *The Catholic Mind,* 121-25.

⁶ Pius XI, *Christian Marriage* (Casti Connubii), 5th ed., pp. 7-8.

⁷ Arnold W. Green, "The 'Cult of Personality' and Sexual Relations," *Psychiatry,* IV (August, 1941), 344-48.

⁸ See among others, Herbert Doms, *The Meaning of Marriage,* trans. George Sayer (New York: Sheed and Ward, 1939); Dietrich Von Hildebrand, *Marriage* (New York: Longmans, Green and Co., 1942). For an evaluation of some doctrinal aspects of their writing, see Carney, *The Purposes of Christian Marriage,* pp. 203-61.

⁹ *The Cana Conference Proceedings,* Vol. I, ed. John J. Egan (Chicago: The Cana Conference, 1950), p. vii.

¹⁰ *Ibid.,* p. 14

¹¹ John C. Knott in the Preface to *The Cana Movement in the United States* by Alphonse H. Clemens (Washington: The Catholic University of America Press, 1953), p. v.

¹² *Ibid.,* p. 3.

¹³ *Ibid.,* pp. 2-3; Francis L. Filas, "Cana Conference Impressions," *Social Order,* II (October, 1949), 349-52.

¹⁴ See Clemens, *The Cana Movement,* p. 3.

¹⁵ Perhaps the outstanding achievement of the Conference has been its integration of the lay apostolate. Article III, Section 1, of the By-Laws of the Cana Conference of Chicago reads as follows: "The Lay Executive Board is the body entrusted by the Ordinary of the Archdiocese of Chicago with the direction of the activities of the Cana Conference of Chicago."

¹⁶ In the Foreword to *The Cana Conference Proceedings,* Vol. II, p. vii.

¹⁷ See Gerald P. Weber, *Chaplain's Manual* (Chicago: The Chicago Federation of the Christian Family Movement, 1952), p. 7.

¹⁸ See Bob and Wilma Senser, "Families Work for Christ," *Social Order,* II (September, 1952), 298-300.

¹⁹ See *For Happier Families: How to Start a CFM Section.* (Chicago: The Christian Family Movement, 1953), pp. 14-16.

Index

IMPRIMI POTEST

Daniel H. Conway, S.J.
   Provincial

IMPRIMATUR

✠ Joseph E. Ritter
   Archbishop of St. Louis
   August 26, 1955